9-(1)(b)(2)

S. O. DAVIES—A SOCIALIST FAITH

S. O. Davies—A Socialist Faith

ROBERT GRIFFITHS

GOMER PRESS
1983

First Impression—May 1983

ISBN 0 85088 887 5

Griffiths, Robert
S. O. Davies—a socialist faith.
1. Davies, S.O. 2. Politicians—Wales—Biography
I. Title
942.9'085'0924 DA722.1.D/

ISBN 0-85088-887-5

Printed by
J. D. Lewis & Sons Ltd., Gomer Press, Llandysul, Dyfed.

CONTENTS

FOREWORD

No Welsh Member of Parliament this century occupies a revered place in as many hearts and minds as S. O. Davies. Yet it is also a fame and affection unmarked by royal honours or offices of state.

What has earned him this unrivalled esteem ? Quite simply, he was a man of inexhaustible and incorruptible loyalty: to his adopted locality—the Borough and constituency of Merthyr Tydfil ; to his class—those who live by their labour ; to his nationality—that of the Welsh people ; and to the international cause of Socialism.

For more than 50 years, he flew courageously into the eye of almost every major political and industrial storm. S.O. was one of the inevitable petrels : not very often a cardinal or prominent one, but one distinguished by the sincerity of his faith, the steadfastness of his principle and the tenacity of his argument.

Writing the life-story of such a figure has been a privilege, albeit a daunting one. I could not have fulfilled the task at all, however imperfectly, without the help of many friends and acquaintances. My special gratitude is due to Sephora Davies (' Mrs. S.O.') and her ever-ready hospitality ; to Mary Green, her marvellous memory and to her family ; and to Harri Webb, who has been a prolific source of information and encouragement from the outset.

I am also enormously grateful to the following, whose assistance has been invaluable : David Bevan, archivist at University College Swansea (where the S. O. Davies Papers are lodged), Gwerfyl Arthur, Stuart Barber, Pennar Davies, Aled Eirug, Hywel Francis, Cherie Hoyle, Heulwen Huws, Alun Morgan, Hubert Morgan, John Osmond, John Plumpton, Ben Wathen and Dafydd Williams, and the staffs of the Glamorgan Record Office and Cardiff Central Reference Library.

Many other people have helped me with information, documents, typing and the such-like; to them, I express my thanks and apologise for preserving their anonymity. No doubt a number of historians will also recognise some fruits of their own research in my text. I have tried to record my indebtedness to their work wherever practicable ; without their contributions to our commonwealth of historical knowledge and understanding, my own addition would not have been possible.

At the same time, though, I must take full and sole responsibility for the contents of this book. In particular, readers might detect a lack of ' balance ' in my reporting of the great controversies in which S.O. was embroiled. This has been deliberate on my part. As a Socialist, a Welsh patriot, an upholder of the Soviet Union, and in most other fields, S.O. stood in opposition to the English ruling-class . . . whose views on all these matters have hardly suffered from under-exposure ! This book, then, is one of those rarer occasions when an ' anti-establishment ' case—S.O.'s views—can and should enjoy preferential treatment. Thus I have concentrated upon those facts and arguments which illuminate S.O.'s standpoint in its most favourable light—including on those issues where I do not subscribe to his position myself. In doing this, nevertheless, I have endeavoured not to stray outside the dominion of truth.

The years I have spent researching and writing this biography have been an education and inspiration to me. My fervent hope is that this product of my efforts will perform the same service to some, at least, of the readers ; comments, enquiries and criticisms will be most welcome.

My only regret is that I failed to finish this book within the lifetime of Dai Francis, who had written a Foreword for it. Like S.O., Dai was in that magnificent tradition of Welsh political and trade union leaders : men who were of the working-class, widely-read, Welsh-speaking and deeply cultured . . . flag-bearers of international Socialism. They leave to succeeding generations the challenge of holding those banners aloft.

33 Lochaber Street
Plasnewydd
Cardiff

Robert Griffiths
April 1983

ABBREVIATIONS

A.A.M.	Amalgamated Association of Miners
A.E.U.	Amalgamated Engineering Union
C.I.A.	Central Intelligence Agency (U.S.A.)
E.A.M.	National Liberation Front (Greece)
E.E.C.	European Economic Community
E.L.A.S.	National Liberation Army (Greece)
F.B.I.	Federal Bureau of Investigation (U.S.A.)
G.I.	General Infantryman (U.S.A.)
G.K.N.	Guest Keen and Nettlefold Ltd.
G.M.W.U.	General and Municipal Workers Union
I.A.D.L.	International Association of Democratic Lawyers
I.C.F.T.U.	International Confederation of Free Trade Unions
I.C.W.P.A.	International Class War Prisoners Aid
I.L.P.	Independent Labour Party
I.R.C.	International Red Cross
I.S.C.	International Scientific Commission
I.S.P.	Italian Socialist Party
M.F.G.B.	Miners Federation of Great Britain
N.A.T.O.	North Atlantic Treaty Organisation
N.C.B.	National Coal Board
N.E.C.	National Executive Committee (Labour Party)
N.H.S.	National Health Service
N.U.M.	National Union of Mineworkers
N.U.R.	National Union of Railwaymen
P.A.C.	Public Assistance Committee
P.L.P.	Parliamentary Labour Party
R.I.L.U.	Red International of Labour Unions
S.E.T.	Selective Employment Tax
S.W.M.F.	South Wales Miners Federation
S.W.M.I.U.	South Wales Miners Industrial Union
T.G.W.U.	Transport and General Workers Union
T.U.C.	Trades Union Congress (Britain)
U.A.B.	Unemployment Assistance Board
U.N.(O.)	United Nations (Organisation)
U.S.A.F.	United States Air Force
U.S.S.R.	Union of Soviet Socialist Republics

ILLUSTRATIONS

My thanks are due to the following for helping with the above illustrations : Mrs. S. O. Davies, Mary Green and family, Hywel Francis and the South Wales Miners Library, John Plumpton, Cardiff Central Reference Library, David Watkins of Dowlais Library, Bill Hyde, Malcom Llywelyn, Harri Webb, Idris Cox, Dafydd Williams and Gwasg Tŷ John Penry. Photographs are also from the files of the *Western Mail*, *Merthyr Express*, *South Wales Echo*, Devon News Service Ltd., the *Miner* and *Daily Herald*.

Chapter One

LLWYNOG O'R GRAIG

In the 1870s Cap Coch, now known as Abercwmboi, was a mining village of two hundred or so houses, two chapels and two pubs. Although a few of the inhabitants earned their living in the local stores, most of the men and older boys laboured in the nearby collieries. It was a close Welsh-speaking community so typical of the South Wales coalfield at that time, but knit all the more tightly in its relative isolation in a *cwm* branching away from the Cynon Valley. Two miles northwards lay the valley's chief town, Aberdare, whilst a two-mile hike over Mynydd Gwyngul to the west would arrive at the head of the Rhondda Fach, the neighbouring valley.

Not surprisingly, the letter which appeared in the weekly Welsh language paper *Tarian y Gweithiwr* (' The Worker's Shield ') on October 6, 1876, swiftly became a topic of conversation—and speculation—inside the taverns and outside the chapels. A pseudonymous correspondent, signing himself *Llwynog o'r Graig* (' the Mountain Fox ') had offered his services to the paper, promising to report regularly on the intrigues and scandals abroad in his territory, Cap Coch.

Sure enough, his first letter remarked upon the local men's preference for slaking their thirst rather than saving their souls, and went on to describe the conflict between Cap Coch's Jewish pawnbroker and his impoverished debtors. During the following months *Llwynog* (' the Fox ') broadened his sights to fire barbs at the Aberdare Board of Health for neglecting its public responsibilities and at the Co-operative stores for its undemocratic management.

Such scurrilous articles marked a departure from the normally staid journalism of the *Darian*, a progressive ' Lib-Lab ' paper whose serious and sympathetic coverage of labour affairs had built up a respectable circulation of 11,000 since its first issue in 1872. *Llwynog*'s racy, gossipy style was soon copied by other columnists. But by the end of 1876 he was stalking a new quarry, one which was to win him a fame and notoriety outside Cap Coch and even beyond the Cynon Valley.

For thousands of Welsh miners condemned to wage slavery, struggling to organise against their appalling working conditions, the 'gaffer' was the Devil's willing accomplice and advocate. It was the job of the gaffer—the overman or foreman—to drive the toil and extract the sweat. Claiming experience of gaffers at Middle Duffryn and in the Rhondda pits, *Llwynog* flailed them with his customary combination of exposure and ridicule. A typical jibe was the one in his column of 15 December 1876 :

> *Set ddrud i'w cadw yw lot o gaffers : y mae yn rhatach pesgi cant o foch nag un gaffer. Ond er cymaint yw y gost, y mae rhai ohonynt yn pesgi yn dda. Byddaf yn gweled rhai ohonynt yn pasio'r graig yma, ac y maent mor grwn a Devonshire dumplings.*
>
> An expensive set to keep are a lot of gaffers : it's cheaper to fatten a hundred pigs than one gaffer. But whatever the cost, some of them have fattened well. I see some of them passing the mountain here, and they are as round as Devonshire dumplings.

He published details of the privileges and abuses indulged in by the gaffers, even calling upon the coalowners and ironmasters to sack them and distribute the wages thus saved among the 'real' workers !

Llwynog reacted gleefully when reports reached him that 'gaffer sycophants' (his words) were calling meetings to discuss how best to run the fox to earth. Just how strongly they felt can be gleaned from a gaffer's letter in the *Darian* on 5 January 1877 complaining that, instead of light-hearted ribbing, *Llwynog* is 'full of malice and envy. One detects in his tales a vindictive undercurrent . . . *Llwynog* should remember that his jealous reports do not harm the gaffers, but rather—by spreading the animosity already present, and creating suspicion and bad, uneasy feelings between one person and another—they damage those whom he wrongly calls his dear fellow-workers.'

The hunt for the *Llwynog* hotted up to the extent that at the beginning of 1877 the scourge of *y dyn byr, tew*—'the short fat man' as *Llwynog* dubbed him—was able to claim that a team of Merthyr solicitors had been hired for the princely sum of seven shillings to track him down and sue him for libel. *Llwynog*'s response on January 19 was predictably contemptuous :

Pe bae y gaffers yma yn gorfod lladd gymaint o'r corff am eu harian ag y mae y gweithwyr yn gorfod wneud, ni fyddent mor barod i'w gwario rhwng cyfreithwyr.

If the gaffers were compelled to flog their bodies as hard for their money as the worker has to do, they wouldn't be so ready to spend it on solicitors.

As the efforts of the '*cwils*' (solicitors) to discover the name behind the pseudonym proved unsuccessful, so the *Llwynog* became more daring in his raids. In August 1877 he demanded to know why the manager of Penygraig colliery in the Rhondda Valley had not been convicted of manslaughter after his negligence had permitted the drowning of men underground. *Llwynog* pointed to the similarities between the circumstances at Penygraig and those surrounding the lethal flood at Tynewydd in the same valley, where the manager had at least been sent for a retrial on manslaughter charges following the jury's inability to agree the first time.[1]

Not that *Llwynog*'s hostility towards gaffers and criminally-inept managers blinded him to the real profiteers from human misery in the coalfield. The coal barons were mercilessly pilloried for their rotten tied-cottage system and their recruitment of cheap, unskilled labour in vital jobs such as that of fireman. Yet running through these bitter indictments there was a sardonic twist of humour. For example, in a letter of September 20, 1877, he outlined his 20-point plan to get rich : buy a coalworks in the Rhondda, bring in brothers, cousins etc. to do specialist tasks associated with managing, like accounting ; appoint members of your tribe to key workplaces—ideal to carry tales ; put men in the weighing-house who can be corrupted and manipulated ; sell powder and candles to the men, compulsorily of course, at high prices ; build houses at company expense and compel the employees to buy them ; build a schoolhouse with money from a religious denomination ; buy back houses at half price when workers are obliged to move elsewhere—perhaps because you have sacked them ; and do not forget to hold *eisteddfodau* regularly—the men and their families will do all the work, you just keep the profits.

Throughout these devastating tirades against 'oppressive and unjust Bossism' his victims made frantic attempts to unmask and silence the *Llwynog*. The refusal of *Tarian*'s managers to divulge his true name prompted his enemies to offer £400 for information leading to his discovery. Miners suspected of being the *Llwynog* were sacked and the editors of *Tarian* were often called upon by suspects to absolve them in print of any such connection. In fact the editors estimated that in just 18 months no less than 110 people had been wrongfully accused of being the *Llwynog*.[2]

By April 1878 a watch on post offices was being mounted in order to identify those people who posted letters to *Tarian y Gweithiwr* ; post office officials were bribed to open the letters and check the handwriting. How desperate the coalowners and gaffers finally became was revealed by *Llwynog* in his penultimate letter, published on 23 August 1878. There he related a journey made earlier that month to Llanwrtyd Wells in mid-Wales, and undertaken upon hearing of an attempt about to be made on his life. Clearly by that time the identity of the *Llwynog* had been discovered by his chosen adversaries ; he had no realistic option but to discontinue his diary in the *Darian*. His final article, on August 30, must have been a jubilant occasion for some : *Llwynog* had made enemies with his attacks on excessive drinking, religious bigotry, the Aberdare School Board and the coal interests. He had been harangued and threatened in the Tory *Western Mail* and in *Y Gwladgarwr* ('The Patriot') or, as he renamed it, *Y Gwladfradwr* ('The Traitor'). Nonetheless, for many workers in the coalfield *Llwynog*'s demise was a source of sadness : he had become something of a folk hero, with readers writing in begging him to visit their village or pit and expose the corruption there. One old miner expressed the feelings of many in a letter to *Tarian y Gweithiwr* on 2 March 1877 :

> *Credwyf mae y Llwynog yw prif hero yr oes hon yn ein plith ni fel glowyr, am ei fod yn anturio i ddod allan i ddadorchuddio twyll a gormes y gaffers yn yr amser caled hwn, pan y mae y glowyr gymaint o dan draed—pan y mae y trechaf yn treisio, a'r gwanaf yn gwaeddi* [sic], *ond heb neb ond y Llwynog i wrando ar ei gwyn.*

> I would say that the *Llwynog* is the major hero of the age amongst us miners, because he dares to come out and unveil the deceit and oppression of the gaffers in these hard times, when the miners are so downtrodden—when the strongest can oppress and the weakest shout out, with nobody except the *Llwynog* to listen to their plea.

Llwynog o'r Graig's real name was Thomas Davies, a native of Cefneithin in Carmarthenshire who had forsaken farmwork for the Rhondda and married a young shop assistant, Esther Owen, from Maenclochog in Pembrokeshire. The couple moved back to the village where Esther had, until then, spent most of her life—Cap Coch. Thomas continued to work in the pits of the Rhondda and Cynon valleys, at the same time assuming his *alter ego* of *Llwynog*. Many of his *Tarian* tales were drawn from personal experiences underground, although he would also relate events in the first person that had happened to someone else, provided he could verify them.

In the Rhondda, Thomas Davies was one of the thousands of miners who flocked to join the Amalgamated Association of Miners, the second serious attempt to spread trade unionism in the South Wales coalfield. Following a successful strike in 1870 for more pay, some 9,000 unionists in the Rhondda and Cynon valleys were organised into Lodges and Districts by mid-1871. The Association's credibility was further enhanced by a partially successful strike later in the year, notable for the A.A.M.'s ability to afford strike pay. But the employers, too, were becoming convinced of the virtues of organisation : in 1873 the Steam Collieries Association was reformed to include all the south Wales ironmasters with coal interests. Their six month lock-out of ironworkers and miners from January of that year did not extract the full 10% reduction in wages they had been demanding, but it played a large part in bankrupting the A.A.M. The miners' union knew another employers' offensive was being planned and so resolved to strengthen its organisation and win new members between July 1873 and January 1875. William Abraham (' Mabon ') was made secretary of the Rhondda District where one of his most militant and enthusiastic helpers was Thomas Davies. Meetings held to recruit men to the union were rowdy affairs, often broken up by the police ; after one particularly violent rally Thomas fled to Dowlais for three weeks in order to escape the Rhondda Constabulary.

The first rumblings of the expected offensive were heard in 1874 when the coalowners and ironmasters—now organised in the South Wales and Monmouthshire Collieries Association—forced two wage reductions with only minimal resistance. Then, on December 1, notices were issued of a 10% reduction in pay. When the men rejected the demand, the owners scorned an offer of arbitration and locked the workers out. The screw was turned the following April when the reduction was increased to 15%. The men eventually returned to work in May, accepting a three months reduction of 12½% and the introduction of a sliding scale linking wages to coal prices. Another victim of the struggle was the A.A.M. itself, which collapsed partly through bankruptcy and partly because of growing Welsh resentment at sending levies to England where they would be administered by English officials. At the same time, the delay in setting up an autonomous Welsh union inside or outside the new Miners' National Union dealt a serious blow to trade unionism in the coalfield, one from which it took twenty years to recover.

The factionalism and localism in the coalfield could not have occurred at a worse time : the coal trade was contracting and, not unnaturally, the bosses sought to maintain their profit margins by cutting wages or enforcing longer hours. Another reduction was squeezed from the workers in 1877. But there were still men who strove to keep the banner of trade unionism flying. In February of that year Mabon had moved to the Rhondda as a full-time organiser, shortly afterwards setting up the Cambrian Miners' Association. The *Llwynog*, Thomas Davies, implored the workers of south Wales to unite :

> *Pe baem ni fel gweithwyr mewn undeb cariad a'n gilydd, nid yn rhwydd y gallai rhai fel y 'byr, tew' hwnnw ein gorthrymu am eu bod yn teimlo yn genfigenllyd tuag atom. Mewn undeb mae nerth ac mewn nerth mae llwyddiant. Pan ddaw yr egwyddor o undeb yn egwyddor lywodraethol ein bywyd, ceir gweled tipyn o lwyddiant eto ym myd y gweithwyr.*[3]

> If only we workers were together in a union of brotherhood, it would not be so easy for those like the gaffer to oppress us because they feel jealous of us. In unity lies strength and in strength lies victory. When the principle of unity becomes a governing principle in our lives, then shall we yet see some success in the world of the workers.

It was inevitable that his trade union membership, his repeated rejection of company houses and his refusal to accept undersized pay packets often resulted in Thomas Davies getting the sack—and sacked he was, at one pit after another. As an agitator he

Thomas Davies—*Llwynog o'r Graig*

Tarian y Gweithiwr.

"Nid Amddiffyn ond Tarian." "Goreu Tarian Cyfiawnder."

Cofnodydd Helyntion Gweithfaol, Llenyddol, a Gwleidyddol, yn nghyda Newyddion Cymreig, Cyffredinol a Tramor.

Rhif 119 [REGISTERED FOR TRANSMISSION ABROAD.] Gwener, Ebrill 27, 1877. [Pris Ceiniog.

Y LLWYNOG.

Wel, wel, mae wedi dod yn *grand* o'r diwedd. Tra yr wyf fi yn nodi allan bechodau pobl y lle hwn, mae rhyw rai mewn lle arall yn gwisgo'r cap ; ac os yw yn ffitio, y mae iddynt bob croesaw i'w wisgo y dydd i gadw y gwres allan, a'i wisgo y n s i gadw breuddwydion erchyll i ffwrdd ; waith os ydynt yn euog o'r pethau bryntion hyn, tra yn ceisio ymddangos i'r byd fel dynion crefyddol, mae yn rhaid fod breuddwydion dychrynllyd yn myned trwy eu penau yn ystod y nos.

Ond hyn sy'n capso'r cyfan fod gwraig i gaffer yma un ochr i'r stryd, a gwidw yr ochr arall i'r stryd, yn hela ac yn gwaeddi 'Tali ho' bob yn ail pan fydd personau neillduol yn myned heibio. Y mae yma siarad yn ein cymydogaeth ni am gael cyfarfod cyhoeddus er nodi dau neu dri i fyned i lawr i Benybont i edrych os oes yno le i ychwaneg o fenywod wedi colli eu *senses*. Mae lle i ofni fod cwpwl eto bron yn barod i'r gwallgofdy. Ond y mae yma ofyniad yn cyfodi yn meddyliau amryw yn y lle hwn, sef, 'Pwy fydd yn rhaid eu cynal yn y gwallgofdy?' Ni a obeithiwn y bydd i'r trueiniaid uchod ddala y Llwynog cyn bo hir, fel y bydd iddynt gael hamdden i wella, waith bydd yn well gan y Llwynog fod yn y ddalfa ei hunan na bod yn achos i fenywod mor *respectable* ac mor gryfion eu synwyrau i gael eu hunain yn Ngwallgofdy Penybont.

Yr ydych yn coflo fod gwobr wedi ei chynyg yn Eisteddfod y T'w'llwch, am y traethawd goreu ar y 'Cysylltiad sydd rhwng gwallgofrwydd a bywyd anllad a ffug grefyddol.' Wel, i'r rhai sydd yn bwriadu cystadlu ar y traethawd uchod, dymuna y Llwynog gyflwyno y stori uchod iddynt. Y mae stori arall, llawn mor darawiadol ar y pwnc, yn adnabyddus yn y cymydogaethau hyn ; ac os bydd rhyw rai o bell yn bwriadu cystadlu, cant yr hanes, gyda throad y post, oddi wrth un sy'n gwybod yr hanes yn dda, sef ysgrifenydd Eisteddfod y T'w'llwch

Heblaw hyny, bydd y Llwynog, yn mhen ewpwl o fisoedd, yn debyg o fyned i mewn i fanylion yr hanes, a'u dadlenu ger bron holl ddarllenwyr y DARIAN : a chewch weled ei fod yn hanes dychrynyd iawn.

Yn y papyrau Seisnig yr wythnos hon cair y newydd pruddglwyfus fod Brigham Young wedi marw. Pan welais yr hanes yn y papyr, fe fu fy nghalon bron neidio allan o'i gwisg, gan ofn mai Brigham Young Cwm Rhondda, oedd wedi marw. Chredwch chwi ddim, Mri. Gol., y fath le fuasai yn Cwm Rhondda, cyn pen pedair awr ar-hugain, pe buasai y Brigham hwn wedi marw. Mae y Llwynog yn meddwl y byddai cymaint o gylch y ty yn wylo am eu gwr ag sydd o amgylch ambell bwll ar ol tanchwa. Y mae'r Llwynog yn dychymygu eu clywed y fynyd hon,—un yn dolefain, 'O! fy Mrigham anwyl, beth a wnaf; O! beth a wnaf? Cyn i mi a'm plant bach symud i'ch ty chwi yr oeddym yn methu yn lan a thalu y *rent*, ond wedi symud, yr oeddwn i a'm plant bach yn cael tamaid i fwyta, a dillad i wisgo, a chwithau byth yn gofyn am y *rent*. Adenydd myrddiwn o angylion a'ch cysgodo, ac os oes gwreica a gwra yr ochr draw, gobeithio y bydd i chwi gael digon o wragedd, waith welais i neb erioed mor *fond* o honynt. O! Brigham, Brigham anwyl, beth a wnaf?'

A typical column by the *Llwynog*

The Co-operative stores and Bethlehem Congregational Chapel, Abercwmboi (Cap Coch) in 1982

Esther Davies, mother of S. O. Davies

Mrs. Mary Green, (S.O.'s sister) now in her nineties

39 John Street, Abercwmboi—bricked up in 1982

would use his column in the *Darian*, for example in this appeal to men in a Rhondda pit :

> *Yn awr, fechgyn, ma's a'r tools bob copa walltog a mynnwn ein hiawnderau . . . Ymarfogwn o ddifri bob glowr trwy'r lofa ac nid gadael i ryw un dosbarth i ymladd ar ei ben ei hun, fel y mae wedi bod yma lawer gwaith yn flaenorol, a thrwy hynny golli y dydd. Safwn yn ddisigil yn y ddwy wythien, a dangoswn ein bod yn ddynion am unwaith, neu bydd yn rhaid i ni cyn hir dalu am weithio os bydd i ni gymeryd bob peth fel ag yr ydym yn ddiweddar.*[4]

> Now, boys, away with the tools every man-jack of you, and we will demand our rights . . . We will recruit every miner throughout the pit, not leave one class to fight on its own as has been done so many times in the past, so ending in defeat. We will stand firmly in both the seams and show for once that we are men—or before long we will be paying to work, if we continue to accept everything as we have been doing lately.

The revelation that Thomas Davies and *Llwynog o'r Graig* were one and the same person obviously intensified the efforts of coalowners and colliery managers to blacklist him throughout the South Wales coalfield, and this they succeeded in doing. For a period of ten years Thomas was hounded out of one colliery after another, or refused even a start if the colliery manager knew of his pen-name ; but he earned small amounts of money by adjudicating at *eisteddfodau*, while his wife turned the parlour of their home at 39 John Street, Abercwmboi, into a shop selling home-baked bread. *Thomas Dafis y Llwynog*, as he later became known, had always been a popular character in the village : when he suffered a serious accident in the pit the local Co-operative store held a raffle to raise money for him and his family. Therefore it was no suprise that when he finally found a job, it was as a very successful agent for the Pearl Insurance Company. Exactly how the *Llwynog*'s identity became known and who betrayed it remains a mystery to this day. However, Thomas always suspected that it was a gaffer and chapel deacon by the name of Henry Davies who received the treacherous information and thereafter transmitted it to his masters.

Thomas was also a devoutly religious man, attending Bethlehem Congregational Church in Abercwmboi. Many years later he was still remembered by Joshua Bowen Davies as one of the chapel's stalwarts :

> *Yr oedd gan yr Efengyl afael rhyfedd arno, oblegid gwelais ef ddegau o weithiau yn ddrylliog iawn ei deimladau dan y weinidogaeth. Gwrandawai yn wresog, a chlywsid ei "Amen" o bell. Gweddïai yn ddwys a gwlithog. Nid oedd yn gerddor gwych ; yr oedd ei gryfder yn fwy fel athraw yn yr Ysgol Sul.*[5]
>
> The Gospel had an awesome hold upon him, because I saw him emotionally shattered by the ministry tens of times. He would listen warmly, and one could hear his "Amen" from afar. He would pray intensely and with tears in his eyes. He was not a brilliant singer ; his strength was more as a teacher in the Sunday School.

But Thomas' militant Socialist convictions were destined to trespass upon his religious activities with dramatic effect. In 1904 Wales underwent its greatest religious revival since 1859 when a young preacher, Evan Roberts, toured the coalfield chapels drawing huge congregations. Claiming to hear the ' Divine Voice ', Roberts won tens of thousands of ' sinners ' to the Lord and away from drink, football and card-playing. Cynics saw in his sermons a mixture of theatre, hysteria and demagogy ; he pleaded with his audience, coaxed them, explained to them why they should reject materialism, malice and hatred. But whereas the sincerity and selflessness of the ' Wesley of Wales ' was never in dispute, the motives of some of his backers and publicists were more of this world than of the next. Nothing could have pleased the capitalists more than a pacifistic work-force, happy with their lot and pledged to turn the other cheek. The *Western Mail* afforded generous publicity to the Revival, joyfully pointing out in a pamphlet that : ' Workmen are more satisfied with their wages and surroundings, and the Revival has exorcised the evil spirit of disaffection from the mine and the workshop. Collieries in many instances have been turned into temporary places of worship.'[6] For the record, it should be noted that the underground hymn-singing services were held before the shift began —and not during working time !

This euphoric mood of harmony and conciliation was wholly contrary to the class militancy promoted by Thomas Davies and his confederates. Even after he had hung up his pit boots for good, Thomas was a familiar figure at political and trade union gatherings, denouncing the coalowners and exhorting the workers to organise. The deacons of his local chapel, many of them colliery officials, eventually gained their revenge by excommunicating him during the Revival—nearly 30 years after his last article as the *Llwynog*. At the same time prayers were said for his family that they might return to the ' straight and narrow '.

The narrowness and sectarianism of the churches, his own and those of others, had received their fair share of attention from the *Llwynog*. Nevertheless Thomas Davies endured the persecution, his religious faith undimmed, and eventually he was elected a deacon of Soar Chapel in Mountain Ash. Esther Davies shared her husband's religious convictions—her brother was a renowned preacher, the Rev. William Owen—but music was the ruling passion of her life. She was a leading soprano in the legendary *Côr Mawr Caradog*, a huge amalgam of south Wales choirs under conductor Griffith Rhys Jones (' Caradog ') which swept to the National Prize at Crystal Palace in 1872 with the unanimous approval of the music adjudicators.

After the wage rises won between 1870 and 1873, the standard of living for the majority of people in south Wales dropped continuously for six years. The early 1880s witnessed another upturn, bringing living standards close to the level of 1874, before another decline occurred to about 1888. With Thomas Davies so ruthlessly victimised throughout much of this period, his young family must have experienced greater hardship than many others in the village. But the children of Thomas and Esther Davies had been born into a remarkable household : the ingenuity and hard work of their mother, the humour of their father, and music, culture and the chapel all lightened their burden. It would be the opposite of the truth to claim that the material hardship of those years bequeathed a sourness or resentment to the children. On the contrary, theirs was a very close, cheerful family with the fullest admiration for the father and the deepest love and affection for their mother who, when still young, suffered several strokes. Although both parents could speak English, Welsh was the language of the home as it was of the whole village : few *eisteddfodau* or concerts were held in the district without at least one member of *Thomas Dafis y Llwynog*'s tribe taking part. Altogether Thomas and Esther Davies had six children :

Catherine Rachel was the home-loving eldest daughter with an excellent voice that won many prizes at *eisteddfodau* ; her husband fractured his spine in a mining accident, leaving her a widow before the age of 30 with five children.

Mary became a nurse in Merthyr Tydfil, before moving on to Whitchurch Hospital, Cardiff, and Leeds; she survived all her brothers and sisters.

William Owen was the eldest son and the quiet member of the family ; another fine singer, he spent most of his life in Abercwmboi working in the mines.

David also worked in the pits until his asthma obliged him to find a job with an insurance company ; after moving from Mountain Ash to Ammanford he returned to the mine.

Thomas Gibbon followed his elder brothers underground ; he later moved to Carmarthenshire where he became a checkweigher in Tumble and achieved prominence as a militant miners' leader ; after many years service on Carmarthenshire County Council he was elected chairman.

All the family were members of the Independent Labour Party at one time or another, so that politics joined culture and religion as powerful influences in their lives.

But it was in the third son, *Stephen Owen,* that the most explosive fusion of these elements occurred, attracting to the name S.O. Davies a popularity and notoriety far wider even than that gained by his father, Thomas Davies senior—*Llwynog o'r Graig.*

NOTES

[1]See *Disaster at Tynewydd* (1975), a pamphlet by Ken Llewellyn.
[2]*Tarian y Gweithiwr*, 29 March 1878.
[3]*Tarian y Gweithiwr*, 16 March 1877.
[4]*Tarian y Gweithiwr*, 5 April 1878.
[5]*Meysydd Bethlehem* (1915) by Joshua Bowen Davies.
[6]*The Religious Revival in Wales* (No. 3, 1905), a *Western Mail* supplement.
[7]The name ' Gibbon ' reputedly ran in the Davies family ; S.O. Davies claimed the blind ballad singer and composer Levi Gibbon as a relation. Levi Gibbon hailed from industrial Carmarthenshire, and some of his songs told of the cruelties of the workhouse. With his daughters he sang at the market and fair held every quarter on Y Waun, above Dowlais. Legend has it that his ballad kept the workhouse out of Merthyr for a generation, and gave the workers heart for the 1831 Merthyr Rising. He died in 1870 in the parish of Llanwonno, Aberdare, aged 63. See the *Dictionary of Welsh Biography* (1959) ; and *The Merthyr Rising* (1978) by Gwyn A. Williams.

Bibliographical Note

The letter from ' Llwynog o'r Graig '—*Llith y Llwynog*—appeared almost every week in *Tarian y Gweithiwr* from October 6, 1876, till August 30 1878 ; S. O. Davies recalled some of his father's exploits in the *Merthyr Express* (November 9 1918 and November 23 1918), *Y Cymro* (May 13 1970) and in the *South Wales Echo* (April 9 1970). Details of the Davies family history have been provided by S.O.'s sister, Mrs. Mary Green, in letters and conversations with the author from June 1977 onwards. The accounts of industrial conflict and trade unionism in the coal industry have been distilled from *The History of the South Wales Miners* (1926) by Ness Edwards, *The Miners of South Wales* (1961) and *Mabon* (1959) by E. W. Evans, and *South Wales Miners* Vol. 1 (1967) by R. Page Arnot.

Chapter Two

NONCONFORMER

The fourth child in the Davies family, Stephen Owen, was born on November 27 . . . but the precise year of his birth is a matter of dispute ! Throughout his life it was publicised as 1886. Yet when Stephen himself completed his registration form for entry to University College, Cardiff, he gave his date of birth as November 27, 1883—three years earlier. He mentioned in later life that his mother, Esther, had registered the birth after the required time limit ; therefore she might have written 1886 instead of 1883 in order to avoid any legal repercussions. Subsequently, Stephen never claimed those three extra years to which he was probably entitled.

From the five-roomed terraced cottage in John Street it was a short uphill walk to Capcoch Elementary School, which Stephen attended from the age of three and a half. He shared the two-roomed infants unit with over one hundred other children : the overcrowding was appalling even by the standards of the day. One consequence for the staff of three or four was a degree of difficulty in enforcing discipline—a feature not unnoticed by Her Majesty's Inspector of Schools. Likewise, the school curriculum probably inflicted tedium rather than Victorian terror on the pupils ; with his classmates young Stephen endured endless rounds of singing, recitation and ' object-learning '. Or at least they did so whenever the school was not closed for elections, village fairs, strikes, colliers' holidays or chapel tea-parties. But by far the severest scourge of the attendance register was sickness : every day up to one-quarter of the children would be absent with chicken pox, scarlet fever, measles or some other contagious disease.[1]

In all this, life at Capcoch School was unremarkable. Yet there was one practice, general throughout Wales, which with hindsight deserves some mention. This was the policy of teaching all subjects through the medium of English regardless of the fact that nearly all children spoke Welsh as their mother tongue, and indeed most had it as their only language. Stephen Davies fell into the second category, even though both his parents could speak English if called upon to do so.

Although outlawed under the 1536 Act which incorporated Wales into England, no serious effort was made to ' extirp ' the Welsh language until after the Industrial Revolution. With the rise of Capitalism, the working-class being forged in the ironworks, coal mines and woollen mills was mostly monoglot Welsh-speaking ; most of the employers, landlords, soldiers and State churchmen, meanwhile, were English or so anglicised as to make no difference. A series of Government and Privy Council reports in the 1830s and 1840s detected the national-linguistic tension beneath the surface of such social and economic protests as the Rebecca Riots, the Merthyr Insurrection of 1831, and the Chartist agitation. The Report of the Queen's Commission on the Administration of Justice in Wales remarked :

> The people's ignorance of the English language practically prevents the working of the laws and institutions and impedes the administration of justice.

Welsh was alleged to be one of the major causes of popular unrest, ignorance and immorality. Privy Councillor the Rev. H. L. Ballairs hit upon the answer when he concluded that ' a band of efficient schoolmasters is kept up at a much less expense than a body of police or soldiery'.[2] The Welsh language would be shamed and beaten out of children in the schools. From 1870, and for at least 20 crucial years, the State-supervised elementary system and its education codes made it financially and administratively prohibitive for schools to find a place for the Welsh language in the classroom.[3]

One of the most zealous Anglophiles was the principal mistress of Capcoch's infant school, Margaret Howard. She had convinced herself that the youngsters of the village would never ' get on ' in the world without first ridding themselves of the Welsh language. Stephen was only six years old when Mrs Howard banned the use of Welsh in the school. One of the first victims of her ban was young Stephen ; he retaliated by folding away his writing paper, sitting back in his desk and announcing to his classmates : ' *Bois, dwy'i ddim yn mynd i wneud rhagor o waith i hon !*' (' Boys, I am not going to do any more work for her !'). The rest of the children followed his lead and downed their pens. Only later in the day, after the school's headmaster had overruled the infants' headmistress, did work recommence—with the teaching still in English, but the chatter once again in Welsh.[4]

In his report on Capcoch Elementary School for 1893, Her Majesty's Inspector observed that :

> The children seem to come from Welsh homes and would be benefitted by some bilingual teaching.

His advice was not heeded—but perhaps Stephen Davies' first strike played some part in prompting this, the only reference to the Welsh language in H.M.I.'s Report for at least a decade.

The junior school, with 180 pupils in three rooms, was no less cramped than the infants' section. Subjects such as geography, mathematics and craft-work had been added to the curriculum, which Stephen now worked through with enthusiasm ; he was one of the brightest boys of his year, habitually competing with a friend for first place in the class. The encouragement received from headmaster William Halket Jones gave him an appetite for learning that would never be satiated.

Nevertheless his earliest schooling came to an end in the inevitable way when, at the age of 12, Stephen joined his brothers underground at Cwmpennar pit, overlooking Mountain Ash on the opposite side of the valley. On his first day he was asked whether he had any objection to working with the pit's sole Englishman, one Joby Whale from Wiltshire. Stephen jumped at the offer : back in Cap Coch he had braved the taunts of the other youngsters when befriending the only English boy in the village, James Dole. Through this friendship the two lads had learnt a little of each other's language ; now Stephen grasped the opportunity to master English fully.

So he went to work at the three foot three inches seam as Joby's *crotyn*, or young helper. Once Joby had filled a ' curling ' box (or scoop) with up to half a hundredweight of coal, it was Stephen's task to run or pull it to the main stall roadway, unload it into the tram and bring it back in time for Joby to begin filling it again. Meanwhile another full box would be ready for hauling along the low, black tunnel to the waiting wagon. When the one-eyed overman Twm Edmwnd came around on the first ' measuring day ' to assess the pair's work, he began cursing Joby in Welsh ; Stephen acted as interpreter, also seizing the opportunity to tear the gaffer off a strip for taking advantage of a man whom he knew did not understand the language. This precocious intervention earned the youngster a salvo of eloquent and fiery abuse from Edmwnd—and a golden sovereign from his ' butty ' Joby Whale, four pennies above the normal fortnightly rate. Stephen recalled many years later :

> *Roedd Joby Whale yn un o'r cymeriadau mwyaf caredig gwrddais i erioed. Roeddwn i'n mynd yn ffyrnig pan ddwede rhywun bethe cas amdano—fel roedden nhw'n tueddu i ddweud am Saeson yn gyffredinol* ![5]

> Joby Whale was one of the kindest characters I ever met. I used to be furious when somebody said a hateful thing about him—as they tended to do with anyone English !

Shortly after the coal reserves at Cwmpennar were exhausted the family moved to Pyle Villa, Aberdare Road, Mountain Ash. Stephen, who actually enjoyed working underground, started new employment at Nixon's colliery where the manager, W. S. Davies, urged him to continue his education. The intelligent, hard-working newcomer told him of a fondness for adventure stories, whereupon Mr Davies snatched a lump of coal, held it to the young collier's face and said : ' There's more adventure in that piece of coal than there is in all the adventure books on the market '.[6]

After a talk to his father, Stephen enrolled for night classes in mining engineering at Aberdare. He began to spend more and more of his leisure time studying and, when the pit was idle for six weeks following an accident, he swotted for the advanced section of his first major examination paper. Unaware of his extra effort, Stephen's friends sat the elementary section while Stephen successfully tackled the advanced questions. He had undoubtedly developed a facility for passing exams—but it was founded upon exhausting study. After a full day down the pit he would work at his books until two o'clock in the morning, have a short sleep and then return to Nixon's by 6 o'clock for the early morning shift. He eventually reached the stage of insomnia, and his mother was compelled to make up a bed in his study so that he could at least be tempted into an occasional cat-nap. This situation persisted for more than a year until—at the age of 23—Stephen tottered on the verge of a nervous breakdown. Thomas Davies then decided that enough was enough, whisking his son off to recuperate in Blaenau, Carmarthenshire, with some relatives. Stephen's cousin Emily nursed him well, standing no nonsense from him.

He was soon strong enough to earn his keep, which he did firstly with a job at Caebryn colliery, Llandybïe, and then in Emlyn colliery, Penygroes, where he supervised half a dozen boys screening the coal. But all the while Stephen pined for the books he had reluctantly left behind in Mountain Ash ; so when his young charges expressed a desire for education, they found a willing teacher. In fact it was while at Emlyn colliery that Stephen himself studied for his London Matriculation Certificate for entry to university.

Following his recovery in Carmarthenshire, Stephen left home for only the second time in his life, travelling to the Royal College of Science in London where he sat examinations in mining engineering and colliery management—and sailed through them with honours. From this he won summer scholarships enabling him to tour European coalfields and examine different mining techniques. After a visit to Belgium he wrote an influential paper on the activities of the bark-beetle, a pest which exposes the tree trunk to weakening and disease by furrowing just below the bark : indeed it later became the practice in British mines to strip all timber pit-props of bark before allowing them underground.

Once his travels were over he returned home to Mountain Ash to consider his future in conference with the family. Which path should he take ? From that first week in the pits when—at the age of 12—he had paid his trade union dues to the South Wales Miners Federation lodge secretary, Stephen had taken an interest in Socialist politics. With his brothers he used to attend the Saturday night meetings in Aberdare Square, enjoying the Socialist evangelism of such pioneers as Robert Blatchford. All the family had thrilled to the heroic tales told by Thomas Davies, and many decades later Stephen could still recall his first trip to the polling booth—to vote for James Keir Hardie, the founder of the Independent Labour Party and 'father' of the modern Labour Party.[7] The Merthyr Borough parliamentary constituency (at that time including the Cynon Valley) altogether returned Hardie at four General Elections between 1900 and 1910, thus establishing itself as one of Britain's Socialist crucibles.

Religion, too, was waxing a powerful influence in the moral and intellectual development of Stephen Davies. He had spent some of his west Wales convalescence at Gwynfryn School in Ammanford, a preparatory institution for students wishing to pursue theology and, in time, to enter the ministry. Now the young man with a strong voice and an even stronger social conscience was eager to find a platform for his radical views : the pulpit—the focal point of Welsh chapel democracy—seemed both obvious and ideal. So, prompted by his father, he applied for entry to Brecon Memorial College, run by the second largest of the Welsh Nonconformist denominations—the Independents (or Congregationalists). They would sponsor him as a student in University College, Cardiff, whereafter—having gained a B.A. degree—he would read theology at Brecon itself. Like all other sponsored students Stephen would be ' on probation ' for his first year at Cardiff after which he would study there and later in Brecon as a full student of the Memorial College. Even though he refused to sign a form accepting their articles of belief, Brecon agreed to pay his university fees and award him a grant. Stephen found digs in Lisvane Street, Cathays, and began his college career in October 1908. All going well, he should become a minister of religion shortly after his 30th birthday.

During the first year of his three year course he immersed himself in the study of Greek, Latin, Hebrew and the Scriptures, in accordance with the Memorial College's required B.A. curriculum. But outside those academic cloisters the industrial, political and religious life of Wales was in turmoil : the chapels were losing their grip on working-class life as the gains of the 1904-05 Revival evaporated; the Welsh language retreated before the flood of job-hungry Midlands and West Country immigrants ; ownership of industry and finance was becoming concentrated in fewer and better-organised hands ; labour was consolidating itself in the trade unions and in the infant Labour Party. In south Wales the I.L.P. was recruiting thousands of men to a militant—but thinking and feeling—Socialism : between 1901 and 1910 the number of I.L.P. branches in Wales soared from eleven to 104.[8]

Against this background the churches appeared to be increasingly irrelevant. When they took a position on industrial or political matters, it was often an ambiguous or downright reactionary one. Radical Christians now attacked the old theology which considered God to be utterly above and apart from his creation ; a basic material standard of living, they argued, was required before spiritual enlightenment and salvation could be achieved ; the slums and sweat-shops, paupers and unemployed, were symptoms of a social order that was anti-Christian as well as anti-social . . . ' the standard of Christ and the standard of the commercial world are not the same ', declared the Rev. R. J. Campbell. The system founded on selfishness would have to be destroyed—' we want Collectivism in place of competition '. In his hugely influential book *The New Theology*, Campbell maintained :

> The moral movements of the age, such as the great Labour Movement, are in reality the expression of the Christian spirit, and only need to recognise themselves as such in order to become irresistible. The wagon of Socialism needs to be hitched to the star of religious faith.

This was the same gospel preached by Stephen Davies as a student in the chapels of south Wales. The passionate young man cut an imposing figure in the pulpit : six feet tall, smartly dressed and with a steady, powerful voice which could convey the zeal of his convictions. Chapels began asking specifically for him as a guest preacher, offering him fifteen shillings a time instead of the customary ten. But the message he was spreading did not enjoy the same rapturous reception from the Memorial College authorities. Wherever Stephen preached there would be someone in the congregation charged with the responsibility of reporting back to Brecon.

Growing discontent with the outspoken first-year student became formalised in January 1909 when the Memorial College's Executive Committee set up a five-man sub-committee ' to interview Mr. S. O. Davies as to certain rumours abroad respecting certain phrases used by him in public worship '.[9]

After meeting Stephen the sub-committee announced their dissatisfaction with him on three counts : firstly, he had failed to provide testimonials from his past chapels and had refused to endorse the College's articles of faith ; secondly, his theological statement to the sub-committee was ' extremely unsatisfactory ' (' he having refrained from committing himself to any fundamental Christian doctrine ') and thirdly, his defiant behaviour when appearing before the committee had deeply offended many of the members. On January 30 the Executive Committee accepted the sub-committee's unanimous recommendation that—instead of being accepted by

Brecon College as a full student from that summer—Stephen's probationary period in Cardiff should be extended beyond a year. In fact the sub-committee came close to proposing that the College sever their links with him altogether, only deciding against such a drastic step for fear that it might be misinterpreted as a witch-hunt against Socialists and those Christians with unorthodox theological views. It was not that the College 'establishment' objected to Christian Socialism as such : after all, its basic principles of social justice, fairer distribution of wealth, opposition to imperial wars and support for trade unionism were not incompatible with Christianity. Nor did they resent the injection of a mild dose of 'materialism' into the faith. No, it was the particular strain of Stephen Davies' Christian Socialism which they could not accept : for whereas most Christian Socialists adhered strictly to constitutional methods, social reform, pacifism and progress through concensus and brotherly love, he was one of the 'physical force' group advocating class conflict, militant trade unionism and social change by revolution if needs be. Moreover, he held rigidly to Campbell's 'New Theology' including those tenets of it which—as we shall see—were clearly in breach of Christianity's fundamental beliefs (and which Campbell himself later repudiated).

Characteristically, Stephen Davies persisted with the same convictions and 'phrases' that had prompted the creation of his very own sub-committee ; the sub-committee therefore remained in existence. At a meeting of 25 November 1909 it demanded and duly received a fuller statement of his views on the principal doctrines of Christianity. On fundamental points Stephen's opinions were at odds with the accepted dogma. For instance, he only regarded Jesus Christ as the Son of God in the sense that all mankind are God's children :

> Man is God's highest self-manifestation, and Jesus is Man at his best—Man as Son of God, Man expressing the divine love.

Jesus was God incarnate—but so was every beautiful life. Nowhere did Stephen even mention the Resurrection : Jesus was a mortal, albeit an ideal one—the paragon for all men. Similarly, he told the sub-committee that the Atonement (Christ dying on the cross to save mankind) was a 'symbol' to teach us that redemption would come through a suffering love. When all mankind learnt this and applied it then we could indeed achieve heaven on earth.

After considering this statement at a further meeting on 5 February 1910, in Merthyr, the sub-committee reported to the Executive that in their judgement :

> Mr Davies' views on the Central Truths of the Christian Religion do not seem to be those generally held by the Churches which maintain the Institution into which Mr Davies seeks to gain admission.

As to what the College should do with him, the sub-committee did not wish to take responsibility for recommending any particular course of action.

A final showdown with the Memorial College authorities was now inevitable ; it came on 23 February 1910 in Brecon, when Stephen was summoned to tell the Executive Committee why they should continue to sponsor him at the University College in Cardiff. At a full meeting of the Executive, with nigh-on a hundred members present in the Memorial College library, Stephen refused to beg for their patronage : instead he reaffirmed his determination to speak his mind, in the pulpit and outside. They could do whatever they wanted with him, it would make no difference : 'Anyway, one day I'll have a bigger congregation than any of you—and long before I am your age !' he informed the older reactionaries. Some of the younger Committee members spoke up on his behalf, but in truth Stephen had put himself beyond the pale : he had flagrantly defied the old guard and was utterly unrepentant.

Hence it was no surprise when he received a letter from the Memorial College shortly afterwards, dated 25 February 1910, informing him that his probationary period with the College was at an end and that he could consider his connection with them to have been severed. Thus ended what many people believed was destined to be a brilliant vocation in the ministry.

For his part Stephen now realised that Welsh Nonconformism could not be the agent of fundamental social change : its nature had been irrevocably conditioned by the very system that needed to be destroyed. He regarded Welsh Nonconformism as the product and expression of working-class life : the lack of beauty and joyous optimism in the chapels was but a reflection of the homes of the masses. The ugliness of working-class dwellings, the never-ending monotony of domestic life and the paucity of education were all reflected in the dispiriting gloom which pervaded the chapels. For him, Christianity should have joy as its inspiration and beauty as its expression ; it should seek to break out of ugliness, pain and oppression. But this interpretation was beyond the comprehension of those who condoned or praised the prevailing social and economic order. Such were the people who determined the ' official ' character of the church. A few years later they were to be typified by a fictional deacon, Price, in a play reviewed by Stephen Davies in the *Llanelly Mercury* :

> His 50 long years of hard, grinding anxious toil had, in conjunction with his belief in a cruel and loveless God, embittered and hardened his life to a painful degree. His God was the God of the Old Testament theology, and his religion was that of a rigid, frozen Calvinism. He, notwithstanding his being a deacon at Horeb, had utterly no conception of Christianity; not a ray of the Sermon on the Mount seemed able to penetrate his petrified spirit. He had without question, accepted as a worker the capitalist system, which had robbed him and a million others of most of the fruits of their labour . . . We find many a Price today in our big pews and pulpits ! . . . In the old man, Price, oppression had found a victim and a supporter. It had deprived him of the very elements of education, and had enslaved him from childhood. But, in the name of God, he protested against Change.[10]

Thenceforward, although he never forsook chapel attendance altogether, Stephen spurned membership of any specific religious denomination. When asked to outline his religious faith he would simply answer : ' My religion is the Sermon on the Mount '.

When the fateful letter arrived, Stephen was living at 34 Gelligaer Street, Cathays, with his mother and sister Mary. Thomas Davies senior had died the previous August, aged 65, after which Esther sold Pyle Villa and moved down to Cardiff where she could watch her son with pride as he progressed through college. Nobody was more distressed than her when Brecon announced their decision ; but more than anything else she admired her son's stand for his principles. Whereas Stephen's first reaction was to talk of abandoning academic life and returning to Ammanford to work full-time underground, neither his mother nor Mary would hear of it. Money was the main problem : Stephen's fees had been paid up to the summer, but withdrawal of the grant from Brecon had left him with no source of income—and little hope of paying future fees. There was no option : he would travel down to Carmarthenshire and work in the local mines during his college holidays.

While waiting to change his university course, Stephen threw himself deeper into local politics. Since coming to Cardiff he had joined the I.L.P., going with his sister to the party's meeting place overlooking St. John's Church in the city centre. Now he took on a job as part-time organiser for a few months, earning a small but much-needed wage in return. The Cardiff I.L.P. had begun challenging the Tory-Liberal duopoly of municipal politics by contesting the city council elections.

Stephen—or ' S.O.' as his friends and comrades were now calling him—was himself addressing more and more public meetings, helping to build a Socialist labour party as the successor to ' Lib-Labism '. In college he began studying economics, sociology, ethics and psychology ; he developed an enthusiasm for Aristophanes, even appearing himself in one of the Greek satirist's comedies at Cardiff's New Theatre. During vacations he worked underground in south-west Wales where his talents as a public speaker, trade union activist and agitator for Socialism attracted considerable respect and attention.

When Esther died in February 1912, just 60 years of age, Mary took up the fight to keep her brother to his studies. Stephen's desire was to drop out of his course and begin earning a proper wage ; he would not agree to take lodgers at their house, in Gelligaer Street. But on this occasion Mary proved too clever for him : she recruited a family friend to help convince Stephen that two young students were desperate for accommodation. They moved in and—unknown to him—payed Mary a modest rent.

Towards the end of his college life, S.O. was eventually cajoled, against his will, into fighting the Cardiff Board of Guardians elections in April 1913 as an I.L.P candidate. The ward chosen for him was Grangetown, an overwhelmingly working-class area of the city. S.O. and his helpers set about testing the appeal of Socialist ideas to the ordinary worker, addressing open-air street meetings and distributing leaflets. In particular, Stephen tried to woo the large Irish vote : ' I am perfectly with you on the Irish nationalist question ', he assured them. When the result was finally announced on April 7—two days after polling—S.O. and his comrades had achieved what was probably the best Socialist vote in any Cardiff municipal election up to that time :[11]

Mrs Cantillion	379
Rev. J. Williams	365
Rev. W. A. Peters	329
Mr W. J. Hall	292
non-elected	
Mr S. O. Davies	246

He had failed by just 47 votes to sit on the Board of Guardians where, undoubtedly, he would have demanded the maximum outdoor relief for all claimants as a prelude to replacing the Poor Law and its network of workhouses with a comprehensive, more humane system of social welfare.

That S.O. and his father had both been disowned, at one time or another, by the church was gleefully referred to by his election opponents. Nor was this the only occasion upon which S.O. came under attack for his departure from the straight-and-narrow ; a controversial essay by the anti-Socialist crusader the Rev. W. F. Phillips, printed in a prestigious magazine in 1911 and reprinted in a well-known book two years later, contained what many people took to be a veiled reference to S.O. :

> *Trwy garedigrwydd un o'r eglwysi, cafodd bachgen o lowr addysg uwchraddol. Ar ei ddychweliad i'w gartref ymosododd yn llym ar yr eglwys a wnaeth gymaint caredigrwydd ag ef, ac ar y gyfundrefn grefyddol y magwyd ef ynddi. Enwir y bachgenyn anniolchgar hwn fel un o aelodau seneddol y dyfodol ! Anaml y clywir Sosialydd yn annerch cynulleidfa yn Neheudir Cymru heb wrandaw ar ddatganiadau gwrth-grefyddol a gwrth-genedlaethol. Wel, dyma'r dynion sydd yn pregethu Sosialaeth yn ein gwlad.*[12]

> Through the kindness of one of the churches, a young miner received higher education. Upon his return home, he sharply attacked the church which had shown him so much kindness, and the religious order in which he had been reared. This ungrateful young man has been named as a future member of parliament ! It is not very often that one can hear a Socialist addressing an audience in South Wales without also having to listen to anti-religious and anti-national statements. Well, these are the men who are preaching Socialism in our country.

Phillips fulminated against the 'infidel, ambitious foreigners' such as Keir Hardie, who were allegedly corrupting the Welsh labour movement with anti-Welsh and anti-Christian ideas. He also referred in another article to the 'black sheep' occasionally elected to the Diaconate, men who acquired their intellectual and speaking skills in the church—only to place those skills at the disposal of this alien creed, Socialism. Perhaps he had Thomas Davies in mind!

S.O. finally gained a B.A. degree in social sciences in 1913, that same year moving down to Ammanford with his brothers David and Gibbon. Within months of restarting work at the Great Mountain colliery, Tumble—where he had spent his college holidays—S.O. was elected a checkweighman by his fellow miners. This was a position of immense responsibility and trust, only tolerated by the coalowners and managers after decades of bitter wrangling. The miners' checkweigher would frequent the weighing house, ensuring that the coal dug by the men was not being weighed 'light' in order to rob them of their wages. S.O.'s skills as an orator were not wasted either: he began lecturing to local I.L.P night classes as well as fulfilling the usual round of speaking engagements expected of any trade union official. Indeed, so keen were the workers of the area to utilize fully the extraordinary talents of this 30-year-old firebrand that the following year they chose him as the Labour Party's parliamentary candidate for the Llanelli Division. S.O. responded conscientiously to the men's trust and enthusiasm. With forceful fluency he voiced their aspirations, using every available platform to argue for social justice, better working conditions, trade unionism, international peace and, of course, for the real emancipation—Socialism.

His letters to the *Llanelly Mercury* and *Amman Valley Chronicle* were models of lucid advocacy.[13] One notable debate in the *Chronicle*'s columns in the autumn of 1914 concerned the philosophy of Socialism, with S.O. showing how best to counter an adversary's arguments and expose his tricks. He deflated one Lewis Jones with the sharpest wit, commenting on Jones' previous letter as follows:

> I trod painfully upon split infinitives, entangled myself in mixed metaphors, floundered in bogs of ambiguity, and wandered around and around circumlocutory paths, along which I had started with hope, but returned with never-failing precision to the point of my departure.

Elsewhere and in more serious vein he launched a swingeing campaign against Carmarthenshire's appalling record in education. His widely-published open letter to the Carmarthenshire Education Committee in 1915 laid the blame firmly at their feet, telling them that :

> By underpaying your teachers you have succeeded in placing the education of the children in the hands of people 60% of whom have no, and cannot have any, pretensions to being educated themselves. I presume that you are aware that taking hopelessly unprepared young women of 18 to 22 years of age from their domestic duties, and placing them at the head of big classes of children, has become a scandal in our county.

As he pointed out, Carmarthenshire's classroom conditions were worse than those in 219 of the United Kingdom's 288 education authorities ; 419 of the county's 495 Elementary school teachers had no qualifications ; and in Glamorgan the education committee spent two and a half times more on each pupil than did Carmarthenshire. Besides calling for support for the National Union of Teachers —which only admitted qualified teachers to its ranks—he warned that his own union, the Miners' Federation, would run the education system if the Education Committee could not execute its responsibilities.

Typically, S.O. also linked his criticisms of the Committee with the great issue of the time—the First World War—by addressing them thus :

> I see, gentlemen and ladies, that many of you at present find the recruiting platform more congenial than the education problem. I read your eloquent denunciations of German militarism, and the invective you pour upon German Kultur. But, believe me, modern German kultur has not descended further from the noble ideals of Fichte, Schiller, Heine and many others, than your conception of education and progress has from the ideals and apirations of Griffith Jones, Llanddowror, and Vicar Prichard. If German kultur, as positively expressed in militarism, is destructive, your policy in the negation of all that makes for progress is equally so. The physical deprivations of underpaid workers, and the intellectual starvation of young children, 90% of whom leave your schools hating rather than 'loving' knowledge, and therefore, spending the remainder of their days grappling blindly with superstition, is ultimately as destructive as the sword of militarism.

In fact Germany's superior education system had played no small part in creating the preconditions for war. Compared with the situation in Britain, Germany's working-class was a skilled and well-educated one. The resulting efficiency in production had enabled German industry to make inroads into traditional British and French markets, even reviving the call in some British ruling-class circles for trade protectionism. This sharpening conflict beween ' modern ' German capitalism and the older imperialisms, the competition for territory and ' spheres of influence ', made war virtually inevitable. The pretence for launching military hostilities proved to be the assassination of Archduke Ferdinand. In the resulting confrontation, France and Russia sided with Serbia, while Prussian Germany eventually lined up with Austria-Hungary. When the Kaiser's troops began to cross Belgium on 4 August 1914, Britain entered the war against Germany. With breathtaking audacity Britain, France and Tsarist Russia—the gaolers of countless nationalities—now claimed to be fighting for Peace, Freedom and the Rights of Nations !

The resolve of Europe's Socialist Parties to sabotage any plans for an imperialist war, announced in the Basle Declaration of 1912, crumbled to dust under the stampede of national ' patriotism '. Labour and trade union leaders joined the ' class enemy ' in their respective countries to boost the war-drive. Those solemn pledges to proletarian internationalism were dumped in favour of the jingoistic battle-cries : ' Defend the Motherland !' . . . ' A War for Civilisation against Barbarism!' Thus the majority of labour's leaders in England, Germany and France wrote the epitaph of the (Socialist) Second International—and of millions of European workers. Among the honourable exceptions were James Connolly (Ireland), John Maclean (Scotland), Karl Liebnecht and Rosa Luxemburg (Germany), Friedrich Adler (Austria), V.I. Lenin and Leon Trotsky (Russia).

Almost alone amongst the left-wing parties in Britain, the I.L.P. refused to support the mass slaughter. But its propaganda for peace was swept aside by the deluge of chauvinism and British nationalism unleashed by the ruling-class Press. Welsh workers rushed to the ' Colours ' in numbers that deserved a smile from Lord Kitchener on his recruitment posters. Welsh national sentiment was cunningly enlisted through establishing Welsh Regiments and harping upon the plight of small nations such as Belgium, Serbia and Luxembourg.[14]

Even so, the S.W.M.F. Executive Council was prepared to endanger war preparations by rejecting an Admiralty request for greater production of steam coal—although threats from the King and Government soon persuaded them to recommend that colliers work an extra hour every day. Nevertheless, threats of legal sanction or public disapproval did not deter a large minority of Federation activists from opposing the war from beginning to end. One of the minority was S.O. Davies ; another was a Maerdy checkweigher, Noah Ablett. During those years of continental holocaust the South Wales miners joined the Clydeside and Dublin workers in defending hard-won trade union rights against the attacks of big business and the State. S.O. was only one of many in the South Wales coalfield who bitterly resented the way in which the coalowners had used the war to increase coal prices by over 300%, whilst trying to keep wage increases below 20%. In July 1915, 200,000 Welsh miners defied their Executive's recommendations, the Munitions of War Act and a Royal Proclamation : their strike met with the loudest chorus of hate ever orchestrated by Fleet Street. It also compelled the Government to step in and accept most of the men's demands on behalf of the South Wales and Monmouthshire Coalowners' Association, which had refused to negotiate with the union.

At the same time as the newspapers were characterizing the strike as the work of German agents, they were also stepping up the campaign for conscription. Eventually the Military Service Bill was pushed through the House of Commons in January of the following year, requiring able-bodied men to enlist in the armed forces. An S.W.M.F. special conference voted against the Bill and called for strike action to force its repeal ; the M.F.G.B. annual conference merely opposed the 'spirit' of conscription and, rather than campaigning for its abolition, committed British miners to 'vigilant scrutiny' of any extension of the Act. Writing in the *Llanelly Mercury* on February 24, 1916, under the title 'Why Conscription should be opposed by the Workers !' S.O. did not mince words :

> No Act of Parliament so callous, unjustifiable and so uncalled-for has found itself in our statute books during the last 100 years. Nothing has so violated our best traditions, nothing has so

shattered the noblest hopes of our people, nothing has so damned the potentialities of our free institutions as this crucifixion of our civil liberties by the god of war . . . Conscription is nothing but a conspiracy of its initiators to deprive the emancipating masses of the workers of their growing freedom, and to sound the death knell of their industrial organisations.

Furthermore, he challenged the conscriptionists' contention that the measures were needed in order for Britain to make a fairer contribution to the Allied war effort : S.O. pointed out that under conscription Britain would have 14½% of its population under arms, compared with 11½% in France, 6½% in Russia and 6% in Italy. Within a week of the Act coming into operation, he was exposing the abuses and deliberate misinterpretations of it. For example, the representatives of labour on the Military Tribunals were all pro-war : people who should have been exempted from enlistment under the Act were, S.O. claimed, being bullied and forced into it. Conscientious objectors were also being press-ganged into the forces, their pleas brushed aside with scorn and contempt. In particular, S.O. vigorously defended the right of Christians not to participate in the ' organised mass killing '.

Naturally his stance attracted the interest of the authorities. On one occasion his lodgings at the home of a Mr and Mrs Lloyd, in the village of Saron, were raided by the local constabulary. They scoured his bookshelves for seditious literature but, curiously, the most subversive publications in S.O.'s possession were the Old and New Testaments and—to the bafflement of the police sergeant—texts in Hebrew ! When the Government proposed conscripting 21,000 young colliers early in 1917, an S.W.M.F. special conference voted against any such scheme, but the South Wales miners eventually decided to toe the majority M.F.G.B. line in favour of the ' comb-out '. Although S.O. and his comrades called for strike action against this wider casting of the Military Service net, the rank-and-file rejected such a course in a November ballot. S.O. then devoted his energies to attacking the way in which colliery managers and the travelling Medical Boards were summoning exempted classes of miners for examination and enlistment. Desperately he watched the flower of working-class manhood being plucked from the Welsh coalfield only to be trampled into the Flanders mud. By June 1918 the Government had demanded another 75,000 British miners for the Front. In between such headlines as ' Hun Brutality ' and ' German Camp Horrors—British Soldiers Starved, Flogged and Shot ', the pro-war paper *Llais Llafur* (' Labour Voice ') exclaimed on May 5, 1918 :

> The patriotism of the Welsh coalfield has been vindicated once and for all. The rush to the colours during the last week, the fine spirit of the recruits, and the hearty send-off they have received, all testify to the fact that the old Welsh spirit is still alive.

Meanwhile history had been unfolding dramatically on the far side of Europe : the Russian Tsar had abdicated and his autocracy overthrown in the revolution of February 1917. A Provisional Government under Alexander Kerensky had taken power with the promise of parliamentary government and a policy of military efficiency. In Britain the revolution was welcomed even by the Tory and Liberal newspapers, thankful at least that Kerensky and not Lenin had been the one to replace Nicholas II. Yet even while the Bolsheviks were at best only a semi-legal organisation, Kerensky's short-lived reign was characterised by a situation of ' dual-power ' whereby the Provisional Government and its agencies co-existed with the more powerful workers committees (*soviets*) and soldiers committees. It was this strategy of soviet power which excited the imagination of Britain's Socialists. Russia was poised for a Socialist take-over, for the creation of the world's first Workers' State. Public meetings throughout south Wales hailed the triumph of democracy and progress in Russia.

On June 3, 1917, 1,150 delegates from trade unions, Socialist societies, Trades Councils and political parties gathered in Leeds for a Convention of Labour, Socialist and Democratic organisations. Besides congratulating the Russian workers and peasants, the Convention resolved to ' establish in every town, urban and rural district Councils of Workmen and Soldiers' Delegates for initiating and co-ordinating working-class activity '. The South Wales Workers and Soldiers' Council would be set up following a district conference in Swansea on Sunday, July 29.[15]

At this point it should be pointed out that the Socialists now calling for soviets in Britain were also those opposed to the war. They saw the Bolsheviks and Russian soviets demanding peace ; in Germany, too, workers and soldiers' councils were being established in defiance of the central government. It looked as if the strategy of the Second International to sabotage the imperialist war was finally being realised, albeit under very different leaders.

Tension mounted as the Swansea newspapers, right-wing trade unionists and a local branch of the Discharged Soldiers League (the ‘ bit-badge ’ men) declared their opposition to the forthcoming conference. By the early afternoon of Sunday, July 29, over 500 pro-war demonstrators had congregated outside the Swansea Elysium, determined to emulate fellow-jingos in London and Newcastle who had wrecked similar district conferences the day before. Armed with an assortment of vicious weapons the mob then surged into the hall and ejected the hundred or so remaining delegates with considerable violence. A *Western Mail* report of July 30 explained what happened after the victorious rabble had sung ‘ God Save the Queen ’, ‘ Rule Brittania ’ and ‘ Tipperary ’ :

> The bit badge men invited the crowd assembled outside to come inside the hall, and an impromptu meeting was held on the other side. During this a protest was raised by one of the delegates to the peace convention, who said he represented a branch of the Miners Federation. He protested against what had been done that day, and said if they would wait till next Thursday they would see what the Miners Federation of Great Britain thought of it. He was not allowed to proceed any further, and beat a retreat through the doors, followed by angry ‘ chuckers out ’.

The courageous miner who had stayed behind, alone, to challenge the warmongers was S. O. Davies. Two days later he and other Swansea delegates were pilloried in the *Western Mail*'s editorial column as ‘ a gang of sedition-mongers which has for some time past been engaged in poisoning the minds of the workers in the South Wales coalfield ’. S.O. always considered it just as important to have the right enemies as the right friends.

NOTES

[1]' Capcoch Infants and Mixed School Log Books and Returns ' (Glamorgan Record Office).

[2]The reports by Ballairs and others were extensively quoted by Coventry M.P. William Williams in his notorious House of Commons speech of March 10, 1846 (*Hansard* Vol. lxxxiv) ; see in particular the Minutes of the Committee of Council on Education 1839-40, Appendix II : *Report of Mr. Seymour Tremenheere on the State of Elementary Education in the Mining District of South Wales* ; and the *Report of the Commissioners of Inquiry for South Wales* (1844). In the book *The Historical Basis of Welsh Nationalism* (Plaid Cymru, 1950) D. Gwenallt Jones contributed an authoritative chapter drawing upon all these sources, viz. ' National Movements in Wales in the Nineteenth Century '.

[3]See *Welsh in Education and Life* (1927), a Report by the Departmental Committee appointed by the President of the Board of Education.

[4]This tale was told by S. O. Davies to Ioan Roberts in *Y Cymro* (13 May 1970) and repeated to me by S.O.'s sister Mary Green in correspondence.

[5]Quoted from the interview in *Y Cymro ;* S.O. also recalled Joby Whale in an interview with the *South Wales Echo* (9 April 1970).

[6]*Y Cymro* and *South Wales Echo* (as above).

[7]*South Wales Echo* (as above).

[8]Annual General Conference Reports of the I.L.P. ; see also the essays ' The New Liberalism and the Challenge of Labour etc.' by K. O. Morgan and ' Working-Class Leadership in South Wales 1900-1920 ' by Peter Stead in the *Welsh History Review* Vol. 6 No. 3 (June 1973).

[9]Executive Committee Minutes and Annual Reports of the Brecon Memorial College (now lodged with Coleg Coffa Abertawe/Swansea Memorial College).

[10]This article (undated) is in the S. O. Davies Papers, Swansea (Ref. : 1C, *i*). The play being reviewed is ' Change ' by J. O. Francis ; written in 1912, it dramatises the conflict between receding Liberal-Nonconformity and rising Socialist-materialism. Although set in Glamorgan during a coal dispute, the play actually reflects the events in Llanelli during the August 1911 railway strike, when two workers were shot dead by the Military.

[11]The election result appears in the *Western Mail* (8 April 1913); memories of S.O.'s I.L.P. activities in Cardiff and of the election campaign were supplied in an interview and letters by Mary Green.

[12]The essay is ' Y Ddraig Goch ynte'r Faner Goch ? ' (The Red Dragon or the Red Flag ?), published in *Y Geninen* (October 1911)

and in the book *Y Ddraig Goch ynte'r Faner Goch* (1913) by W. F. Phillips. T. E. Nicholas wrote a powerful reply to Phillips, ' Y Ddraig Goch a'r Faner Goch ' (The Red Dragon and the Red Flag), in *Y Geninen* (January 1912).

[13]These newspaper clippings are in the S. O. Davies Papers, Swansea (Ref: 1C, *iv*) and many of them are, unfortunately, undated.

[14]See *Wales in British Politics 1868-1922* (1970) by K. O. Morgan, *Lloyd George* (1975) by Peter Rowland and ' Wales and the First World War ' (unpublished, 1979) by Aled Eirug.

[15]' The Swansea Conference of the British Council of Soldiers' and Workers' Delegates, July 1917 etc.' by David Egan in *Llafur* Vol. 1. No. 4 (Summer 1975).

Chapter Three

BRITAIN'S BOLSHEVIKS

The hundreds of miners filing out of the Oddfellows Hall, Dowlais, one dark Sunday evening in November 1918 were in high spirits. As they spilled out onto Union Street, one of the men turned to his workmates and exclaimed above the hubbub : '*Mae'r Messiah wedi dod !*'—the Messiah has come ! Hyperbole of course, but it expressed the elation of the audience. They had just attended a packed public meeting to acclaim the new Miners' Agent for the Dowlais District of the S.W.M.F.

The District's advertisement for a successor to the late John Davies, a popular Labour councillor and chapel deacon, had attracted 45 replies. S.O's name was one of twenty allowed onto the ballot paper ; he set about winning the miners' votes with a combination of cunning and enterprise. From Caeharris station the Dowlais men were transported to and from the collieries in *cwbs*, small and uncomfortable railway trucks. There to greet them one afternoon as they changed shifts was S.O. Together with Thomas Thomas, one of the town's most prominent Liberals, he canvassed the men for the Miners' Agent election. On the leaflets being handed out was a picture of S.O.—sporting an old-fashioned wingless collar which, by mistake rather than intention, identified him as a man of the Cloth.[1] In a district where many of the miners were still 'Lib-Lab' Nonconformists, this image of S.O. did his campaign no harm at all : the miners at Dowlais elected him into the top three on their first ballot. Proof that the contest was warming up came in the second round, when an extra 800 men cast their votes. The front-runners emerged as follows :

W. H. Mainwaring (Blaenclydach)	1,025
S. O. Davies (Tumble)	788
Evan Evans (Penydarren)	542

The top two candidates now engaged in a run-off, which culminated in the third and final pit-head ballot on October 30 and 31. Bill Mainwaring was a formidable foe : the Rhondda man enjoyed the support of the local I.L.P., but his dour dogmatism could not match S.O.'s flair and oratory. A public showdown between the two contenders in the Oddfellows Hall one Sunday afternoon proved decisive. Standing stock-still, Mainwaring spoke first, impressing upon the miners the need for Socialist and class politics. S.O., on the other hand, walked to and fro across the platform, speaking with power and fluency, but—even more important—responding to the mood of his audience. He was only as militant or moderate as the main body of the mass meeting would tolerate.[2]

His flexibility was rewarded in the deciding ballot, where he gained 1,245 votes to Mainwaring's 1,142.

An idea of S.O.'s platform skills at this time can be gleaned from a biographical sketch of him in the *Merthyr Express* :

> As a speaker he is very popular and greatly in demand. He possesses wit, humour, sarcasm, courage, and withal a mastery of the subject without which one must feel the damning consciousness of being a charlatan. With the fire of the orator in every fibre, he has a commanding figure and a resounding voice, which has the true ring of sincerity.[3]

S.O. waited several minutes for the welcoming ovation in the Oddfellows Hall to subside before rising to address the assembled miners. He thanked them for electing him. He reminded them that they were all part of a larger, world-wide Labour Movement. The end of the Great War meant, to him, the beginning of the industrial hostilities—workers must now be ready for a huge and terrific war, one which would demand much more than merely voting Labour at election time. Events in Europe, where Socialist Republics had been proclaimed in Germany and Hungary, showed how time-honoured institutions could be toppled. Workers must destroy the existing social order and build a new one, in which they would control the conditions of their work. Apathy and laziness must be resisted ; working people had to devour knowledge if they were to be noble idealists rather than an incoherent rabble. But this did not require their brothers or sons to attend university—that sort of education poisoned the minds of workers' children against their own class. No, he wanted people to educate themselves inside the Labour Movement. Locally, they should attend the meetings of the Dowlais District. He ended his speech by informing the audience that he had formally resigned as Labour's parliamentary candidate for Llanelli Boroughs on the previous day, November

16, in order to concentrate on his new job. According to the *Merthyr Express*, S.O. resumed his seat amidst ' tremendous cheering '.[4]

Clearly this oration struck a very different note from the preceding ' Lib-Lab ' campaign for the Miners' Agent post. The reason is that S.O.'s overriding concern had been to win the election. Once elected he was virtually irremovable.

A few weeks later, the 80-strong Dowlais I.L.P. branch met above Berni's ice-cream shop in Union Street to discuss, among other things, the ballot result. Half-way through the agenda S.O. stormed into the room, demanding to know why nobody had informed him of the meeting. As the members turned on him angrily to ask what he, a Lib-Lab man, was doing there, S. O. delved into his pocket. With a flourish he produced a fully paid-up I.L.P. membership card. He had been one of them all along.[5] Not surprisingly, many I.L.P.ers disagreed with his election tactics : S. O. answered by becoming one of the Welsh coalfield's foremost Socialist agitators and, moreover, one who could carry the miners of Dowlais with him.

Like many of his trade union contemporaries S.O. saw the immediate post-war period as ripe for struggle on the industrial —rather than the parliamentary—front. Not only did he derive inspiration from revolutionary precedents on the European continent : circumstances at home indicated that the greatest potential for Socialist advance lay with ' industrial ' action. Trade unionism had survived the war, strengthened on the factory floor by an unofficial stewards' network ; workers and their families were demanding wage rises to compensate for inflation and war profiteering ; millions of young men were returning from the battlefield expecting to inherit a land fit for heroes ; and the capitalist bosses of key industries had proved to be so greedy and incompetent that the State had been compelled to take over their responsibilities. At the South Wales miners' annual conference in June 1919, S.O. scandalised the newspapers during a debate on whether M.P.s should be disqualified from the Area's Executive Council, by declaring from the platform that—in his view—there was little use for ' political ' action or Parliament ; he supported industrialism ' out and out '.[6] In February the following year he declined an offer from the Neath Constituency Labour Party to be put on their short list of possible parliamentary candidates.[7]

S.O.'s dislike of universities sprang from his belief that they skimmed some of the brightest working-class children from their communities, stuffed them with a liberal or 'neutral' scientific education and sent them out to scramble for middle-class jobs and middle-class goals. When a motion came before the M.F.G.B. annual conference in July 1920 calling upon the T.U.C. to take over and run Ruskin College, Oxford, he joined Noah Ablett in condemning any such move. S.O. told delegates that his experience at Cardiff had disillusioned him with university education :

> I have had quite enough of a bourgeois and capitalist college, in which category I am compelled to place Ruskin College . . . I dread to place the education of my class in the hands of these people, who have had their names coupled with Lloyd George, Balfour and company, and people of this kind.

The whole atmosphere of such places, he insisted, was enough to poison the mind of a young collier. But the Central Labour College, on the other hand, had grown out of the experience of working-class life and consciousness, thus shaping its curriculum accordingly and desirably.[8]

The newly-elected Miners' Agent moved into Gwent House, Dowlais, early in November 1918, eager to serve the people of that historic town. He was joined there the following year by his bride, Margaret (Madge) Eley, whom he had met at university and married in her native Cardiff on August 23 at St. Luke's Church. While out strolling in Dowlais one day, S.O. happened to meet an elderly ex-miner who, after congratulating S.O. on his new post, recalled how Gwent House had once given refuge to a militant miners' organiser many decades ago : a man named Thomas Davies had escaped there from the Rhondda, to be shielded from the pursuing police by the teller of the tale and his comrades.

Doubtless many houses in Dowlais could claim some such colourful episode in local history. The town stood at the head of the next valley east of Aberdare, on the north-eastern fringe of Merthyr Tydfil. For a period of more than 50 years in the ninenteenth century, Merthyr had been the largest town in Wales, propelled to that position by the siting of four ironworks in its vicinity. Dowlais was dominated by its own huge ironworks and could, with accuracy, have been best described as a 'company town', although it must be said in fairness that in later years the industrial despots of Dowlais ruled with more benevolence than many other ironmasters of the period. The larger conurbation, Merthyr, boasted a political and cultural pedigree second to none in its rich turbulence. During the first half of the nineteenth century the boom-town had been an epicentre of southern Welsh radicalism and republicanism. In 1831 more than a thousand of His Majesty's troops were drafted into the town to crush a popular insurrection. For several decades Merthyr was also a major centre of Chartism in south Wales. Literary and cultural societies flourished ; more newspapers were published there than almost anywhere else in England or Wales. Between 1868 and 1888 the Borough returned Henry Richard, a progressive Liberal and internationally-renowned 'Apostle of Peace', to the House of Commons; the electors later chose Keir Hardie as one of their M.P.s. Merthyr was also the only District in South Wales to favour continuing the Minimum Wage miners' strike in 1912. Long before then, coal had replaced iron as the staple industry of Merthyr and Dowlais : two of the ironworks had closed and much of the Dowlais works had been dismantled and shipped down to Cardiff in 1891, so that by 1906 nearly half the Merthyr labour force was employed in the coal mines.[9]

S.O. began work as the Dowlais Miners' Agent on November 18, moving into the District's offices in East Street. From there he would represent the 5,000 miners of Fochriw (Ras Las and Pwll Mawr), Bedlinog (No.'s 1 and 2), South Tunnel and Nantwen pits in their dealings with the employers, Inland Revenue, employment exchanges, local authorities and the courts. On the wall of his office S.O. proudly hung a magnificent framed testimonial, presented to him upon leaving Great Mountain colliery, Tumble, 'in appreciation of the invaluable services rendered whilst you acted as our esteemed Checkweigher, and as an expression of gratitude for the deep interest you have always taken in the working class of the locality'. He would need all the qualities perceived in him by the miners of Tumble in order to fight the coalowners of Dowlais District—Guest, Keen and Nettlefolds (G.K.N.), one of the mightiest capitalist combines in the South Wales coalfield. Besides a score of collieries in Glamorgan and Monmouthshire, G.K.N. owned the Dowlais and Cyfarthfa steelworks, the Cardiff-Dowlais blast furnaces, Newport chemical works, Rogerstone tinplate works, numerous mines in Spain and four factories in England. In 1917 its assets were valued at £8 million.[10]

One of S.O.'s first tasks in the East Street office was to enlighten two visitors in the pay of G.K.N., one a well-known Tory and the other a Liberal. They had called to give their supposed Lib-Lab lackey his instructions : S.O. and an assistant ejected the pair. But the job was not always so exciting. The surviving letter-books of the Dowlais District bear witness to the enormous burden of paper-work shouldered by the new Miners' Agent. His correspondence dealt mainly with injury cases, medical certificates and the men's complaints about pay and taxes, work conditions, dismissals, and concessionary house coal. Even the pit ponies nudged S.O. for attention—he had to plead with G.K.N. for a supply of nose-bags !

Those first years after the Great War naturally found S.O. immersed in the problems of redeploying demobbed soldiers. He wrote hundreds of letters informing Commanding Officers that G.K.N. would accept servicemen back into their old jobs underground. In many cases this process was made more desperate because soldiers' families were subsisting on a negligible income. Yet S.O. was continually hampered by C.O.'s who were unaware of the redeployment agreements drawn up between the Ministry of War, the coalowners and the M.F.G.B.

Besides revealing himself to be a diligent man of letters, S.O. soon had the opportunity to show his mettle as a man of action. In January 1919 a Dowlais District mass meeting demanded that the company reinstate all conscripted miners ; when G.K.N. refused to re-employ those men who had begun work there only after the declaration of war (and had been called-up subsequently) S.O. led the miners in a three-day strike. Effective picketing helped persuade the company to drop its discriminatory policy, at least until the forthcoming Conciliation Board Agreement was settled. Concessions were also won on union recognition, house coal and working hours. It was S.O.'s first strike—and most of the demands had been secured.

Not that S.O. was an adventuristic hot-head. When the miners of Nantwen colliery voted that same month to strike against the management's disregard of minimum wage legislation, he called a meeting on 9 February where he begged the men not to indulge in an isolated, single-colliery stoppage. They agreed, and mandated

S.O. to negotiate with the company's General Manager for the six pits, Tudor Davies. Following a negative response from Davies and G.K.N., S.O. convened a mass meeting of the whole District, winning the workers to his call for a District-wide strike in support of Nantwen—after cleverly adding the proper delivery of house coal to the original demand. The company had received no customary notice of the strike when pickets took up their positions outside the G.K.N. pits on March 3, 1919. The stokers were kept from the boilers and the enginemen from pumps and ventilating fans. Large numbers of police were imported into the area as the dispute dragged on for five weeks. When Glamorgan Education Authority slapped an £80 bill on the inhabitants of Bedlinog—for feeding schoolchildren in accordance with the Authority's statutory duty—the men of Bedlinog vowed resistance until G.K.N. paid the County for the loan of the latter's policemen ! Faced with a rapid deterioration in the condition of the mines the company eventually agreed to negotiate. Wage increases were conceded ; by November an agreement on house coal was drawn up, with G.K.N. promising to deliver concessionary coal in all areas previously excluded. Even so, the company took enough time compiling its list of eligible householders to ensure that many of them did not receive their first delivery until the beginning of Spring.[11]

At the General Meeting of G.K.N. shareholders in August 1919 the Earl of Bessborough, Chairman of the Board of Directors, complained bitterly about the recent ' sectional and unreasonable strikes ' in Dowlais, singling out the local Miners' Agent as a particularly difficult adversary.[12]

To the people of Dowlais, however, S.O. was already a hero. For the men employed at Lefel Clai tending the water courses in the mountains, he secured the 30 shillings a week plus back-pay money to which these elderly and often dust-ridden miners had been entitled, primarily under the war bonus scheme, for over 9 months. When young George Watkins jumped off the wrong side of the *cwb* in order to take a short cut, he lost both legs in collision with a goods wagon. The negligence was entirely his—but S.O. contested the case in the courts and won £600 compensation for him from the company.[13]

Together with the neighbouring Miners' Agent for Merthyr, Noah Ablett, he raised the industrial and political temperature of

Merthyr Borough to an almost perpetual boiling-point. Both had supported the General Election campaign of James Winstone, the I.L.P. candidate and S.W.M.F. Vice-President ; when Merthyr returned its sitting M.P. Sir Edgar Jones in December 1918 with 14,217 votes, Winstone came a close second with 12,682. This was a remarkably good vote for Socialists in an election where most other anti-war I.L.P. candidates in England and Wales fared badly. The narrow majority for Jones was a tribute not only to the powerful I.L.P. organisation but also, as the *Merthyr Express* pointed out, to the ' scandalous propaganda which had been carried on incessantly since the previous election '.[14] I.L.P. rallies were held every Sunday at Merthyr's Olympia Rink, addressed by the most charismatic and controversial Socialist leaders in Britain. On May Day in 1919 thousands of people flocked to Cyfarthfa Park to hear Ramsay MacDonald, Winstone, Ablett and S. O. Davies. During the summer—in the middle of the official Peace celebrations—I.L.P.ers and ex-servicemen from the British Workers League and the British Empire Union wrecked each others meetings in Merthyr and Aberdare. No wonder, therefore, that Alderman F. T. James was moved to lament : ' Merthyr gets an opprobrious name throughout the whole country, and people think we are the hot-bed of Bolshevism and Socialism of the most violent kind '.[15] The accusation that S.O. and his type were ' Bolsheviks ' was common enough : S.O's only quarrel with the label rested on grounds of inflexion. His Welsh-language upbringing led him to pronounce himself a Bol-*SHEV*ik rather than a *BOL*shevik !

Not that name-calling could stunt the growth of Socialist ideas in Merthyr. In the local elections of November 1919 Labour swept to power in the Borough, at the same time as Manchester, Leeds, Hull, Newport, Neath and other municipalities also elected Labour administrations. S.O. had been active in the campaign, speaking in favour of the Merthyr candidates, and was actually nominated for the town council and the Board of Guardians in a Dowlais by-election. Subsequently he withdrew his candidature in favour of Sam Jennings, a local Socialist. The public meetings continued unabated : S.O. addressed ' Hands Off Russia ' and ' Hands Off Ireland ' rallies, demanding the withdrawal of British Armies of Occupation.

About this time S.O. first came into contact with the young and angry miners' tribune from Tredegar, Aneurin Bevan. They addressed the same open-air meetings, on one occasion sharing an orange-box lent by the local grocer! At such a gathering, S.O. later recalled, Bevan once delivered a blistering peroration on the issue of miners' health, and this in an age when five dead men and boys and hundreds of maimed or injured were carried home from the pits every day. Neither the Government nor the coalowners showed the slightest concern, Bevan accused; crippled victims of the dust were 'callously thrown on the scrap-heap gasping for breath and coughing their lives out until the cold earth took possession of them', Nye told the assembled miners. These were the conditions which instilled in Bevan what S.O. remembered as his 'torrential vituperation, his deadly ridicule and acid wit'.[16]

Within a few years, too, S.O. would be chairing a conference of the S.W.M.F. when Bevan—still struggling to overcome his stutter—was being mercilessly heckled by the irascible Ben Davies of Pontypridd; S. O. turned the delegates against these rasping interruptions, thereby clearing the way for Nye to win a standing ovation.[17]

The terrible conditions that fired Bevan's indignation also ignited a controversy which came to dominate politics and the coal industry in 1919 and early 1920. Back in November 1916 the Board of Trade had seized control of the South Wales coal industry under the Defence of the Realm Act; the pig-headedness of the coalowners had endangered vital coal production. State control was extended to England and Scotland the following year. In 1918 the annual conference of the M.F.G.B. unanimously demanded wholesale nationalisation of the mines, adopting a South Wales resolution: 'That in the opinion of this Conference the time has arrived in the history of the Coal Mining Industry, when it is clearly in the national interest to transfer the entire industry from Private Ownership and Control to State Ownership with joint control and administration by the Workmen and the State'. This was a significant advance on the policy agreed at Swansea in 1912 which omitted any call for 'joint control' and so had left the door open to omnipotent State bureaucracy.

The pressure for nationalisation was stepped up early in 1919 when the M.F.G.B. added it to their demands for a 30% pay increase, a 6-hour day and full pay for unemployed demobbed miners. The union's determination to win this programme was demonstrated in a February ballot for strike action. But in the opposite corner stood a formidable opponent—David Lloyd George, the sharp and slippery orator whose early radicalism had degenerated into power-lusting demagogy. His Government rejected the miners' wage claim, while at the same time Lloyd George promised their leaders a Coal Industry Commission to consider the men's demands. The M.F.G.B. Executive succumbed to the Prime Minister's mixture of threats and promises and so decided to refrain from recommending strike action to the special M.F.G.B. conference called for 20 February, 1919. Nevertheless, South Wales delegates argued strongly for a boycott of the proposed Commission. S.O. reminded the conference : ' The ballot has gone overwhelmingly along the lines we recommended from the last Southport Conference ; and today we are seeking ways and means to undermine that ballot '. Nor did S.O. flinch from condemning his compatriot, Lloyd George, who earlier that week had ordered troops into Red Clydeside to quell the disorder there :

> While this same gentleman was making his speech when meeting the Executive, expressing his sympathy and grave concern as regards the condition of the miners, I at any rate as a coalminer cannot forget the fact that he was the very man responsible for what happened on Clydeside the other day. I hold him as head of the Government responsible. I hold him, the man who is attempting to foist this Commission upon us, responsible for the tactics used : the machine guns, bared bayonets, on the Clyde. I do not think we should accept gifts from the Greeks.[18]

But Lloyd George's gift was accepted by the special conference after President Robert Smillie had made a passionate appeal for the Commission, skilfully attaching a proviso that half the Commissioners be appointed or approved by the miners. Lloyd George granted the proviso ; strike notices were postponed and the Coal Industry Commission began its hearings presided over by Mr Justice Sankey.

Three weeks later, on March 20, the Commission's findings were published in the House of Commons : they included pay increases, a reduction of one hour per day for underground workers, and a judgement on the coal industry that ' the present system of ownership stands condemned ' and that ' the colliery workers shall in the future have an effective voice in the direction of the mines '. The Tory leader in the War Cabinet, Bonar Law, told M.P.s and the outside world : ' The Government are prepared to carry out in the spirit and in the letter the recommendations of Mr Justice Sankey's Report '.[19]

A reconvened M.F.G.B. special conference resolved to ballot the union's members, with a majority of delegates recommending acceptance of the Sankey Report and cancellation of strike action. Part of the minority, Ablett and S.O. opposed the climb-down, distrusting the Government and believing that the miners should fight for a deal even nearer their original demands. On this occasion, however, the two Agents were in advance of their Districts. The ensuing ballot showed a ratio in favour of Sankey of 9 to 1 in the M.F.G.B. as a whole, 7 to 1 in South Wales, 3 to 1 in Merthyr and —the narrowest margin of any District in the coalfield—1,550 votes to 1,307 in Dowlais.

Sankey was asked by the Government to sit again, this time exclusively on the issue of nationalisation. For several weeks the Commission's public hearings exposed the wealth and greed of the coal magnates ; on 20 June 1919 the majority of the Commissioners (including Sankey) reported their positive conclusion that the mines should be nationalised. On 18 August, Lloyd George rejected the Commission's majority report. Ablett and S.O. were proved correct —the miners had been duped all along.

Exercising extraordinary self-control the M.F.G.B. delayed strike action in anticipation of T.U.C. support. It never came. The T.U.C. merely called upon Labour M.P.s to interview the Prime Minister. Then, at a special congress in December 1919, the unions spurned a general strike and instead initiated a propaganda drive in favour of nationalisation. S.O. threw himself into this ' Mines for the Nation ' campaign, beginning with a well-attended public meeting in Bethania Chapel, Dowlais, on January 13. From there he travelled to all parts of the South Wales coalfield, greatly in demand as an advocate of the miners' case. Sometimes the audience wanted a defiant denunciation of the Government and the coalowners as, for example, at this meeting in Pant-teg Chapel, Ystalyfera :

> Mr. S. O. Davies, miners' agent, was the first speaker and said the condition of a man's employment had more to do with his moral outlook than any factor in his life. It was for this reason that the miners were out to better their conditions. The coal mines now were a capitalist gamble, with no regard to human life. Mr. Davies gave the history of the Coal Commission, and said the Government were pledged to the findings of Justice Sankey, and if they did not recognise this he advocated direct action. Both Mr. Bonar Law and the Premier had given undertakings that the report of the Commission should be accepted both in the letter and in spirit. Mr. Davies said if the miners had adopted his ideas, every coal owner would have been in the bankruptcy court by now. He did not agree with increased production if the increased production was not for the benefit of the community [Applause].[20]

In its editorial *Llais Llafur* commented with a weary indignation that ' as usual, the press came in for a considerable amount of hostile—and ignorant—criticism '. Elsewhere S.O. sensed that his audience desired a calmer exposition of the facts :

> SEVEN SISTERS LOCAL NEWS
> Mr. S. O. Davies, miners' agent, Dowlais, paid a visit to the Reading Room on Friday and delivered an address on ' Nationalisation of the Mines ' . . . Mr. Davies' method of reducing this great subject to a simple round-table talk should have benefited everyone who listened to his address.[21]

All the passion and skills of S.O. and his comrades could not rescue the campaign from failure. The Press and other capitalist interests were implacably opposed to nationalisation, while for their own part the miners were deeply divided. The ' old guard ' leaders, such as S.W.M.F. President William Brace, spent much of the campaign attacking the proponents of direct action and calling instead for a Labour majority at the next General Election. Even the militants were split into different camps, with many of the syndicalists utterly rejecting nationalisation proposals which did not explicitly provide for workers' control of the industry—embodied in the slogans ' Sovietize the mines!' and ' the mines for the miners!'.

A special Trades Union Congress in March 1920 once again declined to call a general strike to force the implementation of Sankey. All it proposed was continuation of pro-nationalization propaganda up to the next General Election, whenever that might be. Thus the campaign fizzled out—condemning the miners to another 20 years under the yoke of the coal barons.

Bread and butter issues came to the fore once again when the Government decided in May 1920 to increase the price of coal by 14 shillings and two pence a ton. The miners, already resentful of the huge profits being made from their labour (80s 7d a ton in south Wales) responded with a pay claim and a demand for the price of coal to be reduced. When the Government refused to concede on either count, a strike ballot showed two-thirds of the miners in favour of a stoppage. More negotiations followed, with the miners offered a ' Datum Line ' productivity deal. This they turned down by more than a 3 to 1 majority. In preparation for the coming conflict, the militant miners of south Wales utilised the local Councils of Action originally set up to campaign against British intervention in the Soviet Union ; the Councils were broadened, the intention being to weave them into a Russian pattern of soviets. In one of its weekly reports to the Cabinet, the Home Office Directorate of Intelligence commented :

> An interesting example of local organisation is provided by the Merthyr Borough Council of Action which has been formed for ' the organisation of industrial workers to function in time of crisis.' The prime mover is Noah Ablett (with S. O. Davies) . . . The Rhondda Council of Action is formed on similar lines, and co-operation between the two bodies has been established. A. J. Cook is prime mover in the Rhondda Council and in conjunction with Davies and Ablett, will use the new movement as a preliminary to the establishment of the Soviet system of government.[22]

The Datum Line strike began on October 16. A fresh offer was also rejected, but this time by too narrow a margin under M.F.G.B. rules to continue the strike. The pit-wheels turned again from November 4.

South Wales had led the opposition to the Datum Line deal and—in this matter at least—Ablett, S.O. and Arthur Cook had led the miners of south Wales. Yet again, the S.W.M.F. President William Brace and M.F.G.B. Executive member Vernon Hartshorn had marched out of step with the men they purported to represent. Bowing to pressure from militant lodges, both resigned their posts in November 1920 ; James Winstone was appointed the caretaker

President and Noah Ablett took one of the vacancies on the M.F.G.B. Executive.

Their immediate concern was the effect of a deepening world economic crisis on the South Wales coalfield, which exported two-thirds of its output. An M.F.G.B. special conference in February 1921 met in the shadow of 80,000 unemployed Welsh miners. S.O. told delegates in Westminster Hall that this trade depression heralded 'the collapse, the irrevocable collapse, of the capitalist system . . . I think we have only one course to take, it should be to go wholly over the precipice, and then we would have to establish a new economic system '. Delegates threw out a South Wales motion—moved by Winstone and seconded by Arthur Cook—for direct action to force the Government to adopt job-creation policies.

Ironically, the beginning of 1921 also witnessed a wages peak for the miners, thanks to a shift bonus paid out in January under the Datum Line agreement. Any euphoria was short-lived, however, as the Government rushed a Bill through Parliament handing the mines back to the coalowners. Certainly the owners had no intention of allowing wages to eat further into their profit margins ; all the men were served with notices terminating their old contracts on March 31. New contracts included massive wage cuts and a full return to divisive district agreements. This the miners could not accept : they vainly insisted upon a National Wages Board for centralised pay negotiations and a national wages pool to help the less profitable coalfields. From April 1, a million miners were locked out.

Rank and file retaliation was swift : the mine pumps and engines were abandoned as pit ponies were brought to the surface. By Royal Proclamation the country was placed under a State of Emergency. The Government appealed to able-bodied men 'who are capable of bearing arms' to join the Army Reserve for military service in the U.K. At the same time as British troops were suppressing Nationalists in Ireland and Communists in Germany, soldiers and special constables were shipped into the British coalfields, taking up positions in south Wales on Sunday, April 11. Naval units arrived at Newport and Cardiff docks, accompanied by a cruiser and a submarine ! Regulations introduced under the 1920 Emergency Powers Act made it an offence 'to do any act calculated to cause mutiny, sedition or disaffection among any of His Majesty's

Forces, or the Police Force or the Fire Brigade, or to impede the distribution of food, fuel or water'.

Much to the disgust of militant miners, their own leaders did not have the same stomach for the struggle as the forces of the State. Following a meeting of the coalowners, the M.F.G.B. Exectutive urged the men to allow engineers and maintenance workers into the pits to prevent flooding. Initially, the miners' Triple Alliance partners—the railwaymen and transport workers—vowed to strike in solidarity but, after postponing the action once, eventually decided against doing so. The miners and their families fought alone for ten weeks.

S.O. spent much of his time addressing meetings, keeping the men informed of endless negotiations between the union, the Government, the coalowners and the Triple Alliance. He worked with the Local Distress Committee in its task of feeding the children. Poor Law out-relief to the strikers had been stopped in fear of a letter from the Powell-Duffryn coal company's solicitors to the Merthyr Board of Guardians ; when the same Guardians proved too generous in granting child relief, running up a bank overdraft of £38,000, they were also threatened by the Department of Health from London. Not everybody was so heartless, though : one Dowlais fish-and-chip shop owner, a Spaniard, gave 975 children a free meal.[23]

The spirit of the mining communities could not be broken. Thousands of men, women and children flocked to the Labour Day rally in Thomastown Park on Monday afternoon, May 2, to hear Jimmy Winstone, S.O. and Councillor Sam Jennings. Winstone called for miners' wages to reflect their worth to society ; S.O. poured scorn on Press rumours that the miners' wives wanted the strike to end at any price.

Throughout May S.O. toured the District, witnessing meeting after meeting where the audience rejected the offers of the Government and the coalowners. A ballot of union members in June produced a large, unrepentant majority for staying out ; yet, within a fortnight, they had heeded the strong advice of the M.F.G.B. Executive to return to work. The terms of the new agreement negotiated between the coalowners and the union leadership represented a crushing defeat for the miners. Conciliation Boards were set up to work out area settlements within the guidelines laid down by a National Board. Even the presence of S.O. and other hard-liners on the South Wales Conciliation Board could not prevent huge cuts in the miners' wage rates. The January 1921 peak of 21s 6d. a shift had crumbled to 9s. 6d. by October 1922. The longer-term consequences of the new 'ascertainments' system, whereby a coalfield's 'surplus' profits were shared out between workers and bosses but deficits were carried forward to the next quarterly account, proved to be calamitous for an industry in decline.

The owners were cock-a-hoop ; victimisation of militant miners swiftly followed in Dowlais and elsewhere. S.O. doggedly contested G.K.N.'s refusal to reinstate 'troublemakers' at Bedlinog, pursuing several cases to eventual success in January 1922.

The depression deepened as Welsh coal exports were further undermined by free coal supplied to the victorious Allies by a penalised Germany. Men were laid off in the Dowlais District (where five of the six pits produced steam coal) from October 1921 as S.O. wrote to G.K.N. asking that either house-coal be delivered to the unemployed or that tips be thrown open for the picking of coal. Never slow to rub salt in the wounds, the coalowners and colliery managers seized this opportunity to disregard minimum wage legislation and to refuse compensation to accident victims. Besides challenging the company in these matters, S.O. increasingly found himself in court—fighting the cases of miners and their families who were being prosecuted for not paying their rent.

One effect of this demoralisation was a dramatic drop in the Federation's membership. In December 1920 the S.W.M.F. could boast 198,000 members ; by the first quarter of 1922 it had lost half that number. For a small minority of better-paid craftsmen, the defeat of 1921 had confirmed their belief in collaboration with the masters rather than confrontation. Consequently the South Wales Enginemen, Stokers and Mechanics Union was set up with the blessing of the coalowners and in flagrant breach of their protocol on trade unionism agreed with the M.F.G.B. in 1916.

The Federation regarded the errant craftsmen as 'non-unionists', placing them in the same category as the thousands of miners who belonged neither to the Federation nor to the craftsmen's association. In May 1922 an S.W.M.F. special conference decided to launch a campaign for 100% trade unionism throughout the coalfield ; Federation members were urged to tender strike notices, first in July and then in October. Both times the notices were withdrawn—

the response in the coalfield had been too weak. Men were reluctant to forego their already scarce wages, and fearful lest the owners give their jobs to non-unionists. In his own District, S.O. faced acute difficulties : 1,650 miners at the Bedlinog collieries had been put on a day-to-day contract, with delegations of non-unionists urging the management to continue this arrangement. S.O.'s response of holding a May Day Rally in Bedlinog and a mass meeting there in June failed to eradicate non-unionism. The Federation's strength and solidarity received another jolt later in the year when Nantwen changed to short-time working.

With the S.W.M.F. having abandoned a coalfield-wide strategy to combat non-unionism, the Dowlais District resolved in February 1923 to mount another onslaught with a special 'Back to the Union' manifesto. S.O. wrote to a comrade : 'this manifesto is the commencement of a big and continuous non-unionist campaign in the District'. He had chosen the right moment to renew this struggle : Continental orders for Welsh coal had been improving steadily since the autumn of 1922. Other Districts followed suit so that by March 1923 more than 60,000 Federation members were engaging in sporadic strike action. Tens of thousands of miners rejoined the union. But in Dowlais District, S.O. had not yet delivered the death-blow to the still-strong craftsmen's union.

The final push began on May 22 and May 23 when mass meetings were held in Fochriw, Dowlais and Bedlinog, addressed by S.O. and his fellow Miners' Agents John James (Cwmgors), Arthur Cook (Rhondda Valley) and Noah Ablett. The advance hand-bill warned :

> From the above meetings, Demonstrations will be formed, and will proceed to the houses of all non-Unionists.
>
> All members of the Federation, who are anxious to avoid a stoppage, are urged to be present at the above Demonstrations.
>
> Devote ONE MORNING from your three days Holidays to your own Cause, and establish once again that POWER which alone can RAISE you above the present-day conditions of slavery.

Although such meetings and demonstrations cowed many non-unionists into signing up with the Federation, stronger tactics were required to deal with the stubborn craftsmen. S. O. spent much of May 1923 distributing strike notices to the Federation men who would hand them into the colliery managers. The strike had two objectives : first, to press the company into employing only card-carrying Federation members and, secondly, to confront non-unionists with the choice of either joining the union or losing pay as the Federation forced stoppages over the issue.

From Sunday, June 3, nobody crossed the picket lines outside any colliery in the Dowlais District except the safety men—and they would be withdrawn if necessary. On Monday, the streets of Dowlais were congested with parades and brass bands. Federation members and their wives called at the homes of all non-unionists.

The craftsmen's local secretary convened a meeting of his association at the New Inn, Bedlinog, on the Wednesday at 5 p.m. Guest speaker and President of the Engineers, Stokers and Mechanics Union, D. B. Jones, ran a gauntlet of hostile miners and women all the way from the village railway station to the hotel. There he addressed an audience of one before again facing the crowd of demonstrators, which by that time had swelled to more than a thousand. Jones and the local secretary, Jenkin Davies, were mauled as the mob overwhelmed the scant police escort. Eventually the two officials were allowed to reach the station after promising to disband their union and urge all craftsmen to join the S.W.M.F. Jones was forced to repeat the pledge later the same evening when another meeting he was due to address, this time in Dowlais, was besieged by 3,000 Federation supporters.[24]

S.O. was delighted with the action : all three branches of the 'scab union' in his District had been routed, and nearly five hundred mechanics and surface workers were now back in the Federation. The *Merthyr Express*, however, took a dimmer view of the events : its chief columnist 'Polonius' railed against 'Trade Union Tyranny', spluttering that, 'No fitter parallel could be found or thought of than that of a big school bully gloating over the defeat and discomfiture of a much smaller boy'.[25] Flushed with victory, the men returned to work on Wednesday night, although the Fochriw daymen went home without descending on Thursday when two colleagues failed to produce union cards at the pit-head.

Thus far the triumph of *bona-fide* trade unionism had been total ; too crushing in fact for the authorities to tolerate without some sort of retaliation. It arrived on June 29 when 16 men and 9 women from Bedlinog were summoned before the Merthyr Stipendiary Magistrates, charged with 'riotously and unlawfully assembling together to disturb the public peace on Wednesday, June 6th last'. Some of the defendants were also accused of assault and incitement to riot. S.O. wrote to his I.L.P. colleague and Merthyr's new M.P. Richard Wallhead on July 10, 1923 :

> The whole prosecution is inspired by political prejudice by certain reactionary politicians in the County of Glamorgan, plus a few others who are energetically exploiting every ounce of reaction within the Miners' Federation.

The charges were not baseless : the police authorities who ordered their constables to protect strike-breakers and enforce Emergency Powers regulations were virtually at the beck and call of the coal-owners. The coal barons and their friends in politics still pulled the levers of power in Glamorgan County. However, in Merthyr Borough—which did not include Bedlinog—the police were the responsibility of the Labour-controlled local authority and, therefore, were not subject directly to the same reactionary political pressures. Of course there were also prominent members of the Miners' Federation who supported law and order at any price—even the capitalists' law and order.

Merthyr magistrates committed 20 of the Bedlinog rioters to trial at the Glamorgan Assizes. During the proceedings, D. B. Jones claimed that at a meeting in Dowlais on Sunday, June 3, S. O. Davies had 'appealed to the passions of the crowd' and that this had led directly to the Bedlinog disturbances. At the Assizes in Swansea on July 25 the prosecuting counsel conjured up a terrifying tale of that eventful day in Bedlinog : the women were 'foaming at the mouth' and their behaviour, he claimed, was 'reminiscent of the terrible days in Paris during the French Revolution'. The judge ignored the melodrama but nevertheless imposed fines of £5 on eight of the men, and £2 on seven women.[26]

It was a small price to pay for the defeat of non-unionism. The sore had been sanitised—but it had not been eradicated. It would fester again, when circumstances could be used to crack the unity of the miners' union.

NOTES

[1]This story was told by S.O.'s friend and former Dowlais librarian Harri Webb ; it was confirmed to the author by Ben Wathen, a contemporary of S.O. who was a blacklisted miner and proud Bolshevik, in an interview at Cefn-coed-y-cymmer in 1977.

[2]Interview with Ben Wathen (see above).

[3]*Merthyr Express*, 9 November 1918.

[4]*Merthyr Express*, 23 November 1918.

[5]Interview with Ben Wathen.

[6]*Llais Llafur*, 21 June 1919.

[7]Letter from S.W.M.F., Neath Constituency (27 February 1920) in S. O. Davies Papers, Swansea (Ref : 1A, *i*).

[8]S.O.'s remarks have been taken directly from the M.F.G.B. Conference Minutes. His speech was reported in *Llais Llafur* (10 July 1920)—but not very accurately. The Central Labour College in London was run jointly by the S.W.M.F. and National Union of Railwaymen from the summer of 1914, having been born out of the Ruskin College students' rebellion in 1909 : see 'The South Wales Miners and the Ruskin College Strike of 1909' by Richard Lewis in *Llafur* Vol. 2 No. 1 (Spring 1976).

[9]See *Merthyr Politics : the Making of a Working-Class Tradition* (1966) edited by Glanmor Williams, and 'Merthyr Tydfil Industrial Development 1870-1918' by John A. Owen in *Merthyr Historian* Vol. 2 (1978).

[10]See the pamphlet *Capitalism in the South Wales Coalfield* (1918) by George Harvey.

[11]The S. O. Davies Papers in the Glamorgan Record Office, Letter Books 1-14, contain much of S.O.'s correspondence as the Miners' Agent for Dowlais from 1918 till 1932.

[12]*Merthyr Express*, 6 September 1919.

[13]Correspondence and interview with Ben Wathen (see Note 1 above).

[14]*Merthyr Express*, 4 January 1919 ; by the end of 1916 the *Times* was habitually referring to the phenomenom of anti-war and left-wing meetings as 'Merthyrism', according to Aled Eirug (see Note 14 to Chapter Two).

[15]*Merthyr Express*, 15 February 1919.

[16]S.O. wrote an appreciation of Bevan which is contained in the S. O. Davies Papers, Swansea, but it bears no date or place of publication (Ref : 1E).

[17]Interview with S. O. Davies on July 14, 1964, by Robin Page Arnot.

[18]*South Wales Miners* Vol. 2 (1975) by R. Page Arnot p. 167.

[19]Letter from A. Bonar Law to the Secretary of the M.F.G.B., March 21, 1919.

[20]*Llais Llafur*, 28 February 1920.

[21]*Llais Llafur*, 17 April 1920.

[22]' Report on Revolutionary Organisations in the U.K., September 9, 1920 ' (Ref : CAB 24/111/1848) quoted in ' The Making of A. J. Cook ' by Paul Davies in *Llafur* Vol. 2 No. 3 (Summer 1978).

[23]*Merthyr Express*, 30 April 1921.

[24]*Merthyr Express*, 16 June 1923 (a letter from D. B. Jones) and 7 July 1923.

[25]*Merthyr Express*, 16 June 1923.

[26]*Merthyr Express*, 28 July 1923.

Chapter Four

IN THE WORKERS' ARMY

Millions of workers around the world thrilled to the second Russian Revolution of 1917. In that fateful November, the Bolsheviks swept away the compromising Kerensky regime and the rotten Tsarist autocracy once and for all. Combining popular agitation with covert conspiracy, stirring the masses with promises of ' Peace, Bread and Land ', the armed workers led by Lenin and Trotsky had demonstrated an alternative way of seizing state power for Socialism. Modelled upon the Bolsheviks, with their centralised and disciplined organisation, guided by the theory of Marx and the practice of Lenin, Communist Parties quickly formed in Germany, the United States, France, Italy and, in 1920, Britain.

S. O. Davies was hardly unsympathetic to the Communist Party's objectives ; nor did he oppose in principle its methods or tactics. Nonetheless, he declined to join the British Communist Party. S.O. felt that the working-class in Britain would only move towards revolutionary socialist politics in stages : he and his comrades had only recently succeeded in weaning the majority of miners away from Lib-Labism, taking advantage of the favourable circumstances. Next, the Labour Party would have to be consolidated as the mass party of the proletariat and imbued with socialist, class-conscious ideas. Within the Labour Party, he regarded the I.L.P. as the socialist vanguard. To risk isolation in a comparatively small communist party *outside* the Labour Party was not the way to fulfil these vital and realistic tasks, S.O. maintained.

In the train of the Bolshevik Revolution, the All-Russian Congress of Trade Unions, the Communist Party of the Soviet Union and the Third (Communist) International resolved to establish a revolutionary Trade Union International to rival the reformist International Federation of Trade Unions, which was based in Amsterdam. Widespread empathy with the young Soviet State, together with Socialist uprisings in Hungary, Bavaria and Hamburg and mass strikes in France, Italy and Britain all boded well for the formation of the new body. The Red International of Labour Unions (R.I.L.U.) was duly set up in Moscow in July 1921, soon followed by the opening

Russia in December, 1922.

By S. O. DAVIES, B.A., Miners' Agent, Dowlais.

My impressions of Russia, you ask, Mr. Editor? A month these times in that remarkable country leaves one almost overwhelmed and inarticulate. I fear I shall require weeks of the humdrum existence of the old country, with its $1\frac{1}{2}$ millions of unemployed and its millions of employed but impoverished workers, before I shall be able to sort out and arrange in proper perspective my impressions of that truly wonderful miracle—Russia in December, 1922! "Humdrum existence," did I say? No; no courageous worker can ever again in this or in any other country, where the workers are grounded under the heel of Capitalism, feel existence 'humdrum" after he has beheld the revelation of Russia. There he will have gazed on his cherished ideal securely and indisputably in the process of realisation, and henceforth the sordid conditions of his own class will have assumed a new significance. For has not the Russian worker shown how fleeting such conditions may be? How the most brutal autocracy can be transformed into a commonwealth where useful work and indispensable service lead not to penury and repression, but to freedom and the exaltation of man in his dominion over material things.

The Transformation.

Even the most hardened working-class sceptic of Capitalist news and literature, detailing the consequences (?) of the Russian Revolution cannot possibly imagine the tremendous magnitude of the Russian achievement until he has witnessed it. What pen can faithfully depict the transformation from 1914 to 1922 Russia? Or, indeed, from 1920, when millions felt the gnawing of hunger, to December, 1922, when food, in vastly increasing quantities, is streaming from our countryside into the towns and cities? Who can hope to picture to the mind of the Welsh miner the depths of that spiritual revolution that the consciousness of freedom has wrought in the Russian people? How the breaking of ages-old shackles of cruel, debasing servitude has given such splendid expansiveness to the mind and let loose boundless energy for creative work? The supreme pleasure that is felt by these emancipated people as they jealously and proudly watch the growth of a new culture, the spontaneous expression of those creative energies pioneering a new world of thought and a new material civilisation? Here, at last, you have a people who know much, indeed, of the "zest of living," who stand confidently and exultingly facing the future, proud of the eternal honour bestowed upon them as pioneers of a new civilisation. The British worker, grounded down in penury at his uninspiring toil, has been left behind by the Russian worker. To the latter the whole material world, with all its unrevealed mysteries, exists, awaiting the application of man's all-conquering mind. No longer shall Nature's bounty be forged by the few into chains for many. Never again, says the Russian worker, shall greed and the exploitation of human life be sanctified into ethical standards, and meek acquiescence in such greed and exploitation be deemed a virtue. Human needs, physical, moral and

S.O.'s impressions of Russia, published in February 1923

DOWLAIS DISTRICT S.W.M.F.

Is there to be a Non-Unionist Strike?

Are the Non-Unionists, now only 5 per cent of the Men employed, going to bring about a Strike at the Dowlais Collieries ?

Will 200 Non-Members render idle indefinitely over 4,000 other Workmen ?

Will the few Mechanical Workers and Craftsmen still outside the Federation, continue in their Sectional Policy, and not only bring about the stoppage of thousands of Workers, but perpetuate the scandalously low wages which the Mechanical Workers and Craftsmen have always paid for their Sectionalism ?

Unless a 100 per cent Membership of the Federation will have been achieved by Saturday, May 26th, all the Dowlais Collieries will be on stop.

DEMONSTRATIONS.

DOWLAIS, Next Tuesday, May 22nd,
At 10-30 a.m. at the ODDFELLOWS Hall.

FOCHRIW, Next Tuesday, May 22nd,
At 10-30 a.m. at the Fochriw Square.

BEDLINOG, Next Wednesday, May 23rd,
At 10-30 a.m., Near the Gosen Hall.

SPEAKERS : Messrs.

JOHN JAMES, Miners' Agent, Cwmgorse.
A. J. COOK, " " Rhondda Valley.
NOAH ABLETT, " " Merthyr.
WILLIAM HOPKINS, Mechanical Agent.
S. O. DAVIES, B.A., Miners' Agent, Dowlais.

From the above Meetings, Demonstrations will be formed, and will proceed to the houses of all Non-Unionists.

All Members of the Federation, who are anxious to avoid a stoppage, are urged to be present at the above Demonstrations.

Devote ONE MORNING from your three days Holidays to your own Cause, and establish once again that POWER which alone can RAISE you above the present day conditions of slavery.

18/5/23. BY ORDER, DISTRICT MEETING.

WALSH PRINTER, DOWLAIS

Leaflet against 'Scab Unionism', 1923

of a British Bureau in London. S.O. stood with most of the other militants in the ranks of the miners Unofficial Reform Committee, working for a fighting leadership and a centralised democracy in the South Wales coalfield. With like-minded activists he set out to win the miners of Britain to revolutionary trade unionism and the Red International. His two most powerful allies in this campaign were to be Noah Ablett and Arthur Cook. The latter, a spell-binding orator, had moved as a boy from Somerset to Merthyr ; thence he worked at Trehafod colliery in the Rhondda, beating an impressive field to become one of Rhondda No. 1 District's Miners' Agents. In February 1921 he was elevated to the M.F.G.B. Executive and later that year joined the Communist Party for a brief period before returning to the I.L.P.

As for the talents of Ablett and Davies at this time, the verdict of their contemporary (and later official historian of the South Wales miners) Robin Page Arnot, is as crisp as it is eloquent : 'These together made a pair of keen and quick-witted debaters, clear-headed, logical and persuasive, a pair that could not be matched from Yorkshire, Durham, the Midlands or Scotland '.[1]

The campaign registered its first significant success in July 1921 when the delegates to the S.W.M.F. annual conference approved a motion urging the M.F.G.B. to 'affiliate and actively identify itself with the Third International '. Upon hearing of this resolution, Lenin commented : ' Perhaps it is *the beginning* of the real proletarian mass movement in Great Britain *in the communist sense* . . . If these miners are not too small a minority, if they fraternise with soldiers and begin *a real* "class war"—we must do all possible to develop this movement and strengthen it '. Consequently, he urged Communists to build the Party in south Wales, and to launch a newspaper there for the working-class.[2] At the British miners' conference on July 19 the following year in Blackpool, S.O. shouldered the responsibility of proposing the South Wales motion in favour of M.F.G.B. membership of the Red International of Labour Unions (or the 'Third International' as it appeared on the agenda by dint of clerical error). He began by outlining the causes of the imperialist World War and the links between capitalist crises, the coal trade and miners' living standards. The Amsterdam Trade Union International was, he asserted, merely an information bureau : it could not organise the miners in action, on the basis of international solidarity. Then he put the positive case for affiliation to the Red International :

> We appeal to this Conference to make use of this real live International, out consciously for fighting, realising the great class struggle which is waged internationally and conscious that capitalism cannot be tackled successfully within the bounds of any particular nation, but that capitalism must be fought in all its ramifications by the workers, organised internationally, and by bringing all its power to bear at any and every point where the workers are attacked . . .
>
> Unless American capitalists, through their Government, French capitalists through their Government, and the British capitalists through their Government join hands in their last efforts to rehabilitate themselves in Europe, to rehabilitate capitalism, we shall certainly see in the near future a crash in Central Europe from the Eastern Banks of the Rhine to Russia, which will mean the crash of capitalism. If they do join hands they can only attempt to perpetuate what we believe to be a dying system at an incalculable cost to the workers of Europe. What have we done along international lines to cope with this ? We have talked and passed pious resolutions. What has happened in our various struggles ? In our last struggle coal was sent here for the purpose of defeating the British miners, as the Welsh coal miner is asked to fill coal for export to America with a view to defeating the American miners . . .
>
> We are hoping that this Conference will pass the resolution to affiliate with the Red International on its industrial side, and to the Third International on its political side, then we shall be affiliated with an organisation which is out consciously to fight for the ultimate overthrow of capitalism and save our people from the awful suffering otherwise in store for them.

Arthur Cook seconded the motion with a blistering assault on the ' Yellow ' Amsterdam International and its President, railwaymen's leader Jimmy Thomas. Only M.F.G.B. Secretary Frank Hodges, a militant-turned-moderate, troubled to reply to the proposing speeches : he defended the Amsterdam organisation, accused the Red International and its supporters of being anti-parliamentarian and splitting the trade union movement, and chastised his native district—South Wales—for wasting time on such ' intangible ' and ' remote ' matters when they could be home in their own back-yard combatting non-unionism instead. Responding to the debate, S.O. challenged Hodges' scares and distortions before reciting the constitution of the Amsterdam outfit as proof of that body's aversion to international industrial action. Following the chairman's refusal to read out the constitution of the Red International as requested by S.O., the conference moved to a card vote : 118 votes were cast in favour of the motion, all from South Wales, whilst the 723 votes of every other District were registered against the Welsh proposition.

Never one to be disheartened by set-backs, S.O. rededicated himself to the task of building support for the R.I.L.U. On October 21, 1922, he chaired a special conference of delegates from trade union branches and Trades Councils convened in Cardiff by the British Bureau : within a week he had joined the endless stream of pilgrims to the world's first workers' State, the Soviet Union. After representing the Dowlais District of the S.W.M.F. at the Second World Congress of the Red International of Labour Unions in Moscow, he toured the Don mining valleys in the south of the Russian Federal Soviet Republic where, at the request of the State Government, he wrote a text-book (translated into Russian) on mining management, technology, and trade union practices.

The trip was the most thrilling and formative one of his life. Upon his return to Wales in January 1923, S.O. immediately recorded his exhileration in the *Colliery Workers Magazine*, the official journal of the S.W.M.F. :

> A month these times in that remarkable country leaves one almost overwhelmed and inarticulate. I fear I shall require weeks of the humdrum existence of the old country, with its 1½ millions of unemployed and its millions of employed but impoverished workers, before I shall be able to sort out and arrange in proper perspective my impressions of that truly wonderful miracle—Russia in December 1922 !

He condemned the intrigues of those capitalist countries like Britain who tried to destroy the Soviet State with trade blockades and subsidised White Russian subversion ; more in determination than exasperation, he asked :

> Who can hope to picture to the mind of the Welsh miner the depths of that spiritual revolution that the consciousness freedom has wrought in the Russian people ? How the breaking of age-old shackles of cruel, debasing servitude has given such splendid expansiveness to the mind and let loose boundless energy for creative work . . .

> The British worker, ground down in penury at his uninspiring toil, has been left behind by the Russian worker. To the latter the whole material world, and all its unrevealed mysteries, exists, awaiting the application of man's all-conquering mind. No longer shall Nature's bounty be forged by the few into chains for the many. Never again, says the Russian worker, shall greed and the exploitation of human life be sanctified into ethical standards, and meek acquiescence in such greed and exploitation be deemed a virtue.[3]

But in Britain, too, the balance of political power was tilting towards Labour: in the General Election of December 1923 the Party increased its parliamentary representation from 142 to 191, with miners occupying ten of the Labour Party's 19 Welsh seats. When James Ramsay MacDonald subsequently formed a minority Labour Government, Frank Hodges was one of several leading officials in the M.F.G.B. who accepted posts in this historic administration. In February 1924 the South Wales miners balloted to choose their candidate for the now-vacant office of M.F.G.B. General Secretary ; the newly-created Miners Minority Movement, which agitated for a 6-hour day, a united Mineworkers Union and affiliation to the Red International, campaigned for Arthur Cook.[4] S.O. was eliminated in the second round of the South Wales poll, with the largest share of his transferred votes going to Cook. The eventual election of the latter as General Secretary of the British miners marked the first major triumph of the Minority Movement. Its influence was further felt in the 1924 pay negotiations when the coalowners' offer was rejected in an April ballot. A special South Wales conference the following month instructed its delegates to the forthcoming British conference to repudiate the terms, a course urged in uncompromising terms by Arthur Horner (a Communist and prominent Minority Movement activist) and S.O. At the M.F.G.B. convention a few days later the coalowners' proposals, now supported by the union executive, were accepted by 473 votes to 311—but with South Wales, Scotland and Lancashire holding out for a better deal.

Agitation on behalf of the R.I.L.U. did not cease either. The South Wales annual conference in June 1924 declared itself for T.U.C. affiliation to the Red International as S.O., Cook, Ablett, Horner and others circulated a forceful and closely-argued leaflet imploring workers to ' prepare for the coming struggles by linking up with the Red International of Labour Unions, which stands for *real* international working-class solidarity against international blacklegging '.

Evidence of the Left's growing strength had been furnished in the spring by a coalfield ballot to choose the three South Wales representatives on the M.F.G.B. Executive : much to the consternation of the ' class enemy ', M.F.G.B. Vice-President Tom Richards would henceforth be accompanied by Noah Ablett and S.O. Davies. A few months later, delegates to the Fed.'s annual conference paid S.O. the highest tribute of his life : by card-vote he was elevated to the Vice-Presidency of the South Wales Miners Federation, receiving 1,726 votes against 999 for Arthur Jenkins. Thus did S.O.'s colleagues acknowledge his decade of dedicated service to the miners' movement, expressing at the same time their confidence in his qualities as a courageous and principled leader.

But any satisfaction S.O. might have derived from personal honours or political developments in the union was swiftly tempered by another, more serious down-turn in trade : the artificial boom engendered by the 1922 American coal strike and sustained by the French occupation of the Ruhr coalfield in 1924 began to peter out. When the short-lived Labour Government endorsed the Dawes Plan and so allowed German coal reparations to undermine the British coal industry, exports from the South Wales coalfield slumped still further.

By the autumn of 1924 G.K.N. had closed the South Tunnel, Fochriw and Bedlinog pits, driving 4,000 miners into involuntary idleness. Fochriw had escaped closure by a whisker the previous autumn, when S.O. wrote in desperation to the company agent offering the men's assistance ' within practical limits ' to keep the pits operative ; Bedlinog had also suffered at least one serious breakdown prior to its demise. Now Miners' Agents tightened up on union contributions as the Fed. launched a scheme of cash assistance for young unemployed miners who were not eligible for state benefits. In the following January S.O. had no option but to withdraw £1,000 of Federation funds from the Dowlais Co-op to finance a fourth instalment of Out-of-Work Grants.[5]

Not just parochial problems were demanding S.O.'s attentions ; throughout Britain more than one hundred pits had been abandoned in this latest recession, itself further exacerbated by the country's return to the Gold Standard. Inevitability foreshadowed the mineowners' demands in June 1925 for a return to the 8-hour day, and their intention to scrap the National Wages Agreement in favour of lower wages and district agreements. With equal predictability, the miners announced their resolve to block any inroads into their living standards. Stalemate ensued as the two sides flexed their muscles in anticipation of the showdown. The M.F.G.B. enlisted the support of the British T.U.C. and trade union organisations overseas.

Throughout July the Tory Government met with the disputing parties, even initiating a Court of Inquiry in a futile attempt to break the dead-lock. Then on July 31, on the brink of the scheduled lock-out, the Baldwin-Churchill Government reversed its refusal to cut the industry's losses, and pledged itself to a 9-month subsidy whilst a full inquiry into the mining industry was conducted.

This triumph for a united Labour Movement has passed into history books as 'Red Friday'. But S.O. like other militants perceived no charity or compassion in the Government's so-called 'concessions'. The coalowners were eager to man the muskets; the Tory Government favoured keeping the powder dry until victory for the ruling-class was certain. Any differences between the two revolved around timing and tactics only: the Government and the Mining Association were as one in their determination to solve the crisis at the expense of the miners. In an article entitled 'The Industrial Armistice' in the *Colliery Workers' Magazine*, S. O. Davies warned:

> The Government capitulated and, in common with all the forces of British Capitalism, it is smarting under the consciousness of defeat. But it is only a very short armistice it has declared. It has, in fact, simply asked for time to prepare its forces to wipe out this disgrace. Prove and expose what we will in the forthcoming Inquiry, it will have not the least weight on the Capitalist Class. Mr. Baldwin [the Prime Minister] has already threatened to use all the forces of Capitalism against the Trade Unions if they dare attempt to use combined action against wage reductions. This can only mean the armed forces and all the strike-breaking organisations that will be generously financed by the Capitalist Class.[6]

Events lent substance to his warnings in a matter of days rather than months: that same September in 1925 the Government unveiled its Organisation for the Maintenance of Supplies, effectively under military command ; local authorities were asked to form ' Citizen Guards ' for the preservation of law and order ; and in October a dozen leading Communists were arrested and charged with sedition. Private strike-breaking organisations (some brazenly fascist) flourished under the paternal wing of the Government, the Press and big business.

Meanwhile S.O., and the rest of the Federation's leaders, were grappling with a fierce conflict in the Anthracite District of south-west Wales. The coalfield had begun to smoulder in May when the Anthracite combines, swallowing up local companies in a drive for rationalisation and profit, swept aside well-established customs and practices. The resulting strikes escalated into bloody, pitched battles between the miners and the police after the latter had brutally ambushed a peaceful march in Glynneath in July. S.O. called for the formation of a ' United Army ', and the Amman Valley miners set up a Defence Corps. Disturbances continued throughout the summer and autumn, culminating in the trial of 198 Anthracite miners—and the imprisonment of 58 of them—just before Christmas.[7] As pits throughout south Wales struck in solidarity, the S.W.M.F. called a special conference for January 2, 1926, in Cardiff.

S.O. was, of course familiar with the issues and the grievances, having himself worked in the Anthracite a decade before. Moreover, one of the most prominent leaders of the Anthracite Combine strike committee was his younger brother, Thomas Gibbon. Chairing the Cardiff conference, S.O. declared at the outset that he knew many of the jailed men intimately, and thought it was near-impossible that they could commit the acts of which they had been convicted. He added :

> The police, like a great many other people, were undoubtedly prejudiced against the strikers. The terms of settlement of the strike, agreed by the Federation and the employers, included a clause that there would be no reprisals. Although the colliery owners are not responsible for the initiation of the prosecutions, it is pretty evident that all the colliery official force was used to secure the conviction of the workmen.
>
> I believe there is a general, ruthless attempt to frustrate the efforts of the working classes, and to cover up the failure of the capitalist system in this country.

On the recommendation of the Executive, the conference decided to press the Home Secretary for the miners' release, rather than launch a militant campaign around the issue. The union would need all its resources for the coming confrontation with the Government and employers. In the meantime, a campaign to support the imprisoned men was undertaken by the International Class War Prisoners Aid, a body linked to the Red International. S.O. chaired the meeting in Cardiff, on February 6, 1926, to set up a South Wales District of the I.C.W.P.A., and the work began of raising funds, providing legal aid and campaigning for the release of the gaoled men. As the Red Friday truce expired, conditions deteriorated still further in the South Wales coal industry. With exports and export prices plummeting, coalfield profits of £5.7 million in 1923 and 1924 turned into a loss of £3.4 million the following year, although Government compensation amounted to £3 million. By March 1926 the monthly deficit had climbed to £600,000.

That same month the battle-lines were drawn by the pen of Sir Herbert Samuel and his Royal Commissioners. Their report juggled the figures to ' refute ' the miners' claim of falling living standards since 1914. Whereas the cost of living had indeed risen by 78% since that year, and wages by only 64% (according to the financial statistics submitted by the M.F.G.B. under S.O.'s editorship), the Commission argued that—taking a five year average from 1909 to 1913 as the base mark—wages had increased by 78% compared to a cost-of-living rise of 76%. Samuel and the other Government appointed Commissioners also criticized the 1924 minimum wage as too high in some areas and called for National and District minimums (to be supplemented by Family Allowances), the extension of piece-work and an end to the subsidy. Not surprisingly, nationalisation of the mines was rejected.

Negotiations between the men and the coalowners broke down in April on the issue of wage levels ; the bosses then demanded an increase in the 7-hour working-day, secured in 1919. In an attempt at mediation Prime Minister Stanley Baldwin chaired a series of meetings with disputing parties. The Government's gossamer-thin pretence at impartiality was subsequently exposed in the diary of Cabinet Secretary Thomas Jones :

> It is impossible not to feel the contrast between the reception which Ministers give to a body of owners and a body of miners. Ministers are at ease at once with the former, they are friends jointly exploring a situation. There was hardly any indication

> of opposition or censure. It was rather a joint discussion of whether it were better to precipitate a strike or the unemployment which would result from continuing the present terms. The majority clearly wanted a strike.[8]

To that end they posted lock-out notices on April 15, giving the miners two weeks to accept lower wages and an 8-hour day. As the trade union movement resolved to support the miners, the T.U.C. General Council's Negotiating Committee met the Government on the eve of the lock-out in a desperate effort to concoct an agreement which, while conceding the owners' demands, could be ' sold ' to the M.F.G.B. When the miners' leaders stood firm the General Council found themselves cast in the role of reluctant revolutionaries, leading a General Strike from May 4. In his detailed account of this unique event in British labour history, Arthur Cook captured the drama and elation of that moment :

> What a wonderful response ! What loyalty ! ! What solidarity ! ! ! From John O'Groats to Land's End the workers answered the call to arms to defend us, to defend the brave miner in his fight for a living wage . . .[9]

Nowhere was the struggle more fateful than in south Wales. The coal barons there claimed that wages were higher than elsewhere in Britain, productivity was lower and therefore no national minimum wage should apply to the coalfield. Steeling their soldiers for the show-down, reinforcing their sense of injustice, Cook, Ablett and S.O. collaborated to produce a pamphlet just prior to the lock-out, *Our Present Plight*.

Urged on by S.O. and Aberdare M.P. George Hall at eve-of-strike mass meetings, the workers of Merthyr responded to the call with an organised fervour almost without equal anywhere else. The local Trades Council took the initiative in setting up a Central Strike Committee, comprising the Trades Council Executive and one delegate from each union's local strike committee. Central strike sub-committees were given responsibility for food, finance, communications, intelligence, permits and sports and entertainments. District sub-committees were also established, including one in Dowlais, with their own family of sub-committees.[10] On the morning of Monday May 4, the whole of Merthyr fell idle ; the strike was solid. The police and the local authority adopted a low-key approach to the whole affair, thus helping to make the Borough one of the most tranquil areas throughout the State of Emergency.

The surviving minutes of the Bedlinog Council of Action testify to the strikers' frantic activities behind the scenes. Problems of picketing, non-unionism and propaganda dominated the Council's business ; S.O.'s services were much in demand as he travelled from one strike committee and one locality to the next.

For nine days spirits ran high ; the men felt confident that they could sustain the struggle until victory. Unknown to them, and even to the M.F.G.B. Executive, the British T.U.C. General Council had agreed to the memorandum composed by Sir Herbert Samuel as the basis for a negotiated settlement of the coal dispute. On May 11 the miners' leaders told the General Council that any proposals which included wage reductions, as these did, were unacceptable. The following day, the General Council abandoned the miners and—to the disgust of workers everywhere—called off the General Strike. Millions of workers throughout Britain took several days to drift back to work, many of them in a stunned daze of anger and bitter dissapointment

The miners, however, remained locked out. On May 20 a readjourned M.F.G.B. delegate conference rejected the Samuel/Baldwin scheme (which resembled the conclusions of the Royal Commission) and the coalowners soon did likewise. The lock-out continued amidst a welter of recriminations around the General Council's decision. Two chief targets of the militants were Labour Party leader Ramsay MacDonald and N.U.R. General Secretary J. H. Thomas, both of whom had displayed a demoralising lack of commitment to the cause even while the strike was in progress.

But S.O. preferred to analyse the surrender of May 12, in a broader, more mature fashion. When a *post-mortem* conference of trade union executives met on January 20 and 21, 1927, to consider the General Council's reports on the General Strike, he made an ' effective speech although in parts it aroused opposition ', according to the *Guardian*. The paper continued :

> Mr. Davies sought to bring the discussion out of the personalities and details which had confused it, and asked the conference to meet the following issues :—
> Did the General Council carry out the mandate of May 1st ?
> Did the conference approve of the unconditional calling-off of

> the General Strike by the General Council ? Was the existing leadership as revealed in that great crisis capable of meeting existing working-class needs ? Had the General Strike as a principle to be abandoned ?
>
> The General Council seemed to have regarded the mining crisis as an isolated episode in working-class life rather than as an expression of a continuous process involving economic and political offensives against the workers. British capitalism could not carry its existing burdens without degrading the workers' conditions. For this reason the policy of the General Council failed in May, and must fail much more in the future.[11]

Nevertheless, S.O. also declared on behalf of South Wales that ' the miners as an organisation believe in the General Strike '.

An M.F.G.B. motion to refer the General Council reports to union branches was ruled out of order ; the miners then lost by the margin of 3 to 1 a bid to reject the reports entirely. S.O. told the *Sunday Worker* :

> In the course of the conference, Mr. Ernest Bevin had to admit that the General Council had made no preparations for the struggle until the conference of executives was called on April 27. This confession of incompetent leadership was sustained by the damning admission by Pugh [T.U.C. Chairman] that the General Council, as a matter of policy, refused help from the Russian Workers. In other words, they were afraid to offend the government and the employing class. The miners know, to their sorrow, that the General Council were always more ready to placate the government and the mineowners than they were ready to fight for the Workers . . . The atmosphere of the conference showed that the present leadership in the General Council was not only opposed to national strikes, but was opposed to any form of industrial struggle.[12]

It is ironic that the Communists and other National Minority Movement activists should have blamed the General Council; after all, the Left itself had urged the vesting of greater powers in the General Council right up to the declaration of the General Strike, knowing surely that the Council remained in the grip of a right-wing bureaucracy. For his part, S.O. had applauded the M.F.G.B.'s decision to entrust the T.U.C. General Council with the handling of its case as a bold and historic step ; he had written back in the autumn of 1925 :

> On July 20th the Transport Workers, at their Biennial Conference, pledged themselves to support the miners. A day or so

> after this the miners put their dispute in the hands of the General Council, and from there on the identity of the Miners' Federation was merged in the larger representative body—the General Council. This was the most profound and far-reaching step taken by the Trade Union Movement of this country during the last 25 years. Here you have traditionally one of the most powerful and militant organisations handing over without demur its executive power to another body that had never previously directed or waged a single industrial struggle. It was an epoch-making realisation that had suddenly dawned upon the consciousness of the British Trade Union Movement, that not only was Craft Unionism dead, but that sectional action by the most powerful Union must now be relegated to the past. The attacks of Capitalism are mass attacks, although these attacks may be concentrated at different points from time to time. This has become obvious, particularly since the miners' struggle of 1921, after whose defeat, group after group of workers were also attacked and defeated.[13]

Events set in train by this transfer of responsibility appeared to justify S.O.'s judgement : a special trades union conference pledged its support for the General Council ; a fortified General Council defended the miners against the Government in more authoritative and threatening tones ; the transport unions announced their refusal to handle coal shipments ; and a conference of trade union executives declared its support for any action taken by the transport and rail unions in solidarity with the miners.

So what went wrong ? Fundamentally, supporters of the slogan 'All Power to the General Council !' had not intended these developments to end where they did, with an omnipotent but unreformed General Council at the apex of an unchanged trade union structure. As S.O. explained in his September 1925 article :

> Our immediate duty is obvious : a fundamental reorganisation of the Trades Union Movement ; the centralisation of all Trade Unions in the General Council ; the abolition of our cumbersome and slowmoving sectional constitutions ; the realisation that even the days of comparative peace in the economic world are gone by, and that the decline of British Capitalism has reached a point that makes every wage demand on any considerable scale a revolutionary issue. Hence our slogans must be : Mass attacks must be met by Mass attacks ; sectionalism is suicidal ; Our Hope is in a mobile, centralised, scientifically organised industrial army, which means all power to the General Council.

Time was too short. The General Strike fell like a guillotine on the evolution advocated by S.O. and the National Minority Movement, and on changes which would almost certainly have thrown up a fighting leadership in the General Council. In the event, in May 1926 the miners allowed the Negotiating Committee of an unreconstructed T.U.C. General Council to conduct discussions on their behalf with the Government and Sir Herbert Samuel. The General Council had then failed to consult the M.F.G.B. at crucial stages of the process. Now the miners and their families would suffer the consequences.

In Merthyr Borough the General Strike machinery swung into action in support of the locked-out miners. District strike committees enlisted the huge sympathy of their local communities to open soup kitchens, seven of them in Dowlais alone ; churches, chapels, trade unions and other voluntary bodies helped swell the Mayor's Distress Fund. Every penny was needed—the S.W.M.F. could not afford strike pay. By early June the Merthyr Board of Guardians had amassed an overdraft of £54,000 in assisting 12,000 men, 13,000 women and 27,000 children. Weekly pay-outs of unemployment or ordinary relief amounted to more than £14,000 in cash and nearly £9,000 ' in kind '. The latter consisted mainly of free meals for thousands of school children, served under the watchful eye of teachers sacrificing their spare time.[14]

But if large-scale destitution was held at bay, widespread deprivation could not be avoided. On Sunday, May 30, S.O. escorted Lady Astor and other parliamentary celebrities through the streets of Dowlais to witness the indigence for themselves ; Lady Astor subsequently broadcast a ' Save the Children Fund ' appeal in aid of the needy.

Feeding the undernourished was only one of the responsibilities discharged with fortitude and efficiency by the strike committees. Morale also had to be maintained, sagging spirits uplifted. In organising sports, music, drama and other entertainments the committees expended enormous energy and ingenuity. S.O. judged carnival and fancy-dress competitions besides presiding at the Dowlais Eisteddfod held in November to raise money for the victims of the lock-out. He also turned his house into a reception centre for donations of cash and clothing sent by supporters of the miners' cause.

Throughout the summer and autumn of 1926, S.O. toured Britain's coalfields with Arthur Cook and other comrades, hoisting the Red Flag of resistance and scorning the white flag of surrender. Both sides knew this was a war of attrition. In July, Parliament passed the Coal Mines Act to suspend the 7-hour day. Colliery shareholder and Prime Minister Stanley Baldwin tried to scuttle an M.F.G.B. fund-raising delegation to the United States by sending a perfectly-timed telegram to the American Press, predjudicing them against the miners' appeal. But aid and succour were forthcoming from one source at least : the Russian Central Council of Trade Unions sent nearly four million roubles (£835,000), collected in the mines and factories, to the British Miners' Relief Fund. Doubtless aware of the mischievous irony in his expression of gratitude, S.O. declared from public platforms : 'Thank God for Russia !'.

At an M.F.G.B. special conference in August 1926 Nottingham leader George Spencer successfully proposed the reopening of negotiations with the owners. Much to S.O.'s surprise and regret, Noah Ablett seconded the proposal. For South Wales, S.O. moved a counter-resolution calling for a fight to the finish. He was defeated, although the hard-liners succeeded in imposing tough bargaining conditions on the Executive : no departure from the 7-hour day, and no regional return-to-work agreements. Within days of meeting the coalowners, Ablett reverted to his belief in a duel to the death. The only other real option, put bluntly to the deputation by Lord Birkenhead, was a 'hell of a hiding' at the vengeful hands of the coalowners and the Government.

By October the men's resistance had begun to weaken, especially in the Nottingham coalfield where thousands of miners were returning to work on the owners' terms. Idleness, hunger and persecution were gradually exacting their toll. The police stepped up their already vigorous harrassment and prosecution of Socialists and trade unionists ; the Ministry of Health clamped down on Boards of Guardians, stopping Poor Relief altogether in some areas. In Merthyr the Board had run up an overdraft of £110,000 in its efforts to help more than 33,000 men and women.

For six months the Press had waged a campaign of vilification against the Federation and its leaders ; in the *Merthyr Express* regular columnists and syndicated specialists praised the 'scab' unions,

' exposed ' Communist subversion and denounced Socialism, in particular the I.L.P. ; the letters pages were crammed with character assasinations of miners' leaders and calumnous allegations of union corruption. It is difficult to resist the conclusion that two of the paper's perennial correspondents, with their highly-sophisticated and detailed tracts, were Government agents of one stamp or another. A fine example of the newspaper's racy but scurrilous style is the following item from the prestigious ' Polonius ' column, which appeared on the editorial page :

> When it was reported in these columns last week that the Merthyr Watch Committee had decided to ask Mr. S. O. Davies, the Dowlais miners' agent, to call his men together and urge upon them to preserve the peace of the district, it must have occurred to the minds of many readers that Satan had been called upon to rebuke sinners. As the originator of the M.F.G.B.'s ' Council of War ', or ' Cook's Travelling Circus ', Mr. Davies was engaged at the time in the congenial task of trying to persuade the miners in the Midlands, who have returned to work in thousands, to give up their jobs and thus help prolong the strike. This must have been known to members of the Watch Committee, and in the circumstances they must have had infinite faith in the inconsistency of Mr. Davies to expect him to preach the gospel of peace at Dowlais so soon after hurling his thunderbolts at Nottingham. It appears from an all-too-brief report which has come to hand that Mr. Davies responded to the call and that he addressed a meeting of miners at the Gosen Hall, Bedlinog, on Sunday, but the nature of the advice he tendered has not been recorded as far as I have been able to ascertain. One would have thought that being among his own people on a mission of peace he would have invoked the aid of the police, but he would not have been S. O. Davies if he had taken that course. He went out of his way to flout and belittle the police by describing them as ' dull, soulless, and brainless, without the intelligence of any ordinary, pale-faced boy who went down the pits '.[15]

In vain did S.O. deny uttering any such remarks ; in his reply he even referred approvingly to the ' extraordinarily happy relations ' between the miners and the Borough's police. Within a month the correspondence and gossip columns of the *Merthyr Express* echoed with well-coordinated sneers at S.O. for drawing a salary and thus, they charged, living on the backs of his unemployed members. In truth, he handed a substantial proportion of his wage back to the jobless and other worthy causes—although he never publicised the fact.

October began brightly enough for the militants : a South Wales special conference demanded an intensification of the struggle for a return-to-work on the terms and conditions prevailing in the coal industry before the General Strike. To this end the M.F.G.B. was urged to threaten the withdrawal of safety men, halt ' coal-picking ' on the hillsides and elicit the support of other workers to prohibit coal imports. This was to be operated behind a propaganda campaign spearheaded by the Labour M.P.s and the T.U.C. The whole strategy was adopted by an M.F.G.B. conference a few days later—only to be washed away like a sand-castle by the battle-weary reluctance of the English Districts.

The miners' resolve evaporated in the face of this defeatism : in November an M.F.G.B. conference authorised immediate District-by-District negotiations, with settlements to be sanctioned within a framework of general principles. S.O., Cook and Arthur Horner spoke for the majority of Welsh miners in resisting this thinly-disguised surrender. Among those who waved the white handkerchief were Mainwaring, Ablett and Aneurin Bevan.

Left alone, the South Wales Federation had no option but to treat with the local coalowners. The agreement reached finally on November 30 included swingeing wage cuts and the restoration of an 8-hour day. No coalfield resumed work later than South Wales did, on December 2, and no District went back later than Dowlais. Some miners never descended a pit-shaft again : as S.O. recounted to the Federation's Cardiff H.Q. in a letter of January 24, 1927, about 130 men were victimised at Nantwen (including his close friend Stan Beynon) and another ten at Brithdir levels. In some cases the resulting ' vacancies ' had been filled by colliers from other pits, while in others G.K.N. argued that the excluded men were ' in excess of requirements '. When the local Chief Insurance Officer awarded benefit to victimised Dowlais miners, dated from December 12, S.O. took the cases to the Court of Referees—and succeeded in back-dating the benefit to December 2.[16]

Another moment of pleasure for S.O. came a few days before Christmas, when he and Sephora spoke at a meeting in the Carmel Congregational Chapel in Fochriw, alongside local M.P. Morgan Jones and the Rev. D. M. Jones. Their purpose was to welcome

S.O. at the Second Congress of the League Against Imperialism, July 1929 in Frankfurt

Dowlais Oddfellows' Hall—later demolished

At the Frankfurt anti-imperialist congress: *back row:* Olive Arnot, Reginald Bridgeman (L.A.I. British Secretary), James Maxton (I.L.P.) and Alex Gossip (Sec. of Furniture Workers Union); *middle row:* two unidentified Russian delegates, Arthur Cook (M.F.G.B. General Secretary) and Harry Pollitt (National Minority Movement Sec. and imminent Gen. Sec. of the British Communist Party); *seated:* Millie Baruch (Communist Party office, London), an unidentified Russian delegate, Shapurji Saklatvala (former Communist M.P. for North Battersea) and S.O.

home nine men and two women who had served prison sentences for rioting ; the felons—' class war prisoners '—were presented with inscribed gold cigarette cases and pendants.

Victimisations were easier because they could be executed in the shadows of a darkening crises: the return to the Gold Standard had increased the price of exported Welsh coal ; the European coal industries profited from their higher levels of technology and productivity, taking a greater share of the stagnant world market for coal. During 1927, membership of the S.W.M.F. fell by nearly half ; the mining valleys were sliding into a dozen years of desperate poverty, joblessness and emigration. By January 1928 S.O. had 1,200 unemployed miners on his books, of whom 720 had been without work for three years or more. The Dowlais District could not even sustain its subscription to the miners' convalescent homes at Porthcawl and Southerndown, or afford to despatch delegates to the Labour Party's annual conference.

At this time the District comprised six branches : Nantwen (Dowlais), Nantwen (Bedlinog), Brithdir Levels, Dowlais Unemployed, Bedlinog Unemployed and Taff-Merthyr. S.O.'s advocacy of branches for unemployed miners had incurred the displeasure of the National Unemployed Workers' Committee Movement, whose organiser Wal Hannington criticized S.O. for organising an alternative to local unemployed workers' committees. The Dowlais Agent defended himself vigorously in the pages of the *Sunday Worker* a week later, on 20 September 1925, arguing that keeping miners together after a colliery closure (as a non-contributory branch of the Federation) reminded employed miners of their responsibilities to the workless, enabled the unemployed to remain active in the trade union movement and, as S.O. pointed out, allowed them to sit on a spectrum of influential welfare and local government committees.

The first-ever hunger march from south Wales to London took place early in November 1927, to coincide with the opening of Parliament. The marchers carried with them the anger felt in Wales at the new Unemployment Bill, and the popular resentment at the Department of Health's dictatorial powers over local Boards of Guardians. Even so, the T.U.C. witheld its blessing from the protest, with the S.W.M.F. Executive following suit. An undaunted S.O. joined Arthur Cook, the Communist Party, a number of Trades Councils and the S.W.M.F. Rhondda District in supporting the march (which included a contingent from Merthyr). One marcher, who died of pneumoconiosis on the way, had previously written home : ' Don't worry about me. Think of me as a soldier in the Workers' Army '.[17]

With an endeavour born of dedication, S.O. and other leaders of labour strove to lift their class out of this, the deepest trough in its fortunes for two decades. Working with the National Unemployed Workers' Committees Movement, he organised pilgrimages of protest from Cardiff to Bristol and London, financing them with flag-days in the streets of Dowlais. When, in 1929, the Merthyr contingent for a London-bound trek could not afford to travel down to their Cardiff starting point, S.O. paid their rail fares from his own pocket. Indeed, through these lean years he did not shirk his share of the hardship and accepted less than his full salary as the Dowlais Miners' Agent. On the positive side, S.O. tried—in vain—to persuade public bodies like the Water Board to spread out work in fortnightly rations ; the Society of Friends employed ex-miners in boot-repair shops.

But a growing problem for the ' Workers' Army ' was its Fifth Column . . . the company unionists. And nowhere were they stronger than on S.O.'s patch. Initially, the opening of a new pit in Trelewis in 1926 by the Taff-Merthyr Steam Coal Company (a progeny of the huge Powell-Duffryn and Ocean combines) had been welcomed as a shaft of light through the clouds of depression. But then, with the favour of the bosses and the organising skills of a local Conservative and a lock-out blackleg behind them, the men there constituted themselves as a branch of the ' South Wales Miners Industrial Union ' in December 1926. From its bases in the Raglan colliery near Bridgend and at Taff-Merthyr, the S.W.M.I.U. extended its tentacles to other pits, threatening the Fed.'s hegemony at a time when the employers owned the whip-hand ; mines were shutting, and the Fed.'s membership was declining.[18] S.O. explained the position as follows in a letter to an Amman Valley lodge secretary on May 29, 1930 :

> The Taff-Merthyr colliery is a comparatively new one, and enforced membership of the ' Non-Political Union ' (established by the Employers) is a condition of employment. The workmen there are drawn from all over the Coalfield, many of them are recruited from the Tory drinking clubs. The Colliery is in a

> virgin part of the Coalfield, outside the boundary of any Federation Districts. It is kept on a Day-to-Day Contract—this is a most effective victimisation weapon. It is no exaggeration to say that since the commencement of this colliery hundreds of men have been victimised because of their resisting the 'Non Pol' Union. The Dowlais District has now assumed responsibility for this Colliery, and we are concentrating upon the wiping out of this 'Scab' union. Recently, we succeeded in obtaining the signatures of between 75% and 80% of the men to a document prohibiting the employers from making any deductions towards the 'Non Pols'. These were handed into the Company by Mr. Tom Richards. But within two weeks most of this work was undone. The workmen were seen individually, and by means of trickery and threats of victimisation many of them were compelled to withdraw their signatures.
>
> We are now concentrating on an attempt to stop this colliery. The Executive Council [of the S.W.M.F.] are prepared to back that policy to the hilt, with full financial support.
>
> Unfortunately, our strongest men there are weeded out by victimisation, and very many of the best have been unemployed for 3 to 5 years.
>
> Nevertheless, we are very hopeful that when the Raglan struggle ends we shall be able to straighten out matters at this colliery.

As it turned out, the Fed.'s 1930-31 offensive, when between eight and ten of its bravest activists were employed to collect Federation dues, failed to eject the company cuckoo from Taff-Merthyr. Some fundamental changes would be required in the Federation's structure, and some ingenuity applied to its tactics, before the next onslaught could realistically aspire to success. When the time came, S.O. would play a key part in planning the victory.

Meanwhile S.O., elected by Penydarren Ward to the Borough Council in 1931 and a member of the Trades Council since 1921, led the day-to-day struggle for bread and shelter in his community. There was no respite from the recession : in 1930 the Nantwen pits had ceased work, killing the jobs of several hundred Dowlais and Penydarren miners. S.O. skilfully negotiated the labyrinth of Poor Law Guardians, Courts of Referees and Umpires to claw back unemployment and welfare benefits for his constituents. On occasions, in the face of a pitiless authority, he found himself checked by the necessity to compromise; for example, in April 1932 he had fought stubbornly to gouge a lump-sum of £475 from the coffers of G.K.N. in aid of an incapacitated miner. S.O. wrote to the unfortunate man in question urging him to accept the settlement rather than go to court demanding more : should he follow the second course, S.O. warned, the case would be heard by a Mr Rowland Rowlands—the son of a Rhondda coalowner :

> Judge Rowlands is most unsympathetic. He contends that if you injured workmen had not received your accident, you would probably be still unemployed, because there are some millions of able-bodied men unemployed today. Of course it is a brutal argument but it satisfies the conscience of this judge who would try your case if taken to court.[19]

The period after 1926 was one of swirling political turbulence, pitting Left against Left as often as Left against Right. The right-wing in the trade union and Labour movement portrayed the Communists and their associates as reckless adventurists, wreckers who had duped responsible workingmen into a hopeless confrontation—and at the behest of a sinister foreign power, the Soviet Union. In 1927 the T.U.C. General Council resolved to excommunicate Trades Councils who identified themselves with the National Minority Movement ; the 1927 and 1928 T.U.C. Conferences strongly condemned the Minority Movement and the Communist Party, launching an inquiry into ' disruptive elements ' in the trade unions. At one of the M.F.G.B. Rules Conferences in 1928, the South Wales representation on the National Executive was reduced from three to two, leaving S.O. and Tom Richards on the executive—but having the intended effect of chopping the Communist, Arthur Horner ; motions were also passed criticising the Communist Party and the tactics of the Miners Minority Movement, especially in Scotland. S.O. added his signature to those of 17 other union officials endorsing a counter-attacking manifesto drawn up by Arthur Horner, all of them thereby incurring the displeasure of the M.F.G.B. Executive. Communists were also being driven out of the Labour Party ; in response, dissident constituency parties enlisted the support of the I.L.P. and Communist Party to launch the National Left-Wing Movement, with S.O. and Arthur Cook sponsoring its campaign for Communist Party affiliation to the Labour Party.

At the same time as making scapegoats of the Communists and their allies, the Labour ' establishment ' (led by Ben Turner of the T.U.C.) and the employers (represented by Sir Alfred Mond) were cooking up a corporatist scheme to reduce industrial strife, boost profits and thus, allegedly, to create more jobs. Socialists responded to the Red-baiting and the Mond-Turner talks in two ways : the Communist Party, repeatedly rebuffed by the Labour Party, abandoned its ' united front ' tactic and—after initial misgivings—adopted the Communist International's ' Third Period ' perspective. This foretold of recurring capitalist crises driving the workers towards socialist revolution and the West into war against the Soviet Union ; to secure the former at the expense of the latter, the working-class must be turned against the social-democrats and reformists who, it was argued, would try and bamboozle the workers into an anti-Socialist alliance with the bourgeoisie.

S.O. and other non-Communist left-wingers, however, decided to stay and fight for Socialism within the mass Labour Party, assembling around the manifesto composed in 1928 by Arthur Cook and I.L.P. leader James Maxton. Revilement in the Communist press was their retribution for refusing to march out of the Labour Party under the banner of the Third International. Cook was singled out for special scorn and subjected, along with S.O. and others, to taunts of collaborating with the ' social fascists ', as the social-democrats were now dubbed.

In the General Election of May 1929, the people settled accounts with the Conservative Government that had enacted vicious anti-working class measures in the wake of the General Strike. The Tories were turfed out of office and replaced by a Labour administration headed by Ramsay MacDonald—but once again dependant on Liberal support. Communist Party candidates received a derisory share of the poll, as much in Wales as anywhere else. Although the new regime undertook some encouraging reforms in its early months (notably a half-hour reduction in the miners' 8-hour day), its hustings courage crumbled as the ' Wall Street Crash ' dragged the world capitalist economy down with it. MacDonald's Cabinet trembled before the sacred testaments of the Treasury and Bank of England, kneeling in awe of the gospels of free trade and the Gold Standard; I.L.P. demands for reflation of the economy were rejected as unemployment doubled within a single year.

As giant election promises shrivelled to morsels of parliamentary legislation, the relations between Communists and Socialists worsened. In Scotland, many militant miners reacted against a rule-rigging right-wing leadership by establishing the breakaway United Mineworkers of Scotland, affiliating it to the Minority Movement. In South Wales a number of Lodges had been warned about their continual infringement of Fed. rules by financing political candidates and organisations other than the Labour Party. The S.W.M.F. Executive eventually expelled Mardy Lodge in 1930 for refusing to give an undertaking not to support Communist candidates in the future : the Rhondda miners had backed Arthur Horner, then a checkweigher in the Mardy pit, in the General Election a year previously. Mardy also persisted with its affiliation to the Rhondda Borough Labour Party after the latter had been expelled for enrolling known Communists in its ranks.

The issue was seized upon by the Communist Party as a stick with which to beat those union leaders who had remained in the Labour Party. Nobody received rougher treatment in the National Minority Movement's pamphlet *Why Mardy Was Expelled !* than S.O. :

> Numerous attempts were made by S. O. Davies, the sham militant, and others of his kidney, to persuade the Mardy miners to drop their affiliation with the dis-affiliated Rhondda Borough Labour Party and re-affiliate to the scab organisation which supports MacDonald and fights against the militants. This proposition was put forward, not for the purpose of convincing the Mardy miners of the need for such a course being adopted, because Davies and his colleagues knew full-well that the Mardy miners were completely disillusioned with regard to the rule of the Labour Government and its supporters. Nevertheless, these officials were given every facility to come and state their case before the Mardy Lodge, and were overwhelmingly defeated. Every attempt at breaking the resistence of the Mardy miners and persuading them from the path of struggle merely had the effect of more openly exposing the pro-capitalist policy of the reactionaries and consolidating the ranks of the Mardy miners in support of its own courageous and fighting leadership.[20]

Predictably enough, the pamphlet detected darker motives behind the banishment of Mardy than mere umbrage at rule-breaking: allegedly, the S.W.M.F. bureaucrats had connived with the forces of 'social fascism' (namely the M.F.G.B., the T.U.C. and the Labour Party) to expel the Lodge because of its pedigree of militancy. No doubt the Labour and trade union oligarchs delighted in the disaffiliation of Mardy for just such an ulterior reason, but to tar S.O. with the same brush was patently absurd. His despair at the deterioration of the Labour Government ran as deeply as theirs ; it was his sympathy with Mardy's position which sent him into their valley on several occasions, pleading with them to agitate *inside* the Fed. for Socialist policies and a fighting leadership : an estranged Mardy Lodge would be a voice wasted in the wilderness, subtracting from the strength of the Left in the union and—indirectly—in the Labour Party. They were splitting the Federation from the left at a time when company unionism was chipping away from the right.

Mardy appealed against its expulsion to a special South Wales conference on February 20, 1930. The Minority Movement's pamphlet reported the events as follows :

> The proceedings of the Conference are a further indication of the desire on the part of the bureaucrats to prove their allegiance to the coal owners and their antagonism to the demands and interests of the South Wales miners.
>
> The conference was composed, as usual, of carefully selected delegates, openly reactionary lackeys who were pledged beforehand to support the line laid down by the bureaucrats. The proceedings were opened under the chairmanship of S. O. Davies, the one-time militant who, along with Cook, professed at one time to take a stand against the very policy which he is now actively carrying through.
>
> The whole conference lasted less than 20 minutes. Davies proceeded to make mis-statements, which were promptly challenged by many of the delegates . . .
>
> Ultimately the conference developed into an uproar, and in the midst of the utmost confusion S. O. Davies took a vote and declared that the expulsion of Mardy was endorsed by 15 to 9.

For good measure, the anonymous author added that this result was false—at least 30 delegates having defended Mardy, while the majority had abstained from voting altogether ! The brief, official minutes of the S.W.M.F. recount a story very different from that of the Minority Movement : S.O. had endeavoured to explain, between interruptions, why the conference had been called ; then the General Secretary began reading out a letter from Mardy Lodge justifying their actions. When Mardy's representatives punctuated their own letter with heckling, exasperated delegates moved that the motion to confirm Mardy's expulsion be put.

Arthur Horner had never argued in favour of Mardy Lodge putting itself beyond the Federation pale. Perhaps decisively, he departed for Russia just before the February appeal conference; from there he wrote a newspaper article in September 1930 joining in the denunciation of the 'pseudo-lefts' S. O. Davies and Arthur Cook.[21] (This did not inhibit S.O. from campaigning for Horner's release from Cardiff prison a year later.) But Horner's autobiography, published in 1960, gives no credence to the Minority Movement's account of the Mardy conference. Instead, he recalls that S.O. 'had planned to make a statement which would give us a chance to withdraw with dignity'.[22] Unfortunately for Mardy Lodge and the Fed., S.O. was prevented from delivering this face-saving statement by the obstructiveness of the Mardy delegates themselves.

S.O. was the first person to recognise that nobody really emerged victorious from the fratricidal Mardy affair : the miners union, even with its new Lodge at Mardy, had been weakened ; the Minority Movement's extravagant damning of major organisations in the working-class movement, and its slanderous assaults on erstwhile comrades, played into the hands of the right-wing. Yet the need for the Communists and left-wing Socialists to co-operate was greater now than ever before. MacDonald's Labour administration had revoked unemployment benefit from many thousands of needy claimants ; public expenditure was being reduced in the period when it was most required. Travelling this road to its logical cul-de-sac, MacDonald and J. H. Thomas surfaced from underground meetings with Tories and Liberals in August 1931 to take the helm of a 'National Government'. In the General Election two months later, the Parliamentary Labour Party was literally decimated ; even in Wales the party lost 10 of its 25 seats to the united Tory-Liberal front, although Labour's share of the vote was higher than before in almost every Welsh constituency. In England, though, a hefty slice of the working-class deserted the Labour Party and fell in behind the Pied Piper tunes of 'national unity' and 'the national interest'. Where should Socialists go from here ? S.O.'s next step opened up before him, carved out by Merthyr Tydfil's seemingly unstoppable slide into utter destitution.

NOTES

[1]*South Wales Miners* Vol. 2 (1975) by R. Page Arnot p. 244.

[2]From V. I. Lenin's letter to Tom Bell, in Lenin's *Collected Works* (Progress, Moscow) Vol. 32 pp. 510-11 ; the letter is also reproduced by R. Page Arnot (see above) pp. 320 and 345.

[3]' Russia in December 1922 ' by S. O. Davies in the *Colliery Workers' Magazine* (February 1923). Following his visit to the Donets basin, S.O. would tell of his meeting descendants of John Hughes of Merthyr : Hughes had founded the first steelworks in Russia, in a town which was called Yuzovka (Hughes-town) in his honour ; after the 1917 Revolution it was renamed Stalino and, since the late 1950s, it has been called Donetsk.

[4]See *Communism and the British Trade Unions 1924-1933 : A Study of the National Minority Movement* (1969) by Roderick Martin.

[5]S. O. Davies Letter Books, Glamorgan Record Office.

[6]*Colliery Workers' Magazine*, September 1925.

[7]The fullest account of this conflict is to be found in ' The Anthracite Strike and Disturbances of 1925 ' by Hywel Francis in *Llafur* Vol. 1 No. 2 (May 1973).

[8]*Thomas Jones, Whitehall Diary* Vol. 2 (1969) edited by Keith Middlemass p. 19.

[9]*The Nine Days* (1926) by Arthur Cook.

[10]*Souvenir of the General Strike* (1976) published by Merthyr Tydfil County Borough.

[11]*Guardian*, 22 January 1927.

[12]*Sunday Worker*, 23 January 1927.

[13]' The Industrial Armistice ' by S. O. Davies in the *Colliery Workers' Magazine*, September 1925.

[14]See ' Merthyr Tydfil and the General Strike ' by Huw Williams in *Merthyr Historian* Vol. 2 (1978).

[15]*Merthyr Express*, 6 November 1926.

[16]S. O. Davies Papers, Swansea.

[17] An account of the 1927 hunger march is to be found in the chapter ' Blind Alleys and Some Exits ' in *The Fed* (1980) by Hywel Francis and David Smith. This history of the South Wales miners in the twentieth century is the source for a number of events involving S. O. Davies.

[18]See ' The Struggle against Company Unionism in the South Wales Coalfield 1926-1939 ' by David Smith in the *Welsh History Review* Vol. 6 No. 3 (June 1973) ; and the chapter ' The Scab Union ' in *The Fed* (1980) by Hywel Francis and David Smith. The autobiography *Incorrigible Rebel* (1960) by Arthur Horner also contains valuable information about this struggle.

[19]S. O. Davies Letter Books, Glamorgan Record Office, letter dated 18 April 1932.

[20]*Why Mardy was Expelled!* (1930), a pamphlet published by the National Minority Movement.

[21]*Daily Worker*, 25 September 1930.

[22]*Incorrigible Rebel* (1960) by Arthur Horner p. 109.

Chapter Five

THE SUFFERING, THE PATIENCE . . .

Along with the rest of industrial south Wales, Merthyr and Dowlais had descended into the dark ages by the beginning of the 1930s. Then personal tragedy fastened itself to the burden already borne by S.O. as a trade union and local community leader : his wife, Madge Eley, died of cancer in February 1932. Sharing his interest in politics, she had served on the local education authority and the St. Tydfil's Hospital committee ; even if their marriage had been less than idyllic—both partners being weighted down by public duties—nonetheless her death deprived S.O. of a loyal companion, and robbed their three daughters, Mary, Margot and Gwyneth, of a conscientious mother.

Surrounded by hardship and now stunned by bereavement, S.O. resisted the urge to withdraw into a cocoon of grief and despair ; that would have been a self-pitying indulgence of the sort condemned by Madge before anyone else. Besides, fate had now left him with three girls below the age of 14 to rear—a task he subsequently performed admirably with the help of kind neighbours and a magnificent housekeeper, Letty Davies. One casualty of this crisis, though, was his Vice-Presidency of the S.W.M.F., which S.O. resigned in 1933. In August 1934 he married again, this time to Sephora Davies, a schoolteacher from Gwauncaegurwen in industrial Carmarthenshire. She had been a friend of the family since joining the staff of Quakers Yard Grammar School in 1927, although she saw less of them after taking an appointment at Glamorgan Training College in Barry.

Having begun the task of rebuilding family life in Gwent House, S.O. found fresh heart for the supreme struggle of the time—that for social justice and dignity. Merthyr Tydfil floundered in a trough of enforced idleness; Dowlais tottered on the brink of utter devastation. The Dowlais iron and steelworks had been scrapped in 1931 ; over the previous decade all the Dowlais District coal mines had been closed, including Nantwen in 1930. Several Merthyr collieries had also shut, while those that remained open did so on short time. Of the 21,000 insured workers in Merthyr Borough, no less than

13,000 of them—60%—were out of work in 1934, and this after 16,000 people had left the area since the Great War. By the middle of the same year, rent arrears to the local authority reached £5,000. The Borough's phenomenal rate of 27s 7d in the £ (of which 15s 7d went towards the amelioration of poverty and deprivation) was the highest in the United Kingdom—and hardly an aid to attracting much-needed industry to the area.[1]

Very nearly all the stuffing had been knocked out of the people of Merthyr : their renowned trade union militancy, their erudite and profound Socialist convictions, had been unable to stave off the slow-motion calamity inflicted upon them by forces beyond their control. The strike, an effective weapon in so many previous crises, had become as much impractical as insufficient ; moreover, the conflict between Capital and Labour echoed ever-louder in a chamber far away from the pit-wheels and factory lathes, namely in the House of Commons. The *débâcle* of MacDonald's Government and the decimation of Labour at the 1931 General Election had concentrated many Socialist minds on the need for strong and incorrigible working-class representation in that institution. Rightly or wrongly, the arguments in Parliament on social and economic matters occupied the newspaper columns : it was at Westminster that the excuses for the *status quo*—and the submissions against it—were rehearsed and widely reported ; there that the rescuers of the old order had come together to form a ' National Government '. On the practical plane, by legislation in such fields as trade unionism, the working-day and social benefits, the Houses of Parliament had demonstrated their ability to worsen the plight of the working-class substantially. Similar measures in the future must be fought—and if possible blocked—at their point of issue : the case against Capitalism should be articulated, and the cruelties of its regime exposed, in the arena that so often seized public attention.

This desire to wage the class war on all fronts prompted Miners' Agents and Marxists like George Daggar, Aneurin Bevan, Ted Williams and Bill Mainwaring to stand for Parliament between 1929 and 1933. Since 1922 Merthyr's voice in the Commons had been that of Richard Wallhead, a solid but unspectacular past-chairman of the Independent Labour Party. When the I.L.P. disaffiliated from the Labour Party in 1932, Wallhead had joined the defection ; he returned to the larger fold the following year, recoiling with horror from I.L.P. conference decisions to co-operate closely with the Communist Party, to support Communists in by-elections and to adopt the Communist Party's revolutionary strategy of building Socialism through workers' councils rather than relying upon a parliamentary majority. When Wallhead died at his Welwyn Garden City home on April 27, 1934, the aspirants flocked to fill his vacant place on the green upholstered benches of St. Stephen's.

Within days the Merthyr I.L.P.'s Executive had shortened its list of possible candidates to two : Jennie Lee (soon to marry Nye Bevan) and the Rev. Campbell Stephen, an unexciting London barrister. Technically, S.O. was himself still a member of the I.L.P. at this time, although for several years his political activities had been confined to the Miners' Federation and the mainstream Labour Party ; he had continued to pay his I.L.P. dues in the diminishing hope that its 'disastrous leadership' might be replaced by one committed to reaffiliation with the Labour Party.

The name of S. O. Davies soon surfaced in connection with the official Labour candidature, naturally enough as the nominee of his union. This was not the first time for him to be mentioned as a possible runner in the Parliamentary stakes. After resigning as the prospective candidate for Llanelli Boroughs he had declined, in 1920, to go forward as the S.W.M.F. nominee to the Neath Divisional Labour Party, telling his would-be sponsors : 'the call of the industrial movement is too strong at present to permit my acceptance'. Then in April 1926 he had been adopted by the Flintshire Divisional Labour Party as their parliamentary contestant, only to relinquish this position in the bitter back-wash of the General Strike.[2]

A bout of internecine sparring preceded the Merthyr Trades Council and Labour Party meeting of Wednesday, May 16, to choose a candidate for the by-election ; the local Co-operative Movement preferred to go outside the Borough in the search for a candidate, complaining that the miners were already over-represented in the Parliamentary Labour Party. The delegates in the Miners' Hall decided otherwise : in a rare fit of parochialism, they selected a local man. By a short head, with 43 votes, S.O. pipped an impressive field of six rivals : the Co-op's favourite, who received 18 votes, was Herbert Lees-Smith—an M.P. on two previous occasions, a Minister in the 1929-31 Labour Government and Chairman of the

Ruskin College Executive. Another contestant was Sam Jennings, a respected Alderman of the Borough who came just three votes behind S.O. According to Jennings, the selection meeting had been rigged to guarantee S.O.'s success—the miners' lodges having sent so many delegates when so few miners were at work in the area. In reality, his quarrel should have been with the Labour Party's own rules, rather with S.O. or the Fed. for taking full advantage of them.

Perhaps one small irregularity at the selection meeting could have helped S.O., had he not already established his credentials throughout the Labour Movement. On the ballot-paper, next to S.O.'s name, one of the poll officials had pencilled in the persuasive qualification ' Min. Fed.' . . . no doubt to steer any undecided delegates in the right direction !

So strong was Labour's domination of Merthyr politics that the actual by-election was almost a secondary affair, a formality once the Party's candidate had been chosen. Nevertheless, the intervention of two other hopefuls portended a month of Left polemics before the polling booths opened on June 5. The Communist candidate, Wal Hannington, mounted a vigorous campaign with the help of Harry Pollitt and Arthur Horner ; Will Paynter moved into an empty shop at the bottom end of the constituency, from where he masterminded the efficient Communist election machine.[3] (Horner's efforts consequently earned him a censure from the S.W.M.F. Executive.) Hannington's programme proposed a ' Soviet Britain ', a united front against Fascism, increased wages, planned production and a shorter working week. S.O. could agree with each of these planks in his opponent's platform ; what he lambasted was Hannington's hesitancy to broadcast the Communist Party's declared strategy for achieving Socialism :

> The Communist Party leaders have the virtue of frankness. The Communist candidate in this by-election is not quite so frank. He carefully avoids mentioning, in his election address, the true aims of the Communist Party.
>
> But responsible leaders of the Communist Party have bluntly told us that the rebuilding of our social system is, in their view, impossible without a bloody revolution. Is that what the people of Merthyr want ? It is not. They want a new and better social system from which poverty and unemployment will be banished. They want security and a decent life for all. They

> want to end war. That is what the Labour Party is out to achieve.[4]

It was rare for S.O. to find a Socialist to the left of him, let alone to criticise one. The explanation for his standpoint lay in events overseas : Nazism had just triumphed in Germany, aided by the refusal of the Communists and Social Democrats there to shelve their differences in the struggle against Hitler ; elsewhere in Europe, in Italy, Hungary, Spain, Portugal and Bulgaria, Fascist movements were either in power or driving towards the goal they were destined to reach. Hence S.O.'s warning against left-wing adventurism : ' The Communist Party stands for a policy of violent revolution, which could bring nothing but bloodshed and disaster to the workers, and further the cause of Fascism '.

Now was the time to unite behind Democracy—even of the imperfect bourgeois variety—instead of undermining it with wild, insurrectionary talk. The current balance of class forces, S.O. maintained, dictated such a position for the workers' and Socialist movement. Nor did S.O. pull his punches with the I.L.P., still immersed in its flirtation with the Communist Party and Third International. Ignoring its candidate, S.O. praised the I.L.P.'s past achievements—but characterised it now as an anachronism :

> The Independent Labour Party has rendered great service to the workers of this country. Its mission was to awaken the consciousness of the masses to the necessity of working out their own political and economic emancipation.
>
> That work has been done. The existence of our great Trade Unions, their policy and objectives, with their political structure which is the Labour Party, makes it abundantly clear that the working class realise that its mission is the control and direction of its economic and political life.
>
> The need for the consolidation of the ranks of Labour is absolutely paramount ; and the recognition of that need is the disappearance of the I.L.P.
>
> It is inconceivable that the workers of Merthyr will dissipate their political power by voting for the candidate of a party whose work is ended.[5]

In fact, the I.L.P.'s presence in the by-election represented the only hope of the *Merthyr Express* and other reactionaries that S.O.'s imminent victory might yet be thwarted : the I.L.P. had performed well in Merthyr's local elections seven months earlier, so brightening the prospect of a strong Liberal-National Government candidate stealing the seat from beneath the noses of feuding Socialists. When the Merthyr Conservative and Unionist Association decided against contesting the by-election, its members were urged to support the Liberal candidate J. Victor Evans—who was recommended to them as ' definitely anti-socialist ' by the *Merthyr Express*. The local paper gave generous coverage to Mr Evans in the hustings : he was boosted as a native of the Borough, a law lecturer at University College, Aberystwyth, the head-boy of his old school (Christ College, Brecon) and an ex-President of the Oxford Union ; and with a good war record to boot. Yes, Evans was indeed ' a Welsh-speaking young Welshman who has had a brilliant career ',[6] as the *Merthyr Express* gushingly informed its less-than-gullible readers : someone who, apart from the Welsh-speaking qualification, was the very antithesis of the wicked Labour candidate, S. O. Davies. ' Polonius ' commented a week before polling day :

> It would be interesting, incidentally, to know what Mr. Davies has ever done to restore the Borough to prosperity. Have his activities as a miners' leader been calculated to reduce poverty, prevent the ruin of businesses, and find work for the unemployed ? As he surveys the landscape from Dowlais Top, can he point to busy works and mines which he has helped to keep going ? The whole Borough knows the answers to these questions . . . One of the indispensable conditions of the restoration of Merthyr's industrial prosperity is a cessation of the chronic agitation which has done far more to impoverish us than the action of any Government. Mr. Davies appears before the electors as an ardent reconstructionist in one breath and a revolutionist in the next.[7]

Nobody took seriously this novel theory that S. O. Davies constituted a major cause of the Great Depression ; by far the most pertinent and damning question was the one asked by S.O. of the resurrected local Liberal Party :

> During the last three years poverty has compelled us to fight every Government Department. We have contended for the liquidation of Government loans that lie so heavily upon our rating resources ; for the more generous administration of the Poor Law and Unemployment and Health Insurance Acts ; and for the feeding of necessitous school children.
>
> We resisted the attempts of the so-called ' National ' Government to destroy our free Secondary Education and to reduce the standard of our Elementary Education.

S.O. meets miners in his constituency

With friends and election helpers, probably 1945

> We have fought for better housing and improved social amenities for the people.
>
> Where, through all this ceaseless struggle, has the Liberal Party organisation been ?[8]

Besides belabouring his adversaries, S.O.'s propaganda was notable for its positive proposals for reconstruction. With a hinterland rich in minerals and other natural resources, he suggested Merthyr as an ideal location for carbonisation and hydrogenisation plants ; local shales and fire-clay could be utilised in brick-making ; petrol could be manufactured from coal slack ; and the nearby agricultural areas could also generate industry in the town—for example, why not set up a bacon factory? Contemplating the Borough's good rail links, abundant industrial sites, ample water supplies and the rest, S.O. applied his fertile mind to the possibilities. Many of his ideas became incorporated into the Merthyr Development Committee's evidence to the Government Commissioner on Derelict Areas in South Wales.

The remainder of S.O.'s manifesto recited a list of Socialist and progressive demands : the public ownership of land, industry and financial institutions ; immediate socialisation of the mines, coal products and transport services ; full maintenance or work at trade union rates for the unemployed ; a shorter working week ; an increase in unemployment benefit and wages to increase purchasing power; immediate abolition of the Means Test; raising the school-leaving age ; and a 'Bold Policy of Disarmament and International Co-operation, especially with Russia'. In particular, he attacked the Incitement to Disaffection Bill (which penalised propagandists aiming to seduce soldiers away from the Armed Forces) and denounced the 1932 Health Insurance Act, which denied State medical benefits to the long-term unemployed.

Certainly S.O. did not take the electors' loyalty for granted : 58 public meetings took place between May 27 and June 1, at which S.O. enlisted the oratorical talents of Clement Attlee, Morgan Jones, Rhys Davies, Sir Stafford Cripps, Dai Grenfell, Nye Bevan, Will John and other Labour M.P.s.

At twenty minutes to two o'clock on Thursday morning, June 6, S.O. knew for sure he would be joining their ranks at Westminster. Eight thousand people heard the returning officer announce the result after one of the heaviest polls—81% of the electors voted—in Merthyr's history :

S. O. DAVIES (Labour)	18,645
J. VICTOR EVANS (Liberal)	10,376
CAMPBELL STEPHEN (I.L.P.)	3,508
WAL HANNINGTON (Communist)	3,409

From the balcony of the Town Hall, S.O. told jubilant supporters of his pride in inheriting the Keir Hardie-Wallhead tradition : ' the attempt to break up the unity of the Labour movement has been defeated ', he declared.[9]

Exactly two weeks later he was standing up in the chamber of the House of Commons, dressed sombrely in a dark jacket, striped trousers, white shirt and black tie, delivering his maiden speech. It was an unremarkable event : S.O. did not demolish a Front Bench giant or terrify the editorial writers of Fleet Street. He began by reminding the Minister of Labour of the debt owed by the country to an area that had hugely accelerated Britain's industrial development. Yet, in his constituency today, miners were suffering mass redundancy whilst Britain imported £40 millions worth of fuel oil every year . . . why not convert home-dug coal to replace it ? Similarly, £60,000 worth of pit-wood had been shipped into the Merthyr valley the previous year—when the hillsides above the coalfield could easily be utilised in a great re-afforestation scheme. S.O. also prodded, politely but incisively, a tender nerve in the Government's strategy for combatting unemployment in south Wales :

> A change of policy is absolutely necessary. The time has arrived when we should consider the possibility and practicality of bringing industry to the people. We see communities with a great industrial history dissolving and disintegrating, and all that the present machinery of government does is to take out a few of the unemployed from those communities, doing nothing, however, to retard the dissolution of the community as a whole.

S.O. returned to this issue—the transference of labour from the depressed areas of Britain to the more opulent regions—towards the tail of his ten minute speech ; the Department of Labour should, he suggested, redirect jobs and investment rather than ' shuffle and reshuffle people over the map of this country '. S.O.

was articulating, in an uncharacteristically sotto-voice, a smouldering resentment in the South Wales coalfield. Between 1921 and 1935 approximately 313,000 people had left the area—16% of the entire population, and most of them aged between 15 and 24. Merthyr Borough had itself waved farewell to 20,000 of its people. Instead of giving the depressed areas a transfusion of capital and work, successive governments had sucked their labour, their life-blood, to the Midlands and Metropolis of England. To induce young people to forsake their communities, Government agencies placed them in jobs elsewhere and offered allowances to ease the uprooting. To coerce them into moving, the rules determining unemployment relief and other benefits were designed to penalise households with more than one able-bodied inhabitant; the 'genuinely seeking work' and 'willing to work' stipulations for unemployment benefit were used to brow-beat claimants into seeking or taking up jobs in England, on threat of losing their benefit should they refuse to go.

The degradation heaped upon the Welsh people by transference and the Depression almost defies description. The facts must speak for themselves: for example, from the *New Survey of London Life and Labour*[10] it was estimated that over 145,000 Welsh girls comprised 1 in 10 of all domestic servants in the London area in 1931 ; once-proud miners entered special Government centres to train as waiters and butlers ; families from the south Wales valleys were coerced into moving to 'Welsh Land Settlements' such as the one near Shotton, on the border with England.

Even when the employment situation began to improve in most parts of Britain, south Wales remained in the doldrums : whereas unemployment levels in 1934 stood at 9% in London, 6% in Birmingham and 5% in Coventry and Oxford, the regional average for south Wales was 28%, rising to 37% in the Rhondda Valleys and soaring to over 51% in Merthyr. Anger spread in the shadow of governmental inactivity ; any illusions that the delay might be compensated for by a strong dose of anti-depressant were swiftly dispersed by the Special Areas (Development and Improvement) Act : this mouse of a measure created a Commissioner for the Distressed Areas of England and Wales, and endowed him with a paltry £2 million to spend within his very limited powers.

This same year, 1934, the Government asked Sir Wyndham Portal to investigate industrial conditions in south Wales. Much of his Report was superficial, patronising and platitudinous—where it was not downright insulting. The Chancellor of the Exchequer in the National Government, Neville Chamberlain, could scarcely conceal his glee with its 'findings' when he presented them to the House of Commons on November 14, 1934. He gloated over Portal's conclusions that south Wales is 'suffering from the disadvantage of not having the outstanding type of people resident in the district that they had in years gone by' . . . and that 'past labour troubles in South Wales have mitigated against the prospects of firms starting in this area'.[11]

S.O. led a pack of South Wales coalfield M.P.s in a prolonged assault upon Chancellor Chamberlain and Commissioner Portal; he delivered a tremendous tirade, brimful of indignation, so very different in tone and temper from his maiden speech. Dealing first with the issue of local calibre and initiative, he exposed the contradiction in Portal's conclusions by quoting from page 127 of the Report, where Portal had written :

> An appreciable percentage of the people whom I met during the course of the investigation were members of local authorities or attached to unemployed or welfare clubs.
>
> I found them very intelligent, with a thorough grasp of all the duties and functions falling on their councils. Both on the county councils and the urban districts, I was much impressed with the fact that they spoke of their subjects without any reference to the permanent officials, which is quite unlike my experience in the southern counties of England. They have been trained in a political atmosphere unlike my experience in any part of England. They know a great deal about national politics and what is going on in other parts of the country. They were very easy to get on with. They have grievances, but, for all that, they are cheerful and, considering most of them have been out of work for a long time, their outlook on life is not as bad as one might expect.
>
> It is also noticeable how very much in touch the local Members of Parliament were with the urban district councils.

Having turned Sir Wyndham's words against their author, S.O. criticised Chamberlain for echoing the damnation whilst neglecting the praise. He then lectured the Chancellor in local history :

> The Chancellor has obviously been misled. The great people who existed in days gone by have been largely imaginary. My constituency was once probably the richest industrial area in the whole of the country. There was, 130 or 140 years ago, mass production of iron and of coal. For the last 100 years not a single person either owner or part-owner of any works in the constituency has ever identified himself with any kind of public service. Not a single man who has been a part-owner or director of any of the local companies has ever taken the trouble even to live in the constituency.

After S.O. had dismissed Chamberlain's proposals for helping 60,000 jobless people by removing slag heaps, increasing agricultural smallholdings and appointing additional commissioners as 'pathetic and distressing', the object of his wrath stalked out of the chamber. Undeterred, S.O. then called for Government help to ease the rate burden, before returning to the offensive: he accused Chamberlain of discourtesy for hinting publicly that Merthyr Tydfil could lose its County Borough status, before any communication had been sent directly to the people or councillors of the Borough. Both Chamberlain and Portal continued to promote the migration of workers as a panacea for the distressed areas ; now S.O. expressed the bitterness this had engendered in south Wales :

> The policy of transferring labour, so far as our coalfield is concerned, has come pretty near to being an absolute disgrace. Possibly I have had as much to do with transference as anyone in the House who has not been connected with any Government Department. For a considerable time I gave all the assistance that I could to transfer labour from my constituency to places where I hoped they would be established with some decent work and some means of livelihood. But over and over again, I should say in hundreds of cases, I have met them walking back from London all the way to South Wales. A job has lasted a matter of two or three days, and in some instances there has been no job at all . . .
>
> I am going to appeal to the Government, if an appeal can carry any weight in this House, to consider the possibility of bringing industry to the people. Why drive them from their homes ? Surely power can be had to prevent industrialists planting their works anywhere they desire. Surely there must be some minds within the Government who must be concerned with the terrific extension in the size of this great city ; men and women being driven from almost every corner of the country, uprooted from their homes, their districts, and no effort being

made to carry on the continuity of their lives in their own districts.

On one particular occasion, the tragedy of the new nomads struck S.O. with an unforgettable starkness : he met thirty men from his own district one evening in a Midlands railway station. Some of them had found work in England, others were still searching. But none could afford lodgings—and so slept rough, to the accompanying clatter of the railway carriages.[12]

As the south Wales valleys smarted under these savage assaults upon their pride, the Government in London was deliberating over a new scheme which would rub salt into the wounds. The 1934 Unemployment Assistance Act established a central Board to imburse those unemployed workers whose entitlement to benefit had expired. These new allowances would supplant the ' transitional payments ' hitherto awarded by local Public Assistance Committees. But in areas such as Merthyr, the P.A.C.s had shown especial sensitivity to local circumstances by disregarding the Means Test on transitional payments—and defying the Ministry of Labour's subsequent admonishments. The Unemployment Assistance Board's centrally-nominated staff, operating a rigid and miserly scale of means-tested allowances, were unlikely to display an equal generosity.

The launching of the new scheme in January 1935 provoked massive demonstrations throughout Britain : on February 3, 60,000 people marched in the Rhondda ; three days later, 6,000 unemployed workers besieged Sheffield Town Hall. S.O. warned mass meetings of redundant miners that any drop in local authority rates (because the U.A.B. had taken over one of the local P.A.C.'s financial responsibilities) would be more than offset by the drop in unemployment payments and by the withdrawal of ' necessitous area ' grants ; purchasing power in Merthyr would be deflated by £1,000 a week—a calamitous prospect which he had tried to ' drive into the thick heads of the ratepayers of the Borough . . . Unless we can destroy this fiendish Act of Parliament and its regulations, trades people and others in similar circumstances are going to be wiped out with us '.[13]

A few days after meeting a Trades and Labour Council delegation led by S.O., Merthyr's newly-arrived U.A.B. officials received a visit of a more violent tenor : on February 4 thousands of protestors descended upon the Board's offices in Isgoed House, Pontmorlais. Windows were smashed; several women were arrested (and speedily released). The demonstration had been organised by the Communist Party and I.L.P., but without the support of the Merthyr Trades Council and Labour Party. S.O. regarded the protestors as an indisciplined 'rabble'—and as a result was heckled at a subsequent meeting in Penydarren Park.[14] Even so, the sectarianism soon subsided as the campaign surged onwards. Neither the admission by Minister of Labour, Oliver Stanley, that the new regulations had caused 'grievance and hardship and a widespread uneasiness not confined to one political party', nor his promise to alter the scales, could quell working-class anger.

S.O., sure-footed in the social benefits maze, concentrated his fire on the meagre assistance levels for single men: when the average miner's wage was £2 (40s) a week, the adult male allowance of 15 shillings (less than 10s if he lived with his parents) would not even pay the bill for board-and-lodge. Putting these paltry sums alongside the Government's plans for establishing unmarried men's employment camps, S.O. completed the equation at a mass meeting in Thomastown Park on Wednesday, February 6:

> I am satisfied that the Government has an ulterior motive in its attack on the unemployed single man. Behind these impossible low scales for single men, there is an attempt to drive them into the Army and also, in all probability, to use them as a mobile wage-cutting force in this country.

When the Government presented its measure of repentance to the House of Commons on February 12, restoring assistance to its previous levels, S.O. upset Tory M.P.s with his 'uncharitable' and 'unchivalrous' response. He had told them:

> It is insincere and hypocritical on the part of the Government and its supporters to plead now, when they have had the wind up pretty badly over these protests in the country, that they made a number of innocent mistakes in voting for a string of regulations and figures that they could not understand and could not interpret . . .
>
> I find it extremely difficult to forgive what has been done against the unemployed. I cannot persuade myself that the hundreds who went into the Division Lobby in support of these scales and regulations did it in complete ignorance. If they did, they had better be left to their constituents to deal with.

The Government's stop-gap scheme for the U.A.B. to operate both the new regulations and the old Public Assistance scales simultaneously, making the more generous award in each case, was 'a muddle'. Besides, this fresh wave of militancy had swept people's expectations to a higher mark: even the restored benefit levels were now denounced as niggardly. Rioting in the Monmouthshire valleys on March 21 resulted in prison sentences for local Labour leaders. Later in 1935 an all-Wales conference met to declare its opposition to the miserliness of State benefits.

As in the past, this upsurge of working-class self-confidence in south Wales hinged upon the health of the Miners Federation. In 1933 Arthur Horner had launched a fortnightly rank-and-file paper, *South Wales Miner*. By early the following year a reorganisation of the Fed. (long espoused by S.O. and other left-wingers) had been carried through: the coalfield's 20 Districts were amalgamated into 8 Areas, each Area to elect one member of the Executive Council per 6,000 miners; a new leadership, more representative and in touch with the Lodge activists, quickly developed. The useful role of Unemployed Lodges and the unofficial Combine Committees also won wider recognition. This revamped organisation would, S.O. argued, 'substitute for the old, isolated and independent action in one place, action directed from the centre, in order that its results may become the common property of the whole Coalfield, and thereby derive from it a common advantage'.[15]

The new mood's undercurrents broke the surface in a fresh crusade against company unionism. A branch of the 'non-political' South Wales Miners Industrial Union had been established at the Emlyn colliery, Penygroes, during the 1926 lock-out; unsuccessful attempts had been made to dislodge it in 1931. But now, from March 1934, it received the undivided attention of the Federation's Organisation Department . . . headed by S. O. Davies. He worked with the local Miners' Agent, (Arthur Horner) and neighbouring Fed. lodges to recruit S.W.M.I.U. members into the union. By the end of April, most of the 'Non-Pols' were also covert members of the Fed. From this position of unity, they then moved swiftly to dissolve their branch of the company union. Spurred on by this victory, the Fed. engineered a 6-week strike in the scab union's show-piece, Taff-Merthyr, in October: a settlement eventually conceded the right of miners to join the organisation of their choice, thus ending the automatic deduction of S.W.M.I.U. dues from every pay packet. By April 1935 the Fed. felt strong enough to call its first major strike over wages for four years. Just how much the men had mended their mettle was further demonstrated in the following October when 'stay down' strikes against the Non-Pols and non-unionism were initiated at more than eleven pits. During the most celebrated of these subterranean sit-ins, at Nine Mile Point in Monmouthshire, the railway unions in S.O.'s constituency collaborated to stop the 'ghost trains' carrying blacklegs from Merthyr and Dowlais to the colliery.[16]

S.O. played his part in the campaign, addressing meetings, writing propaganda and providing expert advice. But he and the County Borough of Merthyr Tydfil also faced another, more local, challenge : early in April 1935 and true to Chancellor Chamberlain's threats, Prime Minister MacDonald announced the establishment of a Royal Commission 'to investigate and report whether the existing status of Merthyr Tydfil as a County Borough should be continued, and if not, what other arrangements should be made for its local government, regard being had to its own interests and to those of the surrounding counties and county districts'.

A back-breaking rates burden had caused Merthyr's civic crisis. Not only did County Boroughs shoulder responsibilities for higher education, highways and mental health (functions usually exercised by County Councils) but, since the abolition of Boards of Guardians in 1930, Merthyr had been compelled to fund its Public Assistance entirely from local resources. All this occurred in a period when the area's industrial base was disintegrating ; the population had declined steadily from 80,116 in 1921 to 68,700 in 1934 ; some 12,460 were unemployed—63.6% of the insured workforce. The resulting poverty and rate burden was indicated by this comparison in the Royal Commission's report :

LOCAL AUTHORITY	Rateable Value per Head	Rates Collected per Head
Cardiff	£8 6s	£4 12s
Swansea	£6 5s	£4 9s
Merthyr	£3 8s	£4 0s
Average C.B. in England and Wales	£7 0s	£4 3s

The unsurpassed poverty of Merthyr's citizens did not, therefore, earn them any substantial reduction in their rate bills. At the same time, no major schemes in housing, education or health had been undertaken in the Borough for decades ; many of the roads had fallen to ruin. S.O. spoke for the whole of Merthyr Tydfil when he accused the Government of heaping insult upon injury by sending in the Royal Commissioners. The area's plight and the potential to overcome it had been investigated by Sir Wyndham Portal. S.O.'s remarks in the House of Commons contained a warning :

> The Government have refused to examine the cause of the depression and the poverty, and have refused to place before the House a constructive policy to revive industry. They refuse to adopt any policy which promises hope of rehabilitating the economic and industrial life of those areas. I do not know whether any appeal can move the Government to take a constructive step. I am afraid I shall have to abandon an appeal because the Government have abandoned their duty. One thing is certain. The distressed areas will have to let the country know, not through this House but in other ways, that they are not prepared to accept the policy of abandonment and despair which the Government have forced upon them.[17]

The Special Area incentives had yet to spawn a single new factory in Merthyr Tydfil. While the lone Commissioner for all the Special Areas in England and Wales frugally dispersed his £2 million pocket-money, the Government and its supporters proudly allocated £40 millions for the electrification of north London's railways.

The Royal Commission's report, published in November 1935, recommended the stripping of Merthyr's status as a County Borough and the integration of the area into Glamorgan County for Public Assistance and associated purposes. Muddled and timorous proposals were also produced to lighten local government's responsibilities for maintaining the poor and the workless. Neither course of action was pursued. Had a General Election not been called for November 14, perhaps the National Government would have responded to the Report's findings. In the event, Stanley Baldwin's incoming Conservative administration dallied for six months before announcing that an experienced administrator (John Rowland, chairman of the Welsh Board of Health) would be appointed to advise the Merthyr Corporation. It was further intended that the Royal Commission's conclusions be reconsidered at the end of his period of service. Mr

Rowland received a welcome from the Borough's officials, but the Report was never resurrected : Merthyr Tydfil's status survived the desolation, unmolested.

World peace—and the price of its purchase—was virtually everyone's preoccupation in that General Election of November 1935. For four years the Japanese had been conducting a war of aggression in China ; the Geneva Disarmament Conference had collapsed in 1933 ; and now, during the electioneering, Mussolini's Fascist legions were preparing to conquer Abyssinia (Ethiopia). Should the League of Nations enact military or economic sanctions against this self-proclaimed reincarnation of Imperial Rome? Following the appeasement of Japan by the British Government and others, one section of Labour opinion opposed the fostering of fresh illusions in the League. The pacifists—who were prominent in the leadership of the I.L.P.—feared that sanctions of any sort would ignite a wider conflagration. Not a pacifist himself, Aneurin Bevan spoke for many other Socialists when he declared : ' If I am going to ask workers to shed their blood, it will not be for medieval Abyssinia or Fascist Italy, but for making a better social sytem '.[18] Official Labour and Tory policy, on the other hand, was to urge the League of Nations to protect Abyssinia.

From the outset S.O. was alive to the appalling implications for workers everywhere of Fascism, of this phoenix rising from the rubble of Capitalism. Back in 1929 he had travelled with Arthur Cook to the Frankfurt conference of the League Against Imperialist an organisation which campaigned against colonialism and which warned the world about Fascism's endemic war-mongering. Now he saw no alternative to confronting the League of Nations with its own Covenant—and to demand action in defence of its trumpeted ideals. While he, too, regretted the League's record of impotence, he believed that the Soviet Union's recent admittance would strengthen the League's resolve and authority. Naturally, he placed no faith in the Tories or their social stooges : the National Government had acquiesced in Japan's Manchurian adventure and at Geneva had actually impeded French and Polish attempts to arraign Nazi Germany before the League of Nations for illegally rearming. Unlike some Socialists, S.O. welcomed the 1935 Peace Ballot as an indication of the people's desire for a principled peace based on justice ; the verdict was especially emphatic in Merthyr, where the voting went as follows :[19]

PROPOSITION		YES	NO
1.	International Arms Reduction	28,811	487
2.	Abolition of War Planes	28,201	1,035
3.	Suppression of Arms Traffic	28,336	885
4.	Economic Measures Against Aggression	26,990	1,293
5.	Military Measures Against Aggression	14,868	8,765

On S.O.'s home ground at least, Labour's official policy of multilateral disarmament, an international police force and the abolition of private weapons manufacture and trade mirrored the popular mood. Moreover, the fourth and fifth propositions showed the widespread backing that would exist for League sanctions in support of its collective security system. It was the difference between S.O. and the I.L.P. on this point which prompted the party to adopt Claude Stanfield as their General Election candidate in Merthyr Tydfil. Like Leon Trotsky, S.O. stood by Abyssinia and favoured putting the League to the test once again ; Stanfield did not trust the League to act against Italy and, he argued with duplicity, even if it did act the outcome would only be yet another capitalist war. Therefore, Stanfield misleadingly claimed, he was the only 'No War' candidate standing in the Merthyr constituency. To an indignant S.O., the I.L.P.'s decision to challenge him was 'a childish attempt at disruption in the working-class movement'.

On the domestic front, S.O. reminded electors of the Unemployment Assistance regulations, the reductions in Public Works, increased taxes on food and the vindictive anti-trade union legislation still on the statute book. He described the National Government as 'reactionary Toryism sailing under false "National" colours'. Merthyr and the rest of the country needed a bold policy of Socialist Reconstruction : public ownership of basic industries, direction of industry into the Distressed Areas, economic planning, raising the school-leaving age, higher pensions, earlier retirement and an end to the Means Test. This was the message S.O. took to 30 or more election meetings. He also attended one other, sadder gathering that fortnight—the funeral of Noah Ablett, on November 4 in Pontypridd.

Rain kept the turn-out in Merthyr down to 69% on polling day, November 14, although none of S.O.'s support was washed away :

S. O. DAVIES (Labour) 20,530
CLAUDE STANFIELD (I.L.P.) 9,460

Overall, Labour made modest gains in the 1935 Election, lifting its number of M.P.s from 16 to 18 in Wales and from 50 to 150 in Britain as a whole. But by and large, the voters had swallowed the unequivocal pledges of impeccable Tory gentlemen : that the Conservative-National Government would prod the League of Nations into protecting Abyssinia. When the Tories betrayed the Abyssinians a few months later—as S.O. and others had always predicted they would—the sick feeling in so many stomachs could find no release at a General Election until 1945, ten years on.

In the new parliament, south Wales Labour M.P.s pounced upon the Unemployed Assistance Board and its despised Means Test. With the possible exception of Bevan and Llanelli's new M.P. Jim Griffiths (ex-President of the S.W.M.F.), S.O. surpassed all his colleagues in his expertise and incisiveness in the sphere of social benefits and insurance. For instance, his method of dissecting the U.A.B.'s Annual Report in the House of Commons on June 22, 1936, was as original as it was devastating. First he reminded M.P.s that the Board was headed by a Chairman earning £5,000 a year ; it employed 7,000 staff costing £1,500,000 annually, backed up by 130 Tribuuals and hundreds of regional officers. Their callous disregard of claimant's conditions did not apply to their own bureaucratic comforts, he charged . . .

> I have had an opportunity of seeing how generous the Board has been with public money in putting up offices that are palatial, some of them cheek by jowl with the most rotten houses that no civilised Minister of Health would permit to exist so long.

According to its Annual Report, the Board's 750,000 applicants possessed an aggregate personal wealth of just £175,000—

> That is the value of the capital and property of the three-quarters of a million of working men and working women. The means test pursues that value, draws its toll from it and uses it in the application of scales and allowances. The total value of the property and savings of these people, whose poverty has squeezed them almost dry, does not work out at more than an average of one penny per person per week. Yet they are the people the Board is pursuing, importuning, embarrasing, and then the Minister is called upon to apologise for the Board.

S.O. continued to dig in the same vein : the earnings of between 2½ and 3 million husbands or wives, sons, daughters, mother, fathers, brothers and sisters of all the Board's applicants totalled £47.3 millions—2s 3d per person per week. Presumably it was to prevent these pennies reaching the pockets of Unemployment Assistance recipients that the Board's staff had spent £1.5 millions: ' Is it worth it ? Are we justified in bringing this vast and brutal system of espionage into use ?' he asked rhetorically.

In this same debate Nye Bevan anticipated the new regulations due to be introduced and, amidst cries of ' Shame !', told M.P.s : ' I hope that if the Regulations worsen the condition of the people in my district they will behave in such a manner that you will require to send a regular army to keep order '.

When Lt. Col. Muirhead presented the scales to the Commons on July 21, the key-note of his speech resounded with a deeply offensive cynicism : the Means Test would, he enthused, afford families the occasion to operate that splendid Christian principle of ' mutual family support '. The Labour representatives of the jobless and destitute exploded with fury. Even if the Parliamentary Secretary's breath-taking ignorance and incompetence prevented him from answering specific queries about the effect of the new Regulations on lodgers and members of families, S.O., Bevan, Griffiths and Arthur Jenkins (Pontypool) recited case after case where assistance would be slashed or wiped out altogether. S.O. warned the Government that Wales would not tolerate spiteful treatment on top of its impoverishment. Already, one Welsh person in 18 depended upon Public Assistance (1 in 9 in Merthyr Tydfil), compared to 1 in 30 in England :

> Wales will fight for its culture ; it will fight for the amenities that have been established there ; it will fight for the idealism that has been a part of its life for centuries, it will fight for its language, it will fight for anything and everything that is worth fighting for in its life and its traditions . . .
>
> Not long ago we used to hear one country referred to contemptuously as John Bull's Other Island. Some of us are old enough to know the deliberate, wanton, fiendish acts that were responsible for the depopulation of that island. But this little nation in Wales is not going to accept its immolation in that way. It will fight for the personality that is its own and will express it in such a way that this Government will be sorry for

> the harsh and brutal way it has been acting towards a little nation of that kind.

All this was too much for the Tories sprinkled on the benches opposite : Viscountess Astor admitted that 'Wales presents a big problem', but pleaded wearily with Welsh M.P.s : 'Do not give us any more sob stuff'. S.O. goaded her further by deriding the Ministry of Labour as a tool of the Federation of British Industries and describing the U.A.B. as one of the latter's sub-committees ! The debate broke up the next day in uproar. Three Clydeside M.P.s were ejected from the Commons chamber, extra police were called to the Lobby and the proceedings were suspended for quarter of an hour—before hundreds of Conservative M.P.s materialised from Westminster's nooks and crannies to stamp Parliament's seal of approval on the new Regulations.

Beyond Westminster the protests spluttered, flowed and—every so often—erupted. In that Vesuvian valley, the Rhondda Fawr, one hundred thousand people assembled at Tonypandy to demonstrate against unemployment and the Means Test. To mark the opening of Parliament in November, 2,000 hunger marchers from Cumberland, Tyneside, Scotland and south Wales filed into Hyde Park, where 200,000 supporters greeted them. On the morrow, November 9, 1936, one million signatures collected the length and breadth of the land were presented to the House of Commons. When this petition was debated two days later, Prime Minister Baldwin defended his decision to turn away a deputation of marchers : the prominent Communist presence had fixed the whole affair, in his mind at least, as 'political agitation designed to discredit and overthrow the Government'. M.P.s from the distressed areas reacted angrily to this distortion : S.O., then a member of the marchers' co-ordinating council, insisted that their cause attracted the sympathy of a wide spectrum of social, religious, cultural and industrial bodies :

> Is there a section of the population in south Wales, of any class or any organisation, that has not forwarded to the Prime Minister appeals and resolutions about the sad conditions that are responsible for the marchers coming to London ? As one who knows most of the marchers from south Wales, I protest vehemently against the Prime Minister associating in his mind those persons with the nightmare of vast mobs—which apparently is worrying him—that are a danger to law and order. I consider the speech of the Prime Minister this evening as being

> nothing short of contemptible. There has not been from any place in the country where the marchers have been the slightest complaint coming through to London about their conduct, which should win the approval of all of us. Why add insult to injury ? Why indulge in such language as the Prime Minister used tonight ? Why talk about mobs ? Why talk about civil disorder and strife ? These people are doing all they can to get rid of such a state of things as may cause disorder in this country.

S.O. also pointed out that the organisers had striven to limit the number of marchers : 5,000 foot-soldiers from labour's army could have been despatched from south Wales alone, had insurrection been the purpose. But the self-control, the reasoned rebukes to Baldwin, the meetings with Labour Ministry chiefs . . . they achieved nothing. The regulations were implemented within a week.

1936 was the Depression's trough, breeding desperation and despair in some quarters. One extreme manifestation of this was the much-publicised scheme for national salvation unveiled at a Free Churches Council conference by R. T. Evans, the former Liberal M.P. for Carmarthen. He proposed the creation of a new Glamorgan or Monmouthshire in one of Britain's old Dominions : the ' surplus people ' of Wales could be transported to a settlement similar to those set up by the Jews in Palestine or, indeed, by the Welsh in Patagonia. The notion was not a novel one—late in the 1920s British Prime Ministers and members of the royal family had mooted the possibility of transferring unemployed workers to a colony somewhere in Canada ! An angry S.O. rounded on the quitters, asking in the *Western Mail* :

> Why ignore the vast mineral resources of North and South Wales, with its rich agricultural area intervening ; and why deliberately advocate the wanton destruction of social, religious and cultural institutions in the pursuit of an undefined and unplaced ' will-o'-the-wisp ' ? . . . May I devoutly express the hope that Wales has few such pessimists as Mr. R. T. Evans ? Nothing but disaster and shame can ensue from the destruction of our little nation. Nature has endowed our country with vast mineral riches, and history has handed down to us a heritage, memories of an heroic past, the loss of which would deprive civilisation in these islands of its noblest treasure.[20]

S.O.'s counter-proposals included the direction of private industry into depressed areas, channelling unemployment money into job

As Mayor, S.O. invests Clement Attlee with the Freedom of the Borough in 1945. Sephora Davies is sitting on S.O.'s left

Canvassing local railwaymen

creation programmes, and nationalising the coal industry as the trigger for its expansion. Of course, the Tory-National Government rejected any such measures ; instead, rearmament and the establishment of trading estates fuelled a modest economic recovery—almost everywhere, that is, except in Merthyr Tydfil. Whereas every other Special Area had begun to pull out of its nose-dive by the end of 1936, the Borough remained stagnant. Between 1932 and 1938 Government incentives attracted 235 firms into distressed areas—but none to Merthyr. Meanwhile, 2,000 factories had opened in the Midlands and Greater London.[21] True, Merthyr's unemployment rate relaxed to 37% in October 1937, but this was due primarily to a readjustment of the Ministry of Labour's base figures or —less charitably—to a statistical sleight of hand. Within months the rate had returned to its usual range of between 40 and 50 per cent. Over the same period, the jobless level in much-vaunted Jarrow stood at 20%.

The spectre of defeatism cast its shadow again in March 1939, in the Political and Economic Planning unit's *Report on theLocation of Industry*. This team of eminent experts concluded that Merthyr Tydfil should be abandoned and its population moved in whole to the coast or into the Usk valley ! Once more, S.O. condemned the well-intentioned, would-be undertakers, although the irony is that financial hardship had already compelled him to forsake 'Haddington', The Grove, in Merthyr, for London. A Parliamentary salary of £400 a year had proved insufficient to support him and his family, lodgings in London, a house in Merthyr and the weekly travelling to-and-fro. Reluctantly, therefore, he moved in 1937 with Sephora, their three daughters and infant son Alyn Stephen (born in June 1935) to a London county council flat in Clapham, returning to his constituency each weekend.

The idea that Merthyr could be dismantled and its people dispersed might seem fantastic today, but in the midnight of the town's existence it did not appear to be so preposterous a suggestion—at least to outsiders. After all, had not 23,000 people already left the Borough between 1918 and 1939 ? And the remainder might well have been shifted out eventually . . . had it not been for World War Two.

Hill's Plymouth colliery closed in 1940, but by then the hostilities between Britain and Nazi Germany had already produced new job opportunities : increased production in nearby coal mines and steelworks drew workers from Merthyr Tydfil. The bombing of industrial installations in the London region prompted S.O. to propose the construction of ' shadow ' factories in outlying areas : the first such buildings went up in his constituency, with I.C.I. taking a site in Dowlais and munitions factories springing up elsewhere in the Borough. Thanks to such developments—and to military recruitment—the homes and streets of Merthyr were no longer occupied by thousands of aimless, jobless men. Yet this was a fragile revival. Once the war in Europe had come to an end, in May 1945, most of the workers and demobbed soldiers began returning to the dole queue, swelling it to more than 7,000 within 12 months.

Even so, the General Election campaign of June that year was dominated by a popular determination never to go back to the deprivations of the 1930s. This mood was informed and reinforced by the Beveridge Report, which called for a comprehensive social insurance system and the eradication of poverty. S.O. had passionately supported Sir William Beveridge's ' great enterprise ' in the House of Commons on 17 February 1943, delivering one of his most eloquent indictments of Capitalism and the ravages it had unleashed in the previous decade :

> It was a policy based upon the efforts to rehabilitate a worn-out and decrepit economy, a policy that proceeded on the assumption that the more profound and widespread material poverty became among our own people, the better the system would function. It was a policy of scarcity that was attempted in order, presumably, to bring about prosperity. What was the result of that policy ? . . . Poverty that I never dreamt I should see in this country. It was a policy that brought about the destruction—the wanton, wicked, mean destruction—of hundreds of millions of pounds of capital values. Many hundreds of collieries were closed down, not because any one of them had been exhausted. Many hundreds of factories and workshops were closed down, not because those workshops and factories, with the collieries, could not have responded to and met the prime material needs of our people at that time. Many of our shipbuilding yards and engineering works closed down. The people of this country and the world were deprived of that great craftmanship that these engineering works and shipbuilding yards possessed at that time. Hundreds of thousands of acres of first-class food producing land were forced to become waste land . . . This was private enterprise, which we have

> heard so many appeals and prayers from the other side of the House during this day that it should be given another chance.

In Britain, S.O. pointed out, huge bank deposits had been laying idle alongside 3 million unemployed workers : in the United States, massive gold reserves had been accumulated as 12 million people cried out for work. Such a situation would not be tolerated again, he warned—

> We are asked to provide social security for our own people on the broken, withered reed of an obsolete economy. I warn the Government that when our people are demobilised from the Forces and from the war industries they will not stand the kind of cruelty that was perpetrated against them after the last war . . .
>
> Sir William Beveridge says in effect, ' This scheme of mine must be reared on one outstanding fact, a job of work for every man and woman in this country who can work '. But can private enterprise guarantee that ? Did it after the last war ? Why the colossal failure ; why the disaster after the last war, and what assurance can it give that the disaster after this war will not be far greater ? I say, deliberately, that the Beveridge Plan demands a great adjustment of our economic policy and of our economic structure.

Taking advantage of the widespread pro-Russian sentiment existing in Britain at the time, S.O. finished by referring M.P.s to the Soviet Union where ' the vastest and most successful economic planning in human history has been achieved '.

The Labour Party entered the post-war General Election campaign on a bold programme of reform : the coal, electricity, gas, transport and steel industries would be nationalised, along with the Bank of England ; private monopolies would be controlled, national economic planning could begin, full employment would be achieved ; a national health service and a social insurance system would form the basis of a Welfare State ; a whole range of meaures would be taken to improve and extend the education system.

With great enthusiasm S.O. endorsed these plans—although he would have preferred to go all the way, on to Socialism. Only one other name appeared on the ballot paper in Merthyr Tydfil : that of Alderman Sam Jennings. He had fallen out with the local Labour

Party in 1934, protesting at the conduct of the selection conference to choose Wallhead's successor. Whilst describing himself as an 'Independent Labour' candidate, Jennings focussed his campaign almost exclusively upon S.O.'s personality. At the Merthyr Trades Council and Labour Party meeting of June 30, 1945, Jennings alleged that his opponent was in arrears with his union dues—and thus was no longer a member of the union which sponsored him, the Miners Federation. The Dowlais Lodge replied that S.O. had kept up to date. But S.O. gave as good as he got in the personal exchanges, and told his constituents :

> My selection was made by the unanimous vote of all Working Class Organisations in the Borough. I am the only Official Candidate in this Constituency of the great Trades Union and Political Labour Movement of the country . . . the I.L.P. have declared their support for the Official Labour Candidate, and they have called for a United Front of all Socialists and Progressive Forces to assure the defeat of all reactionaries in whatever words they may describe themselves . . .

When the result was announced on July 5, S.O. had amassed an enormous 81% of the votes cast :

S. O. DAVIES (Labour)	24,879
SAM JENNINGS (Ind. Lab.)	5,693

This handsome victory was the first of two honours bestowed upon him that year by the citizens of Merthyr Tydfil ; two months later S.O. was made Mayor of the Borough. When he resumed his seat in St. Stephens, it was on the Government side of the House amongst the largest-ever group of Labour M.P.s . . . 393 in all. In addition, the Government could count on 6 other left-wingers in any crucial confrontation with the 213 Opposition M.P.s. In terms of seats won, this 1945 General Election had been an avalanche for Labour, although it is often overlooked that the number of pro-Socialist votes barely outnumbered the non-Socialist total.

Still, the monumental task of reconstruction could begin. In Merthyr and Dowlais, Ministry of Works factories were taken over by Triang Toys and Hoover respectively ; the Merthyr Borough Industrial Estate was constructed, and in 1947 work started on the massive Hoover complex to the south of Merthyr town. Other companies such as Thorn's Electrical, Teddington Aircraft, Kaysor Bondor, O.P. Chocolates and the Dowlais Button factory arrived in the area—transfusions which revived historic communities, cutting the Borough's unemployment level by more than half. In this triumphant effort, S.O.'s mountainous correspondence with Government Ministers, civil servants, businessmen and others is an ample testament to his own heroic contribution. He also encouraged the industrial estate established at Hirwaun, in the neighbouring constituency of Aberdare, which provided work for many commuters from Merthyr ; in appreciation of his services, the Sobel company offered S.O. a free television set—but he declined, his scrupulous refusal of all such ' perks ' standing in stark contrast to the unprincipled rapacity of some parliamentary colleagues !

Above anything or anyone else, S.O. acclaimed his Labour colleague Hugh Dalton as the architect of Merthyr Tydfil's salvation. As a Minister in the war-time Coalition Government, Dalton had drafted the 1945 Distribution of Industry Act which empowered the Board of Trade to buy land, build factories, make loans and to clear land ; most importantly, the Act introduced building control regulations to push new industrial development into the distressed areas (which themselves were positively re-designated as ' Development Areas '). Beforehand, and without publicity, Dalton had visited S.O.'s home and constituency from where he derived the inspiration for his view that ' industry should be made far more mobile than communities of men, women and children '—thenceforth propagated as the ' Dalton Principle ' by S.O. who, twenty years later, remembered Hugh Dalton as ' the greatest friend that I and the Merthyr Borough ever had '.[22]

Not that S.O. was ever satisfied with the progress made in these post-war years ; he was continually suggesting imaginative ways to reduce unemployment still further. Although the number of registered jobless workers in Wales had fallen to 40,000 by 1948, the unemployment rate of 5½% was twice that of any other part of Britain. S.O. took the lead in compiling a memorandum to the Prime Minister, Clement Attlee, which he presented on behalf of the Welsh Labour group of M.P.s in the summer of that year.[23] He called for :

1. More Remploy factories (for disabled workers) ;
2. The National Coal Board to initiate the manufacture of colliery requisites and equipment in south Wales ;
3. New and improved trunk roads ;
4. The clearing of coal waste tips for amenities and recreation, using powers under the Distribution of Industry Act ;
5. Positive discrimination in favour of Development Areas in awarding Government contract work ;
6. The Forestry Commission to pursue reafforestation schemes ;
7. More consistency in Government capital investment projects ;
8. A Welsh Committee of Government Ministers (Trade, Labour, Supply, Fuel and Power, Works, Transport, Health and Treasury) to co-ordinate and execute the above programme.

Had such a plan been implemented, it would have enhanced the longer-term prospects of the Welsh economy, transforming the environmental and transport infrastructure, inducing State agencies to bring modern research and technology to Wales.

Nevertheless, much of Labour's General Election manifesto, *Let Us Face the Future*, was fulfilled between 1945 and 1951. S.O. extended an especially warm welcome to the massive housing programme pioneered by a new and dynamic young Minister, Aneurin Bevan. Merthyr Borough had been unable to afford any significant housing improvements for more than a decade, hence S.O.'s call in a Commons speech back in March 1945 for the creation of a national housing authority, with the resources to build millions of temporary and permanent homes—and with the powers to eliminate profiteering in land, building materials and labour. In this field as in most others, he supported the Government whilst wishing to go further. Thus he voted for every item in Labour's shopping-list of nationalisations—while criticising the generous compensation paid to dispossessed shareholders, and voicing his fears that the new State bureaucracies were as unaccountable to Parliament as they were to their employees ; S.O. also took a close interest in the parliamentary legislation to set up the Welfare State—but bitterly attacked the retention of Means Test tribunals in the unemployment benefit system, and sternly opposed Bevan's concessions to private consultants in the National Health Service.

All in all, though, S.O.'s pride in the Attlee Government's reforming achievements bloomed with the passing of time ; so too, perhaps paradoxically, did his belief in the possibility and the necessity of Socialism. Not for a moment did he think that Capitalism had been transcended : but it had at least been restructured and humanised. A Labour Government had given it a new lease of life, and in the process had rescued the communities of Merthyr Tydfil from extinction.

Nobody celebrated the Borough's salvation in more simple and moving terms than the Rhymney poet, Idris Davies. He had been angered by the remarks of South Croydon's Tory M.P. Sir Herbert Williams, who had regaled the Commons with his ' memories ' of Merthyr Tydfil in the 1930s.[24] *Hansard* recorded the exchange in Parliament as follows :

SIR H. WILLIAMS : Merthyr Tydfil indulged in extravagance while existing on the charity of the rest of the country.

MR S. O. DAVIES : May I be permitted to describe that statement as an unmitigated lie ?

THE CHAIRMAN : That expression is not permissible and I must call upon the hon. Member for Merthyr Tydfil to withdraw it.

MR DAVIES : Very well, Major Milner, I will withdraw the noun but not the adjective.

SIR H. WILLIAMS : The last time I went to Merthyr Tydfil the cinemas were full, the shops were full, 70 per cent of the people were unemployed, ruined by the reluctance—

THE CHAIRMAN : The hon. Member must not pursue that line of argument.

EARL WINTERTON : On a point of Order. May I point out that I have sympathy with my hon. Friend [Sir H. Williams] ? What is sauce for the goose is sauce for the gander. He has been blackguarded, and it is well that hon. Members should know that if one side uses hard language, the other side is entitled to do so also.

Nearly two years later, in March 1946, Idris Davies wrote to S.O. and enclosed these two verses, hitherto unpublished :

MERTHYR TYDFIL

(To the Memory of Keir Hardie)

They have talked of Merthyr Tydfil
wherever men were free
To honour those who toiled and died
for human liberty
And men have told her troubled tale
to spur the sons of men
When hopes were faint or flagging,
to lift their hearts again.

They shall talk of Merthyr Tydfil
in the centuries to be
Of her suffering, her patience,
her moral victory
And her foes shall be forgotten,
and her honour shall abide
And her children shall remember—
And they shall walk with pride.[25]

NOTES

[1]See ' Earning a Living : Industrial Development from 1918 to 1939 ' by Alun Morgan in *Merthyr Historian* Vol. 2 (1978) ; the *Second Industrial Survey of South Wales* (1937) published by the National Industrial Development Council of Wales and Monmouthshire [sic] Vol. 1 p. 406 (Migration), p. 425 (Unemployment) and Vol. 3, pp. 127-141 (Labour Supply and Demand). The *Report of the Commission of Inquiry into the Status of Merthyr Tydfil as a County Borough* (November 1935) Command 5039, contains much information on population, unemployment and local authority rates ; other information about rate levels, rent arrears etc. comes from the *Merthyr Express* for May and June 1934.

[2]Telegraph from S.O. to the S.W.M.F., Neath Constituency, March 1920, in the S. O. Davies Papers, Swansea (Ref : 1A, *i*) ; his acceptance and speech to the Flintshire Labour Party was reported in the *Merthyr Express*, 24 April 1926; on March 31 1926 the Cardiff Central Labour Party wrote to S.O. inviting him to become their Parliamentary candidate (S. O. Davies Papers, Swansea, Ref : 1A, *i*).

[3]See *My Generation* (1972) by Will Paynter.

[4]*S. O. Davies Election Special*, a four-page newspaper to be found in the S. O. Davies Papers, Swansea.

[5]As Note 4 above.

[6]*Merthyr Express*, 26 May 1934.

[7]*Merthyr Express*, 26 May 1934.

[8]As Note 4 above.

[9]*Merthyr Express*, 9 June 1934.

[10]See the *Second Industrial Survey of South Wales* (1937) Vol. 2 p. 81.

[11]*Report on the Investigation into Industrial Conditions in Certain Depressed Areas* (1934), Command 4728 ; a useful summary of this and other reports is to be found in the chapter ' Wales's Locust Years ' in *Rebirth of a Nation : Wales 1880-1980* (1981) by K. O. Morgan.

[12]*Y Cymro*, 13 May 1970.

[13]*Merthyr Express*, 19 January 1935 ; an informative article about the 1935 national assistance scales, ' The Politics of Need ' by Tony Lynes, appeared in *New Society*, 8 December 1977.

[14]See the accounts of this march on Isgoed House in the *Merthyr Express*, 9 February 1935 ; in the *Daily Worker*, 9 February 1935 ; in the *Western Mail*, 21 February 1935 ; in ' Eye-Witness : Mary Morgan Says No ! ' in *Rebecca* (February 1982) ; and in *My Generation* (1972) by Will Paynter. Paynter deals quite extensively with the various assistance regulations of the 1930s and the campaigns against them.

[15]*Miners' Monthly*, April 1934.

[16]Sources as listed in Note 18 to Chapter Four above. Will Paynter's *My Generation* (1972) also contains some valuable information and analysis about the struggle against Company Unionism. A final settlement was reached between the S.W.M.F. and the scab union in the Taff-Merthyr colliery early in 1938, involving the gradual dissolution of the S.W.M.I.U. there. During these negotiations, S.O. stood firm in demanding that the Fed. take control of a local £2,000 fund for a workers' institute ; he won the argument with the 'Non-Pols' and the coal company, and the money was speedily used to build one of the finest small halls in the South Wales coalfield. See the recollections of Edgar Evans in *Strike—A Live History 1887-1931* (1973) edited by R. A. Leeson. Evans, a Communist councillor and ironmonger in Bedlinog, was gaoled for 9 months in 1936 following clashes with blacklegs ; S.O. helped organise a mass campaign in support of him and other defendants. Evans was also stripped of his political liberties for 10 years.

[17]Debate on the Unemployed Assistance (No.2) Bill, House of Commons, 9 May 1935.

[18]*Aneurin Bevan : A Biography* Vol. 1 (1962) by Michael Foot p. 238.

[19]*Merthyr Express*, 19 January 1935.

[20]*Western Mail*, 30 July 1936.

[21]'Earning a Living : Industrial Development from 1918 to 1939' by Alun Morgan in *Merthyr Historian* Vol. 2 (1978)

[22]Notes written by S. O. Davies in 1968 for an article on industrial development in Merthyr Borough, in the S. O. Davies Papers, Swansea (Ref : 1E).

[23]S. O. Davies Papers, Swansea (Ref : 1A, *ii*).

[24]Debate on the Town and Country Planning Bill, 12 July 1944.

[25]Letter from Idris Davies to S.O., 6 March 1946, in the S. O. Davies Papers, Swansea (Ref : 1A, *i*).

Chapter Six

A WAR FOR FREEDOM ?

Much though he craved for Peace, S.O. never claimed to be a pacifist : 'Turn the other cheek . . . ' had been no motto for a miners' leader in south Wales. Rather, he shared the prevailing attitude of his class towards war and violence which was essentially a pragmatic one : they declined to make a fetish of either violence or non-violence, they preferred to avoid bloodshed—but would fight if the cause was necessary and just. The Great War had underlined in red the terrible truth that it was S.O.'s people, the working-class, who were the first and foremost casualties in any war. He would refer to the 10 million men killed, and the 30 million injured, between 1914 and 1918 ; in the first battle of the Somme 5,000 fathers, sons, husbands and brothers had perished during each hour of daylight. 'And did this help the workers ? ' S.O. asked, 'No, on the contrary, when it was over we witnessed violent upheavals and attacks on the working-class.'

It was never the trade union and labour organisations that demanded or declared war : this was the prerogative of the State and its ruling-class. Thus in 1939 the British State—that political and economic conspiracy to exploit and subdue S.O.'s class—called upon its citizens to combat the Nazi and Fascist menace. Of course, S.O. yielded to nobody in his loathing of the Hitler and Mussolini regimes : but he refused to fall in behind his domestic enemies, to be fooled by their bogus philanthropy, their fake indignation and their hypocritical moralising. Not for one second did he believe that Britain's capitalists cared for anyone's rights and freedoms but their own ; the tyrants of the peace were now masquerading as the angels of the war. 'Capitalism has never fought for my or your freedom. This war fought by Britain and France is not for the working-classes ', argued S.O. at the outset. Capitalist crises had spawned Fascism, showing the readiness of industrialists and financiers to ditch bourgeois democracy in order to save their system from collapse or Communism ; Fascism would make the world safe for Capitalism, at least temporarily, by shattering the Labour movement and destroying the 'surplus ' productive forces that had created gluts and colossal unemployment side-by-side with hyper-inflation. War would destroy, on a grander scale, the over-capacity whose products could not be consumed smoothly by Capitalism's increasingly impoverished masses.[1]

There was no fundamental conflict between Capitalism and Fascism, S.O. therefore maintained. He had spent his life resisting both—without ever receiving help from the former against the latter. Along with other Socialists, he could not forget or forgive the Tory-National Government's refusal to support democracy in Spain. In 1936 the reactionary and Falangist forces of General Franco had launched an insurrection against the elected Republican Government. Yet at the same time as Italian legions marched into Spain to aid the insurgents, as *Luftwaffe* bombers obliterated towns and villages in Euzkadi (the Basque Country), the British Government denied munitions and non-military supplies to the democratically-elected governments in Madrid and Guernica. This non-intervention policy could not be budged by the enormous 'Arms For Spain' demonstrations in solidarity with the Spanish Republic. Sharing many a platform with other Socialists, Communists, Liberals and churchmen, S.O. implored the National Council of Labour to organise political strikes against the British Government's stance. Nor was the Chamberlain administration moved by the sinking of more than a dozen British ships bound for Spain with food and equipment ; some Tory M.P.s actually cheered when these Italian outrages, costing scores of civilian lives, were announced in the House of Commons.

Conservative complicity in Franco's advance, and Labour's tame and ineffectual opposition, provoked a fresh outburst of 'Popular Frontism' in January 1939 : the memorandum presented by Sir Stafford Cripps to Labour's National Executive called for Labour unity with the Communist Party and other political groups, in defence of democratic and working-class rights at home and abroad. Cripps paid the penalty for attempted heterodoxy—expulsion. Prominent Labour figures like Nye Bevan, Richard Crossman, G. D. H. Cole and S. O. Davies signed a letter protesting at the N.E.C.'s lightning-strike against Cripps, and criticising the sluggishness with which that same body engaged the Tories. The National Petition for a Popular Front, initiated by Cripps, received an early boost in March when the National Government bestowed diplomatic recognition upon Franco's victorious dictatorship. Yet still Transport House persecuted Labour's ' crypto-Communists ' with more zeal than it pilloried the appeasers of Fascism. The two M.P.s who refused to withdraw from the Popular Front petition, Bevan and George Strauss, were despatched to the same purgatory as Cripps. Yet, to the *Western Mail*'s chagrin, S.O. escaped any such punishment ; on April 6, 1939, the newspaper's Editorial complained :

> Mr. S. O. Davies, M. P. for Merthyr, while he has not appeared on a platform in support of this heretical faction, has publicly announced by letter that the Popular Front campaign has his unqualified sympathy and support.

In his reply S.O. could not pass up the opportunity to poke fun at the Labour leadership and its most recent Conservative allies :

> I am impressed by the touching concern shown by the *Western Mail* for the orthodoxy of official Labour. Is it to be hoped that the latter will appreciate a new champion of the cause ? Will the new and startling role of the *Western Mail* as the guardian of the true Socialist faith be welcome at Labour Party headquarters and will it be felt there that this intrusion is helpful ? Is this another variant of the Popular Front in which the champion of capitalist interests, of Tory political theory and practice, is aligning itself with the official custodians of Labour interests and Labour political theory and practice ?[2]

Few left-wing M.P.s could match the acidity of S.O.'s invective against those whom he called ' the "Inner Council" of the Cabinet, the self-proclaimed saviours of the nation ' ; speaking in Norwich early in November 1938, he began with the Chancellor of the Exchequer, Sir John Simon, who as Foreign Secretary in the first National Government had ' glossed over ' the Japanese invasion of Manchuria when addressing the League of Nations . . . here was the man who had ' sneered ' at the Peace Ballot : he was ' an inveterate enemy of the League and of Collective Security, a wrecker of World Peace '. Then there was the Home Secretary, Sir Samuel Hoare, who had as Foreign Secretary connived with the French Prime Minister and Fascist-collaborator Pierre Laval to abandon Abyssinia to the Italians in 1935. As for the current Foreign Secretary, Lord Halifax, he had ' behaved shoddily ' in Geneva in 1938 when efforts were made to exclude Abyssinia from the League of Nations. S.O.

pointed out how eagerly Halifax had filled the post vacated (at Mussolini's insistence !) by his predecessor, Sir Anthony Eden. S.O. contrasted Halifax to the dispossessed but dignified Emperor of Abyssinia : ' How small, puerile and contemptible a figure he cuts side-by-side with that frail, sick man brutally robbed of his country and tens of thousands of his people massacred '.

Before them all, though, paraded the Prime Minister himself, Neville Chamberlain, who had expressed his ' perfect good faith ' in Mussolini's promises, swallowed Hitler's assurances at Munich in September 1938 and then had regurgitated them to an adulatory House of Commons. ' We have not forgotten the speech delivered to Parliament by the Prime Minister on February 22, when he threw Austria to the Fascist wolves,' S.O. remarked. ' Nor have we forgotten that at the very moment Austria was being destroyed, he dined with that genial gentleman, Herr von Ribbentrop.' These were the four men who had set up the Cabinet's ' Non-Intervention Committee ' ; their Mediterranean Treaty with Italy in April 1938 had marked ' another victory for the Rome-Berlin Axis '.[3]

Many Tories had looked on with admiration as Fascism invaded Manchuria, China, Spain and Austria ; they approved and found excuses for the extinguishing of democracy, the crushing of free trade unionism and the imposition of totalitarian dictatorship. Here, for example, is Winston Churchill paying tribute to Mussolini in 1927 :

> If I had been an Italian I am sure I should have been wholeheartedly with you in your triumphant struggle against the bestial appetites and passions of Leninism . . . Italy has provided the necessary antidote to the Russian poison. Hereafter no great nation will be unprovided with an ultimate means of protection against the cancerous growth of Bolshevism.[4]

In a series of articles in the *Evening Standard* in August and September 1936, Churchill praised General Franco's crusade against ' squalid Communism ' (even though the early Republican Government in Spain did not contain a single Socialist or Communist).[5] In tandem with these and other apologetics, the English Tory press disparaged every international effort to check Fascism. On home territory, however, most members of the ruling-class believed it possible and desirable for their system to survive the 1930s without jettisoning bourgeois democracy. At the same time, just beneath the surface lurked a network of anti-Socialist, anti-trade union, anti-immigrant, anti-Semitic, pro-Empire and crypto-Fascist organisations, bristling with retired diplomats and military men, titled aristocrats and Tory M.P.s.[6]

It is no wonder, therefore, that S.O. regarded the British Government's indecisive and unconvincing war preparations with a cynical eye. In the Commons on December 6, 1938, he told Sir John Anderson why his official scheme for National Voluntary Service would raise no popular enthusiasm : ' It is no use expecting the country to forget such names as Abyssinia, Munich and Spain. Those names will be extremely lively in their minds, and this Government will never be able to shed its responsibility as far as perpetrating the tragedies that those three names stand for in our memories '. S.O. called upon the Government to show some humanitarian concern for its own people, by abolishing the Means Test and increasing unemployment benefit. Under such improved conditions, he had no doubt that the British people would defeat any ' totalitarian slave-State '.

Czechoslovakia having been added to the list of capitulations, Chamberlain's Government finally decided in August 1939 to resist Nazi aggression, to come to the aid of Poland and democratic rights. But the ensuing self-righteous clamour rang hollow to S.O. and other anti-Fascist Labour M.P.s : they believed that England's ruling-class was acting primarily out of self-interest, fearful for the future of their Empire, their investments and their prestige. In the major Commons debate of October 12 that year, S.O. demanded a clear statement of Britain's war objectives—as distinct from the ' high-sounding generalities ' about ' fighting for democracy, self-determination, freedom of thought and expression, and for the rights of nations to the forms of Government that their people desire '. Yes, Fascism trampled upon these principles. But had not our closest ally, France—with whom we were supposedly in ' perfect accord '—just proscribed 70 Communist members of its National Chamber? Was this to be a war for parliamentary democracy and free expression, or was it not ? Had the British Government been consulted about the ban? Did it agree with the French Government's action? No answers were forthcoming, although the Deputy Speaker of the Commons intervened twice to demand that S.O. desist from this line of inquiry. The discordant Member for

Merthyr Tydfil then repeated his call for humanity and compassion to be shown to the poor, the old and the unemployed of Britain. Morale on the domestic front was important for military success : ' We look for justice first at home, before being bidden to fight for it abroad '.

S.O. further stated his position on 13 May 1940 on a Commons motion to welcome the formation of a Coalition Government ' representing the united and inflexible resolve of the nation to prosecute the war with Germany to a victorious conclusion '. He expressed his grave misgivings about the action of Attlee, Morrison, Bevin and other Labour leaders in joining the new all-party Government under Winston Churchill ; they had, remarked S.O., crossed a great gulf ' that some of us believe will never be bridged until radical changes take place in the social structure of this country '. The Conservatives represented a ' harsh and cruel ' society, whereas he and other Labour M.P.s spoke for the poorer and oppressed classes who would suffer in war as they had suffered in peace-time : ' If this is a war for democracy, it can be waged and won only when democracy is experienced by our own people ', he declared. The anti-trade union Trades Disputes Act remained on the statute book ; the Government was persisting with the ' contemptible ' Workmen's Compensation Bill ; profiteering was rampant in the manufacture of arms, food and other essentials. Under these circumstances, S.O. concluded, he could not countenance co-operation with the Tories. His colleagues had crossed the Floor of the House without so much as a transfer fee ! Nor would the war be won by ' stultifying and hamstringing opinion in this House of Commons ' : voluntary totalitarianism was as unacceptable as the compulsory Fascist variety. He closed the debate on a resolute and defiant note :

> We shall watch this Government critically and anxiously. Their task presumably is to mobilise the men and resources at our disposal ; but will they be able to do it ? I am confident that they will not be able to do it unless the dead hand of the past is removed, and until the crippling weight of organised profiteering is lifted and the ' Patriotism Ltd.' of high finance, of the money changers and gamblers on our stock exchanges is completely eliminated. These are the powers—and we have no illusions about this—which brought Nazism into being and the powers which will bring Nazism into being in this or any other country if their dominion is to last much longer. We on

> these benches are as prepared to fight Nazism as is any representative in any part of this House, whether that Nazism is partially concealed in this country or blatantly open elsewhere. We shall do so, but not at the price of sacrificing the principles which have ever been dear to us, namely, the interests of our own people who have placed us in this House.

It was in this spirit, too, that S.O. declined to support the Merthyr Tydfil War Weapons Week in 1941, informing a Mr Thackeray on January 16 :

> I regret that I am unable to give my unqualified support to this cause. I could not possibly reconcile any appeal I might make to the patriotism and generosity of the people in order that they may contribute towards the cost of armaments with my life-long agitation against profiteering in the tragic experience of war. I consider the rampant profiteering that is now taking place, when women and children figure so prominently in our war casualties, as the most sordid and disgusting of crimes against humanity. No appeal of mine for contributions towards the payment for war weapons can conceal the fact that out of every £100 given towards the cost, say, of a Spitfire, over £50 go in profit, rent and interest . . .

Emotionally, S.O. viewed the war with pessimism ; on 4 April 1942 he expressed his feelings and trepidations in a letter to Miners' Agent S. O. Thomas, whom he addressed as ' My dear fellow-S.O.' :

> We are in a catastrophic war, where old systems and social relationships are dissolving around us. Colossal and most vital problems are immediately confronting us ; problems whose solutions will determine the well-being, or otherwise, of almost the whole of humanity for generations to come. I am alarmed at the indifference of our Movement respecting these problems. It will be far too late to consider them once this war is over. The manner in which this war is conducted will determine the nature of the Peace. They are inseparable. Private ownership, with its rabid profit-seeking, is as arrogant and insolent in the saddle these days as ever it was in the past. In fact, it is more deeply entrenched now than it was in pre-war days. How can the class in power, deriving its sustenance, its pomp and splendour, from human exploitation, ever establish the basis of permanent peace ? Our class has already been deprived of most of its cherished achievements. Its freedom has been whittled away to an alarming degree. A Labour Home Secretary, who has been in the past notoriously keen in suppressing minority

and progressive views within our own Movement, is now most evilly engaged in restricting the freedom of the Press and of opinion. Are these facts not of supreme and urgent importance? Is not the vast drama at this moment being enacted in India, with its 400 million souls, a matter of profound interest to all of us? I could go on enumerating life and death issues arising from the corrupt heart of modern Imperialism. Unless our Movement is revived, and becomes militant once again, all our past gains will go with our priceless local government. We must wake up.

Yet the adherence of S. O. Davies to the Marxist theory of dialectical development induced in him an optimism of the intellect: whatever his heart might feel, his head reasoned that the construction of a war-economy under Capitalism would prove to be a progressive step for mankind. S.O. argued that Imperialism faced rivals abroad as well as the left-wing enemy at home—and that 'this double task entails changes in the economics and politics of present-day Capitalism'. The Second World War, S.O. noted, was compelling the State in Britain to: (1) control capitalist industry and (by rationing) the market-place in order to avoid crises and the under-feeding of labour; (2) step in and manage the distribution of raw materials to protect key war industries; and (3) regulate labour, wages and transport. S.O. quoted Lenin:

War, by extraordinarily expediting the transformation of monopoly capitalism into State monopoly capitalism has thereby extraordinarily advanced mankind towards Socialism . . . State monopoly capitalism is the complete material preparation for Socialism, the prelude to Socialism, a rung in the ladder of history between which and the rung called Socialism there are no intermediate rungs.[7]

But S.O. was equally sure that the guardians of the old order would try anything to abort the future; after all, the capitalists were still in the saddle: he pointed out that the Controllers sitting on the Councils of Supply, Exports, Raw Materials and the rest were businessmen and financiers almost to a man. The duty which S.O. shared with other Socialists, he insisted, was to protect those domestic rights and freedoms that would ease the birth of Socialism. His overriding fear was that 'War will establish fascism in Britain much sooner than Hitler will in the absence of war'; thus S.O.'s supreme priority between 1939 and 1945 was the maintenance of hard-won civil and political liberties. The English ruling-class should not be permitted to erode democracy at home under the cover of battles being fought elsewhere. In short, S.O. adopted the slogan emblazoned across the Government's own posters : ' Your freedom is in danger ; defend it with all your might '.

Not surprisingly, the first freedom to disappear was that hitherto enjoyed by aliens and immigrants. Public opinion applauded the internment of Germans, Italians and others in 1940, whereas a few Labour M.P.s like Rhys Davies (Westhoughton) withstood the clamour of jingoism. In particular they objected to the rounding-up of anti-Fascists, including Jews and even Socialist ex-members of the German *Reichstag*, convicted by their nationality alone. In Parliament S.O. raised the case of a constituent, Guiseppe Conti, who had been interned and then deported—consequently losing his life at sea and leaving behind a widow and two young children in Treharris ; the Government's unsubstantiated excuse for setting the tragedy in motion was that Conti was ' reported to be a member of the Fascist Party '.[8]

A more celebrated cause was the War Cabinet's decision to suppress the Communist *Daily Worker* newspaper. Since the staggering Nazi-Soviet pact of August 1939 (prompted by the capitalist powers' rejection of an anti-Fascist alliance with the Soviet Union) the British Communist Party had pursued a policy of ' Revolutionary Defeatism ', to turn an imperialist war into a civil war. As a result, the Communists sought to inflate legitimate grievances and urged the working-class to step up their struggle for trade union rights, better wages and for other aspirations that might impede the war effort. Peddling more softly, the *Daily Worker* spent most of its columns criticizing the curtailment of liberties, countering anti-Soviet propaganda and exposing the undoubted inadequacies of the Home Office's civil defence and safety precautions. In January 1941 the Home Secretary, Herbert Morrison, closed down the *Daily Worker* and a Communist weekly journal under Defence Regulation 2D. S. O. Davies added his voice to the considerable outcry, although he did not wholly agree with the Communist Party's attitude to the war : he opposed sabotage and gratuitous strikes, and was not so much anti-war as deeply cynical of ruling-class aims and motives—especially in this, the ' phoney-war ' period. It was because he put domestic working-class politics and freedoms before the shadow-boxing with continental Fascism that S.O. defended the *Daily Worker* with such gusto. He joined six other M.P.s to vote in its favour in the Commons following a statement from Morrison, whom S.O. accused of ' treating the House with contempt, exploiting its prejudices—all to the accompaniment of a barrage of cheap and reckless vituperation '. Writing in the Communist-front magazine *Labour Monthly* in March 1941, S.O. linked the suppression with the introduction of industrial conscription and the recent release from prison of prominent Fascists, concluding :

> This act is tragically reminiscent of the destruction of liberty in Germany, Italy and France. It therefore behoves us, at whatever personal cost, to guard our hard-earned liberties with the unshaken conviction that a war that is made the excuse to rob us of any of these liberties cannot be a war for freedom and democracy.

Alongside Bevan, H. G. Wells and Liberal-Left M.P. Richard Acland, S.O. castigated Morrison for gagging the *Daily Worker* under Regulation 2D, instead of taking it to court under 2C and thereby permitting the paper to defend itself against specific charges.

It was S.O.'s unapologetic championing of such causes as the Popular Front and the *Daily Worker*, his willingness to work with Communists and anyone else on the Left, that prompted allegations that he was a ' fellow traveller '. Yet he did not toe the Communist Party line in several important matters : for example, after the German invasion of the Soviet Union in June 1941 the British Communist Party became the most zealous prosecutors of the war, participating in production committees with unrivalled enthusiasm, opposing strikes, abandoning independent working-class electioneering, calling for a ' Second Front ' against the German Army, and even praising Winston Churchill. S.O. underwent no such overnight conversion : maintaining civil liberties and the autonomy of the Labour Movement remained paramount. Of course, as a Socialist and an admirer of the Soviet Union he desperately wanted the world's first workers' State to escape the Nazi yoke ; nor was he any the less keen to see Britain defended. Indeed, he and his family had been victims of the blitz in September 1940, driven from their devastated flat in Clapham to the haven of Merthyr Tydfil—to ' Gwynfryn ' in Park Terrace. Nevertheless, the disarmament of the working-class, politically and industrially, would be a price fraudulently-asked and foolishly-paid for the purchase of a military victory. On these grounds S.O. could not support the mass conscription of his class into the Armed Forces in April 1939 ; two years later he accused the National Service Bill (which plugged ' loopholes ' for conscientious objectors and introduced compulsory recruitment into the Civil Defence Services) of ' making inroads into our liberties, violating every socialist principle '. Working with Stan Beynon, he persuaded the Merthyr Trades Council to oppose the measure also.[9] Braving the taunts of ' defeatism ' and ' fifth columnist ', S.O. and a handful of Socialist M.P.s argued consistently that the economic organisation of the war should be in the hands of the workers : the Labour Movement must control production, industrial conscription, manpower allocation and all the other levers that would enable it to win the Peace after winning the War.

On the political front, too, S. O. Davies could not accept cold-storage of the class war. Labour's leaders had arranged an electoral truce with the Conservatives for the duration of hostilities, whereby the party in possession of a particular parliamentary seat would be given a free run at any by-election that might occur therein. So when the King's Norton Divisional Labour Party was suspended early in 1941 for leafletting against an unopposed Conservative candidate in their constituency, S.O. jumped to their defence. He believed the N.E.C.'s retaliation to be ridiculous and disgraceful, and wrote to a correspondent :

> The National Executive is becoming more and more prone to panic decisions, all directed to the complete stultification of the Movement. That way lies the destruction of all we have fought for, and all imperialist Britain pretends to be fighting for these days. The most painful of all experiences today is to contemplate objectively the enforced sacrifices of our class while, on the other hand, we see the Capitalist class more deeply entrenched in class power and privileges than ever before.[10]

Nowhere was goodwill squandered more recklessly than in the coalfields. Coal was essential to the war effort ; but the Government only recognised the axiom reluctantly and belatedly, taking the mines out of the coalowners' hands and placing them in the trust of State-appointed Controllers in March 1942. Naturally, the owners would continue to draw their dividends—and at one time the

Coalition even proposed a National Wages Board to boost profit margins. The timidity with which Labour's spokesmen tip-toed around this opportunity to nationalise the coal industry incensed S.O. : the coal barons were utterly discredited in the public's eyes, having grown fat on the profitable coalfields, neglected others regardless of strategic requirements, and killed off rationing schemes in collusion with back-bench Tory M.P.s. Yet the Board of Trade President, Hugh Dalton, and Minister Dai Grenfell had let the owners off the hook, abetted by workers' leaders afraid to rock the ship of state. S.O. knew that the new arrangements would disgust many ordinary miners ; voicing the sentiments he had gleaned from pit-head meetings, he tore into the Government's 1942 White Paper :

> This White Paper—apply it any way you like, wrap it up with all the eloquence and rhetoric that you can—will not produce an extra ton of coal. I am more than tired of this insincere, pettifogging and piffling treatment of the mining industry. My mind has been going back very vividly over 30 years of a very active life in the industry. Every commission and every committee of inquiry for 30 years has condemned the conditions responsible for the disorganisation of the mining industry. I am not using language that is too strong when I say that for sheer wicked, irresponsible and wanton 'wastrelism', this industry has suffered more than any other industry in the country. Now we talk about rationing. Twenty-three years ago to this very month a great Commission was at work inquiring into the wholly inadequate organisation of the mining industry. We had this pronouncement made by the Sankey Commission : 'I recommend on the evidence before me that the principle of State ownership of the coal mines be accepted'.
>
> What has happened since then ? Nearly 500,000 men have been driven out of the industry, and we have lost about 80,000,000 tons of coal a year in output. And here we are crying and panicking for coal today. The miners cannot be blamed for the loss of a single ton of coal and for the displacement of a single worker. We have preached, appealed and written and cajoled all the powers that be for well over a generation, and these are the results : 500,000 men have been driven out of the industry, and hundreds of collieries have been closed down. The abandonment of a colliery means, in general, that it is completely ruined. Communities have been made derelict, families have been broken, homes have been uprooted and indescribable poverty and despair have been experienced by thousands. Do the Government think that the miners have forgotten all this ?[11]

He wanted nationalisation, higher wages, rationing and refused point-blank to accept any responsibility for the Government's plans. His sincere concern was for a productive, efficient industry ; the dead hand of the oligarchs had to be removed once and for all. On this issue S.O. clashed with his friend and ex-miner Dai Grenfell on numerous occasions. When Grenfell defended the Coalition's approach in the House of Commons on 17 March 1942, S.O. derided his efforts as 'most disappointing, pathetically unreal, foreign to all his experiences and, I regret having to say it, even to the profound convictions that he holds with regard to the industry'. Feigning incredulity, Grenfell listened as S.O. showed how the screening process and price-list system wasted up to one-third of the coal cut: because the owners refused to pay for the lumps of coal that passed through the screening bars (although they would often sell much of it afterwards!) the miners themselves would leave small coal underground. Then S.O. exposed the way in which the owners profited from making bogus distinctions in work-grading ; he cited an important agreement negotiated with the S.W.M.F. of which the Government, apparently, knew nothing.

Here were major sources of grievance—and yet the authorities pleaded ignorance. The men's resentment deepened with the imposition of an Essential Work Order, shackling them to the coal industry. On top of this the Government decided in 1943 to conscript young men—'Bevin Boys'—into the pits, to fill the places vacated by miners conscripted to the battle-front two years previously. As S.O. and other mining M.P.s predicted, production began to fall and unrest increased ; unofficial strikes broke out in 1943. Churchill's eloquent appeals to the miners' patriotism did not sweeten his refusal to nationalise the mines. When the Government and the coalowners declined to finance the whole pay award recommended by the Porter Tribunal, the militant coalfields erupted in February 1944. Within a month more than 100,000 men had stopped work in south Wales alone. The press accused the miners of treason, and M.F.G.B. President Will Lawther inflated the fantasy that 'Trotskyists' had instigated the rebellion. It required the combined efforts of the union, the Labour and Communist Parties, and the miners' M.P.s to soothe the men and end the stoppages.

Meanwhile the Minister of Labour, Ernest Bevin, had gone into a huddle with the Employers' Federation and the T.U.C. General

Council, emerging with their approval for new and tougher anti-strike legislation. Regulation 1AA—swiftly christened 'Bevin's Penal Servitude Regulation'—decreed that: 'No person shall declare, instigate or incite any other person to take part in, or shall otherwise act in furtherance of, any strike amongst persons engaged in the performance of essential services . . .' The penalty for an offender stretched to 5 years imprisonment, a £500 fine, or both. S.O. regarded the measure as a monstrous provocation : 'Bevin is primarily responsible for the most harsh and reactionary measure inflicted on the workers since the repeal of the Anti-Combination Laws', he told Merthyr trade unionists, 'Bevin is preparing the way for Reaction to be in the saddle after the War. He will be their excuse and their justification. He is presenting the ruling-class with the most effective instrument to bludgeon the workers, including the Ex-Servicemen, at the end of the present emergency'. The door was being opened even wider to black-legging, strike-breaking, company unionism and *agent provocateurs*.[12]

Bevin tried to justify his big stick before the Commons on 28 April 1944, exaggerating the incidence of wild-cat action and hinting at the omnipotence of a handful of Trotskyists. He was cheered by the Tories and by crypto-Communists like D. N. Pritt. But the independent M.P.s Bevan, Acland and others flayed the Minister for Labour and his Government : 'They seem to be breaking under the strain' remarked S.O., 'the ease with which they become panicky is not a good example to the people of this country in days of crisis'.

Long before this, the course of the war had compelled S.O. to share the popular desire for an Allied triumph. What began as a localised 'phoney war' had, by 1942, ignited into an international struggle between Fascism on the one side, and an alliance of the Capitalist Democracies and Socialism on the other. Belgium, France, Denmark and Norway had fallen to the Nazis, who were now laying siege to the Soviet Union ; and in December 1941 the Japanese had stung the U.S.A. into action by obliterating Pearl Harbour. The conflagration had spread to four continents. Towns and cities in Britain blazed under aerial bombardment, and prepared to resist a German invasion. Confronted by such perils at home and abroad, S.O. could do no less than urge the successful prosecution of war by Britain and the Allies. He travelled the south Wales valleys with Nye Bevan and assorted Communist speakers, calling for the establishment of a Second Front : the time was ripe for a massive Allied land offensive in north-west Europe, now that the bulk of the German armed forces were engaged in an epic tussle with the Soviet Red Army.

Yet still his watch-words were ' Trust the People ' ; the censorship, suppression and industrial serfdom that had been imposed on Britain were unnecessary as well as dangerous. Socialists should, S.O. maintained, argue for people to have *more* rights and freedoms to defend, not fewer : let the working-class take control of industry, government and the mass media. If they were to defend the country, it should be theirs to defend ! S.O. pointed to the courageous resistance of the Soviet people, and contrasted their ' Great Patriotic War ' to the hypocritical and self-defeating policy of the English ruling-class towards India. He challenged the House of Commons with his underlying principles on 27 January 1942 :

> In view of the tragic and gloomy picture which the Prime Minister drew today about the Far Eastern situation, what do the Government intend to do ? Is their present mishandling of the situation in India to continue, or do they prefer that India should fall a victim to the Fascist forces of the Far East rather than grant India that necessary measure of freedom to defend herself ? . . .
>
> What are the Government fighting for ? Is it to make the world safe for free peoples ? Are they fighting for the principles that are laid down in the Atlantic Charter ? If so, India has the first call on them, not merely humanly speaking, but strategically speaking also. Or is this a war simply to perpetuate the miserable *status quo* in India and in many other parts of the Empire ? Is it a war to make profit-seeking safe ? Is it a war for cheap labour ? Is it a war for raw materials ? Is it a war, once again, for unrestricted markets ? Or is it a war of liberation ? . . .
>
> I have no illusions as to what might happen at the end of the war. There are two alternatives confronting our people. This war must be either a war of liberation or a war of extended suppression. What is it going to be ? Shall we fight and win the new world, or shall we fight and die for the extension of Fascism ?

No other tract of Empire preoccupied the minds of Britain's Socialists so much as India. S.O.'s grasp of India's history and its contemporary predicament was firm and thorough. Since 1600

India's bountiful store of raw materials had been plundered to feed the Imperial Motherland and to build up England's industries at the expense of India's own.

When British capital eventually invested in India, it did so with the minimum installation of machinery and the maximum exploitation of dirt-cheap labour. By 1939 some 70% of Indian industry was owned by British capitalists, most of whom exported the profits overseas and paid their taxes to the British Treasury ; at least £1,000 millions were siphoned out of India between 1830 and 1930. On the other hand, and in order to facilitate the tapping of the sub-continent's labour and raw materials, about the same amount had been ploughed into India's industries, railways and irrigation system. Even so, the net result for the natives was a low-paid, largely illiterate and disease-ridden workforce ; nine-tenths of the 350 million population subsisted on the land and agriculture—in an agrarian sytem dominated by feudalism and usury. And all this was being suffered by a country abundant with precious metals, copper, manganese, bauxite, coal, iron, salt, oil, cotton, mica, jute, tea, tobacco and water-power. No wonder that Britain opposed full self-government for such a colony ! Never was the White Man so reluctant to put down what he arrogantly referred to as his 'Burden'! The English ruling-class clung tenaciously to its Raj, quelling rebellions there in 1919, 1921, 1930 and 1931, ever-boastful of its own wisdom and philanthropy.

The former Lieutenant-Governor of the Punjab, Sir Michael O'Dwyer, declared :

> Historically and morally we have a better right to rule India than the Hindus or any other race. We alone have proved our capacity to protect, unite and develop it.
>
> We cannot, in justice to the Indian peoples, of whom only 8% are literate, transfer ultimate responsibility for their welfare and advancement to Indian control.
>
> Any attempt at such a transfer to the urban Hindu oligarchy, who wrongly claim to represent the Indian peoples, over 90% of whom live in villages, would inevitably lead to civil war.[13]

The paradox of India's condition—severe deprivation in the midst of plenty—did not escape the Indian nationalist movement, spearheaded by the Congress Party with its leaders the Mahatma Gandhi and Pandit Nehru. From 1927 they demanded full independence for India, with Indian control of the Armed Forces, an independent foreign policy, more protectionism for domestic industry and the right to secede from the British Empire. Such a programme went considerably further than the Dominion Status first promised to India in 1929. It was the straightforward nationalist replacement for the patchwork-quilt of Provinces, Administered Areas and Native States, stitched together by Britain according to the classic colonialist principle of ' Divide and Rule '.

In the 1937 elections to the provincial assemblies, provided for in the Government of India Act two years previously, Congress swept to power in six of the eleven Provinces and formed the largest single party in a seventh. But the Congress Ministries resigned in November 1939, in protest at the omission of Indian independence from Britain's list of war aims.

In the face of Gandhi's latest campaign of civil disobedience, the British Government postponed any significant constitutional developments behind a smoke-screen of petty reforms ; the situation deteriorated in 1941 when Churchill announced that the Atlantic Charter drawn up by himself and the U.S. President Roosevelt, with its clarion call for the self-determination of all nations, did not apply to India.

With mounting anger and exasperation, S.O. watched the Coalition Government trample on the ideals with which it had lured the working-class to war, frittering away the willingness of most Indian Nationalists to assist the anti-Nazi effort. He hurled his passionate invective at the British Government's Bill in 1941 to cancel elections in India and Burma, concentrating upon the official excuse for the cancellations : the danger of worsening communal tension between Muslims and Hindus. He declared in the Commons debate on September 11 :

> To attempt to justify the postponement of the elections because there is alleged to be much communal feeling is really absurd. The Right Hon. Gentleman [Leo Amery, Secretary of State for India] answered a question as to the number of political prisoners now in Indian prisons. Those political prisoners are the leaders of the Indian masses. The appalling figure given to us was over 12,000. Can it be said that the imprisonment of these leading personalities among Indians has anything whatsoever to do with communal feeling ? The Right Hon. Gentleman knows very well that the answer is ' No '. How can we

> reconcile a statement of that kind—without by the way, any attempt to justify that mass imprisonment of Indian thinkers and Indian leaders and patriots as great as any of us—

At this point the Speaker of the House of Commons interrupted S.O., admonishing him for ' extending the debate far beyond the scope of this Bill ' ! Unabashed, S.O. stood his ground and went on to conclude :

> I object to the Bill because I regard the war as one of liberation. I am accepting every word of our Prime Minister and President Roosevelt, in their Declaration to the world the other day. Because of that Declaration we are under the most solemn obligation to apply the Charter to the Indian people. When I remember the great effort that our country is making today in this war of liberation, I believe that what the Prime Minister meant was liberation from exploitation, from economic insecurity and privation, from disease and hunger and from ignorance and superstition. We want to believe that we are fighting for that kind of liberation.

Under pressure from the Left, public opinion and from the U.S. Government to break the Indian dead-lock, Labour leader Sir Stafford Cripps was despatched to Delhi in April 1942 ; as Lord Privy Seal he was empowered to offer the Indians the prospect of a post-war Indian Union, with full Dominion Status and the right to secede from the Empire. But the Nationalists, mindful of the growing threat from Japan, demanded immediate independence and Indian control over the Indian Armed Forces ; nor would Congress countenance the right of unelected Native Princes, or of Provincial administrations elected on a limited franchise, to take their territories out of an independent India. Thus Cripps flew back to London, his mission having failed.

In response, the Viceroy and the British Government's India Office thickened their conspiracy to split the Indian people along religious and cultural lines, chiefly by inflating the status and credibility of Mohammed Jinnah and his Moslem League. In the early 1930s the British Intelligence Services had channelled financial and intellectual resources into the notion of a breakaway Muslim state, to be called ' Pakistan '.[14]

Unlike other M.P.s on the left of the Labour Party, such as Tom Driberg, S.O. was not fooled for a second by the Government's protestations of good intention and all-round philanthropy. Nor did he stand in awe of such ‘ darlings of the Left ’ as Cripps had once been, as is shown by this exchange in the House of Commons on 11 September 1942 :

S. O. DAVIES : Has there been as much anarchy in India since the Mutiny as exists at this moment ? Can the Government depend upon any representative section of the Indian population today ? They know they cannot. That is why the Secretary of State and the Lord Privy Seal have worked so hard in pretending that Congress have no influence in India.

SIR S. CRIPPS : Oh, no.

MR DAVIES : The Lord Privy Seal denies it. May I ask him whether he wrote the deliberately misleading article which appeared in the *New York Times* ? It has his name to it, but apparently he has forgotten it.

SIR S. CRIPPS : I never said that Congress had no influence in India at all. Congress is one of the big parties in India.

MR DAVIES : The Right Hon. and learned Gentleman worked very hard to show that Congress had shed all the influence it may have had in India.

SIR S. CRIPPS : Oh, no.

MR. DAVIES : Did not the Right Hon. and learned Gentleman say that every one of the 90,000,000 Moslems in India were against Congress and were supporting him and his Government here ?

SIR S. CRIPPS : No.

MR DAVIES : I have the article here. The Right Hon. and learned Gentleman said that the whole of the 90,000,000 Moslems were not supporting Congress.

SIR S. CRIPPS : What I said was that if any issue of Islam was raised, the whole of the Moslem population would support the Moslem League.

MR DAVIES : The Lord Privy Seal must be getting into a very difficult situation over this Indian business. I used to know him when he held a great respect for facts and truth. He knows that that statement is incorrect and that Congress represents far more Moslems than the Moslem League ever has represented. Those with the most elementary knowledge of India know that. What criterion does the Right Hon. and learned Gentleman use in coming to his conclusion ? The best criterion as to the extent of the influence of Congress was the 1937 elections. The talk of the Secretary of State for India will impress no-one who knows the facts. The Lord Privy Seal knows very well that in those elections only 4.6% of the Moslem electorate voted for the Moslem League. It is a fact of simple arithmetic.

SIR S. CRIPPS : Certainly.

MR DAVIES : Then on what ground can the Right Hon. and learned Gentleman contend for a moment that Congress was not supported by the Moslems when the party had Congress Ministries in Provinces, particularly the North-West Frontier Province which was overwhelmingly Moslem ?

Cripps remained fixed to the Front Bench, silent. Nonetheless, S.O. was too angry to desist from a bitter denunciation of this erstwhile comrade, describing Cripps as ' a fake socialist who travelled with indecent speed from obscurity on the backbenches up through the Left and then back to the Right, in anticipation again of high office '. In the same speech S.O. called also for the Burmese and Malayan people to be granted independence—' freedom to defend the countries that are theirs '.

True to the traditions and necessities of Socialism, S. O. Davies was an internationalist to his bones. He argued and campaigned for causes in Asia and the Far East with a passion and a familiarity undimmed by distance. For years he bombarded the Government and the Press with questions and statements, arguing and exposing the real effects of British Imperialism. Relentlessly, he harried Ministers about imprisoned Indian Nationalists ; he fought the banning of Soviet Aid and anti-Fascist meetings in India ; he condemned the official censorship of Congress proceedings and resolutions in the Indian and English newspapers (and even in the House of Commons library !) ; he questioned the treatment of Indian evacuees from Burma ; he deplored the execution of four Indian peasants accused of killing a policeman . . . especially when the judge who had sentenced them admitted the absence of incriminating evidence.

S.O. celebrated India's emergence as an independent Dominion in 1947 with special gratification. At the same time, he grieved the ransom that had been extorted by Amery, Churchill, Jinnah and their allies in the British and Anglo-Indian Civil Service: a separate Pakistan was carved out of the North-West and North-East of India, conceded by Congress but still baptised in the blood of half a million victims butchered in the progroms unleashed by Pakistan's founding dictator and Governor-General, Mohammed Jinnah. Britain had retained its foothold in the Indian sub-continent . . . or so Churchill imagined.

The Second World War had changed course in 1943 when, for the first time, the Axis powers were turned onto the defensive; having routed Germany's Panzers at Kursk in July, in by far the greatest tank battle in history, the Soviet Red Army began its long drive to Berlin: the Baltic States and Ukraine were re-occupied and the pro-Fascist regimes in Roumania, Hungary and Bulgaria swept away. The resistance movements (as distinct from the bourgeois 'governments-in-exile') which emerged in Italy, France, Greece, Yugoslavia, Bulgaria and elsewhere were largely led and staffed by Communists, Socialists and radical peasants. Amongst them and their many supporters, the conviction grew that the only way to kill Fascism—to lay it in its coffin permanently—was to drive a stake into its heart, to destroy Capitalism. With the Red Army occupying more and more of Eastern Europe, pro-Soviet regimes being installed, mass Communist Parties taking to the streets, and resistance movements liberating their countries piece-by-piece (with Allied aid), the Western powers were haunted once again by the spectre of Communism in Europe. The Allied Military Governments manoeuvred desperately to turn the tide of workers' factory-occupations and the seizure of land by the peasants. In Italy, especially, right-wing elements and collaborators with Fascism were installed in power at local levels, whilst workers' and peasants' organisations were forcibly dissolved.[15]

But it was in Greece that British intervention was most decisive. With the Nazis driven out, the next power struggle was between the Monarchist-controlled Greek Army and the National Liberation Front (E.A.M.-E.L.A.S.). Civil war erupted on 4 December 1944, and for two months the Liberation forces took on the Army, the Police and the pro-Nazi National Guard; so strong and popular was the E.A.M. that they could have overcome even these odds. But what they could not withstand in addition were the R.A.F. 'Spitfires', the British tanks, two divisions of Britain's North African Army and the Anglo-Indian units which bombarded the working-class quarters of Athens and overran the other towns and villages.

Back in the House of Commons, Coalition leaders sought to justify Britain's role and the right-wing regime in Greece with all-too-familiar ploys and arguments: on 19 January 1945 Foreign Secretary Anthony Eden produced a document purporting to show that the Greek Socialist Party had withdrawn from the E.A.M.

in protest at the Front leadership, whom it called ' deadly enemies of our country ' for provoking war with the Allies. S.O. interrupted Eden and challenged him about the document's authenticity ; the Communist M.P. for West Fife, Willie Gallacher, attacked the declaration as a clumsy fake : no Socialist Party in Europe, certainly not the one in Greece, would have the ' central committee ' and ' political bureau ' apparatus claimed for this one—this was the structure adopted by Communist Parties. Eden retreated, with Gallacher and S.O. in pursuit :

MR GALLACHER : I still think it is a fake.

MR EDEN : I admit that the conditions in Athens are disturbing. I admit the difficulty of substantiating exactly what this or that section of political opinion feels in a city which has been through what Athens has been through, but I submit to the Committee that the document I have read out, and the circumstances which I have described of its presentation to us, are at least a strong *prima facie* case that it represents something of substance in Greek Socialist opinion.

MR S. O. DAVIES : Can the Foreign Secretary explain why the names of Professor Svolos and Professor Angelopoulos are not among the names [i.e. signatories] he read out because they are, and have been, accredited leaders of the Greek Socialist Party ?

MR EDEN : Professor Svolos was a member of E.A.M., but I do not know his present whereabouts, and I cannot tell why he was not a signatory to this document. All I can tell the Committee is that this is the report which came to us through our Ambassador.

More audacious, even, than this crude attempt to divide the National Liberation Front's supporters outside Greece was Churchill's campaign to belittle the massive part played by the Front's armed wing (E.L.A.S.) in driving out the Nazis. On January 18 he referred sarcastically to the ' fierce mountaineers who had been so tame and idle against the Germans ', and characterised the E.L.A.S. forces in Athens as a ' ferocious and well-armed, well-directed mob '. In response, S.O. accused Churchill of ' slander against the Greeks '. For once, he was guilty of understatement. Highly-esteemed war correspondents around the world have recognised and recorded the predominance of E.L.A.S. in the Greek resistance movement, from the *Times* man in Smyrna to Mr William

Shirer (author of the classic *Rise and Fall of the Third Reich*). Shirer wrote:

> Though Mr. Churchill vehemently denied it, I think there is little doubt that the principle resistance movement in Greece was the E.A.M., with its combatant branch known as E.L.A.S. The secret documents of the German High Command which I saw at Nuremberg left no doubt that the German Army considered E.L.A.S. as almost the only serious armed resistance movement it had to deal with.[16]

Another authority, William McNeill, made the following estimation:

> By the time of liberation E.A.M. numbered about two million members, out of a population of over seven million. They were incomparably superior to all rivals in their organisation and enthusiasm, and had every reason to suppose that once the Germans were out of the way that they would be able to take over undisputed control. There seemed nothing that could hope to stand against them.[17]

Throughout their struggle for Socialism and democracy in Greece, the partisans received no material support—and not much moral succour—from the Soviet Union. As we now know, the Greeks had been sacrificed on the altar of Stalin's *Realpolitik*. In October 1944 he had met Churchill in Moscow to plan the final stages of the war and, with an eye to the future peace, to carve up the European continent into 'spheres of influence'. In his war memoirs, Churchill records how an historic bargain was struck: how Britain was allowed '90% influence' in Greece, Russia was given 90% in Roumania and 75% in Bulgaria, while Yugoslavia and Hungary were to be shared on a 50-50 basis between the Western Powers and Russia.[18]

The Moscow Pact (like the tripartite agreement reached at Yalta four months later) was born of Capitalism's desperation to contain Communism—and of the Soviet Union's determination not to suffer another European invasion, least of all one of the same enormity as this last one. The magnitude of what the Soviets call their 'Great Patriotic War' against the Nazi invaders has never been appreciated by most people in the capitalist world; Churchill, however, noted that in 1943 the Red Army faced 185 German Army divisions while the Western Allies were 'playing about' with six German divisions.[19] It is the tilt with the six which features in so many cinema films about the European War. Meanwhile, the

Soviet Union had sustained damages greater than all the Western Allies put together. According to the U.S.S.R.'s Extraordinary State Committee the German forces destroyed 15-20 million Soviet citizens, 15 cities, 1,710 towns, 70,000 villages, 6 million buildings, 31,850 industrial enterprises, 40,000 miles of railway, 56,000 miles of highway, 10,000 power stations, 1,135 coal mines, 3,000 oil wells, 98,000 collective farms, 84,000 schools, 40,000 hospitals and medical centres, and 2,800 churches.[20] To repair this devastation the Soviet State was rumoured to be considering the use of forced labour from Germany in the spring of 1945. When angry Tory and Labour M.P.s raised the matter in the Commons on 11 April 1945, S.O. admonished them for their hypocrisy:

> Dealing with this question of slavery, I am certain that neither the Hon. Gentleman [Tom Hopkinson, Mossley] nor any of the Members opposite protested against the sheer enslavement of 500,000 of my people in Wales in the inter-war period. Half a million men, women and children, one-fifth of the population, were by force uprooted from their country, driven throughout England, badgered, importuned, and many of them forced to live under conditions no better than will be those of the German worker if he is forced to work in Russia. We had no protest then, when thousands of homes were disrupted and even destroyed, when hundreds of our young people were driven, by the policy of the Hon. Gentleman and the Government of the day, to leave their homes in South Wales and return in a few years to die, literally by their hundreds, of tuberculosis. It happened in my constituency . . .
>
> When we talk about enslavement I suggest to my Hon. Friends most kindly that we try to maintain some sense of proportion in the matter . . . The protestations they have made in the House this evening are protestations on behalf of slaves. The whole working-class of Germany has been enslaved for the last 10 or 12 years. It is no good attempting to build a case by protesting against some rumour or other, by which Russia is supposed to be the guilty nation, on behalf of a nation of people who have not been free for half a generation.

In the event, the Soviets dropped their plans to put 2 million Germans to work in the Soviet Union; instead, they seized billions of pounds worth of industrial plant and machinery from Eastern Europe, especially Germany, to be installed in their own war-ravaged country. Also, an incalculable number of enemy soldiers and home-grown collaborators with Fascism—certainly hundreds of thousands, possibly millions—were incarcerated in Soviet prison-labour camps or executed.[21] The same fate befell many Soviet soldiers and officials who were suspected of pro-Western sympathies or political disloyalty to the Stalin regime.

Not that global affairs caused more than a surface ripple during the British General Election campaign of June 1945. In hustings dominated by domestic issues, all the major parties claimed to support a continuation of the 'Big Three' alliance between the U.S.A., the Soviet Union and Britain. Only a handful of the contesting elements detected a deepening anti-Soviet undercurrent, notably the Communists and their paper the *Daily Worker*, Labour's *Daily Herald* and Sir Stafford Cripps. S.O.'s election address awarded greater prominence than most to the international context ideal for Socialist reconstruction at home; his sentiments were, for once, largely uncontroversial:

> A World of Progress and Peace! . . . No domestic policy, however wisely framed, can succeed in a world still threatened by War. We cannot cut ourselves off from the rest of the World—and we ought not to try. We must consolidate in peace the great war-time association with the U.S.S.R. and the U.S.A. We must join with France and China, and all others who have contributed to a common victory, in a great International Organisation capable of keeping the peace. No nation can enjoy full freedom as long as it keeps others in bondage. To assist in this, full freedom must be granted to India and the Colonies, 'Peace is Indivisible'.

Labour's election triumph sparked off victory bonfires all over Europe: progressive forces everywhere celebrated the 'left-turn' taken by the working-class of such a major capitalist and imperialist power as Britain. Labour's programme for domestic reconstruction was certainly bolder than those promised in 1923 and 1929; S.O. also drew encouragement from the party's 'International Post-War Settlement' policy, with its central emphasis on strengthening the Anglo-Soviet-American alliance as the foundation of a United Nations Organisation.

Yet the obstacles in the path of any Socialist foreign policy for Britain were immense. To begin with, both the Prime Minister Clement Attlee and his chosen Foreign Secretary, Ernest Bevin, had served loyally in the Coalition Government, defending Churchill's reactionary positions in Europe with gusto ; they were unlikely to take up a new broom and sweep away the network of English public-school Tories, blimps and appeasers of Fascism that constituted the central nervous system of Britain's Foreign Office and diplomatic staff. It is from this source that the incoming Cabinet would receive so much of its ' expert ' advice and information. The new Government was also susceptible to American pressure, having been compelled to negotiate a substitute for the Lease-Lend aid so abruptly cancelled by the U.S. Government in August 1945.

From the outset, Labour's foreign policy appeared to be merely a continuation of the Coalition's pro-colonial and anti-Communist approach ; (for example, Indonesia was ' liberated ' from the Japanese—only to be handed back to the Dutch imperialists, with British troops rounding-up the island's insurgent Nationalists). At the Foreign Ministers summit in September and October 1945, Ernie Bevin wrecked the talks with his pig-headed anti-Sovietism : he flatly refused to discuss Russia's call for joint Turkish-Soviet control of the vital Dardanelles straits. The *Guardian* commented on July 9 : ' We who hold strategic bases all over the world cannot begrudge the Russians the right to protect the seaway to their greatest industrial and agricultural area, the Ukraine '.

Soviet-backed and Communist-instigated machinations in Eastern Europe also provided the Red-scare mongers with abundant ammunition : within 12 months of free elections in Hungary, leading members of the victorious Smallholders Party were being expelled on the insistence of Moscow ; in Roumania, the Communist-controlled National Democratic Front remained in power without elections ; in Czechoslovakia, where the Communist Party had won 38% of the votes in the 1946 election, all the key posts in the coalition government were filled by Communists. Bulgaria's Fatherland Front had taken power with popular support in 1944, as the political wing of the anti-Fascist partisans, but by late 1946 it was rigging elections against its non-Communist adversaries (although it permitted some of them to occupy minor seats in the new government). In Poland the governing coalition had been broadened to include right-wing *émigré* politicians, in line with Western demands ; non-Communist organisations there could hold meetings, publish newspapers and even criticise the authorities —but anything considered to be remotely pro-Fascist or anti-Soviet was banned by the Communist-controlled police and interior ministries.[22]

In June 1946 the annual Labour Party conference rejected a motion to permit the affiliation of the Communist Party, to S.O.'s dismay, and went on to insert a black-list of proscribed organisations into the new Labour Party constitution : all the Trotskyist and ' Communist-front ' bodies put on the list would be ' out of bounds ' for members of the Labour Party.

A lower point on the Cold War barometer was reached on 12 March 1947 when U.S. President Harry Truman appealed to the American Congress for aid to the Greek junta in its war against the Left. He argued that the struggle in Greece was a microcosm of the world-wide conflict between two irreconcilable systems : Western Democracy and Communist Tyranny. The timing of Truman's bellicose pronouncement ensured that a Foreign Ministers' summit in Moscow, to discuss the future of Germany, broke up in suspicion and bitterness. Soviet and Communist forces immediately cracked down on the opposition in Hungary, Bulgaria and Poland ; the Americans went into Greece, and in the United States itself loyalty oaths and security checks were imposed on public employees—and the infamous House Committee on Un-American Activities was set up.

Against this back-cloth of deteriorating East-West relations the Labour Government in Britain laid plans to introduce, for the first time in modern British history, peace-time conscription into the Armed Forces. The National Service Bill, given a Second Reading in the Commons on 31 March 1947, compelled men aged 18 to undertake 12 months military training, followed by 5½ years in the Reserves. The core of the Government's case was that demobilisation would leave the Armed Forces seriously depleted by its completion in 1949—when conscription would become operative. S.O. joined scores of Labour M.P.s in opposing the measure from the outset : he deplored the striking of such a belligerent pose in a world held together by a fragile peace ; huge conscript armies had been made redundant, anyway, by military science with its atomic bombs and missiles ; he regarded conscription as a disruptive threat to post-war economic reconstruction (the Government's own Economic Planning Committee had forecast a manpower shortage of 600,000—and still rising—for 1947) ; and, recoiling from the horrors of the recent past, S.O. argued that young men should not be 'trained in the formative period of their lives to kill their fellow-men, women and children'. This was the kind of talk to enrage the Conservative leader, Winston Churchill. Whereas S.O. condemned the Bill as a 'betrayal of the Labour Movement's traditions', Churchill welcomed it wholeheartedly on behalf of the 'Opposition'—congratulating the Government for resisting the 'subversive and degenerate elements in their midst' . . . the 'feckless and crack-pate elements' . . . the 'crypto-Communists and pacifists and other trends of left-wing opinion'.

S.O. also decried military conscription for other reasons. Immersed though he often was in matters of international import, he was forever conscious of his own nationality. Of all the protests against peace-time call-up, none took on the popular character of the campaign that developed in Wales: over 700 organisations, from Young Farmers' Clubs to churches, Youth Clubs to trade union branches, passed resolutions branding conscription as 'an injustice to Wales'. When an amendment to the National Service Bill sought to exclude Wales in the same manner as Northern Ireland had already been exempted, S.O. spoke strongly in its favour. But not for him the special pleading indulged in by Welsh Nonconformist pacifists who, in all other matters, lauded British unity and rule from Westminster. They were easy targets for the jingoistic jibes of Bill Mainwaring and Ness Edwards. Instead, S.O. adopted an unapologetic, Welsh nationalist stance. He challenged the very right of the British State to force its will on the Welsh people and their elected representatives (20 of the 36 Welsh M.P.s having voted against the Bill on its Second Reading):

> Wales hates compulsion from Westminster and Whitehall. It is largely because Whitehall did so little for Wales in the inter-war period. That is what is behind the thoughts of the people of Wales. They were treated abominably by successive Governments, which forced ½ million people away from this small country. We know the mind of the people of Wales. They have long memories, kindly as they are, and they are not likely to forget those years.

He warned the Government that compulsion would create more bad feeling: it was not worth it, especially as many Welsh workers—being miners or farmworkers—would be unaffected by the Bill's provisions, amended or not. Far better to rely on voluntarism, he advised, and take comfort in the knowledge that the Welsh nation had never been slow to fight for a just cause : ' The Government would get far better results by taking the people of this country into their confidence than by attempting compulsion, which is cheap and miserable and would cut across the sense of freedom of the Welsh people '. The amendment to leave out Wales was defeated on May 6 wiith the Welsh M.P.s split three ways : 12 supported the amendment (6 Labour and 6 Liberals); 12 opposed (9 Labour and 3 Tories) ; and the remaining 12 abstained or were absent. As punishment for this opposition to peace-time conscription, S.O. was deprived of the Parliamentary Labour Party Whip for a short period.

The agitation against National Service was closely related in Wales to campaigns against the War Office's seizure of land for military training. In 1946 Emmanuel Shinwell's Ministry of War published its intention to use 500,000 acres of Welsh land as tank and gun ranges. Such a gigantic proportion of the country's land area (about one-tenth) was far in excess of that demanded in England or Scotland. The announcement rang alarm bells throughout Wales, bringing back painful memories of the War Office take-over of Mynydd Epynt's 40,000 acres in Breconshire. On that occasion, in 1940, scores of cultural, religious and trade union bodies had jumped to the defence of the 80 homesteads threatened by the scheme—many of them comprising the last Welsh-speaking communities in that part of Wales. S.O. joined the other M.P.s and local councillors in lobbying the Government to change its mind ; they succeeded in prompting the War Office to reconsider. But after six weeks of official deliberation, it was announced that a small number of local people had been cajoled into accepting transfer, worried that continued resistance would endanger their compensation payments. The united front had been broken, morale collapsed and the opposition crumbled.[23]

Now, six years later, an even bigger threat loomed over rural Wales. S.O. waded into the fray, addressing meetings where he described the proposed training areas as ' the playground of obsolete tanks—tearing the land to pieces—and of the equally obsolete Bren, Field and anti-aircraft guns ' . . . it would all be ' child's play ' in this age of atomic weapons. Other Labour M.P.s, Communists,

Liberals and Welsh Nationalists were swept along on the wave of protest ; by December 1947 the tide had risen high enough to beat the Government back to 105,000 acres in Wales (compared with 70,000 in Scotland).[24] Within a few years the acreage demanded in Wales had shrunk still further to 57,000. The Welsh nation had scored a rare victory—although smaller defeats were suffered at Castlemartin in Pembrokeshire, Sennybridge in Breconshire and at a number of other sites conceded to the War Office in Merionethshire and elsewhere.

On the international front, meanwhile, the 'Superpowers' were setting up their camps for the Cold War : 1947 saw the founding of the U.S. Central Intelligence Agency and the Communist international information bureau (Cominform) ; in February the following year the Czechoslovak Communist Party seized power, flooding the streets with workers as the Soviet Red Army stood guard at the country's borders. The *coup* had been engineered by a combination of mass unrest and back-room intrigue in the Government and Police services. S.O. defended the Prague take-over against the English press reports of terror and assassination—'It was a bloodless revolution', he argued with technical accuracy.[25]

After the collapse of the Foreign Ministers summit in March 1947, the Americans put together a $13 billion package of financial aid for the economic reconstruction of Europe (by-passing the United Nations' own commission). Although the Marshall Plan did not expressly exclude Socialist States from its philanthropy, the terms of eligibility and debt repayment were prohibitive in their political implications. In addition, the precise plan drawn up by Bevin and other Western European leaders appeared to steer the continent towards economic integration—in financial and political tutelage to the U.S.A. Obviously, such a road was unacceptable to the Soviets. They rejected it and embarked upon the 'Sovietisation' of Eastern Europe. The political strings attached to American aid had already been pulled in Western Europe : in the Spring of 1947 all Communist Ministers were expelled from the French and Italian Governments. In anticipation of the Italian elections in April 1948, U.S. Secretary of State Marshall warned that American aid 'will come to an abrupt end in any country that votes Communism into power'.[26]

Labour's National Executive Committee decided to withdraw its traditional fraternal support for the Italian Socialist Party, and to throw its considerable prestige behind the Unity Socialists. The I.S.P.'s crime was to be campaigning in the Democratic Front alongside its war-time anti-Fascist allies, the Communists and left-wing Republicans; the Unity Socialists were a MacDonald-type splinter from the I.S.P., had joined the Christian Democratic coalition government and were now on the Rightist election slate. Thirty-seven Labour M.P.s reacted furiously to the N.E.C.'s craven capitulation to American Cold War-mongering, S.O. amongst them; they sent a pre-election telegram of best wishes to I.S.P. leader Pietro Nenni (although it could not save his party from defeat at the hands of the Christian Democrat bloc). An indignant N.E.C. bullied 16 of the signatories into recanting before sending the unrepentant remainder a letter, informing them that the N.E.C. was 'seriously disturbed by the activities over a long period of time of certain members of the Party which are considered to be subversive of Party Policy', and demanding that the rebel M.P.s give a pledge of loyalty. Blowing the issue up still further, Prime Minister Attlee issued a public statement deploring the action of those dubbed by the press as the 'Nenni Goats'.

Whereas most of his colleagues beat a grudging retreat, S.O. stood his ground: sharing a May Day platform in Merthyr with fellow 'Nenni Goat' Emrys Hughes (M.P. for South Ayreshire and Keir Hardie's son-in-law), he jibed that Attlee 'responded to the panic and nightmarish conditions of the American Embassy in London—and saw Red!' As for the accusation from General Secretary Morgan Phillips that S.O. and his comrades had sent a telegram to the 'Nenni-Communist combination', S.O. wrote back:

> This is a deliberate distortion of a simple message sent to one Socialist by other Socialists. Further, you accuse me of defying Labour Party principles and policy in this matter. But you give no evidence in support of that charge. Will you, if you can, be good enough to tell me in clear, explicit language what these principles and policies are in their bearing on the message sent to the official Socialist Party, giving of course the terms and circumstances under which the resolution was passed by the Labour movement to proscribe the Italian Socialists.[27]

S.O. knew he was on fairly safe ground : the supreme policy-making body of the Labour Party—its annual conference—had passed no resolutions hostile to the Italian Socialist Party. Indeed, as S.O. pointed out, the I.S.P. was still a member of the consultative association of Social-Democratic Parties which, in turn, had an information and liaison office in the Labour Party's own International Department. Nor would he attach too much weight to the deliberations of the N.E.C., especially on matters over 500 miles away and outside the scope of Labour's bans and proscriptions. The editorial writer of the *Western Mail*, however, would not be denied : he grabbed at the straw with which to beat S.O., administering the swishes with threadbare sarcasm :

> He is in fact the only man in the regiment in step, and if his speech has any serious meaning he regrets nothing and withdraws nothing, and is prepared like Ajax to defy the lightning. He seems almost to invite expulsion, unlike MR. KONNI ZILLIACUS and the others who, we understand, are now prepared to toe the line and give further assurances of their respect for the constitution and rules of the party. We rather fancy MR DAVIES will cut a less heroic figure when he faces his accusers.[28]

The parting shot was a dud : of all the charges hurled against S.O., the taunt of ' coward ' was the one least likely to be taken seriously by anybody. Far from quaking before the N.E.C., S.O. tended to treat its members with tongue-in-cheek contempt. The ' Nenni Goat ' affair was more a source of mirth than of fear, and nowhere more so than amongst S.O.'s acquaintances in ' The Crown ' in Merthyr. Every Saturday night S.O. would call into the back-room of this remarkably atmospheric pub for a glass of beer : ' For weeks afterwards ', recalled the local librarian and poet Harri Webb, ' the mere mention, in any context, of a telegram or Italy would set off a whole series of witticisms, whether S.O. was present or not '.[29]

Transport House derived rather less amusement from the epidemic rebelliousness of back-bench Labour M.P.s. One of the most persistent pro-Soviet dissidents, John Platts-Mills, was selected as a whipping-boy and expelled from the Labour Party late in April 1948. He was joined in limbo by another left-wing M.P. in February 1949. Then, early the following May, Konni Zilliacus and another heretical M.P. were excommunicated on the first day of 'Operation Tightening-Up'. Next, on May 19, S.O. and 66 of his parliamentary colleagues received a letter of warning from the P.L.P.-N.E.C. liaison committee, threatening to withdraw their status as official Labour candidates at the forthcoming General Election.

This latest bout of Party punishment had been brought on by the Government of Ireland Bill, a measure which guaranteed Northern Ireland's position as part of the United Kingdom for as long as the Stormont Parliament wished it to be so. S.O. remembered his electioneering in Grangetown, back in 1913, and speaking at the 'Hands Off Ireland!' rallies with his old friend Jim Winstone after the Great War. In those days the working-class movement in south Wales had agitated for independence for the whole of Ireland, unconditionally, in keeping with the wishes of the vast majority of the Irish people. Not until 1920 did 'Northern Ireland' exist in any legal or constitutional sense: it was carved out of the historic province of Ulster, three of whose counties were released to the Irish Free State whilst the remaining six (including two with a Nationalist and Catholic majority) were incorporated into the new Northern Ireland. From its invention S.O. had opposed this artificial, sectarian Statelet, run as it was by Ulster's landowners and capitalists, and enforced by legalised tyranny and prejudice. No three-line whip could compel him (or Cardiff Central M.P. George Thomas) to endorse the creation of such a monstrosity.

Perhaps retribution for the Irish revolt in Parliament would have been more terrible than a stiff letter, had the whole episode not been overshadowed by earth-shaking events on the world stage: the Allies had failed to find a way of implementing the 1945 Potsdam Agreement to reunite Germany; the Western Powers broke the stale-mate by merging their three zones—thereby laying the foundations of a West German state. When the new West German currency was extended to West Berlin, the Soviet and East German authorities retaliated by blockading the Western-controlled sectors of the city, which lay 120 miles inside East Germany. Britain and the U.S.A. replied with a spectacular airlift of provisions to the beleagured West Berliners.

International tension tightened still further in the autumn months of 1948, as Mao Tse-Tung's Communists drove the right-wing Nationalists off the Chinese mainland and onto the island of Formosa

(Taiwan). Military service was increased in Britain to 18 months. America's war fever was contagious ; one of its lesser victims was Aberdare's Labour M.P., D. Emlyn Thomas, who spoke of an 'international situation fraught with danger' and pointed to the cloud's silver lining—that unemployed workers would at least be able to 'find work on a new rearmament programme'. S.O. immediately issued a statement rebuking his colleague, and added :

> No Government in this country could possibly get the people and organised workers of the country to support it in a war against Soviet Russia. Of one thing I am positively certain : the miners and industrial workers in South Wales would never be a party to it. They feel like myself that this country may be torn to destruction by dollar diplomacy.[30]

Ten months into the Berlin crisis, the U.S. establishment succeeded in its ambition to institutionalise the Cold War : the North Atlantic Treaty Organisation (N.A.T.O.) was formed in April 1949, comprising ten Western European states including Britain, together with Canada and the U.S.A.[31] Two months later the four Superpowers negotiated an end to the Berlin blockade : Potsdam was abandoned and the *status quo* in Germany was formally accepted by all sides.

Not that this arrangement—unsatisfactory to all—could halt the sabre-rattling. In August 1949 the Soviet Union conducted its first-ever atomic test, sending shock-waves of panic through the West. Stalin was determined to stay in the nuclear arms race ; his distrust of America had been greatly deepened at the end of the Second World War. Whereas then the Soviet Union had declared war on Japan and occupied Manchuria, as requested by the Allies at Yalta, Stalin had not even been notified of the atomic bombs about to be dropped on Hiroshima and Nagasaki in August 1945. Within four days of the Japanese surrender on August 14, the U.S. Secretary of State James Byrnes was accusing the U.S.S.R. of breaking the Yalta/Moscow concordat by rigging the elections in Bulgaria (which were promptly postponed). The charge was purest hypocrisy : the U.S.A. had already discarded a pledge given at Yalta by supporting the entry of Argentina—a haven for fleeing Nazis—into the United Nations. Indeed, American plans were already underway to outflank the Soviets diplomatically and militarily : a formidable pro-

American voting bloc was being built up inside the U.N., and by 1949 the Russians found themselves encircled by some 400 United States military bases.[32] Spurred on by Soviet acquisition of a crude atomic bomb, the Americans stepped up their development of the hydrogen bomb—a weapon one thousand times more powerful than the device that had flattened Hiroshima.

The British Labour Government's response to the Soviet atomic test was to accelerate the production of a British Bomb. The original decision to develop an independent nuclear weapon had been taken by a secret Cabinet Committee, GEN 163, in January 1947 : Aneurin Bevan and other Cabinet Ministers lacking in enthusiasm for the Cold War were not even informed of the committee's existence. GEN 163's decision to manufacture a British atomic bomb was not announced to the rest of the Cabinet or to the House of Commons until May 1948.[33]

Nests of government and military officials—especially scientists—who had been passing military secrets to the Soviet Union were uncovered in Canada in 1945, in Britain the following year and in the United States from 1948 onwards. With the ' enemy ' inside the gates, the Attlee Government set up a Cabinet Committee on Subversive Activities in 1949 ; Communists had already been banned from the Civil Service in March 1948, and were removed from a large part of Government contract work soon afterwards. The ' Red Menace ' was invoked to justify the use of troops to break a series of Dock Strikes between 1945 and 1949, and the deployment of Special Branch officers to disrupt the work and international connections of the National Union of Seamen.[34]

1950 began with the arrest in England of Klaus Fuchs, a scientist who had also been working in the United States—where he had collaborated with Communist agents to pass vital nuclear information to the Russians. Without any public announcement, Labour Home Secretary James Chuter Ede introduced an under-the-table ban on granting British citizenship to immigrants suspected of Communist sympathies ; he told Cabinet colleagues : ' I cannot help feeling that, on the whole, Communist convictions are likely to find readier victims among persons who have not been born and brought up in this country '.[35] Meanwhile, in the U.S.A. Senator Joe McCarthy and his hench-man Richard Nixon were in full cry against liberals and Socialists ; in the United Nations, the Americans were blocking the admission of Communist China ; in Western Europe the first steps had been taken towards closer economic and political co-operation in a European Coal and Steel Community, with the Euro-federalists now turning their minds to a (West) European Defence Community ; plans were also afoot to re-arm West Germany and to build up N.A.T.O.'s capacity way beyond the requirements of ' defence '.

Such developments were advocated and organised by a myriad of newly-formed movements : their paymasters were American big business foundations, the C.I.A. and the U.S. Military Government in Berlin, often working in concert and using Marshall Aid repayments. One such brain-child of the C.I.A. was the Congress for Cultural Freedom, established in 1950 and which funded the right-wing Labour magazine in England, *Socialist Commentary*, and the influential literary and current affairs journal, *Encounter*.[36] On the trade union front, C.I.A. agents and their collaborators split the organised workers' movement in half, internationally and in individual countries ; thus the International Confederation of Free Trade Unions was reconstituted as a rival to the World Federation of Trade Unions (with the British T.U.C. joining the former and leaving the latter in 1949).[37]

The Cold War had reached boiling-point : the combustion would occur in a matter of months rather than years. S. O. Davies wanted to be a warrior for Peace . . . which, according to the temper of the times, put him into the Soviet camp.

NOTES

[1]Miscellaneous notes in the S. O. Davies Papers, Swansea (Ref : 1E).

[2]*Western Mail*, 13 April 1939. In reply, the *Western Mail* reaffirmed its hostility to the 'official' Labour Party, but declared a preference for the 'democratic principle of majority rule' in the Party—as opposed to 'subversion' in the cause of establishing a 'Crippsian dictatorship' !

[3]Speech delivered in Norwich on November 13 1938, from notes in the S. O. Davies Papers, Swansea (Ref : 1E).

[4]Winston Churchill as Chancellor of the Exchequer addressing a Press conference in Rome, 20 January 1927, quoted by George Orwell in 'Who are the War Criminals ?' in *Tribune*, 22 October 1943.

[5]Quoted by Konni Zilliacus in *I Choose Peace* (1949), together with flattering remarks by Churchill about Hitler in 1938.

[6]See *Fellow Travellers of the Right* (1980) by Richard Griffiths (which also documents Churchill's pro-Fascist utterances).

[7]*The Impending Catastrophe and How to Combat It* (1917), pamphlet by V. I. Lenin to be found in *Collected Works* (Progress, Moscow) Vol. 25 p. 363.

[8]Written Parliamentary Answer, 8 August 1940.

[9]Miscellaneous notes in the S. O. Davies Papers, Swansea (Ref : 1E).

[10]Letter dated 4 June 1941 in the S. O. Davies Papers, Swansea (Ref : 1A, *ii*).

[11]Debate in the House of Commons on Coal Policy, 10 June 1942.

[12]Miscellaneous notes in the S. O. Davies Papers, Swansea (Ref : 1E).

[13]'The Truth about this Indian Trouble' by Sir Michael O'Dwyer in the *Daily Mail Blue Book on the Indian Crisis* (1931). Further information about India has been gleaned from *It's Your Empire* (1945) by Alexander Campbell for the Left Book Club, and from the pamphlet *Why Were They Proud : A Study of Empire* (1938) published by the Pacifist Research Bureau. Around this period, Caste Hindus comprised 52% of the Indian population, outcaste Hindus (the ' Untouchables ') a further 22%, Moslems 24%, and Christians and Sikhs most of the remaining 2%.

[14]As claimed by Husain Azli in *India : From Curzon to Nehru* (1969) by Durga Das, pp. 169-173.

[15]The counter-revolutionary steps taken by Allied Military Governments in Germany, Italy and Greece are detailed by Konni Zilliacus in *I Choose Peace* (1949).

[16]William Shirer in the *New York Herald Tribune*, 22 March 1947, quoted by Zilliacus (see above).

[17]William McNeill in *The Greek Dilemma* (1947) p. 111, quoted by David Horowitz in *From Yalta to Vietnam* (1967).

[18]*The Second World War* Vol. 6 (1954) by Winston Churchill, p. 198.

[19]*The Second World War* Vol. 4 (1951) by Winston Churchill, p. 832.

[20]Official Statement of the Extraordinary State Committee of the U.S.S.R., quoted in *The Cold War and Its Origins* (1961) by D. F. Fleming.

[21]In fact 225,000 Germans were kept in concentration areas by the British Zone military authorities in Germany in 1945, designated as ' reparations labour for the United Kingdom '— although they were not subsequently brought to Britain. See *Memoirs* (1958) by Viscount Montgomery of Alamein pp. 370-1.

[22]Accounts of these events in Eastern Europe are to be found in *Nationalism and Communism* (1964) by Hugh Seton-Watson, *Bureaucracy and Revolution in Eastern Europe* (1974) by Chris Harman, and in Zilliacus (see Note 5 above) and Horowitz (see Note 17 above).

[23]See *Tros Gymru* (1970) by J. E. Jones, pp. 280-283.

[24]For example, see the 'Statement on behalf of the War Office—Western Command' in *Welsh Land : Three Authoritative Statements* (1949), 'Wales' Pamphlet No. 2. *Plaid Cymru* President Gwynfor Evans described and attacked the War Office plans in detail in his pamphlet *Havoc in Wales : the War Office Demands* (1947).

[25]*Western Mail*, 3 May 1948.

[26]See *From Yalta to Vietnam* (1967) by David Horowitz, pp. 82-3 ; the Report of the U. S. House of Representatives Select Committee on Intelligence (1976), chaired by Congressman Otis Pike, revealed that from 1948 up to the mid-1970s the C.I.A. spent $75 millions on Italian election campaigns—most of the money going to the Christian Democrats, but at least $1 million given to neo-Fascists : see *Covert Action—What Next ?* (1976) by Philip Agee.

[27]Quoted by S.O. to the *Western Mail*, 3 May 1948.

[28]*Western Mail*, 4 May 1948.

[29]*Y Saeth* No. 6 (Autumn 1977).

[30]*Western Mail*, 21 September 1948.

[31]See 'The Origins and Structure of NATO' in *State Research* Vol. 2 No. 10 (1979).

[32]Horowitz (see Note 17 above), p. 28.

[33]See the *Times*, 3 January 1978 : in 1958 Attlee explained why he had kept some Cabinet colleagues in the dark : 'I thought some of them were not fit to be trusted with secrets of this kind'. The biography *Attlee* (1982) by Kenneth Harris contains a large amount of information on this issue, and on others dealt with in this chapter and in Chapter Eight. The Cabinet Papers about the decision to manufacture a British atomic bomb will not be placed in the Public Records Office before 1998—at least 20 years later than the norm.

[34]See the *Times*, 3 and 7 January 1980.

[35]See the *Guardian*, 2 January 1981.

[36]'Who Were THEY Travelling With ?' by Richard Fletcher in *C.I.A. and the Labour Movement* (1977) with Fred Hirsch.

[37]In the 1970s former C.I.A. agent Philip Agee named scores of leading officials in the I.C.F.T.U., American Federation of Labour and other Western trade union bodies as C.I.A. agents or collaborators : see *Inside the Company : C.I.A. Diary* (1975) by Philip Agee.

Chapter Seven

HOME RULE FOR WALES !

The zeal with which S.O. lifted his eyes to the international horizon could never blind him to the needs of his homeland, or to the debt which he owed it. He treasured Wales, its culture and its *gwerin* (or working-class). Welsh was the language of his family's hearth at Abercwmboi—as it had been through generations—and S.O. rarely missed an opportunity to converse or sing in his native tongue. He was an enthusiastic *eisteddfodwr*, frequently attending the National Eisteddfod—especially when local choirs were competing. In his younger days he had often adjudicated at local and regional *eisteddfodau*, and at ' penny readings '. He had an abiding appetite for Welsh-language culture and literature : *Y Faner* and *Y Cymro* formed part of S.O.'s weekly reading, alongside his subscriptions to Socialist and international magazines. Favourite works included *Cwm Eithin* by Hugh Evans and the writings of Daniel Owen ; not surprisingly, he greatly enjoyed the poetry of T. E. Nicholas, and found R. J. Derfel's essays timeless and very much in tune with his own heart and mind.

Robert Jones Derfel was one of the Socialist movement's foremost propagandists in Wales in the 1880s and 1890s ; his stirring lecture '*Gwladgarwch y Cymry*' (' The Patriotism of the Welsh ') mercilessly denounced those Welshmen who despise Wales and things Welsh in order to ingratiate themselves with the English, or to ' demonstrate ' their commitment to the international cause of Socialism. Derfel wrote :

> *Mae'r dyn sydd yn casau ac yn esgeuluso ei wlad a'i genedl yn un annhebyg iawn o fod yn caru dyn mewn unrhyw wlad arall. Os nad yw yn caru'r genedl y mae yn ei hadnabod, pa fodd y gall garu'r rhai sydd yn anadnabyddus iddo* ?[1]
>
> The man who hates and neglects his land and his nation is unlikely to love the people of any other land. If he does not love the nation that he knows, how can he love those of which he knows nothing ?

S.O.'s distinguished predecessors in Parliament had been renowned for their international outlooks ; yet, at the same time, both were sincere advocates of Welsh national causes : Henry Richard stoutly defended the Welsh language against its powerful detractors, and Keir Hardie had voted in the House of Commons for Welsh and Scottish Parliaments as early as 1895.

In 1918 the North and South Wales Labour Federations, the North Wales Quarrymen's Union and the British Labour Party had passed conference resolutions supporting the establishment of an elected Welsh Assembly.[2] The arguments in favour were most eloquently expressed by Labour Party Secretary, Arthur Henderson:

> The development of capitalism and of modern trade unionism in Wales proceed side by side, and it is impossible to name a community where the conditions are more ripe than they are in Wales for a bold experiment in the direction of complete political and industrial democracy. Given self-government Wales might establish itself as a modern Utopia, and develop its own institutions, its own arts, its own national culture, its own ideal of democracy in politics, industry and social life, as an example and an inspiration to the rest of the world.[3]

Most I.L.P. activists in Wales believed that Home Rule would strengthen the Socialist movement: the existence in Wales of a large class-conscious proletariat and a politically 'progressive' rural population (compared with that of the English or French countryside), ranged against small native capitalist and landowning classes, would place the control of a Welsh Parliament or Government permanently in the hands of left-wing and radical forces. This was the viewpoint held at the end of the Great War by the vast majority of Welsh Labour M.P.s and trade union leaders. Indeed, following S.O.'s speech at a 'Hands Off Ireland !' meeting in Merthyr on 12 December 1919, S.W.M.F. Vice-President James Winstone had urged not only self-determination for Ireland and the withdrawal of the 'Army of Occupation', but self-determination for Wales too! The Chairman of the Fed.'s Anthracite District also declared himself strongly in favour of Welsh Home Rule, and lambasted the record of the Liberal Party in the matter :

> Their apathy and unconcern regarding Wales's claim to self-government has amounted to a political betrayal of public trust. Unfortunately, it is not only the Parliamentary leaders, to whom personal fortune and social aspiration are the main things, who have forgotten the claims of their native land, but our County Councillors and preachers have been almost equally guilty.[4]

This miners' leader, so eager for progress, was the Labour councillor David D. Davies—Sephora's father.

Throughout the 1920s and 1930s workers and their families battled and begged for food in their mouths and a roof over their heads. A Parliament for Wales was merely a dream, the realisation of which had to be postponed to the uncertain future. In the meantime, the present had to be salvaged from the swamps of impoverishment and despair. True, official policy documents published in 1923 and 1928 reaffirmed the Labour Party's commitment to a ' separate legislative assembly ' for Wales. That the Labour leadership never intended to implement these promises, repeated though they were up to the beginning of World War Two, is glaringly obvious in hindsight. The doctrine of administrative centralism, of ' Socialism ' imposed and managed from the top, grew steadily during the inter-war decades : just as the devolution of political power was one casualty, so the objective of workers' control of industry was another and more controversial one.[5]

Expediency also played a part in the relegation of Home Rule in Labour's programme : the Party's collapse in the 1931 General Election, when its candidates were decimated in England, left little Wales supplying half the Parliamentary Labour Party ; hence any reduction in Welsh seats at Westminster, as the probable consequence of devolution, would remove a solid bed-rock of Labour M.P.s.

Yet, as it turned out, the Depression and the subsequent war did much to implant the economic case for devolution in the minds of patriots like S. O. Davies, people whose hearts were already inclined towards some degree of Welsh self-rule. They had watched in anguish as the slump of the 'thirties sapped the vigour and self-respect of their small nation. They realised also that the war-time production boom (which had eliminated unemployment in Wales by mid-1942) was a pain-killing injection rather than a permanent panacea ; that the Welsh coal industry's problems of mechanisation and world markets would remain after hostilities had ceased ; that the thousands of tinplate redundancies between 1940 and 1943 would re-surface once munitions work had run out, and that the condition of Welsh agriculture and the slate industry would worsen before it would improve.

There was unanimity that the priority in a Welsh post-war reconstruction programme must be to diversify the country's narrow industrial base. But, as S.O. swiftly discovered, the conscientious M.P. and the willing industrialist faced a daunting maze of Government agencies, each one concerned with one aspect or another of industrial development—namely, the Board of Trade, the Treasury, and the Ministries of Fuel and Power, Supply, Town and Country Planning, Works, Labour and National Insurance. Most of them operated from a ' regional ' office in Wales but—incredibly—there was virtually no co-ordination of them on a Welsh or local level. Nor was there any plan or strategy for developing the Welsh economy within which they could work. In related social fields, the suspicion was widespread in Wales that Welsh needs and opinions were being disregarded in the planned reorganisation of health and educational services.

Consequently, the call for a Welsh Secretary of State was revived. The Welsh Parliamentary Party had fruitlessly petitioned for the creation of such a post in 1938 ; now, in 1943, the South Wales Regional Council of Labour and the Association of Welsh Local Authorities renewed the request. The first person to raise the issue afresh inside Parliament was S. O. Davies when, on June 10, he exposed the complacent ignorance of Deputy Prime Minister Attlee about the state of public opinion in Wales :

S. O. DAVIES : In view of the extreme dissatisfaction felt and expressed by the people of Wales with respect to post-war planning and reconstruction, will the Prime Minister now introduce legislation for the appointment of a Secretary of State for Wales ?

CLEMENT ATTLEE : No Sir.

S. O. DAVIES : Is not the Right Honourable Gentleman aware of the deep and profound concern that exists today in Wales, which suffered so grievously after the last war, at the apparent inability of the Government to make any preparations for post-war reconstruction, and has he no better answer to give to these people, who cannot forget their experiences after the last war ?

ATTLEE : That is not strictly relevant to the point that my Honourable Friend [S.O.] put about a Secretary of State for Wales. I am not aware of the feeling to which he has alluded in his Question as widespread, or that there is a general desire at the present time that there should be a Secretary of State for Wales.

A few months later, Prime Minister Churchill refused to receive an all-party deputation of Welsh M.P.s who wished to press for a Minister for Welsh Affairs in the Cabinet.[6] Instead, the Government sought to pacify public opinion by granting Wales an annual day of its own in the House of Commons. This first Welsh Affairs Day, 17 October 1944, witnessed a parade of Welsh M.P.s carping at the shabby treatment meted out to their country. Some speakers pointed out that Scotland had enjoyed a Secretary of State with a seat in the Cabinet since 1926. Others such as W. J. Gruffydd (Liberal, University of Wales), Jim Griffiths (Labour, Llanelli) and, surprisingly, Aneurin Bevan (Labour, Ebbw Vale) went further and called for a real measure of devolution to Wales. S.O. implored the Government and Civil Service to treat Wales as a single, whole unit for administrative and planning purposes.

When the war-time coalition dissolved and a General Election was announced for July 1945, the preceding campaign was marked by the intrusion of specifically Welsh issues into the political arena —an occurrence unknown for two decades. Labour candidates in north-west Wales published a broadsheet, *Llais Llafur* (' Labour Voice '), promising Wales a Secretary of State, an economic planning authority, a radio corporation, an end to emigration and a north-south road link. A policy statement published by the Party's Welsh Organiser, Cliff Prothero, declared with cunning ambiguity :

> Wales is a small nation which, through immense difficulties, has preserved her language and cultural life through the centuries . . . The true freedom of Wales depends not only on political control of her own life, but on economic control as well.
>
> True freedom for Wales would be the result and the product of a Socialist Britain, and under such conditions could self-government in Wales be an effective and secure guardian of the life of the nation.[7]

Early in the life of the new Labour Government, S.O. prepared a memorandum for the Welsh Parliamentary Party on a Welsh Broadcasting Corporation which was duly submitted to the Beveridge Committee. S.O. was unhappy that the Welsh Region of the B.B.C. radio service did not broadcast to all parts of Wales : ' We have been repeatedly told by the B.B.C. engineers that this cannot be remedied because of the mountainous configuration of Wales. To this we reply with confidence that if Wales had its own Corporation these engineering difficulties would long ago have been overcome '. But above all, as S.O. told a meeting of *Undeb Cymru Fydd* (the 'New Wales Union') in Swansea : 'I want an independent broadcasting station for Wales so that any talent Wales has, any gift worth giving, shall be given in its own way, and not determined at Broadcasting House, London '.[8]

But no Welsh Radio Corporation would be forthcoming from the post-war Labour administration, nor would work start on a north-south highway ; and any notion of economic planning on a Welsh basis was dismissed contemptuously by Board of Trade President Sir Stafford Cripps, in the Welsh Day debate of 28 October 1946 :

> There is, in reality, no more specialised a view of Welsh economic problems than there is about those of Durham, or the North-East coast.

On this same occasion Cripps announced the Government's rejection of a Welsh Secretary of State and a Welsh Ministry ; part of his case for doing so was that Wales was not large enough :

> With an area and population to draw upon so small as that of Wales, it would be quite impossible to maintain the standard of administration, in purely Welsh services, as high as that which is possible when these services cover the entire country.

As a consolation he offered M.P.s a closer co-ordination of governmental machinery in Wales : the Welsh Regional Controllers of Civil Service departments would henceforth meet together three or four times a year—in Wales. This sop failed to satisfy S.O. and other Welsh M.P.s ; indeed, it was Aneurin Bevan who, closing the debate for the Government as Minister of Health, remarked :

> It is obvious that as the Government more and more intervenes in economic affairs, we may have to reconsider the whole structure of local government, and consider whether any new constitutional devices are necessary in order to put into the hands of elected persons at the regional level the obligation to carry out a good deal of Government administration.[9]

Following the 1945 General Election triumph, delegations of Welsh all-party and Labour M.P.s interviewed Prime Minister Attlee and Deputy Leader Morrison about their constitutional plans for Wales—and were sharply informed that Wales would receive neither devolution nor a Secretary of State. Meanwhile, back in Wales, the Labour movement was discussing the issue in earnest. Inside the Labour Party a Home Rule wing had emerged, with a number of M.P.s, prospective parliamentary candidates and constituency parties declaring themselves in favour of a Parliament for Wales. Responding to pressure from Welsh members the Communist Party's 1944 congress had approved a policy document—*Wales in the New World*—which advocated a Welsh Parliament.[10] For his part, S.O. was growing weary of the mixture of arrogance and ignorance with which the Houses of Parliament, the Civil Service and the mass media treated his country and its people. Whether it was the seizure of land for military training, the re-arrangement of local government boundaries or the structure of nationalised industries, Welsh public opinion and nationhood seemed to count for nought. As a result, S.O.'s desire for an unspecified measure of self-government for Wales quickly crystallised into support for a Welsh Parliament as part of a Federal Britain.

When M.P.s were considering the Government's annual White Paper on Welsh Affairs on 26 January 1948, S.O. (now the Chairman of the Welsh Parliamentary Party) complained bitterly of the War Ministry's licence to run amock through the Welsh countryside in defiance of the wishes of local authorities and M.P.s. He pointed out that the White Paper dealt primarily with the activities of 19 Government Offices in Wales—and their civil servants imported from outside—who effectively ruled Wales. He outlined an antidote to this bureaucratic affliction :

> The first step that should, and must, be taken is to grant to Wales the right to manage and control its own domestic affairs. We are painfully concerned at the way in which our destinies are determined these days by an alien and unrepresentative people . . . We are—and I do not apologise for it—a proud people. What is equally important, we are a nation of workers. Our whole history shows a high degree of national consciousness. We know our country and we love it. We have no alternative than to demand the largest measure of self-government. This would obviously relieve the appalling congestion of work in this House. It would give to the people of Wales the recognition they have long fought for, that Wales is a country, its people a nation, and that they have the right to demand that their people —through their elected chosen representatives—should con-

> tribute directly in large measure to the government of our country.
>
> This farce of political democracy, rule by outsiders, rule by the unelected, rule by the unrepresentative, should be brought to an end.

In the Welsh Day debate of November 24 the same year, S.O. reacted fiercely to the remarks of two Labour colleagues who had spoken before him: Cardiff Central M.P. George Thomas had described Professor W. J. Gruffydd as 'an enemy of Wales', after Gruffydd had delivered an intensely nationalistic speech. S.O. expressed his 'disgust and resentment' at this attack, praising Gruffydd for his 'solid and splendid contribution to the cause of Wales and the Welsh people'. Then he turned to Aberavon M.P. Will Cove:

> The Hon. Member explained the past economic troubles of Wales, and he referred—I am quoting his words—to the 'indigenous poverty of Wales'. Of all the absurd statements that have ever been made in this House, I think that is about the limit. Wales has exported its wealth for several generations. I remember in my younger days being told by statisticians and economists of repute that for every £1 worth of work brought into Wales to keep its inhabitants alive, Wales was exporting between £17 and £19 worth. This is the first time I have heard of the 'indigenous poverty' of this little country of ours, and I am sorry that it came from an Hon. Member who represents one of the Welsh constituencies.
>
> Further—and I take strong exception to this—he exhorted the whole House not to expect any unanimity in Wales, and I was sorry to see that my Right Hon. Friends on the Front Bench rather enjoyed this jibe. I should expect the members of the present Government to be the last to appreciate a jibe of this kind. Wales has shown far greater political unanimity than any other section of these islands. Wales sends to this House now at least 70% of Members who support this Government.

On this same Welsh Day the Lord President of the Council, Herbert Morrison, unveiled plans to set up a Welsh Advisory Council composed of people from industry, agriculture, education, local government and the cultural sphere—each one nominated by the Prime Minister; they would meet in secret and report their deliberations on Welsh matters to the Government. This proposal received a mixed reception from M.P.s; S.O.'s scorn was without equal:

> This scheme will be worse than useless in Wales. I am amazed at the pathetic ignorance revealed by Government after Government concerning Wales. It is really pathetic. At times I am almost forced to the conclusion that the country in the British Commonwealth about which the Government knows least is Wales. That applies not only to the present Government, but also to a succession of Governments. I am certain that if the Government knew Wales as they should, we would never have seen this emasculated spineless kind of scheme submitted to the House today. I am sometimes forced to suggest that the Government should appoint a commission of inquiry into the affairs of Wales, into its culture, its preoccupations, its intense love of country, its characteristics, its courage, its pride, its sense of independence, and its passionate desire to live its own life as it thinks it ought to live it.
>
> Had I the power, I would insist upon the Prime Minister being the chairman of the commission, and that this commission should be made up entirely of Members of this House.

S.O. said he condemned the proposed Council as a ' devolutionist and federalist ' ; his remarkable outburst was, in the eyes of the *News Chronicle*'s Welsh columnist ' *Llygad Llwchwr* ', ' worthy of Keir Hardie, of Merthyr and Wales '.[11]

In 1948 the Liberal Party reaffirmed its support for a Welsh Parliament ; the following summer *Plaid Cymru* (the Welsh National Party) launched its ' Parliament for Wales within Five Years ' campaign. In the newspapers, on the radio, in the pubs and workingmen's clubs, the arguments for and against Home Rule were rehearsed with escalating passion. But the most concrete proposal came from the distinguished cultural organisation *Undeb Cymru Fydd* in a declaration on St. David's Day, 1 March 1950. The Union would convene an all-Wales conference to organise a national petition for domestic self-government, along the same lines as the hugely popular Scottish Covenant. Welsh M.P.s, political parties, local authorities and religious and voluntary bodies received invitations to attend the conference in Llandrindod Wells on 1 July 1950.

The Conservative Party's attitude to this bold initiative was one of predictable hostility. Of heavier consequence was the scornful reaction of the Welsh Regional Council of Labour. In a press statement issued on March 29, the Council's Secretary Cliff Prothero dismissed what he called ' the frivolous demand for home rule ', claiming that it emanated from a ' small number of people who represent no serious body of opinion in Wales '. His rejection of the Llandrindod Wells convention was endorsed in May by the Regional Council's annual conference. Undeniably, this response from the Labour Party in Wales reduced the credibility of the Llandrindod event ; the Labour Party's domination of the Welsh political scene verged on the monolithic. In the General Election of 23 February 1950 the party had increased its number of Welsh seats from 25 to 27. S.O. swept in on the customary tidal wave, although the nature of his opposition was novel :

S. O. DAVIES (Labour)	29,210
L. F. HADDRILL (Conservative)	6,294
TREFOR MORGAN (Ind. Welsh Nat.)	1,571

Not for 40 years had a Tory contested Merthyr Tydfil in a General Election ; the other candidate had been disowned by the Welsh Republican Movement whose Secretary, Ithel Davies actually wrote to S.O. and apologised for their dissident supporter temerity in standing against such a renowned Socialist and patriot as the incumbent M.P.[12]

In the event, the Llandrindod conference on Saturday, July 1, was—even on its opponents' admission—a triumph of organisation and enthusiasm. Following addresses from a procession of prominent figures in Welsh public life, including J. R. Jones (President, *Undeb Cymru Fydd*), T. I. Ellis, Sir Ifan ab Owen Edwards and Lady Megan Lloyd George (Liberal M.P. for Anglesey), S.O. rose to speak in favour of a motion proposing a National Petition for ' Parliamentary Self-Government for Wales '. He informed delegates that although he spoke as an individual, the Labour Party had not formally forsaken the principle of Home Rule which it had professed up to the 1945 General Election. As a Socialist he welcomed the nationalisation of coal, electricity, gas and other key industries—but now the parliamentary machine was too congested to keep an eye on the State boards set up to run them.

' We are ruled by the Civil Service ', S.O. told the crowded Albert Hall in Llandrindod. ' We shall have to ease the pressure at Westminster in order that parliamentary democracy can work again. Control of their own affairs must be handed to Wales and Scotland. We either do that, or we lose the measure of freedom that parliamentary democracy guarantees to us.' After hearing representatives from *Plaid Cymru*, the Communist Party and the Welsh Republicans, the conference nominated an executive committee to co-ordinate the National Petition for a Welsh Parliament. S.O. had not been the only Labour member present : a few prominent Labour councillors and trade unionists were there also, and the conference enjoyed the good wishes of at least three other Welsh Labour M.P.s.[13] Nonetheless, Labour personalities were scarce in a congregation composed very largely of Welsh Nationalists and Liberals ; one obvious reason might have been the Regional Council of Labour's decision to hold a rally in Newtown that same day. As for the newspapers, their near-unanimous hostility to Home Rule led some of them to portray the Llandrindod movement as a ' Communist front '!

The Welsh Regional Council of Labour was not amused by the activities of the wayward M.P. for Merthyr : its Secretary, Cliff Prothero, gladly received authorisation on September 25 to write to the party's National Executive and to the Merthyr Trades Council and Labour Party, informing them of S.O.'s ' attitude ' on Welsh Home Rule, the Korean War and the all-Britain Peace Petition. Prothero's letter to Merthyr included an allegation that the Llandrindod convention had been ' convened as a result of agitation by the Welsh Nationalists ' and urged an inquiry by the local party into the behaviour of its Member of Parliament. S.O.'s presence on the platform at Llandrindod and his nomination to the Welsh Parliament petition's steering committee were also cited.

S.O. vigorously defended his Home Rule affiliations at the Trades Council and Labour Party meeting on October 25. He pointed out that *Undeb Cymru Fydd* did not pay fealty to any political party ; it had certainly not been placed on the Labour Party's list of proscribed organisations—yet ! As for the Welsh Regional Council of Labour, it was a ' conglomeration of nonentities ' who were ' not in line with the movement in Wales '. In a rare display of personal animosity, S.O. then directed his venom against the Council's Secretary: Cliff Prothero's abusive and anti-Welsh statements had cost Labour two extra seats—Anglesey and Carmarthen—at the last General Election, he claimed. For good measure S.O. also accused Prothero of interfering in Merthyr's local affairs by nominating a local Alderman to the Lord Chancellor for appointment as a Justice of the Peace. The enraged dignitary sent an account of S.O.'s remarks to Prothero who, in turn, deemed them to be of sufficient gravity to warrant an emergency session of the Regional Council on November 6 in Cardiff. S.O. was summoned to attend in order to 'repeat and substantiate' his criticism of the Council and its Secretary. The M.P.'s reply oozed contempt :

> Dear Prothero,
> Your invitation to me to attend a meeting of the Welsh Regional Council on Monday next is, as you should appreciate, unacceptably belated. Possibly, in the future, you may deem it decent to invite me to the Regional Council before my work as a Member of Parliament becomes, on your instigation, a subject for criticism and condemnation.
>
> Yours Sincerely,
> S. O. Davies.

That November 6 meeting—minus S.O.—decided to invite the Council's recalcitrant critic to its next gathering 'at a convenient date'. Faced with his refusal to answer further correspondence, however, the Regional Council appointed a deputation to grill S.O. about his derogatory references to the Council and its Secretary. Only after numerous postponements on S.O.'s part did the Council's Vice-chairman, D. J. Davies, and Secretary Prothero catch up with their quarry, at a Merthyr Trades and Labour Council meeting on 12 February 1951. There S.O. withdrew his 'conglomeration of nonentities' jibe, but would retract nothing else. Nor would he retreat from his positions on Welsh Home Rule and several international issues. The meeting accepted Prothero's assurances of non-involvement in the nomination of a J.P. ; and S.O. ignored the Council's subsequent requests that he substantiate his claim that the Secretary had lost two General Election seats for Labour.[14]

S.O.'s stout defence of his views could not staunch the charges that he was the puppet of Communists and Nationalists : in August 1951 Rhondda West M.P. Iorrie Thomas attacked those Welsh Labour colleagues who backed the Welsh Parliament petition as the dupes of cunning and bloodthirsty nationalists ; Cardiff Tory M.P. David Llewellyn announced that the Labour Home Rulers were hoping to make up on the swings of nationalism what they had lost on the roundabouts of their careers.

Some of the arguments against a Welsh Parliament were, however, worthy of an answer. It had been a source of special disappointment to S.O. and the other supporters of the Petition that Llanelli's talented and influential M.P. Jim Griffiths had turned his back on an aspiration which he, too, had once voiced inside and outside the House of Commons. From his appointment as Minister of National Insurance in 1945, Griffiths—ever an orthodox party man—toed the Cabinet line and obediently opposed the idea. Nevertheless, his case against Home Rule was a coherent one, and moderately expressed. For example, he argued in the Labour paper *South Wales Democrat* in November 1951 :

> What are to be the powers and functions of a parliament for Wales ? Is it to be autonomous from the British Parliament ? Are we to sever the Welsh economy from that of Britain ? Are we to be taken outside the ambit of Britain's Welfare State ? Will our local authorities in Wales have to draw their grants from a Government in Cardiff and not from the Treasury in Whitehall ? . . .
>
> We have no right to ask our people to sign a blank cheque for a Welsh Parliament without the consequences being fully explained to them. That is why I have refused to sign the petition.

S.O. regretted his old friend's desertion of a cause they once shared—although he never resented it.

Meanwhile, the ' Parliament for Wales ' committee was busy with preparatory campaign work, with answering the questions of agnostics like Griffiths and—in the process—clarifying its own arguments and proposals. The campaign's prestige suffered a blow in the General Election of October 1951, however, when its President, Lady Megan Lloyd George, lost her Anglesey seat. *Plaid Cymru* having decided not to fight sitting Home Rule M.P.s, S.O. faced and trounced a lone Tory opponent. But October 25 also marked the end of Labour's post-war reign ; as far as institutional innovation and constitutional change in Wales were concerned, the Attlee administration had been a disapointingly conservative one to S.O.'s mind. It had rejected calls for a Welsh Economic Plan, a Welsh Rural Development Board (proposed by the Council for Wales), a Welsh Reconstruction Council and a Welsh Electricity Board (recommended by the Advisory Council on Welsh Reconstruction). True, Labour did much to improve the immediate lot of the Welsh people—but the adopted strategy stored up dire problems for the future. The over-dependence on coal-mining was not seriously tackled, except to the degree that it was joined by a growing dependence on the booming steel industry ; far from developing a more autonomous and unified economy in Wales, the major Welsh economic regions were made more dependent upon English markets, English capital, an English-orientated communications network and the new English state bureaucracies.

The ' Parliament for Wales ' campaign rumbled steadily forwards as the rallies, posters and petitioning grew in professionalism and intensity. Two of the incoming M.P.s—T. W. Jones (Labour, Merioneth) and Cledwyn Hughes (Labour, Anglesey)—joined Goronwy Roberts (Labour, Caernarfon), Tudor Watkins (Labour, Brecon & Radnor), Roderic Bowen[15] (Liberal, Cardigan) and Clement Davies (Liberal, Montgomery) in supporting a Welsh Parliament. In January 1952 the Welsh Regional Council of Labour announced its intention to investigate ' the needs of local government in Wales ' ; in the summer its annual conference turned down Merioneth's call for a Federal Britain.

Thus far S.O. had played little part in the campaign committee's work. But proof that his commitment to the cause had not faded—on the contrary—was demonstrated dramatically in the House of Commons on 22 January 1953. On that occasion, S.O. made the most passionate plea of his life for Welsh self-government, even brushing aside the Deputy Speaker's strictures for straying from the contents of the Welsh Affairs White Paper ostensibly under discussion :

> There is no reason why we should supplicate in the way we are expected to do on these Welsh days. Wales is well provided with the basic necessities of life ; she has a great deal of raw materials, power and food. I am absolutely confident that were Wales allowed to control and govern its own affairs, it would easily be made one of the richest countries in the world, and that within a generation.
>
> The White Paper is wholly misleading as a picture of what Wales really is. The difference between Wales and the rest of this island is not only a statistical one in relation to population and industrial and agricultural production. In speaking of Wales, one speaks of a nation which is fully conscious of its nationhood, possessing a history, a culture and a tradition

> peculiarly its own. With all humility, I urge my Welsh Hon. Friends never to forget that and never to hesitate to say it in this House, which becomes more alien to me the more Welsh debates I listen to. I often have this feeling, as I have had it today, that Welsh Members are here largely on sufferance. They are here because of past favours granted to Wales and in anticipation of more favours to come. Why should we Welsh people quail at the thought of separation in a wholly political sense from England ? . . .
>
> Wales cannot be ordered, governed and managed successfully by an outside alien body of individuals. Surely on a Welsh Day I am entitled to stress that in a way which I think it ought to be stressed. I urge my Welsh parliamentary colleagues at least to regard these Welsh Days as days of protest by the Welsh people against the subjection of our country by a people of alien tradition, alien culture and alien tongue.

Then, alluding to the Cold War and the violent struggles around the world against American imperialism, S.O. brought his memorable speech to an end :

> The Wales we have been discussing all day strongly objects to this Parliament irrevocably dragging it into the abyss of destruction. We have no quarrel with any people or nation in this world. We are instinctively hospitable and we are a nation of workers. We can feel no enmity against any other people or nation, whatever their colour, creed or religion. We abhor the swashbuckling fire-eating speeches which we have had in this House, and as a Welsh nation we repudiate their sentiments. The heart of our hospitable country goes out to those who are struggling against tyranny and against obstruction, because we know that obstruction has been placed in the way of this little country to which I am proud to belong.

If the ferocity of S.O.'s remarks shocked some of his parliamentary colleagues, the Welsh Nationalists were delighted ; *Plaid Cymru*'s English-language paper, the *Welsh Nation*, reprinted the speech in full, while an editorial in *Plaid*'s Welsh-language monthly, *Y Ddraig Goch*, exclaimed :

> *Dyna iaith y Blaid yn Nhŷ'r Cyffredin ! Nid yw'n syndod fod pawb cydbwys eu barn yn barod i gyfaddef fod dylanwad y Blaid yn cerdded ymhell o'i blaen. Os nad yw Gwynfor Evans wedi cyrraedd Tŷ'r Cyffredin, y mae eisoes yn llefaru'n huawdl yno.*[16]

> This was the language of *Plaid* in the House of Commons! It is no surprise that everyone of balanced opinion is ready to admit that *Plaid*'s influence extends far beyond the party itself. Even if Gwynfor Evans [*Plaid*'s President] has not arrived in the House of Commons, he already speaks with eloquence there.

Rather less enthusiasm was felt for the activities of S.O. and other Labour Home Rulers, though, by the Labour Party leadership. They must have heard with dismay of the massed rally at Rhyl in August 1953, when the Chairman of the Council for Wales and veteran Labour leader in north Wales, Huw T. Edwards, announced his support for the Welsh Parliament petition; the presence there of Goronwy Roberts and fellow-M.P. Tudor Watkins, as chairman, coloured the Home Rule platform a little redder still. But, if these appearances were in breach of party discipline, S.O.'s behaviour the following month filled his critics with indignation and near-apoplexy. On a sunny Saturday afternoon in late September, he attended a 'Parliament for Wales' rally in Sophia Gardens, Cardiff, initially taking a seat with his wife in the audience of two thousand. Then, amidst thunderous applause, he accepted an invitation to join the rally's sponsors on the banner-bedecked stage. The reason why his actions were so scandalous was that this particular event had been organised officially by a rival political party—*Plaid Cymru*. After listening to the Ystalyfera Prize Band and applauding the speeches of Welsh and Scottish Nationalist leaders, S.O. happily joined the huge procession through Cardiff's main streets to the proposed site of a Welsh Parliament in Cathays Park.

Anxious to restore some superficial semblance of unity in Labour's ranks, Deputy Leader Herbert Morrison, General Secretary Morgan Phillips and Welsh Secretary Cliff Prothero hastened to a meeting of the Welsh Parliamentary Labour Group on November 11, where they delivered an ultimatum to the Home Rule M.P.s: the dissidents were solemnly informed that the Labour Party would be producing its own plans for Wales within three months—and that in the meantime they must withdraw their support from the 'Parliament for Wales' campaign or risk disciplinary action at the hands of the Parliamentary Labour Party.[17]

S.O. addresses a 'Parliament for Wales' rally in Cardiff City Hall, March 1951. Third from left is J. E. Jones (*Plaid Cymru* Gen. Sec.)., then Idris Cox (Communist Party Welsh Secretary), Lady Megan Lloyd George, M.P., S.O. and Tudor Watkins, M.P. Seated in the front, furthest right, is the Rev. Gwilym O. Williams (later Archbishop of Wales).

SIGN THE PETITION BECAUSE A

PARLIAMENT FOR WALES

WILL BRING

NEW **AND IMPORTANT INDUSTRIES.**

Wales must have her own motor car aeroplane and heavy engineering plants. These essential economic assets remain outside her borders now, although Wales produces in abundance the materials used in them.

NEW **ROAD, RAIL AND AIR SYSTEMS**

to link the valleys, the East and the West, the North and the South.

NEW **RESPECT FOR WALES AT HOME AND ABROAD.**

● A new deal in every way for an old nation.

FEDERAL SELF-GOVERNMENT MEANS ECONOMIC CONSOLIDATION NOT ECONOMIC SEPARATION

Sign the petition for **A PARLIAMENT FOR WALES** when it comes to your door !

Published by the Merthyr and Dowlais Committee of the Parliament for Wales Campaign.

Printed by "South Wales Gazette" Abertillery.

'Parliament for Wales' leaflet published in Merthyr

Sephora Davies

Plaid Cymru rally in Cardiff, September 1953. *From left:* Gwynfor Evans (President), J. E. Jones (Gen. Sec.), R. E. Holland (Vice-President) and S.O.

Annual South Wales miners' gala in Cardiff, June 1956. Heading the procession: S.O., Will Paynter (South Wales N.U.M. President), Aneurin Bevan, M.P., Arthur Horner (N.U.M. General Secretary), W. H. Crews (South Wales N.U.M. Gen. Sec.) and Dai Dan Evans (South Wales N.U.M. Vice-President).

S.O. welcomes the lobby of South Wales miners to the Commons, February 1963

As the public debate continued, the paucity of official statistics relating to Welsh economic and social conditions allowed all kinds of misconceptions and distortions to flourish. Finally, the Government agreed to publish a Digest of Welsh Statistics for the first time in 1955; but S.O. was not satisfied. In the Welsh Day debate on 2 February 1954 he demanded separate figures to show the precise financial relationship between Wales and the British State. The Home Secretary (and thus the Minister for Welsh Affairs) Sir David Maxwell-Fyfe could not see the need for such detail; producing basic economic statistics for Wales would already be a strain on civil service manpower, he pleaded. At this point the Cardiff Labour M.P. from Portsmouth, James Callaghan, jumped in to caution S.O. and others of the 'danger of becoming so mad on searching for new statistics that we never trouble to apply them to the circumstances to which they are related'. S.O. snapped back: 'That is the point of view of the alien who occasionally visits us in south Wales'.

When *Labour's Policy for Wales* was published in March 1954, six of its eleven pages argued against a Parliament for Wales; as a substitute the pamphlet called for a Minister of Welsh Affairs (in their own right), closer scrutiny and discussion of Welsh matters in the House of Commons, and a revision of the constitution of the 'Council for Wales and Monmouthshire' (*sic*). Far from retracting his support for devolution, S.O. angrily attacked the pamphlet's contents at Party meetings. He repudiated its assertion that fundamental constitutional change was irrelevant in the teeth of social and economic problems. A Socialist government in a Socialist, self-governing Wales could have avoided the calamity that befell the country between the two wars, S.O. insisted. It would never have shut down over 200 collieries and iron and steel works, because capitalist profits per ton would not have dictated closures. Nor would thousands of acres of food-producing land have been abandoned, or half a million people compelled by circumstances to leave their homes. A Welsh Socialist government would have instituted an education and research programme into new products and production techniques for the coal, slate and agricultural industries. And even if the pamphlet was correct in claiming that Wales was not an economic entity—why should it follow automatically that economic problems in Wales could only be solved by powers outside

Wales ? S.O particularly resented the implication that Wales was too poor for self-government. The country had always produced a huge amount of wealth by its labour : ' fortunes have been made by foreigners out of coal, iron, steel and shipping; the profits were carted away leaving just the Dowlais's and Merthyr's '. In this century, too, wealth was being created by the workers whilst profits were reaped by companies such as Hoover and Kaysor-Bondor in his constituency—' And what have we had in return ? Just a few houses built by these companies '. Nor did devolution mean isolation : it was nonsense for the pamphlet to claim, for example, that Welsh administration of railway track in its own territory would be impracticable. The Paris-Constantinople railway ran through more than a half-dozen independent states, so why should services to Shrewsbury and Chester be imperilled by Welsh self-government ?[18]

Typically, S.O. now stepped up his efforts for the Home Rule cause, shrugging off his 70 years to address the multiplying public meetings that took the word deep into industrial, English-speaking south Wales. In Merthyr a ' Parliament for Wales ' committee had been established by the *Cymreigyddion*—a local cultural society—with Sephora Davies playing a leading role in the committee's work ; names were collected for the Petition and leaflets distributed. Large crowds filled halls in Merthyr and Dowlais on 7 May 1954 to listen to Lady Megan Lloyd George, John MacCormick of the Scottish Covenant Association, Tudor Watkins and Gwynfor Evans. The Mayor of Merthyr chaired one meeting, and S.O. the other. Yet this seemingly healthy situation in Merthyr concealed a fundamental weakness general to the ' Parliament for Wales ' campaign : at no time had the Merthyr Constituency Labour Party declared itself in favour of Home Rule, although several of its executive members supported the principle ; and while the local party tolerated S.O.'s activities, there were some activists in Merthyr—and many more outside—who resented the way in which the Regional Council of Labour's decision not to co-operate with the campaign had been ignored by the Home Rule M.P.s. Many stalwarts also objected to Labour M.P.s sharing public platforms with prominent members of a party—*Plaid Cymru*—which increasingly (and often insultingly) denigrated those revered Labour politicians who happened to oppose devolution. Nor did Communist endorsement of the campaign commend a Parliament for Wales to the multitude of Labour supporters who had fallen prey to Cold War propaganda.

Another grave objection to a Welsh Parliament was being popularised by Labour opponents early in 1954 : the possibility that such an institution would seize control of the Welsh coal industry, set up a Welsh Coal Board and lead logically to the creation of a separate Welsh Miners Union—just ten years after Welsh miners had themselves voted to wind up the S.W.M.F. and unite inside the new National Union of Mineworkers.[19] These developments, it was argued, would wreck the unity of Britain's miners, restore District agreements to the detriment of Welsh miners, and spell disaster for the ' subsidised ' Welsh coalfields.

When it was announced that a motion in favour of the ' Parliament for Wales ' campaign would be discussed at the annual conference of the South Wales Area of the N.U.M. on 10 May 1954 in Porthcawl, the fate of the coal industry assumed a central position in the whole devolution argument. Welsh mining M.P.s, with the exception of S.O., hardened in their opposition to the campaign and successfully negotiated speaking-rights for Jim Griffiths and Dai Grenfell (M.P. for Gower) at the conference. Unfortunately, the anti-devolution camp's scaremongering could only have profited from the contradictory replies of Home Rule supporters. In a lengthy press statement, Lady Megan Lloyd George did not ditch the notion of a Welsh Coal Board, but intimated that a Welsh Parliament would merely discuss the N.C.B.'s operations in Wales without interfering with the plans of the Board in London. No Welsh Miners Union was proposed by the campaign nor would a Parliament in Cardiff have the power to establish one ; National Insurance arrangements and wages agreements in the coal industry would continue to be determined on a U.K.-wide basis. Finally, if these assurances were insufficient then she and her campaign committee would accept any changes that the Welsh miners might care to suggest.

S.O., on the other hand, reacted to the fears of his fellow mining M.P.s with an uncompromising statement that sailed far closer to separatism than Lady Megan or her committee would have dared to do. On the morning of the South Wales miners' debate, S.O.'s long letter in the *Western Mail* met the doubting Thomases head on :

> There is obviously much confused thinking in the use of the words 'National' and 'District'. Should Wales be granted self-government the Miners' Union would not be a District Union but a Wales National Union. The miners of Wales, therefore, would not revert to a District agreement. Their agreement in a self-governing Wales would be a national agreement. It is, therefore, not a question of the breaking-up of the National Union of Mineworkers, it is rather that two National Unions will exist, one in Wales and one in England. Certainly there is nothing unusual in this among the Trades Unions of the world.

Whatever the titular designation of a Welsh Miners' Union, S.O.'s predictions for the future under self-government hardly reassured those who treasured the organisational unity of Britain's miners in the N.U.M. But, S.O. countered, it must be borne in mind that a Welsh Parliament would also be a Socialist Parliament, hence:

> One of the first steps that a Welsh Socialist Parliament would take would be to end the present muddled and amateurish way in which the mining industry (and other nationalised industries) is being controlled and directed today. It would end the most rigid monopoly ever created in this country. No longer would the Coal Board be a corporate body, a law unto itself, answerable neither to Parliament nor to the people. These absolute monopolies into which the nationalised industries have been straightjacketed sound the death-knell of Parliamentary Democracy. No question, however important, on the industry can now be asked in Parliament. Complete administrative autonomy has been given by Parliament to the N.C.B. What an absurd position in these 'enlightened' days of our political maturity!
>
> . . . The only reason ever given for justifying the conversion of the nationalised industries into monopolies far beyond the reach of the people, and their elected representatives, was that Parliament had no time to deal with them. Admittedly, the British Parliament is tragically congested with work, almost to the point of stultification. But the cure of this state of things is not by destroying our Parliamentary Democracy by the creation of monopolies, but by easing the pressure at Westminster, by granting Wales, Scotland and England the right to control and manage their own affairs.

In a Socialist economy after self-government, coal prices—and hence wages—would not be held down to subsidise private industry, as they were at present. He pointed to the potential of the country's economic base with its coal, steel sheet, tinplate, oil refining, chemicals and agricultural produce :

> The truth is that in relation to its size Wales in natural and physical resources is one of the richest countries in the world, far richer than any European country.
>
> But Wales can never be fully developed, industrially and economically; its rural depopulation, caused by generations of neglect, cannot be halted ; and its people, generally, with their peasant culture, their schools and university, will never fully express, culturally and spiritually, that genius which is theirs, until Wales is free to govern itself, free and unfettered from the remote control of Whitehall.[20]

S.O.'s was a bold, self-confident case. Had he been permitted to make it at Porthcawl the majority against a Welsh Parliament could conceivably have been reduced. As it turned out, 121 of the 200 delegates opposed the Home Rule motion from Morlais Lodge, ably moved by Cyril Parry and supported by Gwyn Phillips, Ystradmynach, and Dick Beamish, Abercrave. Thirty-four delegates resisted the arguments of the ex-Home Rulers Griffiths and Grenfell, declaring instead for a Welsh Parliament.

This psychological body-blow to the campaign was swiftly followed by a more predictable set-back : the Welsh Regional Council of Labour meeting on May 29, also in Porthcawl, adopted *Labour's Policy for Wales* and decisively spurned a Home Rule amendment by 159 votes to 8. Clearly, the enormous margin reflected more a desire for unity in the party rather than the respective strengths of pro- and anti-devolution sentiment. Nonetheless, the decision marked Labour's official abandonment of Welsh Home Rule.

Spurred on as always by adversity, S.O. travelled the south Wales valleys in the summer and autumn of 1954 addressing public meetings organised by local Petition committees. One of the largest rallies took place in Ystradgynlais Miners Welfare Hall on August 5, when over 800 people—many of them patronising the nearby National Eisteddfod—flocked to hear Lady Megan Lloyd George, Tudor Watkins, T. W. Jones and John MacCormick, the Scottish Nationalist leader. S.O. told the enthusiastic audience : ' I am an uncompromising Socialist, but that Socialism can never materialise in Wales unless we can be free to apply its principles to our own way of life '.

Even now he had not exhausted his reserves of energy and ingenuity in this, a cause that lay so close to his heart alongside international peace and his beloved Merthyr. Early in December his name was amongst the first batch of those drawn in the House of Commons ballot for Private Members' Bills. This is the opportunity for a few lucky back-bench M.P.s to introduce a Bill into the Commons, albeit with only the slimmest chance of the measure eventually reaching the statute book. S.O.'s subject was recorded as the 'Better Government of Wales' and the Bill—still to be published—received its formal First Reading a fortnight before Christmas. S.O. spent the parliamentary recess consulting with colleagues and friends about the possible contents of his Bill. Fundamentally he faced two options : either he could propose some modest changes in Wales' constitutional position—perhaps reforming the Council for Wales or setting up a Welsh Ministry with a Secretary of State—or he could weave his Bill around the central thread of a Welsh Parliament.

While discussions with his allies continued, S.O. approached a young Nationalist barrister, Dewi Watkin Powell, and asked him to draft a parliamentary Bill which would provide for a Welsh Parliament. Labour colleagues, on the other hand, preferred a 'minimalist' approach ; they were uneasy about proposing any major constitutional change in a Private Member's measure. Cledwyn Hughes and Goronwy Roberts urged S.O. to adopt a less ambitious scheme : a Secretary of State for Wales should be instituted immediately, followed soon afterwards by the establishment of a Welsh National Assembly. The Secretary of State would consult the Assembly (which would wield no legislative or executive powers) about the course that devolution should then take. The two M.P.s argued that these proposals could be defended on the basis of existing Labour policy for Wales and, anyway, the National Assembly would inevitably accrete greater powers with the passing of time.

'Your and my instinct is to go for the larger scheme, but it is essential that we should all as a team feel absolutely confident of being able to defend what we put forward', Goronwy Roberts wrote to S.O. at the beginning of January. Cledwyn Hughes begged S.O. to put forward a 'moderate and reasonable measure'. Nevertheless, they and the other Home Rule M.P.s were prepared, if needs be, to support S.O. should he insist on a full-blooded measure for a law-making Welsh Parliament.[21] Confronted by the cooling feet of his comrades, S.O. reacted strongly, pointing out to them that the ' Parliament for Wales ' campaign committee had scornfully dismissed Labour's policy. He continued :

> The question, therefore, arises whether we now betray the only active, organised movement in Wales for self-government, and that, of course, done in my name !
>
> You say that your reason for drafting such a Bill as you suggest is that it 'will win support both in Parliament and in the country '. I gravely doubt its winning any support in Wales because it is too far removed from the desires and commitments of every person, body and organisation actively supporting a Parliament for Wales ; while the opponents of any measurea of self-government will kill it with ridicule, ridicule based on the betrayal of a Movement for Welsh Self-government, on treating the Petition with contempt . . . and, of course, on the superstition that Wales does not know what it wants or—if it does—it can never agree on it.

S.O. insisted that there was no alternative to a Private Member's Bill :

> The present Government is opposed to any measure of Self-government for Wales, and so is the Labour Party for the moment, and this attitude will continue until the demand from Wales will be strong and determined enough to compel a British Government to legislate accordingly.[22]

The Bill drafted by Watkin Powell, and the debate around it, would perform a vital educative function and so could only help the cause of self-government. S.O. knew that his Bill, or any Bill proposing even the smallest measure of devolution, would be defeated in the House of Commons. But merely in advocating it, the Home Rulers could—in S.O.'s own words—' do a real day's work for Wales '.

When the Bill was published towards the end of February, its 50 clauses were arranged around the controversial centrepiece—a Welsh Parliament or ' Senate '. Seventy-two elected Senators would meet in Cardiff to govern the domestic affairs of the Welsh nation : the Senate's powers would be similar to those exercised by the Northern Ireland Parliament, leaving responsibilities for defence, foreign policy and overseas trade in the lap of Westminster. A Joint Exchequer Board would adjust the financial relationship between Wales (with its tax-raising Senate) and the United Kingdom Government ; the Queen would appoint her own Governor of Wales, who would lead an executive committee of Senators as the Welsh Government. The Government of Wales Bill, to record its official title, boasted a list of eleven sponsoring M.P.s: the five Welsh Home Rulers, five Scottish Socialists and, somewhat surprisingly, Newport Labour M.P. Peter Freeman—a Cockney! Leaving aside the substance of these proposals, friend and foe alike agreed that the Bill was a model of coherence and consistency.

Friday, March 4 1955, was the historic day appointed for the Second Reading. This would be the first full House of Commons debate on Home Rule for 33 years ; and not since E. T. John's Government of Wales Bill in 1914 had a Welsh Member introduced such a measure. S.O.'s allies busied themselves in the weeks preceding the big day. Local ' Parliament for Wales ' committees rushed petition forms around the houses : by mid-March over 200,000 signatures had been collected. The national committee claimed that between 70% and 80% of people approached had supported the Petition. In Merthyr, 1,092 adults had been canvassed—and 1,074 of them responded favourably.[23] As the ammunition for S.O.'s proposing speech flowed in, so too did the hundreds of letters, postcards and telegrams congratulating him on his stand and wishing him success on March 4.

Not that the Bill's opponents were idle during the run-up to the debate. The press in Wales was, excepting the small Welsh-language section, virtually unanimous in its enmity : on February 26 the *Western Mail* editorial column rejected the Bill, although hoping that a Secretary of State would rise from its ashes. Even St. David's tolerance must have been tested by the spectacle of M.P.s using patriotic dinners on his day, March 1, to discredit Home Rule and to galvanise parliamentary opposition to the Bill. Arriving home from an expatriate event in England, George Thomas explained to the *Western Mail* : ' we are appealing to English Members, as I did in Yorkshire, to help us to save the Welsh people from themselves '.[24]

Nevertheless, the Welsh Parliamentary Labour Group resolved in its meeting on the Wednesday to allow M.P.s a free hand. No whip would be imposed, Chairman Iorrie Thomas declared, because the Bill was that of a back-bench Member. Expediency in the face of considerable public sympathy for devolution did not, apparently, play any part in prompting the Group's abstentionist decision. Undoubtedly a number of Welsh Labour M.P.s had still not made up their minds on the issue—or were too mindful of popular support for Home Rule to oppose it openly. Indeed, party bosses did not relish the prospect of a vote on the Bill, fearing the divisions it would reopen in the Labour ranks. The week leading up to the Second Reading had been a frantic, pulsating one : Churchill had whipped up a storm with his speech on nuclear war ; S.O. joined the Bevanite revolt against Attlee on military expenditure. He must have been exhausted as he sipped his customary half-pint of beer in the Member's Bar of the House of Commons on Thursday evening ; yet from somewhere S.O. summoned up enthusiasm for the following day. His excitement even spilled over into good-natured bravado as he joked to his friends about the ' trouncing ' that awaited the anti-Home Rulers, especially George Thomas.

At five minutes past eleven o'clock on Friday morning, March 4, S.O. rose from his seat to move the Second Reading of the Government of Wales Bill. Dressed in best senatorial fashion, sporting a spotless white shirt, discreet tie and black striped trousers and coat, he began to address the 15 or so M.P.s scattered around the Chamber:

> Never before has our country been more alive, been more active, more articulate and more finely organised in the demand that a substantial measure of self-government should at long last be given to Wales.

Taunted by Caerphilly M.P. Ness Edwards to substantiate a claim that miners' lodges had joined cultural, religious and youth movements in sending messages of goodwill for the Bill, S.O. read out a telegram from his challenger's constituency: ' Congratulations and best wishes for today—Penallta Lodge Committee, representing 1,800 miners '. While M.P.s lay about the sparsely-populated benches, the packed public galleries listened respectfully as S.O. made his case in a moderate and statesmanlike manner ; he deprecated the congestion of parliamentary business, conjuring up an hypothesis to illustrate the lack of democratic control over vital nationalised industries :

> I have living in my constituency 7,000 miners, working within and outside the constituency. There is not a question of the least importance which I can put to the Minister of Fuel and Power about these miners, as miners. Were there a disastrous mining tragedy, it is only by the courtesy of this House that I would be able to put a question to the Minister. The Minister would express his sympathy and I should accept it sincerely. Then, after consulting the Coal Board, he would inform me, in all probability, that an inquiry would be conducted. It is time that we objected to that procedure so far as miners are concerned, and the same applies to workers in other nationalised industries. As a Member of Parliament, as an ex-miner and mining engineer, there is nothing that I can do for the miners, whether they be alive or dead. Many of us know how stultifying and frustrating all this can be and it is all created and justified by the appalling congestion of work in this House. This Bill provides an opportunity whereby, in the process of time, we may relieve that congestion.

Describing his measure as a ' modest ' one, S.O. proceeded to explain some of the Bill's clauses before closing his speech with a defiant declaration :

> I say that we are entitled to, should have and must have more power to look after our own Welsh affairs than we have had. We know what happened in the inter-war years. We have memories of nearly half-a-million of our young people being driven out of South Wales and we do not want the same thing to happen again. We are quite confident of this : we are the people who are conscious that we live in one of the richest countries in the world.

In a competent seconding speech Cledwyn Hughes referred to the problems of the tinplate industry, the coal ports, rural depopulation, the slate industry and leasehold enfranchisement which—being particularly dire in Wales—merited the special attention of a law-making Welsh Parliament. But his masterful exposition of the Bill's precise provisions was followed by a typically intemperate tirade from Cardiff North's Tory M.P., David Llewellyn. He railed against constitutional schemes that bore no relation to the Bill under discussion, raised the spectre of Glamorgan and Monmouthshire dominating any elected Welsh body, and—departing from reasoned argument altogether—claimed that the ' Parliament for Wales ' campaign preached the same gospel as *Mein Kampf*. Bill

Mainwaring, himself a Welsh-speaking son of the Rhondda, could perceive no difference between Welsh people and their neighbours to the east ; furthermore, he doubted whether Wales could rightfully call itself a nation. Unbelievably, this was the same man who had in previous years told the Commons that ' the national traditions of Wales and her language lead Welsh people, inevitably, to regard England as a foreign land ', who had warned M.P.s that Wales would ' declare war on someone ' if her status and conditions were not improved, and who had once offended the Deputy Speaker by speaking in Welsh in order to demonstrate the distinctive attributes of his nation. Now he attacked the Home Rule Bill because, he claimed, it rested on the ' utterly groundless assumption that people who inhabit England are in some peculiar way wholly foreign and alien to the people of Wales '.

The Home Secretary and Minister for Welsh Affairs, Major Gwilym Lloyd George, repudiated the Bill on behalf of the Government with what appeared to be a sliver of sorrow in his voice. The next speaker, Ness Edwards, cited a compendium of figures purporting to prove that, in a self-governing Wales, miners' wages would plummet, the education system would collapse, railways would be chaotic and local government would go bankrupt ; student supporters of Home Rule lived, he asserted, by the motto : ' Hate the English, but take their money '. This catalogue of impending catastrophies was balanced by a number of more moderate contributions for and against the Bill, before Jim Griffiths concluded the case for the Anti's. Blessed with the authority of the Shadow Cabinet, he outlined an alternative programme of reforms : diversification of the Welsh economy, rehabilitation of the countryside, a strengthening of local government, a more representative Welsh Council, greater administrative devolution and the establishment of a Royal Commission (on the lines of the Scottish one) to review the governance of Wales.

Goronwy Roberts replied to the five-hour debate, imploring M.P.s to consider the common sense of a Federal Britain. Pointing to Northern Ireland, he insisted that devolved government need not rupture the universality of the Welfare State or the organisational unity of the trade unions ; he denied once more that the Bill would partition the National Coal Board. However, all the pleas and arguments in favour of Home Rule proved to be sterile. At 4 o'clock in the afternoon, enough M.P.s appeared from nowhere to refuse the Bill its Second Reading by 48 votes to 14. S.O. and Tudor Watkins counted their supporters in the ' Ayes ' lobby : Fenner Brockway, Emrys Hughes, George Wigg and Ted Willis were there—but why the absence of Peter Freeman and the Bill's Scottish sponsors ? That day the sweet taste of triumph belonged to George Thomas (displaying a daffodil in his lapel) and David Llewellyn as they watched the procession of M.P.s into the ' Noes ' lobby. Those who helped snuff out the flame of Welsh Home Rule included Jim Callaghan, Will Cove, Ness Edwards, Harold Finch, Dai Grenfell, Jim Griffiths, Edward Heath, Bill Mainwaring, Iain MacLeod, Arthur Pearson, Arthur Probert, Iorrie Thomas, Peter Thomas and the Rev. Llywelyn Williams.

It would be an exaggeration to depict this defeat as a shattering blow to S.O.'s dreams. He had laboured under no illusions about the Bill's life-expectancy ; he knew full well that the House of Commons, an institution intensely jealous of its powers, would treat his efforts in its own time-honoured, inimitable way—by showing a contemptuous and deadly indifference. Nevertheless, S.O. returned home to Merthyr on Friday night in sadness : some of his Home Rule allies had deserted him, while none of his anti-Home Rule friends had been persuaded to the cause.

Then there was that small but articulate band of Nationalists who had maintained a disdainful aloofness throughout the Parliament for Wales agitation. A former leader of *Plaid Cymru*, Saunders Lewis, composed this verse to his compatriots' endeavours :

SENEDD I GYMRU

Mor neis fai cael drwy ddeiseb
neu siawns S. O. Davies, heb
gyrchu o neb i garchar
na baw gwaed, ond wyneb gwâr
a gwên fêl yn gofyn fôt,
senedd, Barc Cathays, ynot,
senedd fel dy Deml Heddwch
i rawt cachaduriaid trwch
Cymru boluglot flotai,
nasiwn ben ôl Ness, neb a Nye.[25]

A PARLIAMENT FOR WALES

There's nice it would be by petition
or the luck of S.O. in the draw
Without sending people to prison
or drowning the nation in gore
But to get with smooth vote-catching faces
a Parliament in Cathays Park
'Twould be just like the Temple of Peace is,
where the modern Welsh rabble could nark
A beggarly polyglot farce
for Nobody, Ness and Nye's arse.

More serious still was the impact of the Bill's burial on the morale of the petitioners in Wales, many of whom had harboured an absurd hope that the impossible could happen, that the Bill would be permitted to proceed. The 'Parliament for Wales' campaign bravely battled on until April 1956, when Goronwy Roberts presented 240,652 names (a petition signed by 14% of the Welsh electorate) to the Houses of Parliament.[26] But the Bill's demise, and five years of campaigning against the odds, had irreparably tarnished the once-shining armour of the crusade. The Home Rule movement disintegrated in 1956 and it is significant that when the five Welsh Labour rebels were reported by Cliff Prothero to the Party's National Executive in January for flouting official policy, the N.E.C. decided not to bother with disciplinary action.[27]

S.O. had fought one of the great battles of his career. Defeat did not diminish his standing amongst the people who counted—the workers and ordinary folk of the south Wales valleys and, in particular, of Merthyr Tydfil. There, life continued much as usual. Every Saturday evening S.O. would walk down to the 'Crown' at the bottom of Merthyr High Street. The tavern, gauntly furnished and minimally decorated, was presided over by Tom Thomas—'a landlord of the old school'. The bardic Welsh Republican and 'Crown' regular, Harri Webb, later painted a marvellously evocative picture of post-war Merthyr and of this glowing star in S.O.'s social constellation :

> 'Tom the Crown' was enormously respected, and ran his establishment more like a gentleman's private club than a public house open to all-comers. The front door was kept cunningly ajar so that casual passers-by could not be quite sure

whether the place was open or not. To be fully accepted as a customer of good standing you had to be formally introduced and serve a probationary period. The arrangement was a matter of general knowledge and seemed to cause no resentment.

It derived a certain sanction from the presence on the premises, every Saturday night without fail, of our Member of Parliament S. O. Davies, whom nobody ever called anything but S.O. To say that he held court in the backroom on those nights would be an exaggeration, though there was undoubtedly a nucleus of those who saw themselves as courtiers. But that would be to do violence to the subtle societics of the place . . .

That S.O. was the town's most revered figure was, in this context, almost incidental. Here, he was just a nice old man who had found a pub that suited him and stuck to it, and came down every Saturday night for his couple of glasses of beer. Considering the notoriety of some of his Parliamentary colleagues, he was remarkably abstemious. He could never be coaxed to take more than his usual quota, and nobody could ever remember seeing him the worse for wear. He was looked after the way the regulars of an old-fashioned pub used to look after one another. If some aggrieved citizen came in and wanted to ' have it out with S.O. ' (usually on some issue which was not his responsibility at all) he would be dealt with not only by Tom but by the manifest hostility of the entire membership, and if that did not discourage him, Idwal the postman would interpose his massive frame between the backroom door and the complainant in no uncertain manner.

Among ourselves we would pull S.O.'s leg about the numerous scrapes he got into with the official Labour Party because of his independent line, but there was never any serious argument, because the Crown was not the place for it.[28]

S.O.'s patriotic fervour—derived from his identification with the Welsh working-class, from his belief in their potential—never waned. He remained ever-vigilant on behalf of Welsh interests. When, for example, a list of Parliamentary Labour Party spokesmen was drawn up early in 1956, S.O. noted with disgust the omission of a watch-dog for Welsh Affairs, contrasting this treatment with the appointment of a Scottish spokesman. He scribbled an angry note to the P.L.P. secretary, Carol Johnson :

Wales has either been overlooked or possibly, as usual, contemptuously ignored . . . Why should not a Welsh-speaking Member be allocated the task of holding a constant and constructive watching brief with respect to Welsh affairs ?

Why this persistent affront to the sensibilities of the Welsh people, and why this gratuitous provision of political capital to the opponents of Labour in Wales?[29]

No spokesman was appointed. But S.O. did not lose faith that Wales would one day win self-government and, with it, self-respect. He was refreshed in this conviction by a visit to the National Eisteddfod in Aberdare Park, in the summer of 1956. Strolling across the *maes* in the company of Archdruid Dyfnallt, he received a princely reception in the valley of his birth. A staunch upholder of the all-Welsh rule introduced five years earlier, S.O. drew special inspiration from this popular celebration of national distinctiveness.

On the economic front, too, he protested vigorously whenever he detected any disregard of Welsh claims. By the mid-1950s the Government's fuel strategy was to import oil from the Middle East as a substitute for coal, to sell British coal cheaply to domestic industry, to shut ' uneconomic ' pits and to concentrate investment in a small number of deep-mine projects such as Maerdy and Cynheidre. Although S.O. refuted the economic and political case for substitution, he was not driven by any sentimental attachment to the coal-mining process : indeed, he would admonish the M.P. or acquaintance who dared to romanticise the dirty, dangerous job of digging coal. And when nuclear power emerged as a viable source of fuel, seemingly without the political and economic risks associated with imported oil, S.O. welcomed it wholeheartedly. In March 1957 the Tory Government announced an 8-year, 5,000 milowatt nuclear development programme . . . but none of the 19 projects envisaged were allocated to Wales. S.O. initiated a debate in the Commons two days later, on March 15, when he argued that Wales had all the main prerequisites for nuclear sites : the geological conditions, the water resources, the adaptable labour force, and a university for research and development. He vented the feelings of many political, trade union and local government bodies in the country in demanding an atomic power station for Wales, and warned :

We are tired of being just a milch cow for the convenience and well-being of areas in England. We are tired of seeing Welsh valleys being drowned, and Welsh communities, with all their Welsh traditions and culture, being destroyed for the pleasures of an alien people whose Government is so contemptuous of us.

> Our country is good enough for this and similar Governments to take extensive areas of it and to destroy them for the pleasures of people who are not the people of Wales, using our land as battle-training areas where some people derive peculiar pleasure in playing soldiers as we did back in the days of the Boer War. We are bitterly disappointed and angry.

The burden of the Government's reply, borne by Parliamentary Secretary David Renton, was that Wales had not been overlooked : the reference to 'the English and Scottish Electricity Authorities' in the Government's original announcement also embraced Wales—because 'English Electricity Authority' was merely a 'compendious way' of referring to the Central Electricity Authority which served England and Wales together ! (Scotland and Northern Ireland had their own Authorities). Thus Renton confirmed that Wales would play host to at least one atomic power station by 1965.

S.O. expressed satisfaction with the information he had elicited. But the Government's whole approach had betrayed an attitude towards Wales that stirred popular resentment. It was in 1957 that the Liverpool Corporation seized Cwm Tryweryn in Meirionydd, even though the required Act of Parliament was opposed by 35 of the 36 Welsh M.P.s (including S.O.) ; the Welsh-speaking local community was subsequently evicted and the valley drowned, despite the protests of nearly every political, religious, cultural and trade union organisation in Wales, including the South Wales N.U.M. Such acts of brutal insensitivity and exploitation fanned the flames of Welsh nationalism; and when the conflagration occured less than ten years later, S.O. would be there—unbowed and still demanding Home Rule for his country.

NOTES

[1]' Gwladgarwch y Cymry ' in *Detholiad o Ryddiaith Gymraeg R. J. Derfel* Vol. 1 (1945) edited by D. Gwenallt Jones.

[2]See *Turning to London : Labour's Attitude to Wales 1898-1956* (1980) by Robert Griffiths.

[3]' Home Rule All Round ' by Arthur Henderson in *Welsh Outlook*, June 1918.

[4]*Welsh Outlook*, May 1918.

[5]See the relevant contributions to *Workers' Control* (1970) edited by Ken Coates and Tony Topham, particularly the extracts from the 1932 and 1933 T.U.C. and Labour Party conferences.

[6]See *Pages From Memory* (1969) by James Griffiths, pp. 158-161 ; also the pamphlets *A Secretary of State for Wales* ? (*circa* 1943) by R. C. Mathias, and *Attlee's Reply* (1943) by Iwan Morgan.

[7]*Labour and Wales* published by Cliff Prothero as ' District Organiser of the Labour Party '. Strangely, Prothero makes no mention of this statement in his autobiography *Recount* (1982), although he repeatedly emphasises the unofficial status of the *Llais Llafur* broadsheet. Even so, the book contains useful information about Labour's changing attitudes towards a Secretary of State for Wales and Home Rule.

[8]S. O. Davies Papers, Swansea (Ref : 1C, *ii*).

[9]Bevan's attitude towards Devolution and the Welsh language is discussed in ' *Turning to London* ' etc. (see Note 2 above).

[10]An excellent survey of the Communist Party's position on Welsh questions has been written by Brian Davies : ' Heading for the Rocks ?' in *Arcade* No. 31, 5 February 1982.

[11]*News Chronicle*, 29 January 1948.

[12]Letter from Ithel Davies, dated 2 February 1950, in the S. O. Davies Papers, Swansea (Ref : 1A, *i*).

[13]For a report of the Llandrindod convention, see *Welsh Nation*, September 1950.

[14]For the letters from Prothero to S.O. and to the Merthyr Trades Council & Labour Party, and for S.O.'s notes and letter in reply, see the S. O. Davies Papers, Swansea (Ref : 1A, *i* and 1A, *ii*) ; also see the Minutes of the Executive Committee of the Welsh Regional Council of Labour for 25 September 1950, 23 October 1950, 6 November 1950, 27 November 1950, 22 January 1951 and 26 February 1951.

[15]Bowen indicated support for a Welsh Parliament, although he did not play an active part in the Home Rule campaign.

[16]*Y Ddraig Goch*, March 1953.

[17]*Welsh Nation*, December 1953.

[18]Speech notes in the S. O. Davies Papers, Swansea (Ref : 1E).

[19]See *The Fed* (1980) by Hywel Francis and David Smith, pp. 417-9 and 426; only the Welsh Nationalist Party campaigned against the creation of a National Union of Mineworkers, publishing an appeal *To the Members of the South Wales Miners' Federation* (1944). It should also be noted that within the new N.U.M., the South Wales Area retained many of the powers and resources formerly wielded by the defunct S.W.M.F.

[20]*Western Mail*, 10 May 1954.

[21]Letter from Goronwy Roberts, dated 9 January 1955, in the S. O. Davies Papers, Swansea.

[22]Letter from S.O. to Goronwy Roberts and Cledwyn Hughes, dated 19 January 1955, in the S. O. Davies Papers, Swansea.

[23]Minutes of 'Parliament for Wales' Executive Committee, 19 March 1955.

[24]*Western Mail*, 3 March 1955.

[25]'Senedd i Gymru' first appeared in *Siwan a Cherddi Eraill* by Saunders Lewis (*circa* 1956); the translation is by Harri Webb.

[26]See 'Ymgyrch Senedd i Gymru' by Elwyn Roberts in *Cymru'n Deffro* (1981); Roberts was the chief full-time Organiser of the Parliament for Wales Campaign. Unfortunately, confusion might arise from the fact that his account of the campaign reproduces numerous extracts from this current chapter—without permission or acknowledgement!

[27]Two decades later, Cliff Prothero (now retired as Secretary of the Welsh Council of Labour) was appealing for tolerance to be shown to those rebel Labour M.P.s who opposed Labour's policy for a Welsh Assembly. He did so by rewriting history! Referring to the Labour supporters of the Parliament for Wales campaign in the 1950s such as S.O., he claimed: 'They were permitted to continue with their campaign because of the tolerance exercised within our movement. This did not harm the Labour Party, but may have strengthened it because of the tolerance and respect shown to comrades who were conscientious in expressing their views' (*Western Mail*, 25 May 1978). This fiction—that 'tolerance' was shown to the Labour Home Rulers of the 1950s—is repeated twice in Prothero's autobiography *Recount* (1982), pp. 68 and 116.

[28]*Y Saeth* No. 6 (Autumn 1977).

[29]S. O. Davies Papers, Swansea (Ref: 1A, *ii*).

Chapter Eight

PEACEMONGER

'Free World' orthodoxy has it that the Korean War broke out on 25 June 1950 when the army of Communist North Korea swarmed southwards across the 38th Parallel, the boundary separating the North from the capitalist South. The U.S.A. and its allies, including the British delegation, steered an emergency motion through the United Nations condemning the action as a breach of the U.N. Charter ; American and other U.N. troops were shipped to South Korea to prop up the dictatorial regime of President Syngman Rhee.

When the Labour Government tabled a motion in the Commons on July 5, congratulating itself on ' helping to resist the unprovoked aggression againt the Republic of Korea ', the Conservative Opposition concurred ; S.O., however, tabled an amendment :

> That this House expresses its deep concern at the alarming situation in Korea, and recognises the possibility of another world conflict arising therefrom. It therefore calls upon the Government to withdraw all British naval forces from the affected area ; to give, in accordance with the decisions of the Cairo Conference in 1943, and the Moscow Conference in 1945, full recognition to the claim of the Korean people for the unification and independence of their country ; to repudiate all British commitments which involve on our part any obligations to maintain the present division of the nations of the world into two powerful and dangerously poised hostile groups, and to declare in conformity with the Government's socialist principles our determination to give every encouragement to all peoples aspiring for freedom and self-government.

S.O.'s amendment created a minor sensation inside Westminster, angering the Government Whips in particular ; outside, he received scores of letters and telegrams of support. But the *Western Mail* editorial on July 5 dubbed him the ' Welsh Don Quixote ', deriding his stance as ' the sort of pacifism which has caused many wars, and would in this case strengthen all the forces of aggression in the Communist zone '. Later that day, S.O. began his contribution to the Commons debate by attacking the belligerent speech already delivered by Tory leader Winston Churchill. Standing firm amidst cries of ' Shame ! ', ' Disgraceful ! ' and ' Withdraw ! ', he declared: ' It is fairly obvious to all of us who have known and have paid close attention to his life that the right hon. Gentleman [Churchill] is never as happy as when all hell, in terms of war, has been let loose upon the people of this country '. Not illogically, S.O.'s interpretation of Churchill's position was that the U.S.A. should take advantage of its unique possession of nuclear weapons—and crush the Soviet Union immediately. S.O. also demanded to know why a Labour Government must trot so obediently behind the Americans in its foreign policy :

> Our Government—I say this with profound regret—have aligned themselves on the side of what is very well known to be the corrupt regime of Syngman Rhee and his immediate associates and advisers, with black marketeers, and with collaborators from the days of Japanese occupation and during the last war. This regime has a venal police force reminiscent of Hitler's Blackshirts. That is the crowd—not the people and not the nation—with which this Socialist Government are asked to identify themselves and to plunge this country into war, to sustain and maintain a rotten regime of that kind.

He went on to point out that the Korean people had fought for 40 years for their independence from Japan : such a nation would not tolerate its own dismemberment by an artificial 4½-year-old boundary such as the 38th Parallel. Thus the Koreans, he declared, ' have become impatient and angry, and are now in the process of uniting their country '. At this, Tory M.P. Stephen McAdden could control his heckling no longer and shouted : ' You ought to be locked up ! ' But S.O. was in his element ; next he riled Labour M.P.s with an attack on the U.S. Government and, in particular, on General MacArthur who had ' imposed his will on Japan and has destroyed the freedom which so many working-class people and working-class organisations have the right to enjoy '. (MacArthur boasted of his plans to turn Japan into a bastion of big business and anti-Communism.) This provoked further shouts of ' Absolute nonsense !' and ' Trash !', with one M.P. curiously inviting S.O. to ' take your Blackshirt off !'. As S.O. resumed his seat a few minutes later, Young Communists showered the chamber with ' Hands Off Korea !' leaflets.

The controversial amendment was seconded by Emrys Hughes, the Labour M.P. for South Ayreshire ; but the Speaker would not permit a division on it. The Government's motion was approved without a formal vote.

S.O. found a more receptive audience, though, in Merthyr's British Legion Club, packed to the rafters for a meeting on July 16. The local M.P. recited a catalogue of the atrocities perpetrated by Syngman Rhee's regime : the disappearance and probable execution of 162 Opposition members of the Seoul Parliament, following Rhee's crushing electoral defeat in May ; the incarceration of 14,000 political prisoners ; the summary hanging and shooting of 'suspected Communists' and the murder of 900 people by State Police during the 1948 elections. This was the system being defended so stoutly by the U.S.A., Britain and the Prime Minister of Australia, Sir Robert Menzies—'a fascist, who could hardly wait to rush military aid to the Yanks in Korea'. He also accused the Americans of violating the U.N. Charter by establishing strategic-military areas in Formosa, Japan, Iceland, Greenland and elsewhere. It was an extraordinary speech, even winning front-page status in the *Irish Times* !

S.O. also called for the House of Commons to continue sitting through the summer, to no avail ; during the parliamentary recess that August, British troops were transported to the Korean battlefields for the first time. Speaking in the Miners Hall on September 3, one of the first and few M.P.s to condemn the move was the Member for Merthyr Tydfil.

S.O. was always meticulous in providing the sources of his allegations. They were deployed to illustrate his front-page article in the Trotskyist-run *Socialist Outlook*,[1] under the banner headline 'Withdraw British Forces from Korea!' He quoted authoritative Western papers in denunciation of the Rhee dictatorship. Interestingly, too, besides painting contrasts which were infinitely favourable to the North, he justified the effort to unite Korea on nationalistic grounds:

> In Hiroshima between 80,000 and 100,000 people died from the effects of one atom bomb! At long last WAR has revealed its inherent, developing logic ; it is unrelieved, merciless destruction. Yet there are in this country some individuals, whose souls are so twisted and whose little minds are so bedevilled by fear and prejudice, that they would let loose on humanity these diabolical instruments of death.

> The immediate pretext for this awful threat is that of a nation fighting for freedom and independence. The Koreans were promised all this by the heads of the Allied Powers at Cairo in 1943 and it was endorsed by the same people at Moscow in 1945. But what *really* happened after the war was the division of the country by the travesty known as the 38th parallel. This ignored the fundamental fact that the Koreans were a nation and conscious of their nationhood. It also destroyed the possibility of a balanced economy being developed, for, to the north of the line the country was rich in minerals, while the south was, potentially, equally as rich in food production.
>
> The northern area was placed under the trusteeship of Russia and the south under that of the United States.[2]

Such views did not endear S.O. to *Tribune*, the paper loosely connected to the 'Keep Left' group of Bevanite M.P.s. Co-edited by Michael Foot, *Tribune* dredged up excuses for British colonialism in Africa, backed the anti-Communist campaigns in Malaya and Greece, applauded the banning of Communists from the British civil service and from trade union positions, supported N.A.T.O. as a counterweight to 'Soviet imperialism' and defended Tito's independent road to Socialism in Yugoslavia. By the outbreak of the Korean War, most of the 'Keep Left' M.P.s were toeing the American line : Woodrow Wyatt wondered in *Tribune* whether the atomic bomb should not be dropped on the North as a 'short-cut to peace' ; Michael Foot declared that G.I.'s were dying to uphold Labour Party principles ; those who, like S.O., argued that the American intervention had been illegal were branded as 'legalistic appeasers'.[3]

Back in the Commons, on September 13 S.O. and Will Cove tabled an amendment attacking the Government's decisions to increase arms spending and—under threat of resignation from General Montgomery and his Army Council—to extend military service to 2 years. Attlee proposed these measures in response to the 'naked aggression' inflicted upon South Korea, and they would cost a total of £3,600 million. S.O. was one of the few who challenged the assumptions underlying such a massive dip into the public purse. Heretically, he questioned the assertion that the North had instigated hostilities by invading the South. Why, he wondered, had no precise location ever been given for the North's crossing of the 38th Parallel ? What about Syngman Rhee's broadcast on

May 6, when he had voiced his eagerness to trample on the border and to incorporate North Korea? How could American press reports on June 29 have located South Korean forces in Haeju, five miles inside the North, when a full-scale Northern invasion was supposed to be sweeping all before it deep into South Korea ? (When these same allegations appeared in the *Daily Worker* the Attorney-General, Sir Hartley Shawcross, told the Cabinet that they constituted the capital offence of treason in 'giving aid to the King's enemies'—although neither he nor the Cabinet favoured prosecution).[4] Next in his speech S.O. quoted American newspapers to highlight the corruption and iniquity rife in South Korean society. Above all, he implored his Labour associates to beware the U.S. armaments lobby, the weapon manufacturers—'Patriotism Ltd.'—who saw in the Korean conflict a way of boosting profits and averting an economic recession :

> Surely the Prime Minister has not forgotten all the tricks of the imperialists. War was one of their tricks, and none of my hon. Friends within the Socialist movement should pretend to forget it for a single moment. When organised workers were becoming restive and militant, war was one of the happy diversions the ruling class used, as it is doing in the United States today.
>
> The Government know that there can be no equality of sacrifice among people in a war as long as a possessing class exists. What equality of sacrifice is there where the only bread-winner of ageing parents is conscripted for two years for this wretched purpose for which so much humbug and unction has been shown in this House ? No pay increases can compensate any parent for the loss of a son or any young wife for the loss of a husband, particularly in a war which has nothing to commend or justify it. Rather it is the most contemptible military escapade in the history of war ; the increase in Service pay will be construed by many parents as the most wicked of bribes.
>
> I have sons of my own, and my own personal resentment and disgust at this form of buying, and possibly disposing of, their young lives will be shared by most parents in this country.

S.O. scoffed at those who raised the Communist bogey in Britain : such a ploy was 'perfectly ridiculous' in the wake of the Communist Party's 'puny' performance at the last General Election. Brushing aside the barracking of Labour M.P.s Roy Jenkins, Bob Mellish and others, he insisted that Korea's Communism was Korea's own internal affair ; resolute Socialism at home had nothing to fear from Communism abroad. The amendment, proposed by S.O. to the Prime Minister's own motion, was not allowed to go to a vote by the Speaker.

These two parliamentary speeches, in July and September 1950, grossly unpopular at Westminster, propelled S. O. Davies to prominence in British political life. Altogether he received more than a thousand letters, postcards and telegrams of support : Labour Party members, Trades Councils, miners lodges, religious pacifists, Communists, ex-servicemen urged him to 'Fight, Mr. Davies, in heaven's name fight in the House to prevent the utter degradation and annihilation of us and our country in an atomic holocaust' . . .'Thank God for at least one gentleman among the rats in Parliament'. Mothers in different areas of London organised petitions and letters of support for S.O. ; fathers wrote to him of their fears of another war and its consequences for their children : 'My wife and I are proud of you—the one Member of Parliament who is not bamboozled by propaganda and can bring a clear vision to bear on this Korean business'. Former Communist M.P. Willie Gallacher congratulated S.O. : 'At such a time as this when the Labour Movement and the country are being led to disaster at the command of the ruthless multi-millionaires of America, it is good to know that even one or two are still prepared to stand by Socialist principles, and to refuse to be stampeded or coerced into participation in the betrayal of the cause for which so many of us have given a life-time of service'. One-time leader of the National Unemployed Workers Committee Movement, Nat Watkins, praised S.O. for his stand for 'right and truth', adding: 'In reminiscing, I have recollections of a similar character during M.F.G.B. conferences when the forces of reaction were challenged by the few progressives, and in which you invariably played a leading part'. But perhaps the message treasured most by S.O. was that from his old friend and comrade T. E. Nicholas, who wrote :

Annwyl S.O.,

Llongyfarchiadau i chwi ac Emrys. Dim ond eich dau ar y cychwyn. 'Llef UN yn llefain', ond fe ddaw'r lleill. Y mae eich enw wedi mynd i wefusau'r werin bobl mewn noswaith, a disgwylir pethau mawr oddi wrthych yn y frwydr hon. Dinistrir y Blaid Lafur gan Attlee fel y gwnaethpwyd gan MacDonald, yr ychydig weddill fydd yn cyfrif. Carwn i chwi ac Emrys sylweddoli fod cefnogaeth unol y werin gennych yn hyn o beth. Nid oes gwasg heddiw i ddweud gair, gwasg Cymru yn ail-adrodd celwyddau'r wasg Seisnig. Rhoddwyd taw llwyr arnom ni sydd yn heddychwyr erioed ; ac yr wyf yn rhy hen i fynd drwy'r wlad i siarad ; nid oes ond aros yn dawel a darllen celwyddau'r wasg a gwrando ar gelwyddau'r radio, a disgwyl ambell air gennych chwi a'ch bath yn erbyn y trychineb mawr.

Dinistrio'r U.N.O. yw un amcan, fel y gwnaethpwyd yn helynt Sbaen ac Abyssinia, a dinistrio gwaith Sosialaeth yn Korea er dangos i'r byd fod Sosialaeth yn fethiant.

' Ond na bai fy mhen yn ddyfroedd a'm llygaid yn ffynhonnau dagrau ', dros y trueiniaid bach yn eu gwlad. Daliwch ati, chwi biau'r dyfodol, ac nid rhaid i chwi ofni am eich sedd fel llawer ohonynt.

Cofion at Seph.

Yn gywir, T. E. Nicholas

Dear S.O.,

Congratulations to you and Emrys. The two of you stand alone at the start. ' A lone voice crying . . .', but the others will come. Your name has sprung to the lips of the common people in a single evening, and great things are expected of you in this battle. Attlee is destroying the Labour Party just as MacDonald did, but it is those who remain that will count. I want you and Emrys to realise that you have the unanimous support of the working-class in all this. There is no press today where one can say anything ; the Welsh press merely repeat the lies of the English press. We who are pacifists have always been gagged ; and I am too old to travel the country and speak ; there is nothing for it but to stay quiet, read the lies in the press and listen to the lies on the radio, waiting for the occasional word from you and your kind against the holocaust.

Their objectives are to destroy the United Nations Organisation, as was done in the troubles over Spain and Abyssinia, and to destroy Socialism's achievements in Korea in order to show the world that Socialism is a failure.

' Oh that my head were not swimming and my eyes not welling with tears ', for those poor souls in their small country. Keep at it, you will inherit the future, and you don't have to worry about keeping your seat like so many of the others have to.

My regards to Seph.

Yours Truly, T. E. Nicholas

Spurred on and strengthened by this deluge of support, S.O. took his campaign wherever he could find a platform. In *Labour Monthly* that same September, he ventilated his deepest fears in an article entitled ' Labour and War '. He reminded readers of the tragedy of the First World War, when most of Europe's socialists in the Second International reneged on their pledge not to participate in Capitalism's bloody feuds—and of how the jingos broke Keir Hardie's heart. He warned that ' Yankee millionaires today own nearly a third of the capitalist assets in the south of Korea '. S.O. also dealt with the claims and counter-claims about the U.N. Charter, citing the West's transgressions : in matters of war, the five specified great powers (Britain, China, France, the U.S.A., and the Soviet Union) had to agree for a decision to be valid—yet the United States and its ' satellites ' had vetoed attempts by the (Communist) People's Republic of China to take its seat on the U.N. Security Council ; the U.S.S.R. had withdrawn from the U.N. in protest at the veto ; in breach of the Charter, North Korea had not been invited to appear before the Security Council prior to U.S. military intervention ; and the Americans had ignored the Charter by establishing a military base in Formosa (Taiwan), the island refuge of China's defeated right-wing Nationalists. The article finished with this stirring appeal :

> If we march in line with our forefathers who built up the movement in the fight against capitalist wars, we shall be marching in the right direction.
>
> But when our Movement abandons that fight ; when we allow ourselves to be drawn to support, as we apparently do today, the rabid, blatant imperialism of America ; when, that is to say, we give up our historic task and align ourselves alongside our long-recognised class enemy, we betray everything dear to all socialists, the countless acts of sacrifice, the devoted selfless work of millions, that form the very matrix of our Movement. We are, in fact, moving along the road to its complete extinction.

The turn of events in Korea lent credibility to S.O.'s cataclysmic tone : General MacArthur was now pursuing the North Koreans back across the 38th Parallel, plunging his army deeper northwards towards the Chinese border. He proclaimed a crusade to purge south-east Asia (including China) of Communism, collaborating openly with Chiang Kai-Shek. It was only a matter of time before the Chinese Red Army intervened—a prospect which MacArthur publicly relished.

Meanwhile S.O. was running into a storm of his own . . . the Welsh Regional Council of Labour had decided to contact the Party's National Executive and his constituency party about his stance on Korea, Peace and a Parliament for Wales. In a letter to the Merthyr Labour Party on 10 October 1950, Cliff Prothero indicted S.O. for using the columns of the *Daily Worker* to support the all-Britain Peace Petition and to urge Labour Party conference delegates to break with U.S. foreign policy. At the Merthyr Trades and Labour Council on October 25, S.O. proudly pleaded guilty to these heinous crimes. Should Britain turn its back on American imperialism ? Emphatically, Yes ! It was indeed true that he had addressed 30 meetings in support of the Peace Petition—and was glad to have done so ' for a thousand reasons ' ; he could not recall sharing a platform with a Communist, as Prothero alleged, but he had stood next to many a Liberal and even the odd Tory.

Undaunted by the Regional Council's continuing investigations into his ' attitude ', S.O. compounded his sins by speaking in the Empress Hall, London, on November 12 at a rally organised by the British-Soviet Friendship Society. While the Labour N.E.C. was discussing S.O.'s delinquency, deciding eventually to refer his constant criticism of the Government's foreign policy to a sub-committee, S.O. despatched solidarity greetings to the World Peace Congress in Poland :

> In sending you my best wishes may I also, on behalf of every decent man and woman in this country, express my deep disgust and resentment at the action taken by certain people in sabotaging your original efforts to hold your gathering in Britain.
>
> Even at this early stage, ample evidence has come my way to prove that the action taken by the saboteurs of the conference and of peace is now beginning to recoil upon them.

This statement was loudly cheered by more than 2,000 delegates when read out in Warsaw on November 17. They admired S.O.'s courageous attack on the Labour Government's opposition to the intended Peace Congress in Sheffield ; instead of banning the conference outright, the Cabinet had agreed on a strategy of refusing visas to incoming delegates.[5]

One prominent member of the World Peace Council was Sephora Davies, S.O.'s wife. A member of the Labour Party for decades rather than years, she also played a leading part in the West Wales Peace Committee and was particularly active collecting signatures for the Stockholm World Peace Petition. In October and November 1950 Sephora spent three weeks visiting the Soviet Union with the British-Soviet Friendship Society ; her visits to Russian schools, hospitals, rest homes, theatres and libraries—as well as to the Kremlin—convinced her that the U.S.S.R. was making great strides towards justice and Socialism. Upon her return home she told meetings in Cardiff, Neath and elsewhere of the Soviet efforts to bring art and culture to the people, and countered allegations of anti-religious persecution in Russia with the details of her own visit to a Baptist church in Moscow which ' had 4,000 members and the service was packed '. Mrs Davies refused to be bullied by newspaper allegations that she had been a dupe of the Reds : no cries of ' Communist-inspired ' would compel her to tell lies about the Soviet Union, she declared. She was not a Communist, having been ' nurtured on the principles of Keir Hardie-socialism '. Still, the U.S. Government later refused her and other members of the World Peace Council an entry visa to visit the President of the U.N. Security Council, Jacob Malik of the Soviet Union.

S.O. met Sephora on her return from the Soviet Union (via Czechoslovakia) on November 19 at Northolt Airport. They drove straight to Trafalgar Square where she addressed a 1,000-strong rally called by the British Peace Council, telling of her pride in her husband's ' magnificent stand for Peace and Disarmament '. But it was a stand that had begun to exact a toll in more ways than one : S.O. had been ordered by his doctor to ' take it easy ' for a month. In the middle of this convalescence he received a summons to attend Labour's N.E.C. on November 22. Press speculation was rife about the M.P.'s imminent expulsion, although the *Western Mail*'s Westminster correspondent reported that the parliamentary press lobby believed such a step ' would bring about an acute position in the party '.[6] On November 19, his friend Claude Stanfield, President of the Life Assurance Workers Union, wrote to assure S.O. of the solid support he could always count upon in the Merthyr constituency party ; Stanfield also urged his old friend to compromise—even to apologise—if that was necessary for him to retain membership of the Labour Party. The letter concluded :

' I know you appreciate the seriousness of your position, which has been accelerated by many hidden hands '.

The National Executive contented itself with issuing a severe warning to S.O. about his future conduct ; in the Commons, the parliamentary liaison committee withdrew the Labour Whip from him. S.O. took not the slightest heed of these disciplinary pinpricks. If anything, he was emboldened by the N.E.C.'s loss of nerve—and the Whip had never been much more than a formality in any case. His speaking engagements with such proscribed bodies as the Student Labour Federation and the British-China Friendship Society continued as before. At the showdown with a delegation from the Regional Council of Labour on 12 February 1951 in front of the Merthyr Trades and Labour Council, he conceded not an inch of his stance on Korea, Peace and Welsh Home Rule ; even before the dust had settled, he accepted an invitation to address an all-Wales Peace Conference the following Saturday, February 17. S.O. and *Plaid Cymru* leading light the Rev. R. Tudur Jones were to be the main speakers, with Welsh Republican Ithel Davies in the Chair. Two weeks previously, the Welsh Regional Council of Labour had outlawed the assembly in a circular letter :

> The Welsh Regional Executive Committee find that about half the sponsors are Communists.
>
> We in the Labour Party refuse to become associated with this so-called ' Peace Conference', which is Communist-inspired and is nothing more than Communist Party propaganda. We have decided, therefore, in consultation with the national executive committee, to declare this conference to be proscribed, and under these circumstances support to or attendance at this conference will not be compatible with membership of the Labour Party.

In response S.O. brushed aside the Regional Council as a mere cipher of the National Executive, telling news reporters : ' Transport House from remote London has interfered with the right of any Welshmen who desire to attend this conference. I shall regret it profoundly because Transport House has never shown much understanding of the problems peculiar in Wales and of the reactions of Welsh people to those problems '. As it turned out, S.O. failed to reach the conference in time. An editorial in the *Western Mail* explained the circumstances—in terms which appealed to S.O.'s sense of humour, regardless of the mendacity behind the Biblical barbs :

SAVED BY HIS CAR

> The sad news of the breakdown of the car in which MR S. O. DAVIES M.P. was speeding to the Communist-inspired peace conference at Cardiff reminds us of the precedent of Balaam and his ass. In both cases the hand of Providence was clearly seen, and though the ass had the advantage of the car in that it could speak to warn Balaam of his impending folly, the breakdown saved MR DAVIES from a similar fate. There must have been a god in the machine. Had he reached the meeting, at which he was expected to be one of the chief speakers, he would have defied the official warning of the Socialist Party that association with the Communist peace petition is 'incompatible with membership of the party', and not for the first time he would be in very hot water. He was saved in the nick of time from being cut down by the angel of the Lord personified by MR MORGAN PHILLIPS. We await with renewed interest MR DAVIES's next performance as a political strip-tease artiste.[7]

Days later S.O. received a massive welcome at a Korean War rally in the Holborn Hall, London. Some 400 delegates and visitors had assembled under the aegis of the Socialist Fellowship, a Labour Party grouping which embraced left-wing M.P.s and local branches of Labour and trade union activists. S.O. declined membership of the Fellowship from its inception in the summer of 1949, just as he maintained independence from all other Labour Party factions. Although he agreed with its approach to many domestic and international issues, divergence occurred over, for instance, the campaign for Peace : Socialist Fellowship spurned the Peace Movement because of the latter's emphasis on Peace—rather than Socialism—as the alternative to War. For S.O. this was an unrealistic attitude. Peace was the immediate and practical alternative to War, Socialism was the only permanent safeguard against War ; Peace could exist periodically without Socialism, but Socialism could not be built in the middle of a nuclear holocaust. So he was prepared to campaign for Peace alongside non-Socialists, without forfeiting his right to argue for the permanent antidote to imperialist wars—Socialism.[8]

With S. O. Davies as the main guest speaker, the Holborn rally adopted a clear and unambiguous perspective : resolutions demanded the immediate withdrawal of British forces from Korea, an end to all military alliances with capitalist countries, and the convening of a special Labour Party conference to formulate an anti-war and Socialist policy. The delegates also dedicated themselves to 'securing the complete and utter defeat of capitalism and the Tory Party as our contribution to the building of a socialist world'. Within two months, in April 1951, the Socialist Fellowship was proscribed by the Labour N.E.C. and went into 'voluntary' liquidation.

Yet this event, like so many before it, was overshadowed by the ups and downs of one man on the Labour benches . . . Aneurin Bevan. Amidst a welter of publicity, Bevan resigned as Minister of Labour on April 21 ; by then, it had become clear that the Cabinet could not be dissuaded from introducing charges for National Health Service dentures and spectacles. In vain Bevan had argued that the £13 million thus saved would be better taken from the Defence budget, thereby keeping intact the principle of a free N.H.S. Ironically, he had himself defended the Government's lavish rearmament programme in the Commons two months previously, when bound—not too uncomfortably on this occasion—by the Cabinet doctrine of 'collective responsibility'. But by his resignation speech of April 23, Bevan was sure that spending £4,700 million (14% of Britain's National Income) on armaments over the next 3 years could not be achieved without 'irreparable damage to the economy of Great Britain and the world'. Bevan was also reacting against American pressure to rearm West Germany (conceded in principle by Ernie Bevin in September 1950), to brand China as the 'aggressor' in Korea (pushed through the U.N. in January 1951) following the Red Army's decision to confront the oncoming U.S.-U.N. forces, and for Britain to boost its military budget to £2,000 million a year. Evaluating this new mood, Michael Foot attributed to Bevan :

> . . . the authentic voice of an independent British foreign policy suited to the time : one which appreciated the Soviet challenge but wished to see it defined in much more sophisticated terms than the anti-Communist crusaders employed ; one which sought to sustain the Anglo-American alliance while abating its dangerous crudities and dogmatisms.[9]

How S.O. would have disputed this retrospective assessment! Firstly, the so-called 'Soviet challenge' was largely a propaganda fiction, conjured up to stigmatise every struggle for social justice or national liberation. Secondly, the Anglo-American alliance was, in reality, a pro-capitalist 'Jonah-Whale' alliance. Thirdly, Bevan had merely doubted the 'physical attainability' of the Government's rearmament programme, fearful of its consequences in other areas of public expenditure: he did not question the fundamental Cold War assumptions which lay behind it. In S.O.'s opinion, Bevan and his disciples were still in the pro-American and anti-Soviet camp, albeit as 'doves' now instead of 'hawks'. This was partly out of conviction, but partly for reasons of expediency: the U.S.A. had granted Britain £500 million to ease the balance of payments crisis—conditional upon British rearmament.

The term 'Bevanites' gained currency after Nye's resignation, but S.O. was never one of them. Although he found himself increasingly in their company in the Commons voting lobbies, and was on friendly terms with many Bevanites including Bevan, he would sometimes speak rather dismissively of the group.

The eventful April of 1951 also brought a fresh attempt to gag S.O., this time from Labour Party national agent Ron Windle. Prompted by the Welsh Regional Council, Windle insisted that henceforth the M.P.'s speaking invitations be vetted at Transport House. S.O. gave his customary attention to such demands i.e. none whatsoever. In May he wrote of the oppressive Labour Party regime in a letter to a correspondent, referring specifically to the recent excommunication of the Manchester University Socialist Society:

> I cannot regard the long list of proscriptions from the Labour Party with the least comfort . . . I would never have expelled these young people from the Movement. My faith in socialism is such that I have nothing to fear from the fleeting aberrations of any person. It is only when we discard that faith that we have every reason to fear, and it is that fear that will destroy our movement and expulsions become inevitable.

Neither the warnings, the bans nor advancing age—all 67 years of it—could subdue S.O.'s sallies against American imperialism and the preparations for war. In June 1951, writing on 'Labour and Disarmament' in *Labour Monthly*, he traced the escalation in Britain's military expenditure : £24 million a year in the 1870s ; on the eve of the Boer War it had reached £40 million ; by 1913 it was £86 million ; in 1938 it had been £263 million—and in January 1951 Attlee unveiled his scheme to spend an average £1,560 million annually over the next three years. S.O. assailed the ' dollar war-mongers ' and warned of the social and economic consequences of the ' disastrous alignment with American imperialism '. He also admonished those who strove to suppress genuine divisions of opinion within the Labour Party, arguing that :

> Signs of a fight over policy within the Labour Party are signs of health. Only by controversy within its own ranks as to what is the best policy will the best policy ever emerge. Unity in the working-class is essential. But it must be a real unity, not a surface unity. It must be unity in the fight for a true socialist policy. And in my opinion the only consistently socialist policy is the fight for peace and for disarmament, and never to forget our traditional enemies—capitalism and imperialism.

Predictably, the *Western Mail*'s editorial writer pounced upon the hon. Member for Merthyr's latest ' political indiscretion ', characterising S.O. on June 16 as one of those in the Labour Party ' who are so far over to the Left that they have practically dropped off the end of the platform '.

S.O. was one of only half-a-dozen M.P.s who regularly swam against the tide. Time after time he raised his voice above the taunts and jeers of Tory and Labour M.P.s. Only on some occasions could a Bevanite chorus be heard in the background as, with the courage of their convictions, S.O. protested against such acts as the banning of Professor Joliot-Curie from Britain. One of the world's top physicists, Joliot-Curie was refused an entry visa to address a conference in his capacity as President of the World Peace Council (his ' principal crime ' remarked S.O.). M.P.s were told on July 12 of how Joliot-Curie had been decorated for his leadership of the French Resistance in war-time, praised by the French authorities as a great French patriot, and then, in S.O.'s words :

> In April 1950, after a violent Press campaign, which was of course started in America, poor France—now a secondary strategic base in the American war plans and little more than a financial colony of Wall Street—had to take up this hysterical

> cry against this great man, and he was dismissed from his post as Commissioner for Atomic Energy. I refer to France as a secondary strategic base because, as we all know, we are the principal base. For have we not 20 American air squadrons in this country, with its 50 million men, women and children presumably waiting, thanks to the Government's policy, for the time when they are to be blown to bits . . . destroyed by those who have allowed this country to become the strategic base of the most abominably Imperialist country on earth—that is, America . . .

After being warned by the Deputy Speaker that the U.S.A. was a 'friendly country' and must not be referred to in such hostile terms, S.O. turned his fire on the domestic villain of the peace, Home Secretary Chuter Ede. Here was the man, S.O. reminded the House, who had wrecked the World Peace Congress scheduled for Sheffield, shutting the door to world-famous historians, poets, doctors, church leaders and war-time resistance fighters . . .

> He is possessed by what seems to me to be a paranoiac tendency to condemn every effort to establish good and friendly relations with other peoples, and every possible contribution to avoid the worst of all possible tragedies, namely a third world war.

As in so many debates, S.O. received the support of Emrys Hughes who—having been refused a visa to enter the Soviet Union—expounded his empathy with Joliot-Curie as a fellow *persona non grata*. Emrys deplored England's abandonment of the libertarian tradition which, in the past, had given refuge to Marx, Trotsky and Lenin.

Joliot-Curie's exclusion turned out to be the last in what had been a long series of small-minded acts by a Government never committed to an independent and Socialist foreign policy. Even as Attlee's administration left office in October 1951, it was capitulating to its American masters over the terms of the Japanese Peace Treaty: that settlement subsequently went through the English Parliament without opposition (except from S.O. who called it a 'legalised conspiracy . . . unclean in every line and sentence') and was bull-dozed through the United Nations against the wishes of India and China. Labour had been struggling for 20 months with a slender 6-seat majority in the Commons—although this was probably less debilitating than the absence of purpose and vision on the Government's Front Bench. With foreign and defence policy stamping such an imprint on political, economic and social considerations at home, the breakdown of concensus on military expenditure had dealt a mortal blow to the Government's underlying unity.

Labour tasted defeat on 25 October 1951 with a bitterness intensified by Britain's electoral arrangements : despite winning 14 million votes—nearly 2½ million more than in 1945 and half a million more than the Tories on this current occasion—Labour secured only 295 seats against the Conservatives' 321. S.O. obtained 80% of the votes cast in Merthyr Tydfil :

S. O. DAVIES (Labour)	28,841
J. F. LYNAM (Conservative)	7,405

S.O. composed a *post-mortem* on the election in *Labour Monthly* ; in the article ' Labour's New Fight ' he identified the rocks of Labour's ship-wreck as inflation, deficits, higher prices and wage freezes—all of them bedded in the Government's £4,700 million rearmament drive. His well-developed political antennae picked up these signals during the electioneering :

> The campaign within the Labour movement lacked its traditional *élan* and enthusiasm ; lacked a distinctive and irreconcilable contrast, at this particular moment in our history, with immediate Tory policy. As indeed the people feared war. Their daily worries about the increasing cost of living and conscription tearing their sons away from their homes, some of whom were the principal breadwinners, are all related to rearmament, and that to our foreign policy. Let it not be forgotten this last general election was fought in an atmosphere of war preparations and threatened war.
>
> The Tory Party were not only in agreement with our foreign policy : in fact, they proudly claimed to have been the authors of it and that they had succeeded in forcing its adoption on the Labour government. Many Labour candidates, I know, agree with me when I say that had Labour gone to the country with a Socialist foreign policy, that is, a policy for peace, the Tories would have suffered a defeat more severely than that of 1945.

After an unprecedented six years in power, Labour had had a Socialist Britain within its reach—only to be ' buffeted and browbeaten into the counter-revolutionary movement, led by the last remaining imperialist power within whose orbit are the relics of old imperialist powers, petty dictatorships and petty tyrannies '. Labour mustnow rise from the ashes, beginning with a reconvened Scarborough conference to examine the past and aim for the future. S.O. concluded with the stirring rhetoric that suggests the article, like others in the past, was also the transcript of a speech delivered in such a place as the local miners hall :

> Our first call will be to the workers of the world acclaiming our solidarity with them ; to revive our traditional hatred of imperialism with its tyranny and oppression ; to declare our determination to expose and oppose the machinations of all warmongers ; to extricate Britain from the threat of counter-revolutionary forces, and to identify the British Labour movement with the progressive forces of the world. This calls for a policy of peace, the ending of rearmament, the clearing from British soil of all alien armed forces, the reorientating of British foreign policy towards those populous parts of the world who are struggling to build a civilisation unrestricted by financial oligarchies ever seeking ' spheres of influence ', cheap raw materials, military bases, and ever thwarting the legitimate aspirations of oppressed peoples by armed forces and threats of war.[10]

Trade union bosses Arthur Deakin (T.G.W.U.), Will Lawther (N.U.M.) and Tom Williamson (G.M.W.U.) adopted a somewhat different perspective : they blamed the ' extreme ', ' disloyal ' and ' fractious ' Left for Labour's election defeat—and thus conspired to squeeze Bevan and his confederates out of the Labour Party.

One of the first left-wingers to feel the wrath of the Right was Sephora Davies. On December 19 the Merthyr Trades and Labour Council expelled her from the Labour Party, on the instructions of the National Executive in London. According to local secretary Stan Beynon, she had breached the Party's constitution. He declined to comment further ; it was no secret that the local party organisation did not take the step voluntarily, but had acted under the threat of dissolution from Transport House. No doubt Seph.'s activities with the Peace movement and the proscribed British-Soviet Friendship Society had incurred the displeasure of Labour H.Q.—but many people also interpreted her expulsion as a final warning shot across her husband's bows.

How effective it would be in taming S.O. was shown ten weeks later, on 5 March 1952, when he joined the Bevanites in a 57-strong rebellion on the Defence White Paper. They voted against the Tory Government's rearmament budget in defiance of the Labour Whip's demand for an abstention. The Parliamentary Labour Party's ludicrous line was to support Churchill's military spending plans, whilst declaring no faith in his Cabinet's ability to carry them out ! This contortion had been necessitated by the uncomfortable fact that the Tories were merely proposing expenditure levels projected by their Labour predecessors. The refusal of 57 Labour M.P.s to bend over backwards to avoid embarrassing the Attlee regime nearly resulted in the Party's biggest split since 1931 : Attlee, Deakin and other leading figures demanded loyalty oaths and even expulsions, but they were headed off by influential middle-of-the-road M.P.s who advocated a general reimposition of Standing Orders discipline instead.

Another aspect of military matters to come to the fore in 1952 was Civil Defence. As usual, those who contemplated another world war with such serenity were also the keenest to advocate illusory systems of 'public protection' against nuclear attack. When a Tory M.P. ventilated the issue in the Commons on July 18, S.O. and Emrys Hughes tried to introduce an amendment which warned that 'the establishment of American bomber bases in Britain adds greatly to the dangers of the civilian population'; they wanted the bases to be shut down, and called upon the British Government to 'initiate and support disarmament proposals which will make substantial expenditure on inadequate civil defence measures unnecessary'. Although the Speaker ruled this addendum out of order, that did not prevent S.O. from speaking to the theme in his contribution. He asserted that the concentration on civil defence rather than on disarmament or peace was defeatist : M.P.s seemed to exude a sense of 'helpelessness and hoplessness' in the face of impending disaster. He quoted studies by the Institute of Civil Defence to illustrate the magnitude of damage which Britain would sustain in a nuclear attack : 'we know of nothing that can render relatively harmless either the atom bomb or the napalm bomb', he pointed out, nor had work yet started on counteracting bacteriological agents. In this light, civil defence was a cruel illusion. S.O. finished with an appeal to eject the American nuclear bombers from Britain :

> I take no pride in the fact that this island is referred to by other people as an aircraft carrier—and an unsinkable one at that. We shall be sunk. I take no pride, nor can our people or any self-respecting Government, in the fact that we have been reduced merely to the principal strategic base of a foreign Power who will decide their strategy 3,000-4,000 miles away from this island. We shall have no voice in defending ourselves. It is no use talking about the wretched futile methods of Civil Defence when others will decide the destruction *en masse* in which we shall be involved in the next war.

The back-cloth to such divisions and differences over international and military affairs remained the Korean War. Since defeating Asian-Arab proposals for peace talks in January 1951, and arm-twisting its allies and dependants in the U.N. to brand China as the 'aggressor', the U.S.A. had been carrying out its 'Operation Killer' in Korea. Where U.S.-U.N. forces retreated before Chinese Communist offensives, they implemented a 'scorched earth' policy; massive slaughter ensued as the Americans strove to rebuff the Chinese Red Army's 'human wave' assaults. In August 1951 the U.S. broke off further negotiations. The front-line steadied just above the 38th Parallel, as the U.S.-U.N. summer and autumn offensives became bogged down ; then, in October, the U.S. Air Force lost its superiority in the skies as 'Mig' fighters flew in on the Communist side. The struggle had reached dead-lock by the end of the year, as the number of corpses piled up towards the 3 million mark. The horror and desolation that had descended on Korea was captured in these remarks of General Emmet O'Donnell, head of the U.S. Bomber Command in the Far East :

> I would say that the entire, almost the entire Korean peninsula is just a terrible mess. Everything is destroyed. There is nothing standing worthy of the name . . . Just before the Chinese came in we were grounded. There were no more targets in Korea.[11]

Even in the South, American forces had laid waste to villages, fields and forests on an enormous scale in their efforts to drive the North Koreans back and flush out Southern collaborators. The United States used new chemical weapons and, for the first time, deployed napalm—jellied petroleum which clings to the body and burns its victims alive.

Arguments raged as to the 'morality' or 'inhumanity' of such techniques, only to be subsumed from February 1952 onwards in one of the 20th Century's greatest controversies. Beginning on the 11th day of that month, 50 people died of plague in Bal Nam Ri, North Korea : it was the first outbreak of plague anywhere in Korea for more than four hundred years. Furthermore, the attack happened a full three months ' out of season ' in that part of the world. A few weeks later, a dose of cholera killed 9 people in Puk Myen Region in the North ; before this, North Korea had been free of cholera since the organisation of a medical service four years ago. Similar epidemics were also reported in Manchuria (north-east China), in areas adjacent to North Korea.

At the outset, the Chinese attributed their epidemics to climatic and sanitary conditions. But at Bal Nam Ri, following tests, the carriers of the plague were identified not as rat fleas—but as human fleas infected with *Pasteurella pestis* bacteria : further investigations uncovered sightings of unusual insect-concentrations around Bal Nam Ri shortly before the first casualties occurred. Moreover, the flies, spiders and bugs under examination were then found to be types not indigenous to Korea at all. Strange swarms of these foreign insects were found, out of season and sometimes in the vicinity of American propaganda leaflets and empty containers. On checking, it was found that the epidemics had broken out at times and places in the flight-paths of U.S. combat planes.

On 22 February 1952 the North Korean Minister of Foreign Affairs accused American aircraft of unleashing a bacteriological war against his people, and specified dates, places and insect carriers. Two days later the Peking Government endorsed the allegations. Within days the charges were vehemently denied by the U.S. Government and its military authorities in South-East Asia : initially, they disputed the existence of any epidemics at all ; then they acknowledged their authenticity—but claimed the insects caught by the Chinese and North Koreans were incapable of carrying the pathogenic bacteria concerned; finally, after conceding that the epidemics had indeed been spread by infected insects, the U.S. Military Command blamed the Communist authorities' ' own inadequacies in coping with seasonal epidemics '. On April 3 the Americans dismissed Chinese photographs of alleged ' germ warfare containers ' as a ' childish forgery '—the canisters were, in fact, leaflet-bombs and as such would be useless for the carriage and delivery of germs. Two days later, General Bullene told a U.S. House of Representatives sub-committee : ' The means of delivering germs to enemy territory are simple and involve equipment of a type with which we are now already well stocked—such as containers used currently for dropping propaganda leaflets '. True to form, the Western press hastened to echo U.S. protestations of innocence; when the *Western Mail* published a major editorial on April 1 under the title ' War of Lies ', in which it deplored ' the mendacity of the Communist campaign against the United Nations ', the paper's favourite parliamentary bogeyman replied at length. S.O. referred to the germ warfare laboratories and pilot plants at Fort Detrick, Maryland U.S.A., employing 3,900 people, and continued :

> *Collier's Magazine*, June 1946, quotes General Waitt, chief of the U.S. Chemical Warfare Service as saying of the bacteriological weapon : ' I believe it to be a practical form of warfare which has great potentialities . . . I am entirely out of sympathy with the talk about the humanity or inhumanity of a weapon '.
>
> The Chairman of the United States Naval Appropriations Sub-Committee, Mr Harry Shephard, at the same time boasted that the U.S. Government was ' in an enviable position ' by its progress in germ weapons, and that the Navy's biological warfare research at the University of California had concentrated on how to spread a disease ' which was hundreds of years old, and one of the greatest killers '.

S.O.'s case, substantiated by excerpts from official U.S. reports and statements, was that the Americans had been ready and willing to utilise biological weapons by the outbreak of the Korean War. Indeed, the United States and Japan were the only major powers not to ratify the 1925 Geneva Protocol, which specifically prohibited the use in war of gases and bacteriological agents (on 8 April 1947 President Truman had withdrawn the Protocol from consideration by the U.S. Senate). S.O. accused the Americans of historically ignoring international standards of decency, from their refusal to endorse the 1899 Hague Convention outlawing dum-dum (expanding) bullets, to the dropping of atomic bombs on Japan and, now, the deployment of germ warfare against the Koreans.

In March 1952 a special commission of the International Association of Democratic Lawyers claimed to have examined and found abundant evidence of American violation of international conventions, including the use of bacteriological weapons. S.O. accused the *Western Mail* of ' discreetly ignoring ' these findings : their report could not be simply dismissed by shrieking ' Communist lies '—especially when only one member of the eight-man commission was a Communist. He studied the I.A.D.L.'s two reports and concluded that ' beyond any shadow of doubt the United States has added another grisly crime to the many it has previously committed against international law and decency. It fits in with American practice in war '.[12]

Two Chinese reports released in April 1952 finely embroidered the main charges against the U.S.A. But by far the most impressive indictment was published on August 31 of that year by an International Scientific Commission, appointed by the World Peace Council. The six scientists responsible could boast impeccable professional credentials from their home countries of Sweden, France, England, Italy, Brazil and the U.S.S.R. Nevertheless, it must be recorded that most of them were well-known also for their pro-Socialist views or Peace campaign activities. The I.S.C.'s 330,000-word report was based on an initial study of the history and technology of germ warfare ; they then travelled to Manchuria and North Korea in order to examine 19 copiously-documented cases of infection. In particular the I.S.C. interrogated witnesses, scrutinised records and tested exhibits concerning U.S. Air Force flights, containers, plants and insects, and medical documentation ; alternative explanations for various phenomena—including the deaths and diseases themselves—were also considered. When all this had been done, the Commission concluded that some of the claims contained inaccuracies or confusions, some were ' inconclusive ' as evidence—and others had been supported by corroborating evidence that left no room for reasonable doubt :

> The people of Korea and China have indeed been the objective of bacteriological weapons. These have been employed by units of the United States forces, using a great variety of different methods for the purpose some of which would seem to be developments of those applied by the Japanese army during the Second World War.[13]

S.O. obtained a copy of the I.S.C. report and its volumes of substantiating material. He determined to take the issue into an unwelcoming House of Commons as soon as possible after the restart of Parliament. His chance did not occur until October 23 ;

at half-past eleven that evening he proposed that the House adjourn its proceedings in protest at the American germ warfare programme in Korea. S.O. had begun to describe the U.S. facilities for developing such weapons when he was interrupted by the Deputy Speaker, Sir Charles MacAndrew, who demanded to know whether the matter was the responsibility of a specific Government Department. When junior Foreign Affairs Minister, Anthony Nutting, replied in the negative, the Deputy Speaker declared the debate ' out of order '. S.O. attacked this decision as an attempt ' to suppress discussion in this House on a matter of paramount importance to the people of this country '; after a good few minutes of wrangling, the Deputy Speaker apologised tersely, and S.O. was at last permitted to continue. He switched his attention to England, to the germ warfare plant at Porton Down and to the Press which refused to give readers in Britain the truth. In reply to those outside the House who questioned his knowledge of supposed events thousands of miles away, S.O. pointed out that he had not witnessed the obliteration of Hiroshima or the gassing of Jews in their millions—but he was certain, on the evidence, that such atrocities had occurred. Similarly, whilst he had not seen the infection of Korean and Chinese peasants with his own eyes, the evidence proved that germ warfare had been unleashed against those peoples :

> Why pretend that those responsible for these crimes against humanity could ever have any scruples about germ warfare ? We know that, at the time Japan capitulated in the last war, a cargo of bacteriological agents was on its way to the Marianas to be used against the Japanese. We also know that the Japanese carried on germ warfare against the Chinese in the last war, but it is also known that, on the instructions of the last Commander-in-Chief in Korea, Shiro Ishii, Jiro Wakamatsu and Massajo Kitano, Japanese bacteriological war criminals, arrived in Korea from Tokyo in the winter of 1951 to take part in the planning of bacteriological warfare to be launched by the United Nations, including Britain, against the Koreans. What information has the Under-Secretary of State [Nutting] on that hideous fact about Japanese bacteriological war criminals being brought to Korea ? It is no use the Government telling me they do not know about it.
>
> There was a Telepress despatch from Rangoon dated 5th December, 1951, and a Reuter despatch of 9th December, 1951, both giving identical reports that this was being done.

S.O. then alighted upon a major element in the prosecution's case against the U.S.A.: the confessions of captured U.S.A.F. personnel that they had been involved in the preparation and execution of germ-bombing in Korea. Brandishing photostat copies of their hand-written testimonies and aware of the standard Western retort, S.O. reminded M.P.s that North Korea's prisoners were 'well-fed, well-housed and well-clothed' according to all the accounts from non-Communist sources. This he contrasted to the well-documented massacres of Communist prisoners-of-war perpetrated by the South Koreans (and which British Army officers had occasionally intervened to prevent). S.O. went on to quote the conclusions reached in the I.S.C. report and recommended that a copy be placed in the Commons library. He also jumped into the Red Cross controversy:

> Feeble excuses will be made, and feeble questions asked, such as, for example, why did not the North Koreans and the Chinese invite the International Red Cross to investigate the charges of germ warfare ? The reasons are obvious. When ghastly massacres were taking place in Nazi concentration camps, Red Cross investigators were issuing reports that all was well. Have we forgotten their report on the notorious camp at Auschwitz, of gas chambers fame, that murder camp which—

At this point the Deputy Speaker interjected with a warning that time was running short. Still, the point had been made.[14]

Replying to the adjournment motion, Nutting accused S.O. of making 'outrageous charges' in repeating what was 'an old Communist story'. The I.S.C. was sponsored by the 'Communist-controlled' World Peace Council and was composed entirely of 'Communists or Communist sympathisers'. Nutting found it 'curious' that the only bacteriologist on the Commission was a Russian (in fact the delegation expertise encompassed animal physiology, biochemistry, human anatomy, general biology, parasitology, public health and, from an Italian observer-consultant, microbiology). M. Zhukov might have been the only member whose official post included the word 'bacteriology' in its title, but he certainly was not the only commissioner competent in this field. The Under-Secretary then pointed to Commission member Dr. Joseph Needham's comment beforehand that the allegations of germ warfare were convincing, as proof of prejudgement and bias—hence the I.S.C. report had 'the mark of a Communist fraud'.

Also, the fact that the evidence presented to the Commission had been marshalled by the Chinese Communists (Nutting did not mention the North Korean cases) was clear proof of the report's 'fraudulent nature'. Presumably, Nutting believed that the I.S.C. should itself have tracked down the witnesses, corpses, cannisters and insects. He concluded that not one 'shred of real evidence' had been produced to prove that U.N. forces had used bacteria in the Korean War—hence the Soviet veto on an 'impartial investigation'. As Big Ben struck twelve o'clock, bringing the debate to a close, S.O. offered to send the Minister a copy of the I.S.C. investigation. On that gentlemanly note ended S.O.'s first brave and highly unpopular attempt to confront the British Government with bacteriological warfare allegations.

Four months later, in the train of fresh charges from Peking, S.O. took the floor of the Commons again. On 2 March 1953 he asked the Foreign Secretary: 'When was he informed by the United States Government of their directive to introduce in Korea widespread germ warfare?' Selwyn Lloyd denied that such means of warfare had been used 'by the United Nations forces' in Korea, and declared that talk of a U.S. germ warfare directive was 'complete nonsense'.

Points of order drowned S.O.'s endeavours to fire another salvo; Tory M.P.s were furious that his original question had assumed the U.S. Government directive as an established fact. Now that a senior Government Minister had disputed the existence of any such instrument surely, they insisted, S.O. must withdraw his 'insinuations'. The Speaker, for once ruling in S.O.'s favour, announced that each Honourable Member takes full responsibility for the truth or otherwise implied in a Parliamentary Question: the right of an M.P. to ask a question in his or her own way should be upheld in all but the most extreme circumstances. S.O. stood his ground: 'I still adhere to my facts', he told baying M.P.s. Selwyn Lloyd thought it 'remarkable' that Peking Radio had featured its fresh allegations on February 22—'the exact anniversary of the launching in 1952 of the germ warfare legend'. (A previous allegation had, in fact, been made by North Korea in May 1951!) Lloyd considered it 'significant' that these charges cropped up shortly before the season for 'normal epidemics' began. Unfortunately, the Foreign Secretary did not specify which diseases constituted these 'normal epidemics '—certainly cholera, bubonic plague, smallpox and encephalitis were not ' normal ' in North Korea or Manchuria.

In the course of these exchanges, a Captain Pilkington appealed to the Speaker : ' If the hon. Member [S.O.] cannot be induced to withdraw his disgraceful allegation, can it be made clear that he is in a minority of one ?' Yet, in procedural matters at least, S.O. was not entirely friendless : Labour's Deputy Leader Herbert Morrison defended the Merthyr M.P.'s right to table the question of his own choice ; Frank Bowles reminded those demanding S.O.'s withdrawal (merely because the Government had rejected his premise as ' untrue ') that ' the Chancellor of the Exchequer and the Foreign Secretary all through the Spanish Civil War denied that there were German or Italian troops in Spain at all '. The Conservatives had lied on that issue—so why should their word be treated as Gospel this time ?

Generally speaking, the right-wing newspapers awarded very little coverage to S.O.'s campaign in the Commons; the main exceptions were the *Western Mail* and the *Merthyr Express*. On 4 March 1953 the former assailed S.O. in bitter terms : instead of accepting America's word, he ' prefers to believe the enemies of this country, who avowedly include barefaced lies in their propaganda ' ; he had not produced ' an iota of evidence except for that which the Communists had concocted ' . . . he was guilty of ' gullibly siding with notorious liars '. His local newspaper was no more flattering.

Characteristically, S.O. gave as good as he got through the medium of their letters columns. He emphasised the confessions of U.S. Air Force and military personnel : Colonel Schwable, Chief of Staff of the 1st Marine Air Wing, and Major Bley, an Ordnance officer, had admitted the existence of a Joint Command Staff directive in October 1951 to contaminate North Korea with cholera, yellow fever and typhus ; Col. Walker Mahurin (a World War Two flying ace), Col. Andrew Evans and 30 other airmen had signed testimonies of complicity in a germ warfare campaign, supplying a vast amount of data concerning technical briefings, the names and descriptions of instructors, flight details and much else besides. Stupidly, though, the Communist authorities tacked passages of jargonised propaganda onto several of the statements, thereby providing Western cynics with a brush that could be used to blacken every word as a ' forgery '.

Many of the captured South Korean, American and British troops had been innoculated against cholera, plague and yellow fever—even though the first disease had not manifested itself in the region for four years, the second not for centuries, and the third would never appear because yellow fever is a tropical virus. A number of soldiers confirmed that an air of mystery and secrecy had shrouded these innoculations ; one G.I. claimed to have heard that ' the American 65th Infantry Regiment, 3rd Infantry Division, had used epidemic germ shells against the Communist troops in Korea '. South Korean agents were paraded who claimed their espionage activities had included the monitoring of American-induced disease epidemics in the North.[15]

Fortified by this flood of ' confessions ' emanating from North Korean prisoner-of-war camps, S.O. considered the evidence so overwhelming as to withstand the most prejudiced investigation. Thus at the end of March 1953 he submitted a Written Parliamentary Question urging the British Government to propose a U.N. inquiry into the whole business. By a day or two he had anticipated a resolution of the U.N. General Assembly—supported by Britain and the U.S.A.—to establish a commission for that purpose. The five-power investigation made slow progress in the face of Chinese and North Korean suspicion, and was eventually overtaken on 27 July 1953 by an armistice. The blood-drenched Korean War had come to an end, the two sides had fought themselves to a stand-still along the 38th Parallel. Prisoners were repatriated . . . and the inevitable retraction of confessions began.[16]

But were bacteriological weapons deployed during the Korean War ? To summarise the possibilities : either (1) the Soviet, Chinese and North Korean authorities concocted the most elaborate hoax of the 20th Century, fooling or corrupting many eminent scientists and jurists ; or (2) the Communists and investigating teams misinterpreted phenomena whose origins did not lie in a germ warfare offensive ; or (3) the Communist claims were true—and the American denials were dishonest. Almost alone amongst Members of Parliament, S.O. held to the third proposition . . .

The Korean germ warfare controversy has yet to be resolved. Even so, new facts have come to light which do not improve the U.S.A.'s standing in the dispute. In 1976 a Japanese television documentary uncovered massive detail of Japan's development, during World War Two, of a ceramic bomb filled with insects infected by plague, cholera, anthrax and typhoid ; 3,000 prisoners (mainly Chinese) had died as a consequence of experiments in the camp near Harbin, Manchuria. Eleven Chinese cities were attacked with germ bombs to test their effects. At the end of the Second War, the Americans offered immunity to the commanders of Harbin—in return for their technical data and practical help. In 1949 the Soviet Union convicted the few staff it had captured from Harbin as war criminals ; Russian requests that the U.S. Government similarly prosecute the three Harbin leaders in American custody had been dismissed as a ' Communist propaganda manoeuvre '. These were the three men named by S.O., in the House of Commons in October 1952 as being behind the germ warfare programme in Korea.[17]

Yet even as the Korean War burned itself out, there were other Cold War flash-points to illuminate the horizon. The unearthing of more sets of Soviet agents was feeding American paranoia to bursting-point. The detection of Klaus Fuchs in England in 1950 had sparked a trail which led across the Atlantic to another spy, Harry Gold ; this, in turn, put the F.B.I. on the scent of a messenger, David Greenglass, whose sister Ethel was married to the nuclear physicist Julius Rosenberg. In April 1951 the Rosenbergs were found guilty of conspiring to steal classified Government information, under a law passed by Congress in 1917 that provided for a maximum punishment for peacetime espionage of 2 years imprisonment and/or a $10,000 dollar fine. But the convicted couple were sentenced to death, on the grounds that their offence had occurred during World War Two. The fact that the recipient of U.S. State secrets, the Soviet Union, was a wartime ally rather than an enemy was disregarded as a ' technicality '. Greenglass escaped with a prison sentence.

For two years the Rosenbergs' lawyers strove to commute the death sentence. Around the world, millions marched and even rioted against the court decision ; Western governments pleaded with the U.S.A. to tread the path of mercy ; the Pope appealed for clemency—and the U.S. Department of Justice refused to divulge the words of his message. On 19 June 1953 Julius and Ethel Rosenberg died in the electric chair.

S.O. tabled a Parliamentary Question to the Prime Minister

asking ' if, in view of the widespread revulsion of feeling against the United States Government in this country, he will take steps to have their Embassy and Consulates here closed within four weeks and all United States armed forces withdrawn forthwith from British soil '. When it reached the Commons order paper on 25 June 1953, it quickly became evident that S.O. had stirred-up a beehive of bitter protest. Before the Prime Minister's stand-in (the Lord Privy Seal, Captain Crookshank) could reply, a dozen outraged M.P.s had jumped to their feet ; Labour member Harry Hynd demanded that the Question be ruled out of order, denying that there was ' widespread revulsion ' in the country. But the Speaker upheld S.O.'s right to table a question in his own words. Exasperated M.P. Captain Pilkington then won more cheers when he asked whether there were any limits to ' questions as obnoxious as this one '. The volume of applause grew louder still as Brigadier Medlicott called for the order paper to be protected from its use ' for propaganda purposes ' ; S.O.'s statements were, he cried, ' misleading ', ' malicious ' and ' damaging '. Eventually Captain Crookshank squeezed in to tell a grateful House that the Prime Minister, Winston Churchill, ' does not for one moment accept the mischievous and irresponsible assertion in the question, which is wholly without foundation '. S.O. rose to ask a supplementary question, amidst roars of ' Shame ! ' and ' Withdraw !' :

> I ask for the protection of the Chair, if the yells on both sides of the House can still the consciences of hon. Members. My supplementary question is this : are we to understand from the reply that the Government are utterly indifferent to the horror felt by millions of peaceful British men and women at the cold-blooded murder of Mr and Mrs Rosenberg ?

Curiously, the Speaker then informed S.O. that this second question did not arise from the original one. An unprecedented intervention came next : the Leader of the Opposition and of S.O.'s own party, Clement Attlee, stood up from his front bench and assured the Government that ' the opinions expressed in this Question have no support on this side of the House '. S.O. had been publicly disowned by the Labour Party in Parliament. One fellow left-winger, Sidney Silverman, defied the howling mob by pointing out that many poeple around the world joined with the Pope and the President of France in feeling ' a genuine emotion of horror against some events in the United States in recent days.' Except for this dignified contribution, the chamber echoed with scornful laughter and abuse. Tory M.P. Godfrey Nicholson wondered aloud whether S.O. was 'a Russian agent or merely a lunatic'. In vain the object of this smear appealed to the Speaker for some defence against 'individuals whose presence in this House can be justified only by the care they exercise for their own personal interests'. Only after some prompting from Silverman did the Speaker request—and receive—a retraction from Nicholson.

The following morning, S.O. opened his *Western Mail* to find the expected editorial censure. He read that his questions were 'drawn straight from the lunatic fringe of the Communist Party . . . When the Reds themselves make no impression on the British electorate MR. S. O. DAVIES can always be relied on to espouse their cause'. There followed a list of his most recent 'egregious indiscretions': the Nenni telegram, the Peace movement and the Korean germ warfare charges. The editorial column ended with the query: 'Is not the application of some disciplinary measure long overdue?'

The *Merthyr Express* accused him of attracting 'some very unwelcome publicity in the national Press' with his description of the Rosenbergs execution as 'cold-blooded murder', and by the attitude he was striking on a fresh crisis in Germany. Always anxious to explain his unorthodox standpoints to the people of Merthyr Tydfil, the Borough's M.P. despatched a letter to the paper on July 6. He argued that no proof had been produced to indict the Rosenbergs for stealing or communicating classified secrets; instead, the prosecution had purchased David Greenglass in order to convict the couple for 'conspiring' to do so. S.O. knew that most *Merthyr Express* readers would share his working-class contempt for a stool-pigeon:

> For two years the Rosenbergs were kept in the death cell of Sing Sing prison, sentenced on the evidence of a proven perjurer and an admitted spy; a wretch who, having been caught red-handed, tried to save his miserable skin by becoming a Government witness and lying against his sister and her husband. Of course he was helped by the witch-hunting of Government supporters and the hysteria so assiduously worked up . . . The transcript of the trial proceedings shows that the Judge was not only biased but vindictive and he acted with gross impropriety throughout the trial.[18]

Although disowned on the floor of the Commons by the leader of his own party, it was not the Rosenbergs crisis which blew S.O. to the brink that summer. Also in June 1953, with Stalin barely three months in his coffin, hundreds of thousands of East German workers rebelled against their Communist regime's new economic stringencies. For four weeks, numerous towns and cities were the scenes of riots, demonstrations, curfews and martial law imposed by the ' People's Police ' and Russian tanks ; in the end the Government retracted its productivity norms and reissued ration cards, while the Soviet Union eased its harsh reparations policy against East Germany. Nonetheless, the demands of workers and students for free elections, disbandment of the secret police, the withdrawal of Russian troops and unification with West Germany were not conceded.

With the right-wing Press and politicians in England and the rest of the world egging the strikers, demonstrators and rioters onwards to the overthrow of the system in East Germany—and to the restoration of ' free enterprise ' and bourgeois democracy—S.O.'s inclination was to defend the Communist regime, in defiance of his traditional class enemy. Echoing the claims of East German Socialist Unity Party chief Walter Ulbricht and his Communist newspaper allies in France and England, S.O. tabled a parliamentary motion in late June calling upon the House of Commons—

> To express its disgust at the financing of unemployed workers and neo-Fascists in the American zone of Berlin by offers of monetary rewards, free holidays, jobs in the special police of West Berlin, and other inducements, to act as *agent provocateurs* in East Berlin.

The motion went on to urge the British Government to make representations to the U.S. Government to ' cease its provocative acts, for whose committal large sums of money have admittedly been granted by the American Government '. Reaction to this initiative was swift and severe : Sir William Lawther, President of the National Union of Mineworkers, added S.O. to his list of those M.P.s (chiefly Bevan and his Tribunite supporters) who should quit the Labour Party. Lawther issued this statement from Nottingham on June 26 :

> The attitude of Mr Davies on the East German situation is contrary to the expressed wishes and opinions of the miners. He is one of those who attends the House of Commons only infrequently. There he is out of touch with the facts of the day-to-day situation.
>
> My personal opinion is that he should now resign because his speeches and attendances indicate that he has lost touch with the miners' movement.
>
> It is well-known that for a long time he has been a fellow-traveller of the Communist Party, and I would assure my American colleagues, particularly Mr John L. Lewis, that they must not accept Mr Davies as a representative of the British miners in the House of Commons.
>
> Every one of the 38 miners' M.P.s have signed a declaration appealing to the U.S.S.R. to cease their dragooning and murdering of the East German miners and other trade unionists.
>
> I would suggest to the Merthyr Labour Party, who are responsible for his candidature, if they have any regard for the memory of his predecessor, the late Keir Hardie, to get rid of their present Member at the earliest opportunity.

Not surprisingly, Merthyr's Socialists ignored Sir William's advice. Instead, like miners and other workers in south Wales, they gave S.O. a tolerant audience for his heretical views. In the local Press and public meetings, S.O. repeated his charges that *agent provocateurs* had been sent in to East Berlin to foment riots, commit arson and assault the police—thereby causing the East German authorities to eventually seal off their section of the city ; he quoted the confessions of alleged ' hirelings ' apprehended in the Eastern sector ; American officers had led Fascist detachments in the disturbances, American planes had dropped inflammatory leaflets on East German factories, American lorries had parked at the boundaries of the Soviet zone of the city with loudspeakers and stocks of petrol-bombs ; and, he asked, did not American police help kidnap Otto Nuschke, the Deputy Prime Minister of East Germany ? As for the so-called ' martyrs ' killed in the uprising . . . Willi Goettling was registered as unemployed in a West German employment exchange, no heroic striker he ; Erna Dorne had been freed by a ' mob ' from the Halle prison in East Berlin, where she was serving a 15-year sentence for being a commandant in one of Hitler's concentration camps.[19]

It is highly unlikely that the workers' revolt in East Germany had been instigated by unseen Western hands ; nor, to be precise, did this form the substance of S.O.'s accusations. His charge that Western money, materials and men had participated in the momentous events was well-founded ; even so, the extent of their involvement is rather uncertain—played down by the Western establishment and played up by S.O. Relishing the irony, therefore, he would quote the verdict of that anti-Communist and big business journal, the *Economist*, on the East German earthquake : ' Here, surely, is the kind of climax towards which the propaganda of the B.B.C., the Voice of America and Radio Free Europe has been working for years '. S.O.'s punishment for propounding an identical analysis was very nearly expulsion from the Parliamentary Labour Party. On this occasion, however, discretion prevailed over valour: he revoked his Commons motion, bowing to an ultimatum from the Chief Whip and P.L.P. leadership. This did not extinguish the ire of the *Western Mail* editorial writer who, on July 9, chided the ' Merthyr electors who have shown much docile complacency about the frequent aberrations of their Member ' : the time must surely come, he opined, when they would express their condemnation at the polls.

S.O. withstood the jeers and sneers with humour and an unbroken spirit ; the tactical retreat from Berlin did not alter his overall strategy of breaking the Cold War concensus at St. Stephen's, shaming the Bevanites into resistance and voicing the fears of an unrepresented multitude.

Yet, through all these and other developments, Germany still occupied the centre of the world diplomatic stage. In 1952 the Soviet Union, alarmed at the prospect of a rearmed West Germany entering N.A.T.O., had proposed talks to lead to a united, neutral, non-nuclear Germany ; behind the scenes, the Russians went so far as to warn the East's Socialist Unity (Communist) regime of its pending liquidation, should the capitalist powers broadly agree to the Soviet plan. But the U.S.A. rejected the initiative out of hand ; Foreign Secretary John Foster Dulles would negotiate only from a position of massive superiority which, in this case, meant only after West Germany had joined a European Defence Community or N.A.T.O. A Superpowers summit early in 1954 failed to bring the two sides closer together : Dulles would not accept the Soviet Union's insistence that a reunified Germany remain neutral. The

Soviets also demanded equal status between the governments of East and West Germany in any transitional arrangements. The French shared Soviet misgivings about German rearmament : their National Assembly vetoed the blueprint for a European Defence Community, to include West Germany, later that year. Even so, a new arrangement had been drawn up in the Treaties of London and Paris by October, whereby West Germany would join the European N.A.T.O. powers in a Western European Union as the first step towards full integration into N.A.T.O. proper.

The Labour movement in Britain was divided down the middle on the whole issue in 1954. The P.L.P. had decided by just two votes out of 220 to back the rearming of West Germany; the annual conference of the Labour Party was steamrollered into supporting rearmament by the trade union bloc vote, wielded as in the case of the N.U.M. by right-wing leaders who took no account of their members' views.

So on 18 November 1954, faced with a Commons motion to ratify the London and Paris pacts, the Parliamentary Labour Party resolved to preserve its unity by abstaining in the vote. Ten Labour M.P.s preserved their integrity by opposing the Tory Government. During the two-day debate, S.O. and Emrys Hughes endeavoured to elicit the crucial information from Foreign Secretary Harold Macmillan : would the Treaties entitle West Germany's *Bundeswehr* to handle or possess nuclear weapons ? Macmillan's reply that Chancellor Adenauer had renounced the manufacture of an atomic bomb was exposed in all its evasiveness. The answer, underneath the deceitful blathering, was ' Yes '. That was enough for S.O. and the other nine, who soon afterwards marched into the ' No ' lobby. They did so in the knowledge that their likely penalty would be excommunication from the Parliamentary Labour Party. S.O. felt he had no real option, especially as he was by now the Chairman of the (proscribed) Welsh Peace Council. His spell in the parliamentary wilderness was to last for three months, after which Labour's Chief Whip William Whiteley sought an assurance that the Merthyr outcast would abide by the Constitution and Standing Orders of the Party. S.O.'s short note in reply was the model of principled ambiguity : ' My desire always has been to work in harmony with the Party ', he informed Whiteley.[20]

The disciplinary lash did nothing to subdue S.O. He was back on the war path again, immediately after Winston Churchill told a meeting of his Woodford constituents on 23 November 1954 :

> Even before the war had ended and while the Germans were surrendering by hundreds of thousands, I telegraphed to Lord Montgomery, telling him to be careful in collecting the German arms, to stack them so that they could easily be issued again to the German soldiers whom we should have to work with if the Soviet advance continued.

His remarks punctuated by shouts of ' Shame ! ', Churchill continued : ' I am giving it to you plainly and bluntly so that you may see for yourselves how wisely you are being led '. These revelations in an otherwise routine anti-Socialist tirade caused a sensation. Even the *Times* was moved to comment :

> The remark can be looked at in every way and be put to every kind of test, and in the end it is impossible to see what purpose or good it can serve at this time . . . It certainly will not help to convince the Russians that the Western Powers are straightforward in their declarations of peace today. Nor, by suggesting that we were ready to use Nazi-indoctrinated troops in 1945, will it help the cause of German re-armament now.[21]

S.O. was not so circumspect in his criticism. Speaking within a few days of Churchill's shock statement, he accused the Prime Minister of ' treachery ' :

> He wanted to re-arm the Nazis at the moment the British soldiers were uncovering Belsen and other concentration camps.
>
> Churchill tells us he did not at any time judge the German soldiers by any political label but as people, fighting desperately in defence of their native land.
>
> So the Germans who slaughtered millions of men, women and children on their route to Stalingrad, to Narvik, to El Alamein, Greece, Marseilles and who left behind them gas chambers, the incinerators and the death pits, the war graves and mined cities, were patriots. This they did purely in defence of their country !
>
> It is clear that by 1945 Winston was on the side of the Germans not the Russians.[22]

With the backing of the South Wales miners' Executive, S.O. tabled a motion in the Commons on December 2 calling for

Churchill's resignation, branding the instruction to Montgomery 'a betrayal of the ideals this country fought for'; it explained why 'the Soviet Union and the people's democracies of Eastern Europe place no trust in the sincerity of the approaches made by this Government in the urgent matter of world peace'. The *Western Mail*, naturally, deplored S.O.'s remarks and rushed to Sir Winston's defence. As with Bevan, S.O. was accused of conducting a personal vendetta against Churchill whenever he gave vent to political antagonisms, to a hostility based on class and not on personality. First, last and always, Churchill represented the interests of the English ruling-class. S.O., on the other hand, represented the working-class. No amount of flag-waving or anthem-singing could budge S.O. from that view. Nor would he permit parliamentary niceties to blunt this class enmity. When Westminster celebrated Churchill's 80th birthday on November 30 and Dai Grenfell presented 'the Old Man' with an art and crafts commemoration book, S.O. was one of only 20 M.P.s who declined to inscribe their fond regards. However much the parliamentarians muttered 'bad form, old chap', many workers in south Wales cheered this breach of Commons club rules—just as they had sent S.O. hundreds of petitions, letters and telegrams after his stand against the London-Paris accords. Harri Webb was not applauding alone when he wrote:

> Mr S. O. Davies is a true socialist who can neither be bullied nor bought. He alone of the Welsh M.P.s voted against German rearmament. In doing so he fulfilled his mandate as a miners' representative. The other Welsh miners' M.P.s pocketed the union's money and ignored the union's precise instructions. He alone of the Welsh M.P.s refused to be a party to the sickening Tory propaganda demonstration which marked Churchill's birthday, when even Aneurin Bevan went soft. Churchill's bloody record in Wales makes it a matter of humiliation to us that any Welsh M.P. whatever was involved in this Jamboree. M.P.s of Tonypandy and Llanelly, where the worst outrages occurred, had no qualms about signing Churchill's birthday book.[23]

West Germany entered N.A.T.O. as a full member on 6 May 1955; eight days later the Communist countries banded together under Soviet military direction in the Warsaw Pact—six years after the formation of N.A.T.O. Even so, the Soviet Union had not buried *détente*: that same month Moscow officially recognised the

Federal Republic of West Germany. The West refused to reciprocate, and continued to withhold official status from the Democratic Republic of East Germany.

S.O. suggested ways of breaking the Superpowers stale-mate in his General Election address that eventful month : Peace could only be ensured by negotiation, not by 'H-bomb threats', he argued. To this end, Britain could help relax international tension by reversing its decision in February to manufacture the H-bomb, by abolishing conscription, and by convening another meeting of Soviet, American, French and British heads of State. China must be admitted to the United Nations, and Formosa re-united with the mainland. The British Empire should be swiftly transformed into a Commonwealth of self-governing nations ; Germany should be unified on the basis of neutrality and free elections. He also criticised the Conservatives for their domestic policies and for 'importing pathetic examples of mediocrity' to stand against him. The voters of Merthyr Tydfil duly despatched the hapless Tory back to obscurity on 25 May 1955 :

S. O. DAVIES (Labour)	25,630
ANTHONY D. ARNOLD (Conservative)	7,548

But Merthyr and Wales were not Britain : overall the Tories, with Sir Anthony Eden at the helm, increased their share of the votes at Labour's expense and boosted their Commons majority from 17 to 58. With Eden the Nobel Peace Prize winner so firmly installed at 10 Downing Street, patches of blue sky fleetingly appeared between the clouds of mushroom-grey. The Soviet Union had pulled out of Finland following a pledge of Finnish neutrality ; Kruschev healed the breach with Tito's Yugoslavia.

By this time, too, Eden's trial-by-fire had arrived. President Nasser of Egypt began the proceedings in July 1956 when he nationalised the multinationally-owned Suez Canal Company. This measure was partly in retaliation for the sudden withdrawal of English and American finance from the Aswan Dam scheme ; it was also a logical step in his Arab nationalist-socialist programme. Eden and the Labour Party's new leader Hugh Gaitskell condemned Nasser's action in the harshest terms : even Aneurin Bevan expressed disapproval, although he did so in more moderate language and from an international—rather than a chauvinistic—standpoint. For most commentators, though, England's so-called 'national interest' had been jeopardised : the waterway for most of Britain's oil supplies (and much of western Europe's) would henceforth be in the hands of a regime that spurned membership of the anti-Soviet camp.

From the outset, S.O. upheld Nasser's right to nationalise foreign assets in Egypt ; Labour would be hypocritical to advocate such a policy at home, whilst condemning it elsewhere merely because British assets or interests were involved. He punctuated Eden's major speech in the Commons on 12 September 1956 with sarcastic and contradicting remarks : the Prime Minister claimed that the Suez take-over threatened Britain's legal right of passage, before S.O. interjected: 'We've got it still ! ' Colonel Nasser had destroyed the 'balance' struck by the 1888 Convention, Eden insisted. 'Nonsense ! ' shouted S.O. When the Prime Minister accused the Soviet Union of thwarting efforts to internationalise the issue by perpetually deriding Western proposals as 'colonialism', S.O. cut in with a hearty 'Hear! Hear!' Now that Nasser had rejected a plan for joint control of the Canal which offered 'a fair return to Egypt—and Canal tolls as low as is consistent with their payment', Britain and France had no option but to implement such an arrangement without Egypt's approval, or so the Man of Peace told M.P.s. The debate continued :

EDEN : But I must make it clear that if the Egyptian Government should seek to interfere—
HAROLD DAVIES : Deliberate provocation.
EDEN :—with the operations of the association, or refuse to extend to it the essential minimum of co-operation, then that Government will once more be in breach of the Convention of 1888.
HONOURABLE MEMBERS : Resign !
EDEN : I must remind the House that what I am saying—
AN HON. MEMBER : What a peace-maker !
EDEN : is the result of exchanges of views between three Governments. In that event Her Majesty's Government and others concerned will be free to take such further steps—
S. O. DAVIES : What do you mean by that ?
EDEN :—as seem to be required—
S. O. DAVIES : You are talking about war.

EDEN :—either through the United Nations, or by other means, for the assertion of their rights.
HONOURABLE MEMBERS : Oh !

The ' further steps ' and ' other means ' were revealed on October 31 when French and British planes bombarded Egyptian airforce installations, clearing the way for the seizure of the canal by an Anglo-French assault force on November 5. Ostensibly the mission had been undertaken in order to drive a wedge between the invading Israeli army and the Egyptian defence forces, to safeguard a vital transport route from the ravages of a military collision. In retrospect, it is now beyond reasonable doubt that France and Israel had acted in collusion—that the Zionist invasion, besides being a case of ' retaliate first ', was launched then so that Britain could use it as the pretext for an Anglo-French occupation of the Suez zone. The U.S.A. had not been properly informed or consulted—and was angry ; the United Nations had been by-passed ; almost all of the Commonwealth heads, with the predictable exception of Australia's Robert Menzies, strongly decried Britain's adventurism. So, too, did the Labour Party in Parliament, its members finally catching up with those 30 or so M.P.s (including S.O.) who from the very beginning of the crisis had disputed Eden's approach, doubted his credentials, and suspected that his diplomacy would inevitably be continued by ' other means '. His end was a pleasingly humiliating one : the United Nations ordered a cease-fire and replaced the French, British and Israeli forces within days of their arrival in Egypt.[24]

In a Coal Industry Bill debate on 23 November 1959, S.O. insisted upon adding the human and military costs of the ' mad Suez escapade ' to the price already paid for Middle East oil, twice incurring the Deputy Speaker's wrath for mentioning the matter.

An unintended effect of the Suez conflagration was to draw attention away from the savage drama unfolding in Hungary. The Anglo-French offensive had taken place within hours of the Soviet leadership's acceptance of Hungarian autonomy, a gesture given substance by the withdrawal of the Red Army from Budapest. But, tragically, Imre Nagy's reforming regime could no longer control the virulent anti-Russian and anti-Socialist feelings of a large section of the Hungarian people. When Nagy capitulated to popular feeling and introduced non-Socialists into his administration, followed on

November 1 by his announcement of Hungary's defection from the Warsaw Pact, the Soviet tanks turned around and rumbled back towards the Hungarian capital. Only after 10 days of bloody slaughter was the Hungarian resistance crushed ; although Radio Free Europe incited the ' Freedom Fighters ', the much-awaited material support from Western countries never arrived.

S.O. received news of the outbreak of fighting whilst attending a meeting of the British-Soviet Friendship Society. He maintained a sad silence, in private at the time and in public afterwards. As a Welsh patriot he could understand the Magyars' ardour for national freedom ; but he understood, too, why the Soviet Union and its Communist allies in Hungary would feel justified in quashing a rebellion that threatened the strategic interests of ' the Socialist countries ' (as he called them). He also feared the creation of a pro-Western inroad deep into Eastern Europe via Austria and Hungary. Like the Soviets, S.O. would not forget that the pre-war regime in Budapest had been a crypto-Fascist one with a large following ; during the war it had joined in the German attack on the Soviet Union and later transported over half-a-million Jews to the Nazi extermination camps. If Soviet-Socialist rule were the only sure guarantee against such recurrences in the future—so be it, even though S.O. was never an advocate or an apologist for the show trials and executions deemed necessary by the Communist authorities in Eastern Europe.

Suez and Hungary had the sobering effect of showing each Cold War camp what the other side was able and willing to do in defence of its own interests. Behind the cross-fire of claims, accusations and condemnations, the Superpowers regarded the new destructive capabilities unleashed by missile and flight technology with a deepening foreboding. They were intimidating each other into exploring the avenues of peace and disarmament afresh. But hopes had been raised before, only to explode in an atmosphere of mistrust and intransigence . . .

In 1957, Kruschev called for summit talks to bring about the multilateral abandonment of nuclear weapons and a severe reduction in conventional forces ; the British Communist Party thereupon dropped its demand for unilateral British disarmament in favour of this collective international approach. This, too, became the strategy urged upon the Labour Party's annual conference by

Aneurin Bevan. Nevertheless, local Party organisations had submitted more than 100 motions to commit Labour to scrapping Britain's atomic arsenal unilaterally. Bevan challenged them in Brighton that October : unilateral disarmament would mean the summary cancellation of treaties, responsibilities and obligations entered into with friends and allies; yet, he chided, the composite motion did not even suggest anything positive to fill the vacuum. Britain's future influence for all-round disarmament would be nil and its Foreign Secretary ' sent naked into the conference chamber ', utterly discredited by this negation of statesmanship. Scores of angry delegates frequently interrupted their erstwhile champion, giving vent to their feelings of betrayal with jeers and ripostes ; the unilateralists smarted far more under Bevan's verbal lashing of them and their ' emotional spasm ' than they did from the trade union bloc votes that so overwhelmingly repulsed their resolutionary efforts.

Yet Bevan's departure from Bevanism did not induce bitterness or despair in S.O.—probably because he had never been one of Nye's followers, had never indulged in the hero-worship practised by some of this compatriot's *coterie*. Rather, he expressed his disagreement in an unhysterical and comradely manner at subsequent party and Peace meetings. ' The Hydrogen bomb is neither a deterrent nor a bargaining weapon ' he maintained ; now that the Soviets had narrowed the nuclear gap, victory in an atomic war would lie with whichever side attacked first and wiped out the other's weapons. The next war, therfore, would not be preceded by emergency conferences and formal declarations. ' There is now only one force stronger than those lunatic weapons—and that is Moral Force ' declared S.O., by which he meant the moral force of argument, example and self-denial. He told audiences : ' Aneurin says that we cannot unilaterally abandon the Hydrogen and Atom bombs. Aneurin must accept two things : firstly, that these bombs are no longer a deterrent to the Soviet Union ; and secondly, that the greatest and most lasting achievements in human history were brought about unilaterally. Have we forgotten Buddha, Socrates, Christ and Gandhi ? ' He rejected Bevan's insinuation that the unilateralists wanted to discard Britain's bombs in order to salve their own consciences, while continuing to shelter beneath America's nuclear umbrella—' to benefit by the products of somebody else's guilt', as Nye had put it. That was certainly not S.O.'s position: he constantly reiterated his belief that all foreign bases on British soil should be dismantled forthwith, and that Britain should extricate itself from the N.A.T.O. death-trap.[25]

For a period S.O. appeared to be swimming with the tide of public opinion—a rare experience! Late in 1957 the Soviet Prime Minister, Bulganin, called for a nuclear-free central Europe to be established by removing all atomic weapons from East Germany, Poland, Czechoslovakia and West Germany. Various national leaders in N.A.T.O. responded to the popular support for the initiative, and secured a promise from the U.S.A. to consider the proposal seriously. But the price of such a pledge was that N.A.T.O.'s European members would permit the siting of U.S. intermediate-range ballistic missiles on their territory. This was, in S.O.'s opinion, an exhorbitant price to pay; writing in the magazine *British-Soviet Friendship* in February 1958, he characterised the Alliance as a 'collection of obsequious and brow-beaten Governments brought together to be exploited by American financial interests'. He wished to see the British working-class movement pursuing an independent policy of peace and disarmament and, towards that goal, he urged the Labour Party and T.U.C. to send a delegation to Moscow for a meeting with the Soviet leadership.

In March 1958 the Soviet Union announced its intention to halt nuclear tests unconditionally; Britain and the U.S.A. followed suit and, by December, a comprehensive test ban treaty was being formulated. A year later the Americans withdrew from the negotiations, their scientists claiming to have found a way in which the Soviets could, hypothetically—by an unprecedented and gargantuan feat of engineering—detonate an underground bomb that would evade detection. As with the seasons, though, the diplomatic winter gave way to another spring despite the inclemencies of Berlin and the Middle East. The Campaign for Nuclear Disarmament bloomed in Britain, with S.O. delighted to associate himself with the cause; that Thor of American foreign policy, John Foster Dulles, retired in April 1959; in the autumn an official Labour Party deputation visited the Kremlin; and in the biggest ice-breaker of all, Kruschev toured the United States in September, where in an address to the United Nations he looked forward to universal and complete nuclear disarmament within four years. Public opinion pressed the politicians into welcoming Soviet proposals for a Superpowers summit, which was eventually set for May 1960. A new thaw had begun ; the incoming decade was pregnant with hopes of peaceful co-existence between the Superpowers.

NOTES

[1]*Socialist Outlook* had been launched in 1948 ; according to Mark Jenkins in *Bevanism: Labour's High Tide* (1979) p. 287, S.O. enjoyed a 'close working relationship' with the paper's predominantly Trotskyist management. The paper was associated with the 'Socialist Fellowship' group and was proscribed by the Labour Party N.E.C. in August 1954.

[2]*Socialist Outlook*, August 1950.

[3]See Mark Jenkins (as Note 1 above) p.68.

[4]1950 Cabinet Papers, reported in the *Guardian*, 2 January 1981.

[5]Over 270 delegates were refused entry in this way, with 106 turned back even though they did not need visas ; Foreign Secretary Ernest Bevin called the World Peace Movement 'a Communist body' (source : 1950 Cabinet Papers reported in the *Guardian*, 2 January 1981). Attlee publicly denounced the Peace Movement as 'an instrument of the Politbureau' ; in fact, the Soviet Bloc countries occupied just over 10% of the seats on the Movement's governing Council, although many of the delegates from Western countries were Communists or Socialists—with a fair number of Liberals and religious pacifists as well : see *The Fellow Travellers* (1973) by David Caute.

[6]*Western Mail*, 18 November 1950.

[7]*Western Mail*, 20 February 1951.

[8]On Korea, the Socialist Fellowship M.P.s would not go as far as S.O. by condemning the U.S.A. and advocating Korean unification ; at least one of the group, Fenner Brockway, later regretted not having made the same stand as S.O. : see *Towards Tomorrow* (1977) by Fenner Brockway p.160.

[9]*Aneurin Bevan : A Biography* Vol. 2 (1973), p. 315.

[10]*Labour Monthly*, December 1951.

[11]Interviewed in *The Hidden History of the Korean War* (1952) by I. F. Stone, p.312.

[12]*Western Mail*, 7 April 1952. S.O. referred to some of the 156 reports on germ warfare published from Fort Detrick between 1943 and 1947. Throughout 1950 and 1951 eminent and right-wing journals such as the *Science Newsletter* (8 July 1950), *Look* magazine (21 November 1950) and the *U.S. News and World Report* (21 September 1951) predicted the probable, imminent use of bacterial weapons in Korea by U.S. Forces.

[13]*Report of the International Scientific Commission for the Investigation of Facts concerning Bacterial Warfare in Korea and China* (1952).

[14]Red Cross reluctance to act upon reports of mass killings in Nazi camps is authoritatively investigated in *The Terrible Secret* (1980) by Walter Lacquer ; Nazi sympathisers filled leading posts in the International Red Cross during the Second World War, the German Red Cross was under direct S.S. control and the poison gas Zyklon B had been transported in Red Cross vehicles. Towards the end of the war, an I.R.C. deputation visited Auschwitz ; their report was almost complimentary, the visitors having been kept away from the mass graves and extermination chambers at nearby Birkenau : see ' The Men Who Whitewash Hitler ' by Gitta Sereny in *New Statesman*, 2 November 1979.

[15]Excerpts from these highly-detailed and convincing statements are printed and discussed in ' Bacterial Warfare : Was It Employed Or Wasn't It ? ' (1976) by Jaap van Ginneken. This unpublished paper has been an invaluable source of information and argument concerning the Korean germ warfare controversy.

[16]Physical and mental ill-treatment of P.O.W.s by their Chinese and North Korean captors is generally agreed to have been rare ; instead, the methods used in the camps tended to be persuasion, political lectures and subtle pressures to ' conform '. Many of the excuses subsequently made by those who had written ' confessions ' are flimsy in the extreme. About 30% of British prisoners returned as firm Communist sympathisers, most of the Americans co-operated with their captors and not one of them out of 7,000 escaped—even though security was generally lax. See van Ginneken (Note 15 above), *Korea—the Limited War* (1964) by David Rees, and the report on ' Communist Indoctrination—Its Significance to Americans ' by U.S. Army psychiatrist Major William Mayer.

[17]The *New York Times* (13 April 1951) reported that the U.S. Army was employing Japanese experts in germ warfare centres in Japan and on a special ship ; *Newsweek* (19 April 1951) confirmed that an American ' bubonic plague ship ' had arrived in U.S.-occupied North Korea. The U.S.A.'s recruitment of Japanese germ war criminals, the mass murder experiments carried out in Manchuria during World War Two, and the U.S. efforts to protect the Japanese murderers from prosecution by the Soviet Union have been exposed by John W. Powell in the U.S. *Bulletin of the Atomic Scientists* (October 1981) ; see the *Guardian*, 29 October 1981, 2 April 1982 and 14 August 1982. See also van Ginneken (Note 15 above) and, for a pro-U.S. view of the original allegations, David Rees (Note 16 above).

[18]Letter to the *Merthyr Express* (published 11 July 1953) in the S. O. Davies Papers, Swansea (Ref : 1A, *ii*).

[19]Will Lawther's attack was published in the *Western Mail*, 27 June 1953 ; S.O.'s remarks on the East German crisis are taken from his letter to the *Merthyr Express* (see Note 18 above). For details of the C.I.A. and anti-Communist sabotage and propaganda campaigns against East Germany, see *The Secret War* (1962) by Sanche de Gramont and *The Secret War for Europe* (1968) by Louis Hagen.

[20]The letter from Whiteley (dated 16 February 1955) and S.O.'s note in reply are in the S. O. Davies Papers, Swansea (Ref : 1A, *i*). Seven of the ten dissidents were suspended altogether, including Emrys Hughes and Sidney Silverman. As befitting their station in the rebel aristocracy, however, the other three—Michael Foot, Jennie Lee and J. P. W. Mallalieu—escaped with a respectful reprimand.

[21]Churchill's remarks are quoted from the *News Chronicle*, 24 November 1954 ; the speech was commented upon in the *Times*, 25 November 1954.

[22]These speech notes are in the S. O. Davies Papers, Swansea (Ref : IE). S.O. scrutinised *The Second World War* Vol. 6 (1954) by Winston Churchill, showing how Stalin brought forward the Red Army offensive in January 1945—in response to Churchill's plea and at a heavy cost in Soviet lives (pp.243 & 244). Yet on 1 April 1945, Churchill was proposing to U.S. President Roosevelt that they tear up their agreements with the Soviets and ' march as far East into Germany as possible ' ; soon afterwards he urged new President Harry Truman to break territorial agreements with Stalin in order to ' create a new front against Russia as far east as possible ' (p.400) : see the S. O. Davies Papers, Swansea (Ref : 1C, *iii* and 1E). In July 1946 the British Chiefs of Staff considered plans for a massive nuclear and biological attack on Russia, according to the *Times*, 15 June 1981.

[23]*Welsh Republican*, February-March 1955.

[24]New evidence that the British Intelligence Service M.I.6 was planning to assassinate President Nasser at the time of the Suez crisis—with Eden's tacit approval—was revealed in *Ropes of Sand—America's Failure in the Middle East* (1980) by former C.I.A. agent Wilber Eveland. See the *Guardian*, 29 August 1980.

[25]Speech notes in the S. O. Davies Papers, Swansea (Ref : 1E).

Chapter Nine

A SOCIALIST FAITH

S.O.'s loathing for the Conservative Party was inexhaustible. In public and in private he shovelled scorn upon its ideology, its policies and its leaders. An old-style politician in any case, S.O. viewed the Tory populism of the late 1950s as a debasement of the political currency. He accused Lord Hailsham of ' cheap heroics, cheap dramatics and cheap showmanship ' when the latter appeared as the bell-ringing Quasimodo at a Conservative conference ; S.O. disparaged Prime Minister Harold Macmillan's fancy for homely slang and unconventional dress as ' buffoonery '.

Thus the General Election defeat of 8 October 1959 tasted particularly bitter on S.O.'s tongue. Labour had offered the electors a moderate prospectus of social reforms, an income tax cut and a pledge to nationalise nothing more than the steel industry—for the second time—and long-distance road haulage. But still the party's share of the poll slipped from 46.4% to 43.8% as the Tories scooped 107 seats more than Labour in the reassembled House of Commons. After eight years of having it so good, as Macmillan assured them, the people were apparently keen to enjoy another five—except in Merthyr Tydfil, naturally, where S.O. received his customary endorsement :

S. O. DAVIES (Labour)	26,608
MRS M. GREENAWAY (Con.)	7,885

S.O.'s election address reflected much of the Labaur Party's official manifesto, although he placed special emphasis upon the local unemployment rate of 5% (twice the U.K. average), the Conservative Government's Rents Act (decontrolling rents and removing security of tenure) and the Tories' new pension scheme (which did nothing to help low-paid workers, Old Age Pensioners and childless widows).

He also warned of the threat to the coal-mining industry posed by cheap oil imports : ' I warn the Miners and our Mining Communities that if the Tories are returned as the Government of our country, a very large number of collieries will be closed down next year and thousands of you Miners will be unemployed '. This was a danger not mentioned in Labour's official programme, *Britain Belongs to You.* But sure enough, the colliery closures accelerated in 1960 and, much to S.O.'s disgust, the N.C.B. restricted the output of the small mines licensed from the Board by private interests. The redundancies among private sector miners in his constituency (whose partial disabilities had disqualified them from N.C.B. employment) prompted S.O. to move a motion on ' Coalfield Unemployment ' in the Commons in May 1960. On this and on other occasions he voiced his disillusionment with the Coal Board : it was almost as high-handed and cold-hearted as the dispossessed coal barons of yore.

Throughout the 1950s and 1960s S.O. emphasised the vast potential of coal, especially of the supposedly inferior ' lignite ' ; quoting studies and experiments from as far afield as Germany and the Soviet Union, he urged the N.C.B. and the Ministry of Power to realise the tremendous possibilities of this ' black gold ', to utilise its components and by-products in the manufacture of gas, fertilisers, refrigerants, insectisides, disinfectants, synthetic rubber, plastics, nylon, tar and dyes. He would recall how the anaesthetics used in World War One had been derived from coal—the work of scientists following a meeting between S.O., Munitions Minister Lloyd George and S.W.M.F. President William Brace. At that same time it was discovered that lyddite (a major element in coal) could be deployed as a high explosive. Indeed, S.O. had argued for many of these ideas in his evidence to the Samuel Commission in 1925 ; the ensuing decades saw little progress towards them, until the 1961 Wilson Committee Report obliged the Coal Board to undertake much more research and development. That same year, in tribute to S.O.'s knowledge of the coal-mining industry—probably unequalled in Parliament—he was unanimously elected Chairman of the Labour Group of Miners' M.P.s.

In the aftermath of the 1959 Election, S.O. urged his comrades to cease their apologetics for being in a party of the Left . . . and Labour should also stop pretending that the ' Socialist world ' was not taking great steps forward. He referred to the Conservatives as ' creatures who openly and brazenly fool us, who laugh at us and—let us admit it—frighten us away from socialist policies and our own socialist goal '. S.O. appealed to his audiences : ' Are we true to our basic socialist faith ? Have we lost sight of the class war that is still raging ? Are we not divided, confused and discouraged by conflicting policies, some of which appear to be more concerned in running a capitalist state better than the Tories, than in ending the State and the Tory Party with it ? '[1]

During those six years after the Second World War, Labour had failed to seize its opportunity and establish Socialism ; the economic forces of Capitalism had eventually reasserted their supremacy and brought Attlee's administration to a humiliating and demoralising end. The lesson was clear enough in S.O.'s mind: boldness must be the cutting-edge for victory. Hence his profound disappointment with Labour's strategy *Signposts for the Sixties* adopted at the 1961 annual conference. True, the document declared that ' the economy is still dominated by a small ruling class ' and went on to advocate a tax on capital gains, greater State intervention in industry and science, and the nationalisation of building land. But what S.O. wanted was a statement of Socialist intent, that the next Labour government would sweep away the tycoons, the speculators and the land-owners ; writing in *Labour Monthly*, he called in particular for a massive expansion in trade with the Soviet bloc, China and the peoples ' who are so splendidly freeing themselves from the slavery of colonialism ' . . .

> To talk of co-operation with the British ruling-class is not only sheer superstition but a deliberate refusal to accept the logic of the class war waged by this powerful minority with its obsequious Tory politicians. It is no use pretending that we can meet the modest demands of this pamphlet [*Signposts to the Sixties*] in an economy hurtling from one crisis to another, and at a time when £1,600 millions are squandered on futile and suicidal armaments, or by making gifts of many, many millions of pounds a year to financial jugglers . . . or by ganging up with other reactionary governments in conspiring against the working-classes within the so-called European Common Market.
>
> The pamphlet's very first sentence tells us that we live in a scientific revolution. But neither this nor any other capitalist country is fully exploiting the vast creative potentialities of this scientific revolution in the interests of peace and of raising the standards of life of their people. This, however, is being increasingly done in those countries where the profiteer and financial gambler have been eliminated.

From this internationalist starting-point S.O. proposed the nationalisation of all industries, materials and services devoted to armaments production, the abolition of all nuclear weapons and foreign military bases on U.K. soil, Britain's withdrawal from all power blocs, and rigid control of the banks and financial houses . . .

> Such are some of the Signposts that would attract to the Labour movement very many of our bewildered and confused young men and women. Peace and friendship will be the drive and inspiration to the movement. To this there is no alternative, save the disintegration of a movement that failed to respond to the call of the hour.[2]

High hopes for disarmament had preceded the Paris summit of 16 May 1960. The Soviet Union smoothed the path to progress by announcing beforehand that their armed forces would be reduced by 33% ; the United States then unveiled plans for a fresh series of underground nuclear tests and, on the eve of the conference, placed their forces on a world-wide alert. But it was the shooting-down of an American U-2 spy-plane two weeks previously—1,200 miles inside Soviet territory—which ensured that the summit never left the ground. President Eisenhower's lies, retractions and justifications concerning the mission provoked the very worst display of Khruschevian stubborness and histrionics. The conference collapsed in a matter of days.

In the fresh outbreak of Cold War-mongering which followed, Britain's Conservative Government allowed the Americans to station Polaris nuclear submarines in the Holy Loch, Scotland. Negotiations between the two states had been conducted in secret for nearly a year ; even when Prime Minister Macmillan and Lord Home informed Parliament of their decision in November 1960, they would not permit a vote or a full debate to take place on this life-and-death issue.

Twenty-four Labour M.P.s made their own protest against Polaris in March the next year, voting against the Government's Air Force spending plans. Far more serious, however, was the rebellion which broke out in the early hours of Thursday morning on March 16 : five Labour back-benchers forced a division over the Government's entire military budget, much to the embarrassment of party leader Hugh Gaitskell and contrary to the policy of his Shadow Cabinet. The five then walked into a lobby against the Tory 'defence' expenditure programme, thereby registering their opposition to the Polaris deal (which also included an American promise to supply

Britain with nuclear missiles). In so doing, the so-called ' rebels ' were merely obeying the letter and spirit of Labour's unilateralist and anti-nuclear weapons policy, adopted at the momentous Scarborough conference five months earlier. The five who were in step with official Party policy—but out of step with the leadership and most of their parliamentary colleagues—were Michael Foot, Emrys Hughes, Sidney Silverman, William Baxter . . . and S. O. Davies.

On the Thursday evening they were dragooned before the Parliamentary Labour Party, where they each refused to apologise for their action ; after two hours of acrimonious discussion the assembled M.P.s resolved by 90 votes to 63 to eject the dissidents from the Parliamentary Party. From March 17 1961 onwards, S.O. and his four defiant comrades would sit in the House of Commons as independent Socialists. On foreign matters in particular, they worked closely together inside and—to a lesser degree—outside Westminster. The crises in Cuba precipitated many of the group's boldest speeches and parliamentary interventions.

The Caribbean island provided the latest battle-site in the proxy war between the United States and the Soviet Union. In January 1959 Fidel Castro's revolutionaries had overthrown the rotten Batista dictatorship (which had been armed by the British Government up to the very end) and set about dismantling the Mafia-capitalist oligarchy that had ruled Cuba. Trading links with Communist countries led to the termination of American aid ; Castro retaliated by seizing U.S. and British business assets. Washington's drastic economic retribution drove Castro fully into the Communist camp, which in turn prompted Presidents Eisenhower and Kennedy to prepare invasion plans. The attack on Cuba by thousands of C.I.A.-trained Cuban *émigrés* in April 1961 was easily repulsed by Castro's forces. The episode became known as the ' Bay of Pigs fiasco ' ; it also confirmed the revolution's popularity amongst the downtrodden masses of Cuba. In the Commons on April 26 S.O. joined Zilliacus and others in demanding a United Nations investigation into ' the origins of the armed landings in Cuba, the sources of the supplies in men, money, arms, equipment and transport, and where and under what auspices such men were trained '. The Lord Privy Seal, Edward Heath, repudiated the proposal and tried desperately to defend a speech delivered at the U.N. by the

United Kingdom's representative, who had declared Britain's faith in American denials of involvement in the Bay of Pigs assault.[3]

Tension increased still further in August, with the overnight raising of the Berlin Wall by the East German authorities. But the world's attention switched back to Cuba in October 1962, when the United States revealed that the island had received Soviet missiles which could carry nuclear warheads—and that concealed launching sites had already been constructed ; President Kennedy ordered a naval blockade of Cuba and demanded removal of the missiles and their camouflaged bases. He objected to this ' provocative and unjustified change in the *status quo* '—a *status quo* in which the U.S.A. held massive nuclear superiority, had surrounded the Soviet Union with military installations (many of them as close to Russian soil as was Cuba to the United States) and in which the Soviets had no nuclear bases outside its own territory. Indeed, the Americans even had an Air Force base at Guantanamo, in south-eastern Cuba !

Within two days of Kennedy's declaration, his naval blockade was in place—and awaiting the arrival of 25 Soviet ships. For a few days the world held its breath . . . until Khruschev agreed to dismantle the Cuban bases (against Castro's wishes) in return for an American guarantee not to invade the island. Throughout the drama S.O.'s stance had been to criticise Kennedy's ' over-reaction ', but also to call for a negotiated settlement. While he did not support unnecessary provocation of the U.S.A., he upheld the right of the Cuban government to pursue its own foreign and defence policies. The Merthyr Trades Council and Labour Party took an even stronger line, congratulating the Soviet Union on its ' restraint, courage and wisdom ' in the face of the ' criminally dangerous and irresponsible heroics of President Kennedy and the war maniacs of the United States '. They pointed out that the Americans had, since the fall of Batista's corrupt regime, denied the Cuban people's right to self-determination, operated an economic boycott, imposed an armed blockade that threatened to sink any ship trading with Cuba, trained and equipped Cuban exiles in the U.S.A. and Guatemala, and had encircled the U.S.S.R. with nuclear submarines and bases.[4]

S.O's attitude to the Soviet Union itself had not changed since his visit in 1922. He stayed in touch with developments there through its English-language publications and the Friendship Societies ;

in 1961 he played host at ' Gwynfryn ' to visiting Russian journalists, proudly showing them the sites of his historic town, boasting of its peerless tradition in progressive politics. When, in March 1962, he was invited to write an article in *Soviet News* to celebrate the 50th anniversary of *Pravda* (the Soviet Communist Party's daily newspaper) he thrilled to the task :

> I watched the Soviet Union being consolidated over one-sixth of the land of this planet, and among peoples of many races speaking many different languages and dialects. I followed with avidity the Soviet Press on the amazing way the U.S.S.R. solved the problem of nationalities that confronted them. There was no enslavement and exploitation of defenceless peoples, so characteristic of the imperialist powers. Rather, they were assisted by devoted scholars and thinkers whom I personally saw 40 years ago leaving Russia for these countries east of the Urals : Musicians, Philologists and Geologists. I distinctly recollect spending some time with them on the evening before they left on their long trek to spend some years among peoples, some of whom had never evolved a written language. They were people whose history was largely preserved in legend, in their folk-lore and folk-music. These philologists and musicians preserved their cultures in a permanent form, and the geologists and other scientists who followed them sought for and helped to develop the mineral and other resources of these countries. Today, these peoples are proud members of their autonomous republics, which are equally proud members of the U.S.S.R.[5]

The inspiration S.O. still derived from the Soviet Union is also reflected in the message he wrote for Radio Moscow in October 1962 :

> Forty years ago to this day I was with you . . . To any, if they exist, who doubt the enormous success of your revolution I would advise them to study conditions existing in pre-revolutionary days and compare them with life in the Soviet Union today—its dazzling successes in the scientific world, its vast educational and productive achievements, and its social system in which the overwhelming emphasis is placed on the sacredness of human life. And please remember, particularly you my young Soviet friends, that all this has been achieved in a hostile, jealous, and an extremely dangerous world.
>
> It is only in a Socialist State that war and the preparations for war bring profit to no-one. Nor do you profit on the hunger

> and oppression of others. Hence, may your Socialist State, your class-less society from which the profit-monger has been eliminated, be the inspiration of the working-classes the world over to fight with you for World Peace and world comradeship.[6]

S.O. continued to associate with the British-Soviet Friendship Society, with *Labour Monthly* and with other pro-Communist bodies in flagrant breach of Labour Party rules. Yet he did so with impunity. Perhaps his expulsion from the P.L.P. had assuaged the witch-finder generals Prothero and Phillips. His energetic participation in a campaign against N.A.T.O.'s training of West German soldiers in Pembrokeshire, in the summer of 1961, displayed once again his disregard of Transport House edicts.

In May that year S.O. attended a conference in Porthcawl convened by the South Wales N.U.M. and the Glamorgan Federation of Trade Councils ; the assembly in the Pavilion approved a resolution calling for the banning of German troops and their Panzer tanks from Britain, and established an All-Wales Campaign Committee. S.O. led the Committee's first deputation to the House of Commons and the Ministry of Defence. In the Commons he told the Prime Minister that ' the people of Wales are not in the least impressed by the Government's feeble efforts to mask this evil intention by attributing to N.A.T.O. virtues which we in Wales know to be wholly non-existent '. The next day, May 31, he was on his feet again, criticising the visit to London of West Germany's extreme right-wing Defence Minister, Franz-Josef Strauss. Especially provocative was the fact that more than 120 senior officers in the *Bundeswehr* (West Germany's armed forces) had served loyally under the old Nazi regime. Moreover, many of these men now filled major posts in N.A.T.O. itself : for example, the Commander-in-Chief of N.A.T.O.'s ground forces on continental Europe, General Hans Spiedel, had previously been in charge of the war-time Nazi occupation of Paris. Ex-Nazis still occupied leading posts in West Germany's present-day judiciary, police force and state bureaucracy.[7]

War-bombed Swansea played host to an impressive demonstration against the ' bloody ghosts of Hitler ' on 16 July 1961. The crowd marched behind the Seven Sisters Band on that sunny Saturday, carrying banners saying ' *Y Gân nid y Gwn i Gymru* ' (' A Song not a Gun for Wales ') and ' *Croeso i Walia ond nid i Ryfela* ' (Welcome to

Wales—but not to make War '). South Wales miners' president Will Whitehead introduced the speakers outside the Guildhall : Harold Davies, Leo Abse, Tudor Watkins, S.O. and a representative from Haverfordwest Trades Council.[8]

When the German troops arrived in August, Abse led thousands of trade unionists to the military headquarters in Pembrokeshire. Later that month Cliff Prothero issued a statement reiterating why the Welsh Council of Labour had refused to endorse such demonstrations—despite its policy of opposing the Panzers' presence in Wales : ' The Welsh Council of Labour is not in any way associated with the anti-German troops campaign committee ', Prothero explained, ' which from all appearances savours of Communist sponsorship . . . I don't want the Council mixed up with it '.[9] Even so, in the course of 1961 the British T.U.C., the N.U.M. and the General and Municipal Workers Union all added their voices to the protesting chorus. So worried did the War Office become that it attached an extra complement of public relations officers to the Army, charging them with the task of justifying the *Bundeswehr*'s annual forays into west Wales. S.O. mocked these ' miserable and wretched attempts ' to open the hearts of the Welsh people. At the same time, he was ever-anxious to disavow any ill-feeling towards the German people as a whole and would point out that ' within a short distance of where the Panzer lads were brought we have a considerable number of Germans engaged as miners '. With some crude exceptions, the campaign against the troops was conducted in an internationalist spirit ; indeed, the revival of militarism in West Germany met the opposition of millions of that state's own citizens, thousands of whom took to the streets to protest against rearmament, newly-introduced conscription and the outlawing of the Communist Party there.

Eventually the active dissent in Wales died down ; the War Office abandoned its propaganda and the German troops came and went annually without any fuss on either side. Plans to expand their exercises in Wales and England were quietly dropped. Abse and other M.P.s received a severe reprimand from their parliamentary colleagues ; had S.O. been a member of the Parliamentary Labour Party at the time, no doubt he too would have suffered this equivalent—in his eyes—of a slap on the wrist.

On 1 February 1962, the lone and—in this respect—familiar voice of S. O. Davies rang out again in the Commons chamber: this time he was attacking the establishment of a Territorial Army extra reserve force. The Speaker ruled out of order his repeated attempts to challenge Defence Secretary John Profumo's claim that the creation of the force was necessitated by the 'cold war'. S.O. wished to know what offensive role these additional part-time soldiers would fulfil in the event of a nuclear conflagration. With similar scepticism, he sought further information on April 17 about the Government's plans for population dispersal to Wales in antici-ation of an atomic strike against English cities. How could hund-reds of thousands, possibly millions, of refugees be accommodated in view of the serious housing problems in Wales? Parliamentary Secretary Dr. Hill promised S.O. a list of Welsh reception areas, assuring him in the Commons that the number of evacuees would be 'commensurate with the accommodation there'. How much central government assistance would be provided to help Welsh local authorities ensure ample shelter for them?—'None', came Dr. Hill's reply: existing accommodation would suffice. How completely S.O. thus exposed this cruel confidence trick upon the doomed inhabitants of targeted English conurbations!

Problems within Wales—as well as those outside—also demanded attention. Imminent publication of the 1961 Census had fanned fears of the future of rural Wales and the Welsh language. In anticipation of its gloomy revelations, S.O. proposed a Commons motion on April 4 concerning depopulation and unemployment. No longer, he quoted an eminent journalist, were these 'the days when the countryside was plentifully sprinkled with cottages, all with large families, all contributing to schools, entertainments and chapels and, in time, to talent and scholarship'. S.O. himself commented:

> We cannot make English-thinking people appreciate that Wales overwhelmingly owes its culture to the shepherd, the small farmer, the farm labourer, the village schoolmaster, the preacher, the miner and the iron-worker. It was from such workers that the inspiration and drive for higher education in Wales came. In no part of this island—I hope that my Scottish friends will not take umbrage at this—did the Intermediate Education Act have such a tremendous reception and impact as it did on the people of Wales . . .

> But the large majority of those who graduated, many with distinction in our universities, had to seek employment outside their own country, and this has hurt our Welsh sentiments over the years. The sacrifice entailed in getting our young people by their thousands into different universities before there was much State help was enormous.
>
> Economically and industrially our towns and villages were, and still are, cruelly neglected. The younger men and women had to leave their homes, but the sick, maimed and crippled, together with the older people, were tied to their homes and villages. This was responsible for a tremendous struggle on the part of our Welsh local authorities, with their meagre resources, to care for those who needed care most.

He contrasted the drop of 85,000 in the Welsh population between 1921 and 1959 with an increase of millions in England ; Merthyr Tydfil's population had declined by 21,000 over the past 50 years. He also attacked a recent speech delivered in Birmingham by Henry Brooke, the Minister of Housing and Local Government (and hence for Welsh Affairs !), who had cast a thirsty eye over the upper reaches of the River Severn in mid-Wales. S.O. sniffed another Tryweryn-style take-over in the air (as proved to be the case with the subsequent drowning of Clywedog) and warned :

> It is not a bit of good Ministers telling us that Wales is not being neglected. It is, and the figures of our depopulation and unemployment make it abundantly clear. We are not only getting tired of it. We are getting more and more angry that our country —and Wales is ours—is regarded just as a milch cow whose skills, talents and knowledge, even its towns, villages and its very existence, are used to cater for the pleasures, the needs, the whims and the idiosyncracies of people who are not of our country.
>
> Our country has natural resources and potentialities that could maintain happily and prosperously three times the largely stagnant population that we have today in the whole of Wales.

He challenged the Government to send somebody who was not ' fossilised in Tory traditions ' to witness the achievements of the Tennessee Valley Authority in fructifying large tracts of once-barren land ; better still, why not send an openminded person to see how the Soviet Union had transformed sandy deserts into fruit- and crop-growing lands ? As for the south Wales valleys : they would never be suitable ' dormitories ' for new industry on the coastal strip. Instead, the jobs should be brought to reinvigorate the valley communities in line with the 'Dalton Principle'. In his Ministerial response to the debate, Henry Brooke displayed characteristic patience and courtesy; he recited the sewerage and housing improvements carried out in 'the Principality'—speaking as if these were bounteous acts of Government charity for which the natives should be eternally grateful.

With the reorganisation of the water industry in 1963, S.O. and his Welsh Labour colleagues spoke out strongly in favour of creating a Welsh Water Board to control the nation's rich resources. Yet again, they were overruled by hundreds of English M.P.s, including Leeds M.P. and Minister for Welsh Affairs Keith Joseph.

By 1963, too, unemployment had reached 6% in Wales—and even 14% in parts of the southern coalfield. On February 13, a thousand Welsh miners and railwaymen marched through the streets of London to a rally in Soho Square; their placards bore the slogans: 'Jobs for Welsh Youth' and 'Not a Man on the Road'. When they lobbied Westminster at 3 o'clock that afternoon, it was S.O. who laid down the 'Welcome' mat for them.[10]

S.O. had been attending the Commons as an independent M.P. for more than two years, until the election of Harold Wilson as Labour Party leader prompted him to apply for readmission to the P.L.P. He announced to journalists in February 1963 that he would be sending a 'brief note' to the Chief Whip, 'as a gesture towards unity in the party under Mr Wilson'. Asked if he would be prepared to give a guarantee of good behaviour, if it was made a condition of readmission, S.O. replied: 'I do not think behaviour is the right word. I have always been prepared to go as far as is humanly possible to co-operate with other sections of the Labour movement, whether on the political or trade union front'. But, he added, 'I do have certain profound, life-long convictions as to the principles that should guide and inspire the Labour movement in this country'.[11] He posted his application on February 19; not until May 29 did the party's Parliamentary Committee approve his re-entry, and then only after he had promised not to defy the P.L.P. in Commons votes.

Under Harold Wilson's vigorous leadership, the Party entered the 1964 General Election campaign in high spirits. As always, S.O.'s election address mirrored his internationalist outlook. He had welcomed the Test Ban Treaty between the atomic superpowers in August 1963 ; now his manifesto reflected Labour's commitment to reduce East-West tension still further :

> LABOUR WILL APPOINT A MINISTER WITH SPECIAL RESPONSIBILITY FOR DISARMAMENT: IT WILL TRY TO STOP THE SPREAD OF NUCLEAR WEAPONS AND STOP THE PRIVATE SALE OF ARMS.
>
> Labour will definitely strengthen British influence in the United Nations and will urge the calling of Regular Summit Meetings. TALK, Yes ! But NO WAR !

S.O. dismissed his two challengers in Merthyr Tydfil with a faintly tongue-in-cheek indignance : that these upstarts should dare trespass upon his Socialist fiefdom ! He wrote of his ' annoyance and disgust when an arrogant, ambitious stranger, such as the present Tory candidate, aided and abetted by our own Merthyr people, comes along and pours his contempt on everything of which we have reason to be proud '—this after Sidney Doxsey, a Cardiff city councillor, had applauded a proposal from the Local Government Boundary Commission that Merthyr be deprived of its County Borough status and thus merged with Glamorgan County Council. S.O. pointed out that vital services would henceforth be governed from Cardiff, including Education in which the Borough could boast such a fine record ; moreover, the town would also lose its own fire service, police force and control over two-thirds of its revenue.

The second candidate was Ioan Bowen Rees of *Plaid Cymru*. Welsh Nationalists hoped for a high vote in Merthyr, their expectations fuelled by three victories in Borough Council elections two years ago. At that time, perhaps unfairly, S.O. had publicly questioned the sincerity of their patriotism—pointing out that most of *Plaid*'s leading figures in Merthyr were not Welsh-speaking. As for Mr Ioan Bowen Rees now :

> The other Candidate calls himself a ' Welsh Nationalist '. This apparently justifies him in opposing me in this Election. All I need to tell you is that I am Welsh and Welsh-speaking, and that it was I who introduced in the House of Commons the most comprehensive Bill in the history of the British Parliament on Home Rule for Wales. This Bill was debated for a whole day, and it will again, at the first opportunity, be submitted to the House of Commons. LABOUR—ON ITS RETURN AS A GOVERNMENT—WILL APPOINT A MINISTER FOR WALES WITH FULL CABINET RANK.

Harold Wilson moved into Downing Street that October as Labour ended the 'Thirteen Years of Tory Misrule', although his overall majority in the Commons was only 5 seats. In Wales the Labour Party took a record 28 of the 36 constituencies ; yet again, S.O. reaped three-quarters of the votes in Merthyr Tydfil :

S. O. DAVIES (Labour)	23,275
S. DOXSEY (Conservative)	4,767
I. B. REES (*Plaid Cymru*)	2,878

Although Labour had ditched its policy of unilateral nuclear disarmament back in 1961, after just 12 months, the Party's 1964 Election manifesto instilled some optimism in S.O. As pledged, Prime Minister Wilson duly appointed a Minister for Disarmament —Lord Chalfont—and the negotiations began which eventually led to a Non-Proliferation Treaty, limiting the spread of atomic weapons to other countries. But Chalfont, in common with the rest of Wilson's Government, remained totally committed to N.A.T.O. and the capitalist camp. Only the most terrible of wars succeeded, eventually, in shaking Britain and Western Europe's hitherto slavish support for American foreign policies.

Britain's Labour Government endeavoured to extricate President Johnson from this deepening morass, although refusing all the while to condemn America's intervention in Vietnam. As the horrific civilian casualties mounted in North Vietnam, where the U.S. Air Force was dropping three times as many bombs in a single month than had been unloaded upon Europe throughout the whole of World War Two, and as the torture of captured 'Vietcong' in the South was exposed beyond question, waves of protest swept across the world. To S.O.'s mind, it was Korea all over again ; he was particularly outraged by the widespread devastation of houses, hospitals and schools in the North, and by the obliteration of entire villages in American 'search and destroy' missions in the South. In August 1965 he sent this message to a 'Peace for Vietnam' rally in Aberafan :

> The Mass Murder by the U.S.A. Government of the politically uncommitted peoples of Vietnam is a shocking commentary on the so-called civilisation of the United States. We tell them to turn their attentions to the millions of starving coloured people in the GHETTOES of their own country . . . To the

> Americans we say : Go home, end your humbug and hypocrisy about Freedom and Civilization in other parts of the world until you have established them in the lives of the American people. Then we may respect you.[12]

The Communist-led national liberation struggle in Vietnam had been launched anew in late 1959. Having resisted the war-time Japanese invaders, and driven out the French colonialists (for the second time), Ho Chi Minh's forces had established a free state in the North. They then set about overthrowing the unpopular dictatorship imposed on South Vietnam by the U.S.A. in 1954. When an American-backed military coup in 1963 failed to stabilise the South, U.S. troops began to arrive in their thousands : by mid-1965 more than 150,000 of them occupied that part of Vietnam to the south of the 17th Parallel. With guerilla war raging in the South and American bombing intensifying in the North, the U.S.A. had committed its international prestige to this crusade against Communism.

Atrocity was piled upon atrocity in Vietnam. The Americans deployed napalm, incapacitating gases, phosphorous bombs, defoliants and anti-personnel shells, wiping out rice fields, forests and human beings with unbridled ruthlessness—moving the U.N. Secretary-General U Thant to describe the Vietnam War as ' the most barbarous in history '.[13] By 1967, Labour Party and T.U.C. conferences were condemning U.S. policy in Vietnam, demanding the withdrawal of all foreign troops and calling for the country's reunification. These had always been S.O.'s sentiments ; in December 1969 he and 50 other Labour M.P.s voted for them—against the Government and in defiance of the Parliamentary Labour Party. But still Wilson and his administration held Uncle Sam's hat and coat, as dogged as the Americans who were heading for such a bloody, humiliating defeat.

Labour had muddled by with its single-figure majority in the Commons since the 1964 General Election, until Wilson picked an opportune time to strengthen his Government's mandate : on 31 March 1966 a million additional voters swung over to Labour, giving the party an overall superiority of 98 M.P.s. Arithmetically, there was no room for such a dramatic shift in Merthyr ; nonetheless, S.O.'s election address gave the sacrificial Conservative candidate a merciless roasting :

Again the Tories are opposing me and the Labour Movement in this historic Socialist Constituency. Already the Tory Candidate, an utter stranger to this Borough, has, in his complete ignorance, found everything we have tried to do for you to be worse than useless. The presumption of this fellow, who never, until he came here to try to get you to give him your votes, took the least interest in the many problems that our long history has left us. The population of Merthyr and Dowlais, 120 years ago, was as big then as it is today. Thousands of the houses built in those days, with their primitive services, have to be demolished and their sites re-planned and modern houses with modern services provided for our people . . .

MANY OF YOU WILL REMEMBER, AND FEW OF OUR LOCAL TORIES WILL FORGET, THAT WHEN I WAS FIRST ELECTED TO PARLIAMENT, THE GREATER PART OF OUR BOROUGH WAS IN RUINS. THANKS TO TORY GOVERNMENTS WE THEN HAD OVER 13,000 OF OUR PEOPLE UNEMPLOYED, AND 17,000 HAD BEEN COMPELLED TO LEAVE US BECAUSE OF UNEMPLOYMENT. BETWEEN THOSE TWO WORLD WARS OVER 25,000 OF OUR PEOPLE WERE DRIVEN FROM THEIR HOMES IN THIS BOROUGH DESPERATELY LOOKING FOR WORK ELSEWHERE.

We Merthyr people, with our memories of broken homes and broken hearts of those terrible days, do find it difficult to forgive the arrogance of those ignorant and pompous creatures who merely visit us in the hope that they might fool us to vote for them.

IN OUR LAST PARLIAMENTARY ELECTION THE TORY CANDIDATE GOT BY FAR THE LOWEST VOTE EVER POLLED BY A TORY CANDIDATE IN THIS CONSTITUENCY. THIS TIME WE SHOULD DO BETTER STILL BY TREATING HIM AS YOU HAVE THE WELSH NATIONALIST CANDIDATE. *DO SEE THAT BOTH LOSE THEIR DEPOSITS OF* £150.

The Tory escaped with his money—just :

S. O. DAVIES (Labour)	21,737
G. L. PREECE (Conservative)	4,082
M. STEPHENS (*Plaid Cymru*)	3,361

Only S.O. could have talked to the people of Merthyr in those terms in his election address. At the age of 82 he had long become as much a fixture in the town as the Miners Hall, his campaign headquarters under the direction of Stan Beynon. Indeed, S.O.'s Edwardian style of dress dated from the same period as the building: the wide-brimmed homburg hat, the white silk scarf, black jacket, pin-stripped trousers and long black overcoat constituted his 'uniform', and no occasion could cause him to modify it. When the National Museum of Wales invited him to an annual dinner, S.O. declined 'because of their punctilious insistence that my presence could only be suffered when garbed in evening dress—and that further adorned by decorations'. He mocked those who acquired and displayed medals as a 'means of giving more pronounced and conspicious physical evidence of their vanity'. With a mischievous relish he released his letter of refusal to the press, discussing the merits of a Latin adage while so doing.[14]

On this and many other occasions, S.O.'s companions in the 'Crown' slapped their thighs in mirth, enjoying his erudite and cutting wit. There were also the tales about the man himself, especially his legendary fondness for cars with souped-up engines. How numerous the times when friends had been recruited to push-start his 1950s model, a Morris family saloon! Suddenly the car would spark into life, roaring off apace and leaving a heap of exhausted helpers in the roadside. The secret of S.O.'s explosive departure, according to one of the survivors, was 'a 10 horse-power engine under an 8 horse-power bonnet'. Nor could a richer conversationalist than S.O. be found anywhere: from football to the fall of the Roman Empire, his was an expansive seam of quotations, anecdotes and opinions. 'Old S.O.', everyone agreed, 'he's great value for money!' He looked and sounded—indeed, he comported himself—like one of those American elder statesman, the hometown hero, kind and incorruptible, the 'goodie' in a Warner Brothers movie. When two young women—American postgraduates—called at the 'Crown' one afternoon and announced: 'We've come to see the Senator' . . . the misnomer seemed to suit S.O. more perfectly than the title 'Member of Parliament'.

But even the 'Crown's' reign as the chin-wag capital of Merthyr came to an end; Tom Thomas passed away and his successor laid out a 'Welcome' mat to all and sundry—including women. Their unofficial club now disbanded, disgruntled regulars searched elsewhere for a tap-room they could call their own. S.O. dubbed them '*Y Cymry ar wasgar!*' ('the Welsh overseas!'). Many of the wanderers eventually found domicile in the ' Lamb ', a tavern spartan in everything except atmosphere. S.O. joined them less frequently for his glass of ale ; he was still to be seen often enough, however, strolling along Merthyr High Street, doffing his hat to passers-by, pausing every few yards to listen to a grievance or to make a polite enquiry. These were his ' surgeries '—the High Street, and ' Gwyn-fryn ' with its ever-open door and never-silent telephone. Visiting journalists from Cardiff and London were told not to bother making a note of the M.P.'s address or how to get there; they simply arrived in Merthyr, stopped the first person they saw outside the railway station and asked : ' Which way to S.O.'s house ? ' In a town of 50,000 people, the reply was unfailingly prompt and accurate.

S.O.'s partiality to a glass of beer , and his enjoyment of public-house conviviality, never lessened his distaste for alcoholic excess. Like Keir Hardie before him, he warned against the debilitating effects of too much drink on social responsibility and personal self-respect. S.O.'s distrust of this opiate of the masses led him, for instance, to oppose the 1961 Licensing Act which permitted pubs to open on a Sunday and provided for the wider sale of intoxicating liquor. As he explained at the time :

> My vote on the Second Reading of this Bill was not merely against Sunday opening in Wales, but against the whole Bill ; a Bill that is utterly irresponsible, anti-social and immoral ; a Bill that will immensely increase facilities for selling and drinking alcohol, that will inevitably spread drinking habits, particularly among young people.
>
> The Bill is a brewers and distillers Bill.

Some of his friends were pub licensees ; to them he said : 'The solution is not a seven-day week enslavement to this profit seeker, but in a reasonable return for the service you now render '.[15]

S.O. had created an image for himself which was nonetheless true to his own tastes, feelings and beliefs ; it was larger-than-life and yet he lived up to it. He took a playful pride in his venerability : one journalist, anxious to interview S.O. about some breach of the Party line, rang him and received the reply—' Yes, this is S.O. speaking, or what's left of his old bones ! ' With slightly self-mocking grandiloquence he habitually referred to himself not in the first person, as ' I ' or ' me ', but in the third person—as ' S.O.' For example, he once explained his rebelliousness to *Western Mail* correspondent Peter Tinniswood thus :

> When the voters of Merthyr elected him as their M.P., they knew what S.O. was like. They knew full well that old S.O. wouldn't sit back and follow the party whips like a sheep. If S.O. feels something is wrong, he says so. And that, Tinniswood, is that.[16]

This ' S.O. phenomenon ', and the town that hosted it, attracted its share of feature writers, too. Richard West visited Merthyr Tydfil to draw a truculent portrait of the place and its people in the early 1960s ; he asked Tal Lloyd—a ' shrewd, wary official of the A.E.U.'—why the borough continued to return its ' old-fashioned ' M.P. Lloyd told him :

> We're very loyal here in Merthyr. Some people might call it sentimentality but we call it loyalty. And S.O. is wonderfully fit both physically and mentally. Personally I think an M.P. should retire at 65, but if I had to vote on this I wouldn't vote against S.O. It would break his heart to be rejected.

Not even as right-wing a commentator as West could entirely escape the spell :

> Mr. S. O. Davies has an unshakeable majority and an unshakeable belief that the ideas of Keir Hardie need no modification for 1961. ' Esso the Petrolman ', as he is nicknamed by the irreverent, has probably talked more nonsense than any Labour M.P. in the House, not excluding Mr. Zilliacus. But his extreme age and extreme goodheartedness excuse his extreme left-wing foolishness.[17]

S.O.'s presence impressed itself on any social or private engagement. There were very few spheres of community life with which he was not closely connected. As a patron of the local rugby club he was the honoured guest at its dinners, the sporting target of a speech-making quip or two ; and many were the Saturdays when he walked to nearby Penydarren Park, to cheer on Merthyr Town Football Club. Whether at a family wedding or a funeral his nephews and nieces eagerly awaited the appearance of ' Uncle Stephen '. Of course, by now his own children had pursued their different paths away from ' Gwynfryn ' : Margo was a doctor in

London ; Gwyneth had raised a family of her own in Yorkshire, where Alyn would soon become the Principal of Bretton Hall College of Education ; S.O.'s younger son David Stephen, at the age of 23, was a computer programmer ; and Mary had taught at Cyfarthfa secondary school before cancer took her from her husband and children in 1960. Holding education in such high esteem, S.O. rejoiced in his offspring's achievements : it is a rare miner who prays for his son to inherit a pit-helmet, or for his daughter to marry one.

'S.O. is Merthyr and Merthyr is S.O.' ran the local saying which expressed the indivisibility of the town and its M.P. S.O.'s involvement in great international controversies never caused him to neglect the welfare of his constituency. Of paramount concern was the area's economic and social infrastructure. Early in the decade he had participated in the campaign against Dr Beeching's massacre of the railway network; when the axe fell upon the passenger service through Quakers Yard Tunnel, it severed the line that ran across the south Wales valleys at their northern end. S.O. precipitated an adjournment debate in the Commons on 22 April 1964 when the British Railways Board decided to close the Quakers Yard sidings, and the tracks to Ocean and Taff-Merthyr collieries. He outlined the injurious consequences for the distribution of coal and general goods, deploring also the redundancies that would ensue. In reply, the Tory transport spokesman Tom Galbraith declared his Government's impotence to intervene in British Rail's freight policy ; 'the Beeching Report', he predicted, 'if it is fully implemented will actually reduce the total road traffic'. As for the redundancies, all the men had been offered alternative emplyoment—although he ignored S.O.'s challenge to specify the location of the jobs.

In the course of his response the Transport Under-Secretary had admitted that 'the roads in the area are not all they might be'. Over many years S.O. had written letters, led deputations and made speeches in testimony to that under-stated fact. The new Heads of the Valleys road was, with its three lanes, extremely dangerous over several stretches. He also battled for extensive improvements to the A470 trunk road between Cardiff and Merthyr. Nowhere else in Britain can there be two historic industrial and commercial centres so close together in mileage—and so far apart in travelling time. As S.O. pointed out, statutory provision had been made in 1946 for the development of the A470 as a national carriageway linking north, mid and south Wales. Yet virtually nothing had been done in over 30 years.

With its disadvantageous communications and environment, Merthyr's economic health worsened rapidly in the 1960s when a drastic run-down of the coal industry began. S.O. had long warned of the follies and delusions of a ' cheap fuel ' policy based on imported oil ; the Labour Government speedily embarked on just such a course. By 1968 more than 25,000 miners had vanished from the N.C.B.'s pay-roll in south Wales, a couple of thousand of them in and around Merthyr Tydfil. Emigration was wiping nearly 1,000 names a year off the Borough's electoral register ; but even that did not prevent the local unemployment rate climbing to 5%—three times the British norm. Without decisive resistance from the miners union, S.O. again feared the collapse through anaemia of his beloved mining communities with their ' passion for education and culture '. On 25 November 1965 he initiated a Commons discussion of the coal crisis, arguing for the maintenance of jobs as the supreme priority :

> Those collieries where the taking is not exhausted must be kept going until alternative employment is there, right in the heart of these communities. They are the most thoroughly established communities in this island of ours. What is the use of destroying all that is dear to them and, at the same time, creating a psychological reaction there if we do not do the right thing in the time now left to us ?

S.O. quizzed the Government about the redeployment and retraining of miners, pointing out that few collieries in south Wales could absorb extra labour. In truth, while miners were being sacked in their thousands, they were only being redeployed in hundreds and retrained in dozens. For his own patch, Methyr's M.P. called for more Government contract work, especially for the Teddington Aircraft factory.

Besides mass unemployment, emigration and the collapse of local communities, another spectre of the 1930s rose again : schemes to abandon the valleys altogether. Early in 1967 the Secretary of State for Economic Affairs directed the Government's Central Planning Unit to investigate possible sites for a mammoth new town, to be bounded to the east by the River Severn and to the south by the Bristol Channel. S.O. opposed the notion from the start, as did many M.P.s and local authorities in south Wales. He forced a parliamentary debate on the ' Severnside Scheme ' on April 24, voicing the anger and apprehension of many thousands of Welsh people :

> I and many others in South Wales, particularly in the industrial valleys, wonder whether the Government, in considering this vast and uncalled-for expenditure, have given a fleeting thought to the cruel and disastrous effect of such a new Severnside city on our valley communities. We do not think they have. They have certainly forgotten the exceptionally vast industrial and economic contribution which those valleys have for generations made to the well-being of the country at a great cost to life and limb. It is also obvious that the Government have ignored the outstanding political contribution made to our movement, which brought the Government into being, by the South Wales miners in particular.
> . . . Hence the importance to this Government of keeping the South Wales valleys alive in their Socialist faith. I do not apologise for using that expression. I know that it belongs to a terminology which is becoming more and more alien and forgotten. Why talk of spending £1,000 million on piecing together an aggregation of one million people who will be strangers to one another, with no common social or industrial bonds ?

Three months later the Government's Welsh Office plan *Wales : The Way Ahead* proposed the massive expansion of Llantrisant, to suck the people and industry out of the valleys and into a ' New Town '. The Severnside plan never reached fruition, while the growth of Llantrisant was officially stunted a few years later. Saving money, rather than saving the valleys, was the decisive factor in both decisions.

In S.O.'s opinion, the Government's insensitivity to the plight of the valleys was exceeded only by its culpability for the decline of Merthyr Tydfil. On the eve of the T.U.C. conference in September 1966 he wrote to the General Council urging workers to vote against Labour's incomes policy and Selective Employment Tax. Restricting wages was reducing the demand for consumer goods such as toys and washing machines—the manufacture of which was the mainstay of his constituency's industrial base. Redundancies arising from this and from the imposition of S.E.T. on service industries would, he claimed, turn Merthyr into a 'ghost town' (hence his consistent refusal to endorse these measures in the Commons lobby). On this occasion the Trades Union Congress ignored S.O.'s advice, although the following year delegates emphatically condemned the drift of Labour's economic policies—especially pay controls.[18]

It became a source of deepening unease in the working-class movement that Wilson and his Deputy Leader George Brown had surrounded themselves with a *coterie* of industrialists: men like Frank (subsequently Lord) Kearton of Courtaulds, George (subsequently Lord) Cole of Unilever, (Sir) Siegmund Warburg and John Berkin of Shell wielded enormous influence over the Government's economic strategy. The Chairman of the National Prices and Incomes Board established in 1965, Aubrey Jones, was even a Conservative M.P. and a director of G.K.N.! In his earliest days as Prime Minister, Harold Wilson had come face-to-face with the realities confronting a reforming Labour Government in a capitalist society. His plan to finance higher social expenditure by intensifying the taxation of wealthy individuals and companies antagonised the international money markets. Worried about the resulting 'disincentive' to top managers and investors, finance capitalists who held their assets in pounds sterling retaliated by selling their English currency or speculating against it—thereby pushing down the value of the pound and forcing up the bank rate. With the international capitalist community demanding public spending cuts, Wilson attended a significant meeting on the evening of 24 November 1964, which he recorded in his memoirs thus:

> We had our most desperate meeting with the Governor of the Bank of England. Claiming that our failure to act in accordance with his advice had precipitated the crisis, he was now demanding all-round cuts in expenditure, regardless of social or even economic priorities, and fundamental changes in some of the Chancellor's economic announcements.
>
> Not for the first time, I said that we had now reached the situation where a newly-elected Government with a mandate from the people was being told, not so much by the Governor of the Bank of England but by international speculators, that the policies on which we had fought the election could not be implemented; that the Government was to be forced into the adoption of Tory policies to which it was fundamentally

> opposed. The Governor confirmed that that was, in fact, the case.
>
> I asked him if this meant that it was impossible for any Government, whatever its party label, whatever its manifesto or the policies on which it fought an election, to continue, unless it immediately reverted to full-scale Tory policies. He had to admit that that was what his argument meant, because of the sheer compulsion of the economic dictation of those who exercised decisive economic power.[19]

Wilson sought a stronger democratic mandate in 1966 and received it ; but in practice he could still not overcome the self-interest of the financiers and big businessmen. The Government succumbed to their dictates, chopping its spending programmes, instituting a wage-freeze and cutting working-class living standards by raising a higher share of its revenue from indirect taxes on consumer spending rather than direct taxes on income and wealth. S.O.'s disillusionment ran deeper by the month after that General Election ; he disassociated himself from Labour's pro-capitalist policies in a series of important parliamentary divisions. Firstly, the Conservative Opposition moved a motion of ' No Confidence ' in January 1968 ; this followed the devaluation finally conceded by Wilson's Cabinet two months previously, and which had been accompanied by drastic cut-backs in public expenditure (involving the restoration of prescription charges and holding down the school-leaving age). At the end of a two-day debate, on January 18, S.O. and 25 other Labour back-benchers witheld their vote from the Government's lobby. But the retribution demanded by outraged Party loyalists quickly degenerated into farce : Chief Whip John Silkin wrote to the rebels—without consulting the parliamentary liaison committee—informing them that they had ' endangered the existence ' of the Government and would consequently be suspended from all Labour Party activities. Yet no provision existed in the Party's constitution for such a directive ! In the ensuing confusion, the Chief Whip's letter was withdrawn and the defaulting M.P.s agreed—together with their colleagues—to abide by the P.L.P.'s hastily rewritten code of conduct.

Just over 12 months later, on 21 April 1969, S.O. joined 38 other Labour M.P.s in defying a 3-line whip on a crucial Budget resolution ; they were protesting against the third increase in S.E.T. in four years. When asked by Silkin to justify his abstention,

S.O. wrote back describing the tax as 'a contemptible and anti-working class piece of legislation' which had put over 130 local workers out of a job after the last increase. Silkin then selected S.O., along with three others of the 39 with chronic records of indiscipline, for suspension from the P.L.P. This action was approved by the liaison committee but, once more, the long arm of coincidence plucked S.O. from purgatory. On the eve of a P.L.P. meeting to ratify the suspension, Wilson relieved a perplexed Silkin of his post. Appearing before the Party meeting on the morrow, April 30, his replacement Robert Mellish performed an act of inaugural clemency—and granted the four delinquents a free pardon! In any event, by this time S.O. had reached the depths of despondency; he vented his feelings in a newspaper interview:

> The Prime Minister must assume the responsibility for the record of his Government, and I am deeply disappointed in its performance. With all that we know now unemployment should be pathetically obsolete. That we have it now is a crime. You see, this Government has been very, very foolish. In the past eight-and-a-half years there have been 21 changes in purchase tax. When the last one came it threw 1,300 people out of work in my constituency. When S.E.T. was introduced 1,400 people lost their jobs in this area. When he sees this, S.O. cannot sit back and do nothing.[20]

Unlike the Labour Government, S.O. himself had withstood the parliamentary and other pressures to become part of the Establishment; as he informed one journalist: '*Un peth mae nhw ddim wedi ei wneud gydag S.O.—'dy'n nhw ddim wedi gallu gwneud 'professional politician' ohono fe. A Duw a'n helpo i tawn i wedi mynd i'r cyfeiriad hwnnw!*'[21] ('One thing they haven't done to S.O.—they haven't turned him into a professional politician. God help us if I were to go in that direction!'). More than 30 years in St. Stephen's had not dimmed S.O.'s desire for Socialism. He always believed that Capitalism would prove to be obsolete, that people would realise the necessity of replacing it with a more rational and just society. Although such a fundamental change would require the clearly-indicated consent of the mass of the population—which in Britain's tradition would probably express itself at some stage through the ballot box—this did not make him an idolator of Parliament or parliamentarism. He did not rule out the decisive role that might be played by forces outside the House of Commons ; but even they would be bound to have a voice inside as well. S.O. dedicated the second half of his life to being a full-time spokesman for working-class interests, using the platforms afforded him by his status as an M.P. In the Commons he took the part conscientiously, involving himself in the *minutiae* of parliamentary business if it would help secure real improvements for those he represented. Nowhere was this more evident than in the fields of National Insurance, compensation for industrial injuries and the National Health Service. During and immediately after the war he immersed himself in the entrails of Welfare State legislation, making many speeches with that rare combination of technical expertise and first-hand experience. One cause especially close to his heart was the dignity and comfort of retired workers ; he blamed the Depression and Tory policies for preventing the accumulation of life savings. His multiple efforts to achieve decent living standards for pensioners even earned him an accolade from the *Merthyr Express* as ' the Old People's Champion ' : this followed S.O.'s motion—talked out by Tory M.P.s—in 1959 for an increase in pensions, free television and radio licences for the elderly, central government grants to build modern old people's sheltered homes, housing schemes in the community, and home helps and meals-on-wheels at nominal prices. Not surprisingly, he was a popular guest speaker at annual rallies of the O.A.P. Association of Wales—presided over by his old friend and comrade, Dick Beamish.

Early in the summer of 1966 the name of S.O. Davies was drawn, for the second time in his career, near the top of the Private Members ballot. After consulting the National Union of Mineworkers and the mining group of M.P.s (notably Harold Finch of Bedwellte), he introduced a short Bill to aid pneumoconiotic miners who had contracted emphysema or chronic bronchitis. For decades successive Governments had—on the advice of the Medical Research Council—refused to recognise a definite relationship between these respiratory ailments and the men's working conditions : yet miners everywhere knew that whether or not emphysema and bronchitis were actually caused by working underground, they were certainly aggravated by the conditions there—adding considerably to the misery of pneumoconiosis victims.

On 2 December 1966, S.O. presented his National Insurance Acts 1946 and 1948 (Amendment) Bill for its Second Reading. It proposed that chronic bronchitis and emphysema should—like tuberculosis—be treated as if they were the effects of pneumoconiosis where it, too, was present. Thus, for example, a miner suffering 60% disablement from pneumoconiosis and 30% from, say, emphysema would be compensated at a level of 90% disablement—where once he would have been assessed for benefit at only 60%. Explaining his Bill to M.P.s, S.O. estimated that it would cost a paltry £15-20 millions—at a time when the state Industrial Fund had amassed over £320 millions. He paid a richly-deserved compliment to Professor Gough and his team from the Welsh National School of Medicine, for their research into pneumoconiosis and associated diseases ; S.O. contrasted their work to the record of the Medical Research Council's committee :

> In 1934 this Committee concluded that there was no evidence that the inhalation of anthracite or other coal dust caused fibrosis of the lungs in coal trimmers. This conclusion was subsequently proved to be utterly wrong, but unfortunately this wrong and grossly misleading conclusion, which any practical coalminer would have corrected—there is no doubt about that—had most serious consequences among us as coal miners. It was not only extended to coal workers and others exposed to this hazard, but it was reported to the international conference on silicosis in Geneva in 1938 that a Medical Research Council's Committee in this country had concluded that coal dust in itself did not produce fibrosis of the lungs.
>
> I am speaking from experience when I say that this had literally fatal consequences among our miners. For instance, it delayed the suppression of coal dust in mines for almost a generation, at goodness knows what expense in human lives.

S.O. went on to cite authoritative statistics and reports connecting bronchitis and emphysema with the coal industry ; he also pointed out that Australia, South Africa and some European countries already prescribed the two as occupational diseases or hazards. The Ministry of Health and Social Services—whose support was essential for the Bill to become law—was not unsympathetic. Although its advisers could not accept that coalmining actually caused emphysema or bronchitis, they agreed that both complaints would be aggravated by pneumoconiosis in its later stages. The

Minister, Margaret Herbison, backed the Bill—on condition that the disability from pneumoconiosis (including any tuberculosis present) must in each case be more than 50%. Therefore, someone with 40% disablement from pneumoconiosis, plus 20% from emphysema, would continue to draw benefit at the old level of 40% ; but under S.O's measure, a victim of 50% pneumoconiosis, plus 20% from emphysema, would now be assessed for benefit at 70% disablement, instead of the old 50%.

Ironically, though, this improvement also illustrates one of the anomalies and injustices persisting in the compensation. Indeed, S.O. was bitterly accused at the South Wales Miners annual conference of ' missing a great opportunity ' by some of the delegates. He reacted angrily to this charge of timidity : to have insisted upon full statutory recognition of these and other lung ailments as ' industrial diseases ' in their own right would have accomplished nothing. The Government would have rejected the Bill out of hand. As it was, S.O. steered a reform through the legislative process which, within very few years, had benefited more than 2,000 men from the mining communities.[22]

NOTES

[1]S.O.'s comments about the Conservative Party and its leaders are taken from speech notes in the S. O. Davies Papers, Swansea (Ref : 1E).

[2]' Signposts—or Windmills? ' in *Labour Monthly*, October 1961.

[3]For the events and preparation leading up to the Bay of Pigs invasion, see *From Yalta to Vietnam* (1967) by David Horowitz, pp. 194-208, 354-356.

[4]For the Cuban missile crisis see Horowitz (as above), pp. 379-389; the statement issued in November 1962 by the Merthyr Trades Council and Labour Party is to be found in the S. O. Davies Papers, Swansea (Ref : 1A, *ii*).

[5]The full text of S.O.'s message for *Pravda* is in the S. O. Davies Papers, Swansea (Ref : 1A, *ii*) ; a letter of thanks from Jack Woddis of *Soviet News* (dated 6 April 1962) is there also (Ref : 1A, *i*).

[6]S.O. sent the message to Radio Moscow on 22 October 1962 : see the S. O. Davies Papers, Swansea (Ref : 1A, *ii*). The invitation to him was dated 18 October 1962 (Ref : 1A, *i*).

[7]The white-washing of Nazis began soon after the end of World War Two, according to U.S. de-Nazification chief Joseph Napoli in the *Annals of the American Academy* (1949). How the C.I.A. and the West German Government employed Reinhard Gehlen and the German Army's war-time Intelligence Section for anti-Communist work is dealt with in *The Secret War for Europe* (1968) by Louis Hagen. The extent to which Nazi war criminals have enjoyed immunity in Western Europe—but suffered vigorous prosecution in the Communist Bloc—is shown in the *Times*, 1 July 1981. The pre-war Nazi connections of top political and military personnel in post-war West Germany are detailed in, for example, ' The Old Knights Network ' by John Peet in *Labour Monthly*, March/April 1978 and in Hagen (see above). The Anglo-American policy to restore pro-Nazi bankers, administrators and industrialists to top positions in post-war West Germany is revealed in *Blind Eye to Murder* (1981) by Tom Bower. ' Interpol ' was run by Nazis and other European Fascists from 1938 till 1972, according to Alan Sinclair (and Simon Wiesenthal) in ' Odessing Interpol's History ', published by the *Alternative News Service* (1975).

[8]See the poems ' The Bloody Ghosts of Hitler ' by C. Humphreys in *The Miner*, July/August 1961, and ' Ail-Ddyfodiad Hitler ' by T. E. Nicholas in *Rwy'n Gweld o Bell* (1965). The march and rally in Swansea were extensively reported in the *South Wales Voice*, 21 August 1961.

[9]Prothero's statement appeared in the *South Wales Echo*, 26 August 1961. The campaign against the Panzers is vividly recalled in *Private Member* (1973) by Leo Abse, pp. 77-80.

[10]See 'The Lobby' by Dai Francis in *The Miner*, March/April 1963.

[11]*Western Mail*, 18 February 1963 ; S.O.'s letter asking for the Labour Whip to be restored is in the S. O. Davies Papers, Swansea (Ref : 1A, *ii*).

[12]S. O. Davies Papers, Swansea (Ref : 1A, *ii*).

[13]Quoted in *The Cold War* (1969) by Paul Hastings, p. 120 ; by November 1967 some 500,000 U.S. troops were fighting alongside 645,000 South Vietnamese conscripts and 100,000 other soldiers supplied by anti-Communist governments. Yet even against these odds, the 200,000-strong National Liberation Front controlled half of the Southern countryside ; 109,000 troops deserted the Southern Army in a single year to join the N.L.F. (Hastings, pp. 120-1). See also Horowitz (Note 4 above), pp. 138-159.

[14]*South Wales Echo*, 8 March 1957.

[15]*Merthyr Express*, 17 December 1960.

[16]S.O. gave an extensive interview to the *Western Mail*, 16 April 1969.

[17]'A Town Like Malice' by Richard West in *Time and Tide*, 19 October 1961.

[18]S.O.'s attack on the S.E.T. and incomes policy, and his appeal to the T.U.C., were reported in the *South Wales Echo*, 31 August 1966.

[19]*The Labour Government 1964-70* (1971) by Harold Wilson, p. 37.

[20]*Western Mail*, 16 April 1969.

[21]*Y Cymro*, 13 May 1970.

[22]S.O.'s Bill and the technical arguments around it are expertly covered in *Memoirs of a Bedwellty M.P.* (1972) by Harold Finch, pp. 173-185. Miners' criticism of S.O. and his reply to it were reported in the *Western Mail*, 5 May 1967.

Chapter Ten

THE MAN FOR MERTHYR

On the morning of Friday, 21 October 1966, S.O. had just begun work at home on his correspondence and constituency business. It was a sunny day, windless but with a mist obscuring the tips of coal waste piled high upon Merthyr Mountain.

At about quarter-past-nine a roaring, thundering sound was heard in the streets of Aberfan below. Suddenly, a black tidal wave of ash, slurry and colliery rubbish crashed through Pantglas Junior School and a dozen houses nearby. Over 50,000 cubic yards of coal waste had rolled 700 yards down the mountainside and into the village, carrying boulders, trees and trams with it ; the wave was higher than a house. George Williams, a hairdresser, had been making his way to his shop in Moy Road that morning when he heard a noise ' like a jet plane ' ; he was swiftly engulfed by the flood, escaping with his life only with the help of courageous council workmen and a piece of corrugated sheeting. After the tip had fallen, he recalled later, everything went quiet as if a wireless had been turned off : ' in that silence, you couldn't hear a bird or a child '.[1]

S.O. heard the terrible news at 11 o'clock when Mr J. A. Lewis, a schools welfare officer, called at ' Gwynfryn '. Seconds later another friend, Llywelyn John, arrived at the house to drive S.O. four miles down the valley to Aberfan. There they parked as near to the scene as the confusion of cars, crowds and rushing relief vehicles would permit, walking the rest of the way through inches of black slime and mud. Standing on the main section of Moy Road, S.O. could see part of the roof and gable-ends of Pantglas Junior School protruding from a 25-foot-high mound of sludge and debris ; half of the school and an adjacent row of houses had been swamped ; hundreds, later thousands, of volunteers were digging frantically with shovels and bare hands. The danger and devastation precipitated many acts of heroism. Lorries and digging-machines pulled up in growing numbers ; Mines Rescue Service teams worked around the clock. S.O. spent this—the most heartbreaking day of his long life—consulting with the rescue organisers and trying to comfort bereaved parents, many of whom he knew personally.

Towards dusk he watched the flood-lights being set up to illuminate night-time excavations. But the herculean efforts were already too late : after 11 o'clock on the morning of the tragedy nobody was brought out of the morass alive. Entombed in the junior school were 109 children, mostly aged between 7 and 10, and five teachers ; an additional 30 men, women and children also perished beneath the rampaging tip. On Saturday, S.O. began visiting the hundred and more grieving households of Aberfan ; in the morning he showed the the Duke of Edinburgh around the site, accompanied by Cledwyn Hughes (the Secretary of State for Wales) and the Chief Constables of Merthyr and Glamorgan.

The following day, a taut and angry S.O. told the *Sunday Mirror* :

> We've been warning the N.C.B. for years about what could happen, and they took no action. They continued to pile up slag, making the tip even higher. Now the disaster we warned could happen, has happened. Today I saw officials from the Coal Board at the scene looking worried. By God, they looked worried. It is no good disguising the truth. There has been great concern about this tip. Representations have been made over and over again—even in the days before nationalisation—to try and get tipping on the spot stopped.

On Monday, October 24, Cledwyn Hughes acceded to S.O.'s request and delivered an official statement in the Commons : work to stabilise the tip and prevent further slippages was underway ; all other N.C.B. tips were being inspected. Hughes also confirmed the Government's intention to appoint a Tribunal of Inquiry under the chairmanship of Lord Justice Sir Herbert Edmund Davies. S.O. welcomed this news, thanked the Welsh Secretary and the Prime Minister for their prompt visit to the village on Friday night and praised the thousands of rescue volunteers who had rendered unstinting service.

The three-man Tribunal commenced its public hearings in November, beginning in Merthyr Tydfil and moving to Cardiff after Christmas. Seventy-six sessions later, in July 1967, its Report concluded that the Aberfan Disaster had been ' a terrifying tale of bungling ineptitude by many men charged with tasks for which they were totally unfitted, of failure to heed clear warnings, and of total lack of direction from above '. The chief culprit was the

MERTHYR TYDFIL DIVISION

Parliamentary Election, 1966

S. O. DAVIES WHO, AS M.P., HAS SERVED YOU FOR NEARLY 32 YEARS.

With the Compliments of

S. O. DAVIES

LABOUR CANDIDATE

Printed by H. W. Southey and Sons Ltd., "Merthyr Express," Merthyr Tydfil and Published on behalf of the Candidate by Stanley Beynon, Miners' Hall, Merthyr Tydfil, his duly appointed Agent.

General Election manifesto front-page

Aberfan, October 1966

National Coal Board, which bore 'quite overwhelming responsibility for eight years of folly and neglect'.[2]

As much against common sense as against standard civil engineering practice, the murderous Tip Number 7 had knowingly been built from 1958 onwards on top of a surface stream, on land which was punctured by springs and seepages. N.C.B. Chairman Lord Robens had been utterly wrong to claim, two days after the avalanche, that 'it was impossible to know that there was a spring in the heart of this tip which was turning the centre of the mountain into sludge'.[3] Most of the local people could have told him otherwise—as some did at the Tribunal. Over a period of eight years, the waste and rubbish from Merthyr Vale colliery had been piled up to the reckless height of 111 feet. The general instability and high water-content of Merthyr Mountain had been demonstrated time after time : for example, between 1952 and 1965 severe floods afflicted the Pantglas area of Aberfan on at least 11 occasions (the flood-water from the mountain leaving a 'slimy black deposit' on walls, carpets and furniture). More telling still, in 1944 a large part of Tip No. 4 tumbled 600 yards down the mountainside directly above the village. A few years later Tip No. 5 developed an ominous bulge caused by dislocation—prompting the N.C.B. to discontinue its use in 1956. Tips 4, 5 and 7 were the only three, out of seven that were on Merthyr Mountain, to be situated on streams and springs.

Most damning of all, Tip No. 7 had itself slithered several hundred feet into the fields below in 1963. Yet tipping continued there afterwards as if nothing had happened ! In fact, not until the 66th day of the Tribunal's proceedings did the Coal Board concede that the 1963 slide had taken place at all. Moreover, the Inquiry also ascertained that during the six months leading up to the disaster, employees working on Tip 7 reported sinkings, movements and other signs of increasing instability.

The Tribunal sternly admonished the N.C.B. for its time-wasting defence—not abandoned until more than halfway through the hearings—that the calamity could not have been forseen. Emphatically, it should have been anticipated and thus avoided ; the tragedy was *not* due to an extraordinary coincidence of geological factors : 'The only exceptional feature about Merthyr Mountain lay in the fact that it had been used as a tipping site', the Tribunal remarked. No, the disaster stemmed from the Coal Board's failure to operate any general policy relating to the siting, control, inspection and management of tips. In this respect, Cledwyn Hughes had been 'grievously misinformed' by the N.C.B. when he assured Parliament that 'the Coal Board has a regular inspection of all tips on its land'.[4] Because the dumping of colliery waste on hillsides took place almost exclusively in south Wales and nowhere else, Coal Board chiefs in London had never troubled to consider the implications of such an activity; the South-Western Division of the N.C.B., which should have been more vigilant, had failed to take any initiatives at a local level. All that could be pleaded in mitigation was that the Board had inherited its folly and neglect from the old private coalowners.

Characteristically, S.O.'s 2½-hour testimony before the Tribunal was frank and controversial. As someone familiar with the history of Merthyr Vale colliery and its waste deposits, he had long entertained fears that a tip-slide might reach the village. When asked by Sir Herbert Edmund Davies why he had not, therefore, 'taken steps' to forestall such an accident, S.O. replied that he 'had to consider the general feelings and desires of the mass of the people in that ward'. Were tipping on Merthyr Mountain to be stopped or seriously impeded, he had 'more than a shrewd suspicion that the colliery would be closed'—an alarming prospect in a valley which had suffered greater unemployment, poverty and migration than any other area of Britain. Thus miners at Merthyr Vale itself had told him: 'You make a row about that and what will happen? They will close down the blessed colliery'.[5] These forebodings had been fed by the pit's inclusion in a list of endangered coal mines drawn up by South Wales N.U.M. President Will Whitehead in October 1965—but which Whitehead admitted at the Tribunal to have been 'most inaccurate'. Even so, S.O.'s belief that the curtailment of tipping on the mountain would threaten the colliery's future was substantiated by the published correspondence between the N.C.B. and Merthyr Borough Council.

No-one had ever demanded an end to the tipping when, as the N.C.B. insinuated, this would cause the colliery to close. Had he been asked to do so by representative bodies in the area, S.O. would have been prepared to campaign against the tips. As it was—and with S.O.'s knowledge—the Borough Council and the Merthyr Vale Labour Party had approached the N.C.B. about flooding and the instability of the tips—only to meet with bland and sometimes deceitful assurances from Coal Board officials. But nobody would pursue these fears to the point of endangering the pit's future.

Not surprisingly, S.O.'s painful and courageous home-truths attracted severe criticism from some of the implicated parties at the Tribunal. The counsel for the N.U.M., Brian Gibbens, went so far as to suggest that : ' Mr S. O. Davies . . . bears what must be one of the largest personal burdens of responsibility for the disaster '. The Tribunal agreed with Mr Gibbens that S.O. did not appreciate the import of his testimony and had unknowingly allowed hindsight and a faulty memory to affect his recollections ; had they believed otherwise, the Tribunal declared, they would have censured S.O. for having entertained a strong premonition of disaster without doing anything about it. S.O.'s offer to return to the witness stand and substantiate or elaborate his previous remarks was disregarded.[6]

Yet the Tribunal's assessment of S.O.'s evidence is confused and contradictory. One of his two main contentions was that local people, miners in particular, had *consciously* weighed the risk of a substantial but unlikely tip-slide against the need for work at Merthyr Vale colliery. But the Lodge Secretary there, Bill King, denied that his members had worried about their jobs—or had made a conscious choice to put them before the tipping hazards. The Tribunal doubted the authenticity of S.O.'s recollections ; it preferred instead to estimate that fears of pit-closure ' may, and probably did, *subconsciously* colour the attitude and affect the judgement of many at Aberfan '—as if the conscious and subconscious were unrelated and incompatible. But then, Paragraph 253 of the Report continues: ' If Mr S. O. Davies M.P. is accurate in his recollection of events, a passive attitude [i.e towards the tips] was not knowingly adopted by the Union, but was one deliberately taken up after weighing the arguments for and against action '. It then goes on to record the apprehensions expressed by Bill King and the local N.U.M. about tip instability on Merthyr Mountain—and how their public unease apparently vanished after 1963. If anything, this section of the Report lends credibility to S.O.'s original contention that the dangers were known and were deliberately played down by common consent. Protests were made, but nobody would dare to call the N.C.B.'s bluff. On what grounds, therefore, did the Tribunal question his recollection in these matters ? Why should it be so unlikely that the local community, especially those engaged in the mining industry, *consciously* measured precious employment against the hazards which went with it ?

S.O.'s other contention was that his own qualms about the tips perched above the village were more severe than the ordinary, springing as they did from his knowledge of the locality and of engineering. The Tribunal repudiated this confession, supposing instead —and with a presumed charity—that S.O. had not appreciated the gravity of his words. Far from being generous in saving him from censure, such a judgement was misleading and insulting. It misses the tragedy at the core of S.O.'s testimony, namely that the system as a whole had put the people of Aberfan, the miners of Merthyr Vale and their representatives, in a cruel dilemna : that they accept the menacing tips on one hand, or risk losing a major source of employment on the other.

Rather than recognise this dilemna and comment upon it, the Tribunal chose to ignore it. And on what grounds could the three wise men have censured S.O. when the N.U.M., the Borough Council and everyone else who ultimately tolerated the tips escaped the Tribunal's condemnation? Because of his blunt frankness? Because he did not join the queue to be ' fobbed off ' (in the Report's words) by the N.C.B. ? And if the union was ' entitled to assume that tip inspections were being conducted by duly-qualified officials ', could the Tribunal refuse S.O. the same entitlement to assume likewise?

But the controversies following in the wake of Aberfan did not end with the Report. When the House of Commons debated the Tribunal's findings on 26 October 1967, S.O. stunned the authorities with fresh allegations. He began his speech sombrely on this ' the most unhappy day in the very long years I have been an M.P.' He then traced the source of Aberfan's affliction with some reminiscences from his adolescent stint at Nixon's colliery in Mountain Ash, over 60 years ago :

> When I was a young coal miner, working in a colliery immediately to the west of where this disaster occurred, I came up from the coal shaft one Monday afternoon—and Monday was a short day in the collieries—to the beautiful sunshine, and I saw on the mountainside, which must have been beautiful too, at one time, rubbish and debris being tipped from the coal mine. Standing near me on my left was the general manager, a man for whom I had great respect. Indeed, he started many of us as students of mining and of science in coal mining. I

turned to him—his name, like mine, was Davies—and I asked: ‘ Mr. Davies, is that not an absolute scandal, bringing all this rubbish from underground and tipping it on the hillside, instead of scientifically stowing it underground and thus perhaps preventing in the future widespread subsidence in the coal-field ? ’ He was a great mining engineer. His answer was typical of those days. He said, ‘ Stephen, let me tell you, confidentially, that I have to bring it out because it is cheaper to haul it up the shaft and tip it on the hillside ’. Needless to say, I never reported that story while that first-class man held a responsibility under the old dispensation. He was extremely kind to the youngsters in the industry.

The Coal Board has inherited a beastly and unscientific tradition. It accepted what had been done in the old days.

S.O. reminded M.P.s of his long-standing criticism of the form which public ownership of the mines had taken ; at the time of nationalisation he had accused Morrison and Attlee of ‘ lifting the industry out of the [war-time] control of the House of Commons and vesting it in a number of unelected and unrepresentative men ’.

Returning to the present, S.O. shocked his audience inside and outside the chamber with his warning that two other tips on Merthyr Mountain could tumble into the village : they were ‘ glaring at us every day, full of threat ’. On behalf of the people of Aberfan he insisted that these dark, giant cones be removed together with Tip No.7. The Minister for Power, Richard Marsh, interjected to declare his disbelief at this ‘ incredibly serious statement ’ ; he had been advised that all the tips were now safe. Still S.O. stood his ground, repeating local fears and telling the Minister that the experts were discredited. He also rebuked the Attorney-General for having announced, at the beginning of the Inquiry, that no prosecutions would ensue. Those who were guilty—especially the N.C.B.—should have been dealt with by the courts and compelled to make amends. As for the Press, much of its reporting had been sympathetic and responsible, although S.O. deplored the ‘ cold-blooded, cheap journalese exceptions ’.

In his Ministerial reply to the debate, Marsh revealed that senior Coal Board officials had been summoned to the Commons that evening to discuss S.O.’s charges, which had already received publicity on radio and television news. They had assured the Minister that ‘ there is no evidence whatsoever to support the allegation of the danger of another disaster like Aberfan ’. But neither this, nor an invitation from Marsh to visit the tip complex in the company of Mines Inspectors, could placate S.O. ' Merely looking at the tips is no inspection at all ', he told journalists afterwards, ' it is a piece of tomfoolery '. Mindful of the Tribunal's view that old colliery workings beneath No.7 Tip had probably contributed to the instability and thus to the slide, he also pointed out that mines in south Wales tended to be deeper than in other coalfields—and thus the signs of subsidence took longer to appear in the surface tips.

Opinions in Aberfan were divided : some villagers trusted the judgement of engineers working on the site, others echoed S.O.'s call for the tips to be swept away. As far as the latter group were concerned, even the slightest risk would be intolerable and—in the impeccable logic of one resident—' if the tips are not there, they can't slip '. Particularly offensive was the continuing presence of Tip No.7, visible and sinister despite the Coal Board's swift efforts to decapitate and landscape it. The safety work on Merthyr Mountain was stepped up as the campaign to flatten the tips gathered momentum, but by the following summer the Government and N.C.B. could no longer withstand the pressure with any honour or credibility. On July 1, 1968, torrential rain flooded Aberfan ; S.O. wrote to the Secretary of State for Wales, George Thomas, informing him that streams rushing down from the tips had dumped tons of slurry in the village. As the alarm mounted, the Archbishop of Wales joined in the appeal to flatten the tips.[7] On 20 July the Aberfan Parents and Residents Association sent a telegram to the Prime Minister and lobbied George Thomas at the Welsh Office in Cardiff. Within 48 hours Government Ministers had met and approved the removal of the infamous Tip No. 7 ; only one barrier to action remained—finance. The N.C.B. estimated the minimum cost of the job at £750,000, of which it was willing to provide £250,000. Prime Minister Wilson proposed that the Treasury supply an identical amount—and that the remaining £250,000 be raised by ' local donations '. He despatched George Thomas to persuade the Aberfan Disaster Fund Committee to agree in principle to dip into its coffers ; the fund had been opened by the Mayor of Merthyr and within a year had received nearly £2 million from all over the world. This money was intended to help the people of Aberfan rebuild their community, in bricks and mortar as well as in spirit.

The Fund Committee's decision to devote a portion of its receipts to tip-clearance angered the Aberfan Parents and Residents Association, whose representatives were in a minority on the Committee. S.O.'s fury came to a head at a meeting between the Fund Committee and the Secretary of State at the Welsh Office on Thursday evening, August 8. He announced his resignation from the Committee and walked out of the discussions. As he explained to the *South Wales Echo* the next day : ' I still believe not one halfpenny from the fund should be used to clear these tips. In this I have the support of thousands of people in my constituency. I shall continue to fight the fund committee's decision—something I could not have done had I not resigned '. S.O. had been a ' good, loyal and helpful ' member of the Committee, according to its chairman. But the M.P. resisted its appeals to rejoin : he would not have a hand in diverting money away from any of the Committee's excellent projects, which included a new school, community centre, swimming baths and playing fields. He took his protests to Parliament and into its consideration of the Mines and Quarries (Tips) Bill, but to no avail.

Most of all, S.O. reviled Harold Wilson's role in the affair. Immediately after the Welsh Office meeting at which the Fund Committee yielded to the request for £250,000, he wrote to the Prime Minister and told him : ' I hold you personally responsible for enforcing the decision on the committee '—a responsibility confirmed by Wilson's own memoirs. For good measure, S.O. added : ' I have never known a Prime Minister behave so disgracefully in all my 34 years in the House of Commons '.[8] Eighteen months later S.O.'s bitterness had not abated. On Friday 13 March 1970, Harold Wilson was due in Merthyr to receive the Freedom of the Borough; he had been nominated for this civic honour by the executive committee of the town's Trades Council and Labour Party. S.O. waited until the eve of the ceremony—for maximum impact—and then announced his boycott of the forthcoming event : ' I cannot forget his mean action when he told Aberfan residents that £250,000 of the cost of removal must come from the disaster fund or the tips would not be cleared . . . this was the worst piece of blackmail I have ever come across ', he declared on the front page of the *Western Mail*.[9] Vigorously though many heads nodded in support of their M.P.'s gesture, the Trades Council and Labour Party leaders were incensed by his ' irresponsible outburst '—and vowed to take ' appropriate action ' at a later date.

One incident concerning the Disaster Fund characterises the turbulent 1960s in Wales. In July 1967 a coachload of bereaved parents travelled to Westminster with a second petition demanding a public inquiry into the administration of the £1,750,000 Fund ; one grievance was that survivors of the avalanche had, thus far, received a derisory £350. Yet S.O. was not the man the protestors wished to see ; instead they asked for the ' M.P. for Wales ', Gwynfor Evans. As it happened, he was not there to receive the petition and —seriously misjudging the fighting mood of the valleys—sent them a message which stated : ' I am reluctant to take an Arthurian stance over Aberfan, for fear it may be said that I am trying to make political capital out of the Disaster '. Subsequently S.O. and Rhondda West M.P. Alec Jones volunteered to pursue the matter in his place.[10] But the parents' unfulfilled wish to line up with the President of *Plaid Cymru* exemplifies the wave of national feeling surging through Wales. Evans had triumphed in the Carmarthen by-election of July 1966 which followed the death of S.O.'s great friend and Labour M.P. Lady Megan Lloyd George. Whereas the Labour Party hierarchy recoiled from the verdict with fear and disgust, S.O. quietly approved ; and when the first-ever Welsh Nationalist M.P. asked him to act as a sponsor in the House of Commons introductory ritual, S.O. cheerfully braved the sneers of Labour colleagues and agreed to do so. The irrepressible rebel told the *Merthyr Express* : ' I have known Mr Gwynfor Evans for many years and he is a very distinguished Welshman. He has been elected by the people of Carmarthen and they are the best judges . . . I have my roots there. I'm pretty sentimental about that old county '.[11] Gwynfor's other sponsor, Llanelli M.P. Jim Griffiths, accepted the invitation with rather more reluctance.

A month or two later S.O. took issue with some of his Labour colleagues who, led by Leo Abse and Ness Edwards, launched a veiled attack on the National Eisteddfod's all-Welsh rule. Their early-day motion in the Commons implied that using the Welsh language was, in itself, tantamount to banning non-Welsh speakers from the cultural and intellectual life of ' Wales and Monmouthshire '. S.O.'s amendment urged the restoration of Welsh as the tongue of all the Welsh people . . .

> and deeply regrets that Wales has not been granted the power vested in the State of Israel which made compulsory its ancient and historic language [as] its national means of communication, notwithstanding that that language could not at one time be spoken or understood by many thousands of Jewish people when they returned home from many quarters of the world to their old homeland.

Not surprisingly, therefore, S.O. was a vocal supporter of the proposals of the Hughes-Parry Committee set up by the Secretary of State to consider the legal position and future prosperity of the Welsh language. The Committee's report advocated full-blooded measures to promote Welsh, whereas the anaemic Welsh Language Act that followed in 1967 confined itself to a timid, legalistic and formal interpretation of the 'equal validity' principle. S.O.'s anxiety for the survival of his mother-tongue was also reflected in the fight for Welsh-medium education in Merthyr Tydfil. Since the mid-1950s local parents and teachers had launched schemes to promote the language inside the classroom, with Sephora Davies prominent in their efforts and S.O. using his influence in support. Most of the residents of Heolgerrig, a village on the western outskirts of the town, still spoke Welsh as did many of the older folk in Dowlais. Not until the 1960s, however, was the foundation laid for its inheritance by future generations : an *Ysgol Gymraeg* was established on the site of Caedraw School, succeeded by *Ysgol Gynradd Gellifaelog*.

A bombing campaign conducted by Welsh republicans did not prevent *Plaid Cymru* from slashing Labour's majority by more than 14,000 votes in the Rhondda West by-election of March 1967. With public opinion polls in Wales indicating 60% of the people in favour of a Welsh Parliament and 20% demanding full independence, the Labour Party struggled to maintain its balance against the nationalist tide. The party had fulfilled its 1964 Election pledge to appoint a Secretary of State for Wales at the head of a Welsh Office ; the following year the Welsh Council of Labour had called for a directly-elected Welsh Council, albeit one without law-making powers. Nonetheless, even this proposal was too strong for the majority of Welsh Labour M.P.s and for the Cabinet which, in 1967, proposed a nominated Council in preference to an elected one. In the Commons, S.O. reacted by accusing the Secretary of State for Wales of 'depriving the people of Wales of their democratic rights ', and he collaborated with Tudor Watkins, Elystan Morgan (Cardigan), Emrys Hughes and Scottish M.P.s in an unofficial Home Rule group. In July 1967 S.O. went so far as to add his name to the sponsors of a Liberal Bill for a Welsh Parliament.

In July 1968 *Plaid Cymru* sliced 19,000 votes off the Labour majority at Caerffili in another parliamentary by-election. On the eve of Labour's British conference some ten weeks later, the party's Executive rejected a Parliament for Wales, but came out in support of a Welsh Assembly with executive powers. In a survey of Welsh parliamentary opinion, published in the *Western Mail* on October 1, S.O. reaffirmed his standpoint : ' I support a parliament for Wales. To get it we shall have to put fresh pressure on the Government. Wales has suffered badly through governments working from Westminster '. At the end of the month Harold Wilson announced that a Royal Commission would be appointed to investigate a new constitutional settlement for the nations of Britain. The Labour Party in Wales and an influential group of about 13 Welsh Labour M.P.s stood by the policy of a directly-elected Welsh Council; within this camp, S.O. and others pushed for the addition of legislative powers to the Council, but without success. On the other side were ranged the party's National Executive, a majority of Welsh Labour M.P.s and the Secretary of State for Wales, George Thomas : they argued for the Council to be partly nominated. The first group emerged victorious from the internal debates, duly presenting its scheme to the Royal Commission for an executive, all-elected body at the apex of a reformed local government structure—but with this Welsh Council also taking over the functions of the nominated bodies and committees so rampant in Welsh public life.

With hindsight it is clear that the Royal Commission on the Constitution was intended to draw the sting from the political debate inside and outside the Labour Party, and to stifle the nationalist resurgence in Wales and Scotland. Another ploy to take the wind out of Welsh Nationalist sails was the Investiture of the Queen of England's eldest son, Charles, as Prince of Wales in July 1969. But this project—promoted with frightened fanaticism by George Thomas—badly back-fired, provoking a rash of bombs, protests, scurrilous songs and satirical writings. While most M.P.s scrambled for seats at the jamboree in Caernarfon Castle, S.O. stayed aloof.

In private he mocked his parliamentary colleagues for their '*chwarae plant*' (childish antics). Along with Gwynfor Evans and Newport M.P. Roy Hughes he declined to attend the ceremony. S.O.'s old comrades Emrys Hughes and T. E. Nicholas publicly heaped scorn on the Investiture, but this was not S.O's approach.[12] Although he was a republican at heart—and collected factual ammunition against Royalty—he did not regard it as a crucial issue ; the Monarchy, he believed, would wither away as a consequence of the political, economic and cultural emancipation of the mass of the population; attacking the royal family would merely exaggerate their importance and create an irrational back-lash. Anyway, he found it difficult to bear malice towards the Queen personally, having met her ; S.O. referred to her only in the most affectionate and avuncular terms—usually as ' that dear girl '.

S.O. had boycotted the ceremony to honour Harold Wilson in the knowledge that this would put him beyond the pale in the eyes of his Constituency Labour Party. The point of ' no reconciliation ' had probably been reached already : early in March 1970 the local management committee had applied to the National Executive for permission to consider replacing their M.P. at the next General Election.

Disaffection with S.O. had grown inside the Merthyr Labour Party ever since the return of a Labour Government in 1964. Many of the activists who had slogged through 13 years in the Conservative wilderness resented S.O.'s persistent attacks upon the Wilson administration, believing that the Government deserved encouragement and total loyalty to overcome its problems ; and although S.O. was far more accessible than his parliamentary predecessor, younger members of the local party also demanded some control over his activities as an M.P.—that he should be less of a constituency representative, pursuing his own political line, and more of a delegate of the Merthyr Labour Party. S.O., in turn, interpreted these sentiments as an attempt to intrude into his parliamentary duties for which he—in the end—would have to take the responsibility, whoever else might take the decisions.

But most of all there was S.O.'s age. By this time he was supposedly in his 84th year, while rumours—accurate ones!—circulated which reckoned him to be nearer to 90 than that. An increasing number of Labour voters, and at least one party branch, felt that

S.O. was too old to fulfil the demands of his office. Even the South Wales miners' Executive urged him to retire, and it was on the grounds of age that the Merthyr Labour Party asked for—and received—the N.E.C.'s blessing to set the machinery in motion for making their M.P. redundant. The *Western Mail* agreed that Merthyr needed the ' energies of a younger man ' and urged S.O. to ' resign with dignity ' ; even so, the paper's Editorial on the affair illustrates how grace blossoms with the passing of time. It described S.O. as ' a natural successor to Keir Hardie ', and began thus :

> Sadly the long and colourful career of Merthyr's veteran M.P., Mr S. O. Davies, seems likely to end in acrimony, now that the Labour Party national executive has decided to allow his candidacy at the next election to be looked at again. In nearly 40 years in Parliament Mr Davies has been in hot water more than once for his polemical support for unpopular causes. But S.O. has had a background which was virtually bound to make him a rebel. Like many other miners and trade unionists in Wales, he obtained qualifications that sent him to the University of Wales by dint of hard work in his spare time. He was one of thousands whom conditions in the 1920s and 1930s led to adopt a roseate view of Soviet society. But though his defence after the war of the indefensible in Czechoslovakia and East Germany and his support for Communist-backed peace meetings are likely to be seen as major aberrations, he has been a loyal constituency man and a patriotic Welshman.[13]

The constituency party met in the Miners Hall, Merthyr, on Sunday May 10 to debate a motion to retire S.O. and select a new Labour candidate for the next General Election. Prior to the meeting S.O. had told one of the London journalists attracted to this ' human interest ' controversy :

> I shan't even bother to attend. Why should I ? They're behaving like a bunch of ambitious school-kids. I shall send them a message telling them : ' You decide what *you* want and get on with it. I'll decide what *I* want and get on with it too '.[14]

The local party resolved to choose a new candidate; when informed of this verdict, S.O. declared in the *Merthyr Express :* ' The meeting was a waste of time . . . it was not representative of the Merthyr electorate. I am still the Member of Parliament. Let the people of Merthyr decide whether they want S.O. or not '. He had every intention of contesting the next election as an ' Independent

Socialist' candidate . . . 'if I'm physically fit to do my work'.[15] In fact, the only serious bout of ill health S.O. had suffered over several decades was an attack of shingles two years previously. Naturally, he was not as strong as he used to be—but his spirit and tenacity made up for that. For example, in January 1970 he marched at the head of a protest in Cardiff against the visit of the South African 'Springboks' rugby side ; fatigue forced him to drop out at the half-way mark—but even those few hundred yards were more than the many absent Welsh Labour M.P.s had bothered to undertake.

'Informed opinion' in the Borough, notably the editor of the local newspaper, gave S.O. little or no chance in a fight with an official Labour candidate. Indeed, the Party's domination of Merthyr politics was demonstrated in the municipal elections of May 1970—after S.O.'s redundancy notice—when Labour standard-bearers dealt their challengers the customary trouncing. Help for S.O. was on hand, however, and from the most unsuspecting and unsuspected of quarters : Harold Wilson proclaimed a General Election for June 18 and thereby compelled the Merthyr Labour Party to hasten its selection of a new candidate, leaving little time afterwards to sell him to the electors.

A hurried selection conference took place on May 30. Bill King had already withdrawn, leaving Illtyd Harrington and Tal Lloyd in contention for the Labour candidature. Harrington was the local boy who had made good and now occupied a prominent place in London politics ; he predicted that S.O. would win no more than a thousand votes in the forthcoming election. But the man chosen to pick up Labour's title-deeds to the Merthyr parliamentary seat turned out to be Tal Lloyd—area organiser of the Amalgamated Engineering Union and a former Mayor of the Borough. He stood firmly in the Wilson-loyalist camp and enjoyed the support of all the major trade union executives locally, notably the Transport and General Workers Union, the N.U.M. and his own union. Sure enough a long list of Labour and trade union branches and clubs appeared in the *Merthyr Express*, stamping their approval upon Lloyd. But how far did this reflect the feelings of their members ? The Secretary of the Merthyr branch of A.S.L.E.F., the train drivers' union, disputed its inclusion in the list : his men backed S.O., he claimed. Local officials of the National Union of Railwaymen offered S.O. their assistance, Arthur Evans writing to him on May

14: ' As you are aware my organisation is tied to the party machine, but my members are free agents and many of them have indicated that their X will be opposite S.O. Davies if it is his desire to continue as our representative . . . Merthyr without S.O. is like tea without sugar—I don't like it '.[16]

S.O. did not bear malice towards the Labour usurper, preferring to dismiss him with a tongue-in-cheek comment or two. At the time of Lloyd's selection, the General Secretary of the South Wales N.U.M., Dai Francis, asked the unyielding M.P. : '*Pryd ŷch chi'n mynd i ymddeol 'te, S.O. ?*' (' When are you going to retire then, S.O. ? ') He received the reply: ' *Mae hwnna'n dibynnu ar bryd gallan nhw ffindo rhywun gwell i gymeryd fy lle—yr hwn sy' gyda nhw miwn golwg, 'dyw e ddim yn wylia'r Gymraeg, hyd yn o'd!* ' (' That depends on when they can find someone better to replace me—the man they have in mind can't even speak Welsh ! ') S.O.'s determination to challenge the official Labour candidate divided the Merthyr valley and caused many individual agonies : his 77-year-old friend and former election agent, Stan Beynon, confessed to the *Sunday Express* : ' I don't know what I'll do . . . it would be hard for me not to vote for S.O., but we're all dedicated Labour Party here. I'd be split in two down the middle '.[17]

From the beginning of the election campaign, only two of the four candidates were really in the running : Tal Lloyd—' the Official and Only Labour Candidate '—and S.O. the ' Independent Socialist '. All the resources resided with the former ; Lloyd had sixty or more full-time workers, whereas S.O.'s team at the outset consisted of a handful of people. His daughter Gwyneth acted as election agent ; her chief helpers were Arthur Evans and another N.U.R. official John O'Neill, Elwyn Williams (secretary of the Bedlinog Lodge N.U.M.), and Joe Lambert, Glenys Lambert and Megan Phillips from the Cyfarthfa Ward Labour Party. Lloyd's election address made no mention of his main rival, whilst S.O.'s propaganda consisted of a single sheet with his photograph and the caption : ' You know me—I've never let you down. DON'T FORGET S.O. ' There followed a brief reiteration of his well-known distaste for the Common Market, Selective Employment Tax and incomes policies.

Yet there were undercurrents at work ; S.O.'s intellect, courage, charisma and devotion to the constituency all weighed in his favour.

Then there was the public's sympathy for an underdog—something probably stronger in Merthyr, with its pioneering political tradition, than anywhere else in the country. Furthermore, justifiably or not, many people resented S.O.'s teatment at the hands of the local party machine. He also reaped the benefit of negative factors that militated against his arch-opponent. Lloyd had sat on the Borough Council for 25 years, thereby lashing himself to the butt of Merthyr's famous political humour. These were the councillors of whom it was said: 'They wanted to buy a gondolier and put it on the lake at Cyfarthfa Park. Then they decided to get two—and breed them . . .' and : 'The Council intended to have a chandelier in the Town Hall—but they couldn't find anyone who could play it'. Tal Lloyd was tarnished by this image of long-serving councillors as dull and self-important.

Another episode which did nothing to boost Lloyd's credibility was the 8-week unofficial strike at the Hoover domestic appliance works in 1969 and early 1970. The factory, which employed 5,000 people and formed the core of Merthyr's industrial base, grinded to a halt over the Christmas period in a dispute over staff favouritism. Bitterness grew as workers and their families were refused strike pay by their union—the A.E.U. Its local representative—and thus the conveyor of union refusals to back the strike—was, of course, Tal Lloyd. The employees eventually returned to work under threat of starvation but with the greatest reluctance ; the union's man-on-the-spot was the obvious target for their cries of 'Traitor !' and 'Sell-out !' S.O., on the other hand, had sided with the work-force from the first minute. When the Secretary of State for Employment and Productivity, Barbara Castle, ordered an official inquiry into the dispute, S.O. accused her of putting the workers on trial, and of consulting unsympathetic union bosses instead of delegates from the strikers themselves. He informed Castle : 'This action of yours was irresponsible and mischievous and pathetically in accord with some of your other provocative blunders'. The sting in the tail referred to her ill-fated White Paper, *In Place of Strife*, which sought to entangle trades unions in a mesh of legal and procedural controls. Not surprisingly, then, posters appeared in the Hoover's works during the election campaign exclaiming : 'TAL LLOYD——THE MAN TO AVOID'.[18]

But the real turning-point in the contest came on Saturday, June 13. The town was already full of excited speculation about the forthcoming election—and the talk was more about who would triumph in Merthyr than about which party would win power at Westminster. Over a dinner-time drink at Merthyr Rugby Club, a group of young people decided to have a fling : they designed a few rough posters, acquired an old megaphone and set out in half-a-dozen cars to tour the town centre. Their message was straightforward : 'Don't be fooled—vote for S. O. Davies'. The small convoy met with warm and spontaneous enthusiasm : onlookers clapped and gave the thumbs-up sign. The town buzzed with the news of this zestful and ramshackle display. That Saturday evening the Rugby Club was crowded, a rock-and-roll band in full swing. Suddenly, in through the door strode S.O. and Sephora Davies. Amidst the tumultuous applause, the band struck up an impromptu ditty in support of S.O.'s re-election, with the audience singing along raucously. When the chorus of clapping, whistling and foot-stamping had died down, S.O. went to the stage, took the microphone and quietly thanked those who had organised the afternoon's cavalcade. When he left the room, this was the signal for another mass display of impassioned support. As a participant in these stirring events, local historian Alun Morgan later remarked : 'The great irony of the campaign was clear to all—the man sacked on the grounds of being too old was attracting tremendous support among the young'.[19]

Significantly, this would be the first General Election at which 18-21 year olds could vote. Harri Webb recalls the burgeoning alliance between youthful Welsh nationalists and the veteran Socialist :

> Here was an old man, said to be older than he gave out, impeccably garbed in the fashion of the thirties at the latest : the striped trousers, the long black overcoat, the immaculate silk scarf, the venerable white hair under the broad-brimmed black felt hat. And here were his most conspicuous campaigners—a harum-scarum bunch, their leather jackets and blue jeans emblazoned with the Eagle of Snowdon, the Dragon's Tongue and the menacing, sharp-pointed Triban. It was an irresistible combination. The Old Gang did not know what had hit them.[20]

S.O. in 1970

One of the last pictures of S.O.

The unofficial and official campaigns united to give S.O. the strongest, liveliest legion of supporters in Wales ; over one hundred cars and 350 people toured the constituency canvassing for him, backed up by girl cheerleaders, songs and slogans in the most colourful election bandwaggon seen in Merthyr for 40 years. In alarm and desperation some of S.O.'s Labour adversaries opened a dirty-tricks department : they circulated copies of a bogus letter purportedly sent by the Town Clerk to a polling-station attendant, and which reported a fictional decision of the Borough Council to dispense with the paid services of old-age pensioners on ballot-box duty. This resolution, the hoax letter claimed, had been passed after councillors had received written representations from S.O. complaining that as he was being forced to retire, he thought it only fair that other retired people be disqualified from earning money by manning the local polling-booths.[21]

Labour lost the General Election of 18 June 1970. The Party's defeat in Merthyr Tydfil was even more emphatic. Hundreds of S.O.'s followers waited inside the Town Hall and outside in the streets until the early hours of the morning, but they were well rewarded by the Returning Officer's announcement :

S. O. DAVIES (Ind. Socialist)	16,701
TAL LLOYD (Labour)	9,234
EDWARD JONES (Conservative)	3,169
CHRISTOPHER REES (*Plaid Cymru*)	3,076

S.O. had scored a thumping majority of 7,467 votes in the highest turn-out of electors since the 1959 General Election. The jubilant crowd outside chanted ' S.O.! S.O.! ' ; inside the building senior officials of the local Labour Party called the victor a ' traitor ', while Lloyd's speech was interrupted by cries of ' Sour Grapes ! ' and a repeated chorus of ' Hoovers ! Hoovers ! '. S.O.'s address was short and humble : he knew the people of Merthyr Tydfil and had never thought for a moment that they would let him down. He derived a special—but unspoken—satisfaction from the allegiance shown to him by the inhabitants of Aberfan. When asked by journalists to explain his triumph, S.O. replied in a matter-of-fact manner : ' There were two factors—S.O. and Merthyr Tydfil '.

In fact, the result in Merthyr was historic. S.O. had succeeded where D. N. Pritt and many others had failed through the post-war years : he had retained his seat despite having been sacked by the Labour Party. Moreover, he had done so with election expenses of £212—the lowest of any M.P. in Britain. No wonder 'Gwynfryn' was the scene of a celebration that night, with S.O.'s niece providing a bottle of champagne. The house was besieged by telegrams, telephone calls and newsmen anxious for quotes. A delighted S.O. even appeared on B.B.C. network television where, much to the bewilderment of his London interviewer and most of those watching, he delivered replies unthinkingly in Welsh !

Many people of all political hues greeted S.O.'s success with delight. *Labour Monthly* hailed it as 'a well-deserved triumph over a mean and dirty intrigue . . . the Labour Party sought to install a tame Wilsonian candidate as against the ebullient Labour veteran S. O. Davies'.[22] Predictably enough, the glee was not shared by the Merthyr Labour Party, or by Tal Lloyd who vowed to the *Western Mail* : 'We shall have to clean out the Labour movement in Merthyr by weeding out people who pay lip service to Socialism. They must be cleaned out, otherwise the same treacherous acts will be carried out again'.[23] Such vengeful bitterness reinforced S.O.'s belief that the constituency party was 'disintegrating pathetically' ; along with other party members who had campaigned for his re-election, he now favoured the creation of a local Independent Labour Party to contest Borough Council seats. As expected, the Merthyr Labour Party expelled S.O., Megan Phillips, Elwyn Williams and Joe Lambert (who had been a member for 58 years) from the party on July 1. The next day, S.O. sent a letter to the General Secretary of the Labour Party, Harry Nicholas, requesting an inquiry into the selection process and subsequent campaign in Merthyr on three grounds : firstly, S.O. alleged, a valid nomination in his support from the Cyfarthfa Ward party had been ruled out of order for the selection conference by the management committee ; secondly, a large number of other nominations for the Labour candidature had been fraudulent ; and thirdly, a forged document—the 'Town Clerk' letter—had been circulated by his opponents. In response to these charges, National Agent Ron Hayward merely reaffirmed S.O.'s right to appeal against his expulsion. The indignant M.P. wrote back on July 9 :

> The result of my election should have raised a question in your mind that there might have been a great deal of ' dirty work ' in the ultimate selection of the so-called Labour candidate. This was generally known in my constituency, and it had its inevitable consequences.
>
> You will, I hope, on reflection realise how pathetically this action of yours and your Office accords with the rest of the official section of the Labour Party that drove the masses in disgust to place the Tories the Government of this country for the next five years.

Two weeks later Transport House informed S.O. of the National Executive's minute : ' That no action be taken on the request for an official inquiry and Mr. S. O. Davies be advised accordingly '.[24] Time had been too short before the election for him to appeal against his dismissal as the Labour candidate—nor did any clear provision exist in the rules for such a recourse. Later in 1970 the Labour Party conference amended the constitution to allow for such a right of appeal to the N.E.C., but by then S.O.'s hopes for a reconciliation with the party had completely evaporated.

It is an indication of the enigmatic nature of Merthyr politics that in the middle of the acrimonious dispute between S.O.'s camp and the local Labour Party, the council should decide to award S.O. the Freedom of the Borough ! He declined the honour, informing the Town Clerk :

> I very much appreciate this kindly gesture on the part of our councillors, but the confidence which the people of our borough have in general shown me over many years has given me the fullest satisfaction that I could possibly desire to enjoy in my life . . . Please convey to the council my thanks and also, in view of the foregoing, why I consider that the acceptance by me of the freedom of our borough would be superfluous.[25]

S.O. denied that his refusal was politically-motivated. Doubtless he would have been proud to join the company of Arthur Horner, the town's world boxing champion Howard Winstone and others who had been made Freemen of the Borough in years past. But, then, that esteemed award had been devalued by bestowing it upon Harold Wilson.

S.O. resumed his seat at Westminster, on the Opposition benches this time, still amongst Labour M.P.s although no longer one of them. Facing them was a Conservative regime led by Edward Heath and armed with the most right-wing programme of any administration since the early 1930s. S.O.'s attendance at St. Stephen's was more patchy now than it had been in those bygone days ; even so, he travelled up for most of the important divisions. He made a rare intervention on the floor of the House to condemn the Industrial Relations Bill, a measure intended to shackle the trade union movement : S.O. protested in January 1971 that ' the Government are obtruding into the relationship between organised employers and organised workers by laying down certain financial limitations. What is the use of talking about freedom between organised employers and organised workers when we have a Bill of this kind before us ? '

Successive governments in London had also concocted schemes to recast the irregular, multifarious pattern of local government, to replace it with uniform tiers of larger and more centralised authorities. S.O. consistently resisted any attempts to curtail the powers and autonomy of local councils ; he had often demonstrated, too, his jealousy for Merthyr Tydfil's County Borough status. Hence his opposition to the Wilson Government's plans back in 1967 which would have stripped the Borough of this proud badge: the new, larger counties would, S.O. predicted, ' provide the happy hunting grounds for the unelected and the unrepresentative—Wales for the bureaucrats!—and the destruction of our democratic local government '.[26] His suspicion of over-large impersonal units also prompted him to challenge the dissolution of Merthyr's own Probation Service and, three years later, to try and block the amalgamation of county and local constabularies into the South Wales Police. He had warned M.P.s on 26 March 1969 :

> Statistics show the number of crimes detected but they do not show the number prevented, particularly in my part of the world, because of the friendly relations which exist between the police and community . . .
>
> All that unity between the police and the rest of the community will be destroyed. The policeman will cease to be a member of the community ; he will be moved from one valley to another valley, from one county borough to another county borough ; he will become known not for himself, but just because of his uniform, and he will enjoy no local confidences at all. He will become an automaton representing a force, even though part of it is the force which we have and which is such a credit to us.

The latest effort to reform Welsh local government made its appearance in March 1971, in the form of a White Paper ; what aroused S.O.'s anxiety was the proposal to reduce Merthyr Tydfil's standing to that of just one more District Council, with many of its cherished responsibilities—notably for Education—moving upwards to the new county of Mid Glamorgan. Although he voted and spoke against the Local Government Bill, he was happy to receive assurances from the Secretary of State for Wales that Merthyr could retain its old Borough name and status.

Sadness, too, touched S.O. in the spring of 1971; his comrade, contemporary and personal friend T. E. Nicholas passed away at the age of 91. He had already been deprived of his co-rebel in Parliament, Emrys Hughes, two years previously. Still, S.O. struggled on, by now in his 88th year. His sights were trained on the enemy as sure as ever before. The incoming Conservative Government declared its intention to take the United Kingdom into the European Economic Community. S.O. had defied a 3-line whip in May 1967 to register his hostility to this Common Market. Four years later heresy had become orthodoxy as Labour's parliamentary leaders turned against the E.E.C. S.O. set out his long-standing objections in a letter to the *South Wales Echo* on 9 August 1971 :

> The Government's efforts to fool the people to agree with our entry into the Common Market has been one of the most disgraceful and untruthful pieces of propaganda I have ever come across. And the vast amount of the people's money spent on this has been equally disgusting.
>
> Their first claim in the Government's White Paper is that to join the Common Market would add to our international security, and right through the Paper this presumption runs. It says that ' our security has been bound up with our European neighbours for over a thousand years '. (Can you beat it ?) What about the wars from the 17th century to 1815, and later the two World Wars against Germany including the Hitler War when British security meant co-operation with Russia.
>
> The White Paper also claims that the Six [Member States] have a population of 190 millions, and that with Britain it would be near 250 millions. But in the real Europe outside there are about 390 million people ; where is the internationalism in the Government's claim ?
>
> Most of my anti-Market colleagues have already stated in the *Echo* my other reasons for opposing entry into an anti-Parliamentary and anti-working class scheme of this kind.

He characterised the E.E.C. as a creature of the multinational companies, a free market for the exploitation of labour—and the transfer of capital—across the old nation-state boundaries ; it was anti-democratic because massive political and bureaucratic power resided in the unelected Commission in Brussels. Thus, for once, it was with pleasure that S.O. obeyed Labour's 3-line whip on October 28 to oppose Britain's entry into the Common Market. He joined the overwhelming majority of Welsh Labour M.P.s in the ' anti- ' lobby—only to be outnumbered by the pro-Market Tories and a handful of Labour rebels.

As the Conservative Government pursued its hard-nosed policies, one ' saving ' in public spending came to symbolise the callousness of the Cabinet's strategy more than any other : the abolition of free milk for all primary-school children above the age of seven. That this practice had been wasteful and unnecessary in many cases was hardly in dispute ; yet all the evidence also showed that poorer and neglected children benefited enormously from such additional nutrition. S.O. lent his voice and his vote to the protest in the Commons ; back in Merthyr Tydfil the local council refused to implement the measure, and later sought ways to circumvent it. He also began work on an article for *Labour Monthly* exposing the cruelties of the Secretary of State for Education (branded ' Maggie Thatcher —Milk Snatcher ' by her critics). Nevertheless, much though S.O. admired the Borough councillors' stand on school milk, he still found himself on the opposite side in another education controversy: the Merthyr Welsh Schools Committee was campaigning for a Welsh-language nursery school to be established in response to the proven demand—but had met with obstruction from anti-Welsh members of the Merthyr education committee. S.O. promised to see the Director of Education and, if neccessary, the Secretary of State for Wales about the matter. He explained to the *Merthyr Express* on August 20 : ' Of course I am supporting the setting up of the Welsh School. I should be betraying all I hold dear if I did not ! '

Around this time, too, S.O. resolved to contact the young Independent civil rights M.P. for Mid-Ulster, Bernadette Devlin, to offer his help in the campaign against the mass internment without trial of Irish Republicans in the north of Ireland ; he could see in the huge police and army swoop of 9 August 1971 all the mistakes of England's imperial past being repeated. But a bout of ill-health intervened: he experienced chest trouble before Christmas and into the New Year. Not until the middle of January did he feel fit enough to travel, taking the train to London for the new session of Parliament. Naturally, S.O. was dressed in his traditional garb ('it's cheapest because it can be worn all year round' he joked to newspaper reporters at Cardiff Central Station). A relapse brought him back to Merthyr—but within a week or two he was bound for Westminster again, to vote against the Government in a series of motions on the E.E.C. on the evening of Monday, February 21. The following day Sephora deputised for her husband at a rally of the Merthyr branch of the National Old Age Pensioners Association in the Miners Hall. She explained S.O.'s absence, telling the audience: 'He regards the Common Market issue to be of the utmost importance to the senior citizens of this country. If we go into the Common Market, make no mistake about it, prices will shoot up. He was very anxious to vote against the Common Market motions last night.'

S.O. returned home earlier than planned, on Wednesday, having suffered a recurrence of his chest problems. He went almost immediately to bed. On Thursday he came downstairs to attend to some constituency correspondence, after which he warmed himself before the fire, reading, before taking to his bed early in the evening. Sephora carried a cup of tea to his room on Friday morning . . . but could not wake him. S.O. was transferred quickly to the Merthyr General Hospital—where he died later that day, 25 February 1972.

The news that this seemingly unbreakable man had finally yielded to nature's laws—at the age of 88—spread swiftly through the town and beyond. With equal speed, the tributes and condolences flooded into 'Gwynfryn'. Newspapers now lauded a life they had reprimanded so often during its living:

S.O.—THANKS FOR THE MEMORY

> So S.O. the Indestructible is finally gone. And now is the time to mark his passing, before the scrabbling starts to find a successor . . .
>
> Even if you set aside his parliamentary record of achievement, his periodical brushes with the people who attempted to govern his purpose (and, as far as S.O. was concerned, brushes they were, nothing more), his disdain for one-time colleagues who criticised him for daring to think independently, and the strength of character that drove him on for more years

than any man has a right to expect, you still admire him for one over-riding principle from which he never deviated.

Even in his twilight years, he was, above all, a Merthyr man. Or, if you wish to be pedantic about his place of birth, a man for Merthyr.

(*Merthyr Express*, 3 March 1972)

REBEL M.P. FOR MERTHYR TYDFIL

He was one of the left wing ' rebels ', and time and again was a source of trouble to the official Labour Party leadership in the House of Commons. No disciplinary action seemed to moderate his extreme views, and he maintained a stubborn, aggressive attitude . . .

In appearance Davies was anything but a revolutionary. Tall, with a not unpleasing personality, he had an outwardly quiet demeanour. But underneath fires were forever smouldering, and could be fanned into flame at the least provocation.

(The *Times*, 26 February 1972)

THE MAN WHO WAS ' MR MERTHYR '

S. O. DAVIES. It was unnecessary to add ' M.P. for Merthyr '. His name had been so long associated with the town they had almost fused into one.

Merthyr was already a hotbed of industrial unrest when S.O. came there. His own special brand of fiery Socialism found a ready-made response among the miners he came to serve and lead . . .

But through all the storms of political life S.O. went his serene and unruffled way, a dignified, formally-dressed figure typical of another era.

He was sure of his opinions, however quixotic they sometimes appeared to his critics. He was a pacifist, a Socialist and a patriotic Welshman.

That was how he began his career. That was how he brought it to a close. Today even his political opponents will be feeling a pang at his passing.

(*South Wales Echo*, 25 February 1972)

MERTHYR EXPRESS
5979 FRIDAY, MARCH 3, 1972 4p

PASSING OF AN ERA

Merthyr mourns its loss

THE MAN intended for the Christian ministry, S. O. Davies, realised his vocation by fighting for his fellow-men through the medium of politics.

At the funeral service in Soar-Ynysgau Chapel of Merthyr's Member of Parliament for nearly 40 years it was said, "He always insisted that in serving his fellows he was serving his God."

This tribute was paid by the Rev. E. Islwyn Evans Tabernacle, Treharris), who conducted the service in which a number of ministers and clergy took part. Many Welsh Members of Parliament, civic heads, and other dignitaries from many areas outside Merthyr were present as well as representatives of most walks of life within and from far outside the Borough.

The words most on the lips of those taking part were "controversial," "colourful," and most frequent "caring" for all the speakers emphasised S.O.'s love of Merthyr and its workers as the motive behind his long career as miner, scholar and politician.

In the crowded church with its vases of spring flowers as fitting emblems of renewal of life after death, family mourners, including the widow, Mrs. Sephora Davies and sons and daughters and the many friends and representatives, listened as the Mayor of Merthyr, Ald. Gerry Donovan said: "S.O. was determined to educate himself and went to university and obtained a degree, not for self-aggrandisement but to reach the necessary standard so that he could represent the people and the cause that were his life.

"He was," went on the Mayor, "as we are all aware, a controversial figure and an individualist who followed the teaching of 'Love thy neighbur as thyself.' He was highly respected by all for this, even by those who didn't agree with him. On behalf of the people of the County Borough of Merthyr I express our condolences and deepest sympathy with Mrs. Davies and the family.

The service was in the two languages and one of S.O.'s favourite hymns "Arglwydd, gad im dawel orffwys," was sung with intense feeling and power by the large congregation. The singing was a moving and impressive feature of the simple service, other beautifully rendered hymns being "O love that wilt not let me go" and "Rho im yr hedd, na wyr y byd amdano."

Merthyr's Town Clerk, Mr. Selwyn Jones, said: "S.O. was a man of conviction and determination — as exemplified last week when he travelled to London (while in a very poor state of health) in order to vote in the Common Market Debate."

Speaking of the impact made on all by Merthyr's M.P., Mr. Jones added: "It was said that S.O. was Merthyr Tydfil. Mention Merthyr and you were told 'Oh, S.O.'s constituency'. A happy man, his happiness was two-fold, representing his constituency and his family, and he served both with equal charm, grace and kindness. His name is assured as part of Merthyr's history."

The immense cortege with its long line of cars following the hearse with its flower-covered coffin, wound its way through Merthyr town and over the mountain into Aberdare and thence to Mountain Ash, S.O.'s birthplace. Police were on duty controlling traffic in all the built-up areas along which the funeral procession passed.

High on the hill-top Maesyrarian Cemetery, Mountain Ash, with its view of the mountain barrier dividing the two valleys, on a grey February day, S.O., the man of paradox, stormy fighter

(Continued on Page Six)

S.O. — a rebel in the cause of humanity

WHEN MR. S. O. DAVIES was elected to Parliament as Member for Merthyr Tydfil in June 1934, 8,000 people heard the announcement outside the Town Hall at 1-40 in the morning. When he died on Friday, at Merthyr General Hospital, aged 85, the news of his death spread quickly through the Borough.

Mr. Davies had been suffering from chest trouble in recent weeks but travelled to London on Monday of last week to vote against the Government over Common Market legislation. He returned home on Wednesday and stayed in bed. His wife, Mrs. Sephora Davies was unable to wake him on Friday morning and he was taken to hospital where he died later that day.

A left-wing "rebel", S. O. died as he would have wished — "in harness".

He caused a major upset in the 1970 General Election by being returned to Parliament as an Independent Labour M.P., with a majority of nearly 7,500 after the Labour Party had refused to adopt him as the official Labour choice.

S. O., as he was always known (his names were Stephen Owen) was born in 1886 in Abercwmboi. He began work in Cwmpennar colliery when he was 12 but by studying in his spare time, he obtained a Bachelor of Arts degree from the University of Wales.

He returned to work as a collier and in 1913 he became a checkweigher. In 1918 he was appointed miners' agent under the South Wales Miners' Federation at Dowlais. He held that post until 1933. Between 1924 and 1934 he represented the Welsh miners on the Miners' Federation of Great Britain and he later became Chief Organiser to the South Wales Miners' Federation.

ENERGIES

Mr. Davies had to fight a difficult by-election to enter Parliament. His opportunity arose when Richard Wallhead died. S. O. achieved a majority of 8,269. He polled 18,645 votes. His opponents were J. Victor Evans, Liberal, 10,376; Campbell Stephen, Independent Labour 3,508, and Wal Hannington, Communist, 3,409.

From then on S. O. had little trouble in keeping his seat, his majority once (in 19[illegible]) being nearly 27,[illegible].

After the result of the poll, S. O. told the people: "I am proud to have succeeded in keeping up the Keir Hardie-Wallhead tradition in Merthyr.

"I am equally proud to have the opportunity and the power given to me to look after the interests of the people of Merthyr and Dowlais with which I have long been intimately connected.

"I take from them a message of hope to the House of Commons and a claim for the attention of the Government and for help in their dire need. The attempt to break up the unity of the Labour movement has been defeated. My constituency have passed an emphatic

Continued on page 3.

WHO WILL SUCCEED?

IT IS probable that the by-election resulting from the death of Mr. S. O. Davies will be contested by six parties, Labour, Independent Labour, Liberal, Plaid Cymru, Communist and Conservative.

The secretary of the Merthyr Independent Labour Party represented in Parliament by Mr. S. O. Davies, Mr. Joe Lambert, said the decision as to whether to contest the election would be made within a few days.

"We are looking into it but it is too soon to say anything definite," he said this week.

The official Labour candidate, Mr. Ted Rowlands, Member of Parliament for Cardiff North from 1966-70 was Under-Secretary of State at the Welsh Office from 1969. Aged 32, with a son, he intends, if elected, to move from Cardiff to live at Merthyr.

DEFEATED

The Liberals have drawn up a short list of candidates including Mr. Angus Donaldson of Tredegar, Monmouthshire Liberal County Councillor and Tredegar Urban Councillor.

Plaid Cymru are to fight but have not yet selected their candidate. The same thing applies in the case of the Conservative Party.

The Communists will be represented by Mr. Arthur Jones, a toolmaker at Lines factory who is A.E.U.W. branch secretary. He was a Merthyr Borough Communist Councillor for Park Ward for three years until defeated in the May elections last year by Labour Coun. James Burns.

THERE are tributes from S.O.'s fellow-politicians and friends on page 3. The editor writes on page 8.

Front page news

'Who will inherit Merthyr Tydfil from S.O.?'—a *South Wales Echo* cartoon in 1972. The by-election result on April 13 was: Labour 15,562; *Plaid Cymru* 11,852; Conservative 2,366; Communist 1,519; Liberal 765.

COLOURFUL M.P. WHO KEPT THE PEOPLE'S LOYALTY

> In the judgement of history, Mr Davies is certain to be remembered as one of the most colourful, controversial and independent of the M.P.s elected from the Welsh mining valleys . . .
>
> The loyalty to him was based on his long tenure as an M.P. and his consistent advocacy of the case for the valleys and mining communities living in them. In an area where memories of a less humane industrial past are deep-rooted, Mr Davies, with his uncompromising brand of Socialism, spoke in terms which were well-understood.
>
> (*Western Mail*, 26 February 1972)

Two of S.O.'s election helpers, Arthur Evans and Joe Lambert, paid him a warm and moving tribute in the *Merthyr Express* :

> The immaculate dress, the silver locks and the familiar face will no longer be seen in the County Borough. An era has passed.
>
> Countless are the tales that will be told to future generations about the man who gave his life to the town and its people. He was a tall man who walked tall and never bowed to anyone, but treated everyone alike.
>
> His command of the spoken word in English and Welsh was phenomenal. All of us who knew him intimately came under the caress and lash of his golden tongue at some time or other in the full knowledge that whatever he said to us was said with love and respect. Anyone who came from the Borough was his, and he cared for them as a father cares for an only child . . .

The General Secretary of the South Wales miners, Dai Francis, praised S.O.'s work for Peace and Socialism ; in particular, he recalled the ' S. O. Davies Bill ' to help pneumoconiosis sufferers: ' Many of our members benefited from this Act, but perhaps its greatest significance was that it opened the political door for the final inclusion of emphysema and bronchitis in the diagnosis '.[27] Labour historian Glanmor Williams wrote of S.O.'s ' undying hatred for any kind of exploitation ' and of his ' engaging blend of individualism and Left-wing radicalism '.[28]

Plaid Cymru's President Gwynfor Evans remembered S.O. as ' a bonny fighter . . . inspired by a passionate concern for social justice ' ; in order to illustrate S.O.'s deep patriotism, Gwynfor drew a vivid historical comparison :

> In 1911, Keir Hardie had said of the investiture of that year: ' every flunkey in Wales, Liberal or Tory alike, was grovelling on his hands and knees to take part in the ceremony '. In 1969 most of the grovelling was done by Labour men. But S.O. was not among them. Grovelling had no place in his nature. He had idiosyncracies many, which endeared him to people; he was voluble, but not volatile. A man of principle, he stuck up with courage to the end, and for that his name will be remembered with respect as well as affection.[29]

The person nearest to being a contemporary of S.O. in Parliament and in the miners' union was Jim Griffiths. He, too, had fond memories to recount—and some pertinent points to make:

> S.O. was gifted with a pleasing presence and an impressive personality, and had he found it possible to work with the team would probably have attained ministerial office.
>
> However, he always was a lone figure. He did not knit easily and seemed to like being in isolation. The one place where he would relax was at the Welsh Table in the Members' Tea Room at the House of Commons. Many a talk he and I had at that table—always in Welsh—homespun Carmarthenshire Welsh. He would always begin the conversation by asking: ' *Shwd mae pethau lawr 'co?* '—*lawr 'co* meaning the anthracite area in the family and the homeland and with the miners of *Glo Carreg* who launched him on his career in the South Wales Miners Federation—and eventually on the road to St. Stephen's.
>
> S.O. and I were the only survivors of the miners' leaders in South Wales who led the miners during those heroic months of 1926—and through the long, heartbreaking years of the aftermath.
>
> With the passing of S.O. and the loss of a seat in the Rhondda, it now seems inevitable that for the first time since Mabon became Rhondda's M.P. in 1885 South Wales will not have a single M.P. who will have made the journey from the coalface to Parliament. We are nearing the end of an era in Welsh politics . . .[30]

More than four hundred people crowded into Soar-Ynysgau Chapel, Merthyr, on 29 February 1972—a grey Tuesday—to attend S.O.'s multi-denominational funeral service. A resplendent array of spring flowers symbolised life's renewal after death. His family and friends, Members of Parliament and civic dignitaries, mourners from all avenues of life, comprised the congregation which gave such a beautiful rendering of one of S.O.'s favourite hymns, ' *Arg-*

lwydd, gad im dawel orffwys ', together with ' O love that wilt not let me go ' and ' *Rho im yr hedd, na ŵyr y byd amdano* '. They heard the Mayor of Merthyr, Alderman Gerry Donovan, pay tribute to the ' endearing figure who had little respect for man-made rules and regulations ' and delighted in the spirited, moving sermon of the Rev. Islwyn Evans :

> S.O. and I had a lot in common, for we were born in the same valley, played in the same fields and streets. I knew the colliery where he first worked. The Davies family of Cap Coch, as it was known then, bore a name which was revered, and the chapel had a strong influence upon the life of the community both at Aberdare and Merthyr. S.O. worked in the colliery at Cefnpennar—the ' Blackberry Village '—at Mountain Ash, but he set his sights upon the ' Mantle of the Prophet ', and for some time he followed that direction, and his decision to forsake the pulpit shook many, they knew not what had happened to the man.
>
> But he had a great love for man, he believed with the Psalmist that ' The earth is the Lord's and the fullness thereof ', and it was these words, sinking deep into his heart, which made him ' Take up the cudgels for the common man '.

The Minister likened S.O.'s hunger for Peace with the heroic efforts of his parliamentary forerunner, Henry Richard, and reminded any who needed such strictures that both had shared a deep-running Welsh patriotism. ' We have had big industries here and our name is to be seen on the map of the world—great industries and great exploitation—and great men ', he remarked.[31] Afterwards, the long *cortège* of vehicles wound its way around Merthyr town, passing bare-headed crowds who watched silently and respectfully, and crossed over the mountain to Mountain Ash. There at Maesyrarian Cemetery, high on a hill-side, S.O. was lowered to rest in his native earth. It was indicative of his breadth of vision that the ceremony attracted Socialists, Communists, Welsh Nationalists, Republicans and many of no political creed at all, each one heavy-hearted with their loss. One such witness, Harri Webb, had already composed these words in honour of S. O. Davies—on behalf of the oppressed and disinherited everywhere :

TO THE MEMORY OF A FRIEND

The kind old eyes are closed at last
That mirrored memories of a past
When all the valleys rose as one
To see a people's justice done.
He strode those bitter barren years
With pride that banished doubts and fears,
And in the voice that challenged wrong
His father's wit, his mother's song
Rang out again from vanished days
To lead our land in Freedom's ways,
And in the winter of his time
When generous thoughts were held a crime
He put to flight the sons of shame
Who had usurped proud labour's name.
With him, an age comes to its end,
So much has died with this old friend,
But much lives on, his faith, his strength,
His vision that all men at length
Would walk in Freedom on this earth
And a new world be brought to birth.
Old warrior, rest, after long strife,
Yours was no vain or wasted life.
Although the struggle's not yet done,
We promise you, it shall be won.

NOTES

[1]*Report of the Tribunal Appointed to Inquire into the Disaster at Aberfan* (H.M.S.O., 19 July 1967), para. 52.

[2]Tribunal Report, paras. 47 & 179.

[3]Tribunal Report, para. 198.

[4]Tribunal Report, para. 64.

[5]Tribunal Report, para. 61.

[6]The Tribunal Report considered S.O.'s testimony in paras. 60-62, 253 & 254. S.O.'s offer to give further evidence was reported in the *Western Mail*, 22 April 1967, where he also pointed out that the N.U.M.'s Q.C. had had ample opportunity to cross-examine him during his 2½ hour testimony—but had failed to do so.

[7]*Sunday Times*, 7 July 1968 ; a detailed account of the campaign to clear the tips can be found in *Aberfan: A Disaster and its Aftermath* (1974) by Joan Miller.

[8]Wilson's decision to send George Thomas to secure a contribution from the Fund Committee is recounted in *The Labour Government 1964-70* (1971) by Harold Wilson. S.O.'s letter to Prime Minister Wilson is quoted in the *Western Mail*, 14 September 1968.

[9]*Western Mail*, 12 March 1970.

[10]*Sunday Telegraph*, 13 August 1967.

[11]*Merthyr Express*, 22 July 1966.

[12]See *The Prince, the Crown and the Cash* (1969) by Emrys Hughes, and the poem ' Syrcas '69 ' by T. E. Nicholas in *Barn* (November 1968).

[13]*Western Mail*, 26 March 1970.

[14]*Sunday Express*, 12 April 1970.

[15]*Western Mail*, 11 May 1970.

[16]Letter from Arthur J. Evans (dated 14 May 1970) in the S. O. Davies, Papers, Swansea (Ref : 1B).

[17]Feature article on S.O. in the *Sunday Express*, 12 April 1970.

[18]This dispute is dealt with by Alun Morgan (see Note 19 below) ; Castle's reply to S.O. was reported in the *South Wales Echo*, 19 March 1970.

[19]' The 1970 Parliamentary Election at Merthyr Tydfil ' by Alun Morgan in *Morgannwg* (1978). This article is an immensely valuable eye-witness account and source of information about the election campaign.

[20]*Y Saeth*, No. 6 (Autumn 1977).

[21]See the S. O. Davies Papers, Swansea (Ref : 1B).

[22]*Labour Monthly*, July 1970

[23]*Western Mail*, 20 June 1970.

[24]Letter to S.O. dated 22 July 1970 ; the correspondence between him and the Labour Party N.E.C. is to be found in the S. O. Davies Papers, Swansea (Ref : 1B).

[25] *Western Mail*, 30 July 1970.

[26] *Merthyr Express*, 18 August 1967.

[27] The tributes from Dai Francis, Arthur Evans and Joe Lambert appeared in the *Merthyr Express*, 3 March 1972.

[28] *Guardian*, 26 February 1972.

[29] *Welsh Nation*, 3 March 1972 : Keir Hardie's attack on the 1911 Investiture was reported in the *Times*, 2 May 1911.

[30] *Merthyr Express*, 3 March 1972.

[31] *Merthyr Express*, 3 March 1972.

INDEX

GENERAL

PERSONS

NEWSPAPERS & PERIODICALS